Junot Díaz

Junot Díaz

On the Half-Life of Love

José David Saldívar

DUKE UNIVERSITY PRESS
Durham and London 2022

© 2022 Duke University Press. All rights reserved

Project editor: Susan Albury
Designed by Courtney Leigh Richardson
Typeset in Portrait Text and Helvetica Rounded by
Copperline Book Services

Library of Congress Cataloging-in-Publication Data
Names: Saldívar, José David, author.
Title: Junot Díaz : on the half-life of love / José David Saldívar.
Description: Durham : Duke University Press, 2022. | Includes
bibliographical references and index.
Identifiers: LCCN 2021055641 (print)
LCCN 2021055642 (ebook)
ISBN 9781478016083 (hardcover)
ISBN 9781478018711 (paperback)
ISBN 9781478023333 (ebook)
Subjects: LCSH: Díaz, Junot, 1968–Criticism and interpretation. | Díaz, Junot, 1968- Brief wondrous life of Oscar Wao. | Dominican Americans in literature. | Decolonization in literature. | BISAC: LITERARY CRITICISM / American / Hispanic & Latino | SOCIAL SCIENCE / Ethnic Studies / American / Hispanic American Studies
Classification: LCC PS3554. I259 Z88 2022 (print) |
LCC PS3554.I259 (ebook) | DDC 813/.54—dc23/eng/20220225
LC record available at https://lccn.loc.gov/2021055641
LC ebook record available at https://lccn.loc.gov/2021055642

Cover art: Junot Diaz, 2013. Photograph modified from the original.
© Pascal Perich. Courtesy the artist and Getty Images.

I believe I read your short stories first. What attracted me to those stories or whatever I read—I have short-term memory loss, you have to understand, I'm 86, so I get to forget things—was how startled I was by the language. It was so real and intelligent and wild. There was the wildness as well as some deep intelligence, and I didn't think the combination of the two was possible in recent literature. Yours struck quite immediately and it wasn't just the combination of words from Santo Domingo or curse words or grammatical [uniqueness]. It was provocative but there was something so human in the nostalgia and in the knowing of human beings. I don't know anybody who writes like that, the way you do, but it's very fetching, and I look forward to more, and more, and more.

Toni Morrison, on Junot Díaz (2017)

I saw our struggles and dreams all tangled up in the same failure, and that failure was called joy.

> Roberto Bolaño, *The Savage Detectives* (2007)

Preface · xi

Acknowledgments · xix

Introduction · 1

Contents

1
"Wrestling with J. R. R. Tolkien's *Lord of the Rings*":
How Junot Díaz Thinks about Coloniality,
Power, and the Speculative Genres · 27

Part I
**Junot Díaz's MFA Program Era
at Cornell University and Beyond**

2
Díaz's Planet MFA:
"Negocios" · 47

3
Díaz's Planet POC (People of Color):
Drown · 73

Part II
**Understanding Imaginary Transference
and the Colonial Difference**

4
Becoming "Oscar Wao" · 99

Part III
A Legacy In-formation

5
Junot Díaz's Search for Decolonial Love · 151

Conclusion and Coda:
"Monstro" and *Islandborn* · 179

Notes · 191

Bibliography · 225

Index · 239

Preface

In January 2017, President Barack Obama explained to Michiko Kakutani of the *New York Times* that Junot Díaz—along with Dave Eggers, Barbara Kingsolver, Jhumpa Lahiri, Zadie Smith, and Colson Whitehead—had helped him get through his eight vexed years as the first African American president of the United States. Díaz's fiction, Obama said, helped him understand "a very particular immigrant experience" in which Díaz's Dominican American characters longed "for this better place" while also "feeling displaced."[1] And although Díaz's characters found expression in his well-crafted fiction, the story of Díaz himself is still in process: in all likelihood, the writer-activist, professor, and immigrant will in the coming years write more novels, craft more short-story collections, publish more essays, and unveil still-unknown parts of himself: the sources of his lifelong depression, the contours of his inventive imagination. The truths of those works are the future's to unpack: a goal of this book is to help light the way.

I started writing this book years ago, during a historical moment that now feels a lifetime away: January 2010, only two years into President Obama's first term. In one of my early drafts of the preface, I began with a notice: readers attempting to find revelations about Junot Díaz would be disappointed. However, Díaz's autobiographical essay "The Silence: The Legacy of Childhood Trauma," published in the *New Yorker* in 2018, changed everything. In his essay Díaz revealed that at eight years old, he had been raped by a "grownup" that he "truly trusted"; the resulting psychological traumas followed him for decades. As a result of his sexual "violación," as he called it in Spanish, Díaz confessed that he not only had suffered from a lifetime of terror, depression, agony, shame, self-recrimination, addiction, and "asco [disgust]" but that it "casi me destruyó." At eleven, he suffered uncontrollable rage; by thirteen, he had stopped "being able to look at himself in the mirror"; and by fourteen, he had put one of his father's guns to his head. Díaz emphasized that throughout his adolescence he had nightmares about endless rapes: attacks by his brothers, his father, his teachers, and his school friends. By high school, Díaz, once a student enrolled in its gifted-and-talented program, had been booted out for truancy. He returned to Stephen King novels for solace, though to no avail; again, he attempted to kill himself by "swallowing all these leftover drugs" from his older brother Rafael's cancer treatments. By the time he enrolled at Rutgers, Díaz had not only buried the boy who was raped but had also worked to "lock" his traumas behind what he characterized as "an adamantine mask of normalcy."[2] That "normalcy," as one might imagine, was itself a weighty fiction: through his graduate schooling, his professional activities, and his intimate life, nightmares, self-blame, secrecy, and "suicidal ideation" followed.

The immediate responses to Díaz's "The Silence" on Twitter and Facebook were polarized. Some responses were thankful that the essay's narrator, Díaz himself, was honest about having experienced sexual trauma, was open about having been in pain for most of his life. Relatedly, some readers saw in Díaz's piece a larger social body in pain, lost, suffering, living in quiet desperation. However, other responses focused not on Díaz's personal revelation but rather what read as incidental in the essay: Díaz's failed relations with a series of lovers over a ten-year period—women named only with single letters and dashes ("X—," "Y—," or "S—," etc.). These readers of the essay asked why Díaz's partners were so easily reduced to objects, assemblages, and "señales"—objects to be used only as signifiers that helped him come to self-consciousness and, with therapy, to recovery. Why did so many broken men of color (like Toni Morrison's Paul D in *Beloved*) need women of color to be made whole again?

Soon after Díaz's *New Yorker* essay appeared, the writer and instructor of creative writing Zinzi Clemmons stood up at a writer's conference and asked Díaz why he had treated her badly some six years before. A few hours later, she specified the behavior to which she was referring on Twitter, saying that he had forcibly kissed her when she was a graduate student.[3] Her claim then set off another accusation of "enraged" bullying behavior: at the University of Iowa Workshop, Díaz had disagreed with an audience member, Carmen María Machado, who had accused him of being the same as his misogynist fictional characters.[4]

A few weeks later the writer and professor of creative writing Shreerekha Subramanian "outed" herself as one of the former "ghost-lovers." Identifying herself as "S—" in Díaz's essay "The Silence," she claimed he had sworn "her to silence" during their relationship, when she was a graduate student. In her telling, Díaz, some ten years after their relationship had ended, still visited and communicated with her (when he came through her city), "speak[ing] about our past and say[ing] what he already said hundreds of times to one another—my hurt, his apology, his trauma" till kingdom come. She laid out her fuller sense of Díaz's and her own behavior—"I never ran towards him, I never did fully run away"—and claimed that Díaz had broken off their relationship because as a South Asian immigrant she "was not black enough for him."[5]

By these and some other reviewers' accounts, critics posited that Díaz's behavior of bullying, shaming, and aggressive advances was appalling and that his imaginative work thematized and championed patriarchal normalization and uncritical misogyny. Nobody is arguing against Díaz's appalling behavior—myself included. However, I do argue that Díaz's *fiction* allows readers to confront heteropatriarchal dominance in our culture and society. In the words of decolonial feminists Yomaira C. Figueroa-Vásquez and Paula M. L. Moya, Díaz's fiction empowers readers "to bear witness to the ways in which coloniality exerts power over and commits violence upon bodies deemed to be insignificant" (Figueroa-Vásquez) and to theorize "race and intersectionality" in our postcontemporary moment (Moya).[6]

Almost overnight, calls for the boycotting of Díaz's fiction went viral. On Facebook and Twitter, Díaz was cast as a "bizarre person, a sexual predator, a virulent misogynist, [and] an abuser and aggressor."[7] In an op-ed piece in the *Chronicle of Higher Education*, a number of prominent Latinx and South Asian feminist scholars responded to these portrayals by calling for more patient consideration, criticizing the viral admonitions of Díaz's "pathological behavior" as part of a broader infrastructure of snap judgment.[8] And as this book goes to press, the debate about Díaz's behavior and future career has in fact quieted, for Díaz has been cleared by all the institutions with which he works even as detractors have succeeded in marginalizing him.[9] In no uncertain terms, the accusations against Díaz are serious, and he needs to be held accountable for whatever he may have done, may be doing, and may still do. "Sexist behavior, whether slight or severe," philosopher Linda Martín Alcoff wrote in a front-page *New York Times* online opinion, is "never acceptable or excusable. Sexism in every form weakens liberatory movements, fractures solidarity and exacerbates the oppression of the oppressed."[10] In its November 2018 review of the allegations against Díaz, the Pulitzer Board unanimously found no evidence or reason to remove him and invited him back.[11] Assessing the validity of each accusation against Díaz is beyond the scope of this literary study.[12] Addressing the importance and volume of their expression of rage and pain, however, is part of what this book of literary criticism on Díaz's fiction and intellectual formation attempts to describe: the historical traumas passed like cursed heirlooms among our aggrieved communities and the ever-pressing need for decolonial love.

I don't pretend in these pages to look prophetically into the future and critically analyze Díaz's still-unfolding writing career. I mostly look backward (for one can only predict the past) from Díaz's early years in Santo Domingo, Dominican Republic, and his public-school education in Parlin, New Jersey, to the present moment. Through an interpretive commentary that restricts itself to the repertoire of meanings in Díaz's texts, I explore how the role of the imagination is crucial to the functioning of his fiction. He allows us to experience what Winfried Fluck calls a "negative aesthetics" (not something literally represented), compelling readers to provide links across the many gaps, blanks, and páginas en blanco created by the author's suspensions of relations of meaning.[13] What emerges is a book about Díaz as the inventor of an expansive fictional cosmos, an anatomist of coloniality in the Américas, and a tormented and anguished writer staving off depression, shame, anguish, and addiction—and eventually producing *The Brief Wondrous Life of Oscar Wao*, one of the most influential novels of our time.

Here is this book's genesis. In 2003, Díaz, along with Edwidge Danticat, had been invited to the University of California, Berkeley, where I taught at the time, to be the keynote speakers at a conference organized by graduate students in the departments of history and comparative literature. I, too, had been asked by the conference organizers to join Díaz and Danticat as a keynote speaker. Although I had taught Díaz's debut book of stories *Drown* and Danticat's *Krik? Krak!*, I had not met either writer before.

Fast-forward to the end of the decade. Díaz had by then published to great fanfare and critical acclaim his novel *The Brief Wondrous Life of Oscar Wao*. I had moved midyear to Stanford University and had written, during the 2010 winter quarter, a long draft of an essay conjecturing on world literature and Díaz's concept of the fukú americanus. I emailed Díaz to share my essay with him that was about to appear in the journal *Global South*. Díaz read the work and commented on its strengths and weaknesses.

A year later, in March 2011, I sent Díaz a version of another essay in which I discussed a footnote in his novel in which the Dominican American character Yunior de Las Casas observed Oscar de León reading science fiction in the closet and underachieved masculinity and hypermasculinity. Díaz sent me a three-paragraph email response in which he thought my essay was "lit": he explained that the characters Oscar and his college roommate Yunior had had their masculinity "transmuted" by "our post-work stage of capitalism into extreme hypermasculine performance." This "ratchet[ed] up the pressure against things like reading and being smart." He then commented that although some boys of color are being "liberated" by hipsters like Drake, "the rest are being fettered by these identities which don't permit such perversions as 'being smart.'"[14]

With this, I was hooked. Díaz explained that he honestly felt that amid all the essays that were being written, sent to him, and published about his work—for all of which he was very touched and grateful—he had not yet read anyone who was really "digging" into his texts' meat and bones: "I didn't work so long because I WASN'T trying to challenge some of the ways I was to conceive my African diasporic post-colonial Caribbean Dominican poor NJ smart-kid identity."[15] That was when I decided to read all his books and short stories, essays, and interviews. I read everything, including "Negocios," the noncirculating MFA thesis he had completed in 1995 at Cornell, and I was struck by the texts' complex styles, tones, and atmospheres, or what Hans Ulrich Gumbrecht calls "Stimmung," or "mood."[16]

Fast-forward again to late 2011. Díaz's work had by then appeared to global fanfare. He had received a Pulitzer Prize for his debut novel, and he had won a MacArthur Fellowship. Díaz's fiction was receiving worldwide attention. As I taught his work, one thing came into clearer focus. I knew I had to ponder the arc of his immigrant (diasporic) writing career.

To figure this out, I decided, along with my Latinx studies colleagues Monica Hanna and Jennifer Harford Vargas, to invite Díaz to Stanford in 2012 to give a distinguished lecture and to hold the first symposium on his work. After these events, all of us came away amazed with his address on race, difference, and Tolkien's *The Lord of the Rings*, his "decolonial turn"[17] in writing *The Brief Wondrous Life of Oscar Wao*, and his future-leaning imaginative work on zombies and decolonial love.

I did not interview him; however, he agreed to answer my questions about his life and his family so that I might get all the facts straight. In the years since, Díaz read and commented on the penultimate draft of this book while remaining detached, unlike in his early emails, from my interpretations of his work.[18] But I have been extremely fortunate, for Díaz read the draft of my manuscript with care, occasionally correcting some errors about his family and some of my rhetorical infelicities but never confirming or critiquing my literary criticism.

As I have prepared this book for production, I have often been asked why I am attending to the life and work in progress of a living, breathing writer at the peak of his creativity and his fall from grace as one of the leading American writers of his generation.[19] In my first and last books, on the dialectics of the America that is ours and not ours and on trans-Americanity, I attended to something much bigger: those books sought to articulate what such writers as Gloria Anzaldúa, Alejo Carpentier, Sandra Cisneros, Gabriel García Márquez, José Martí, Cherríe Moraga, Toni Morrison, Américo Paredes, John Rechy, Roberto Fernández Retamar, El Vez, and Helena María Viramontes had in common as diasporic and borderlands writers in the Américas. This book on Díaz is a kindred effort, though on a much smaller scale. It focuses on the fluid relations between the immigrant and diasporic ruptures in Díaz's life and on those of the Afro-Atlantic Dominican characters in his books who are connected by diegetic continuities.[20] It sits with, as President Obama noted, the distressing and the hopeful in Junot Díaz's books about Latinx immigrant belonging in the United States.

This book follows the writer through his childhood, through his college and graduate-school experiences at Rutgers, and through his time in Cornell's MFA program, arriving at the writer we know today. The Anthropocene, Anzaldúa and Moraga's "theory in the flesh," Césaire, Cisneros, Fanon, Iser, Mongooses, Morrison, NBC's *Late Night with Seth Meyers*, "negative aesthetics," Sauron, Tolkien, and Trujillo all play their part in this historia. But my framework supports my critical focus on Díaz's work: the short-story collections *Drown* and *This Is How You Lose Her*; the MFA thesis "Negocios"; *Islandborn*, a children's book; the interviews, the essays, and the improvisations; and above all his novel *The Brief Wondrous Life of Oscar Wao*. The resulting findings do not add up to a tidy, neat narrative. Rather, this book tries to put carne on the huesos of my claim—it unpacks a fictional multimundo in which there is a continual dialogue among complex characters, settings, myths, and strategies that continually appear, evaporate, morph, and haunt. And in the process it asks questions embedded in the works and apropos of our moment: Why are Díaz's historias mainly stories of the failure of his male characters' efforts to overcome their misogyny and the violence of the coloniality of gender on the bodies and souls of his female characters? Why do both his female and male characters suffer from "repetitive trauma" and rape?

Like the Chilean Roberto Bolaño's "post-boom" stories and novels about the global abyss of his imagined Santa Teresa, Mexico, in *The Savage Detectives* and *2666*, Díaz's works engage in fictional world making by focusing on how the loser always yields—from a literary point of view—more, far more, than a winner.[21] I am thus interested here in why so many of Díaz's characters are "doomed" and tangled up in the failure of transcending the history of coloniality and the transgenerational history of rape of the New World, or what Díaz ingeniously called the "fukú americanus" in *The Brief Wondrous Life of Oscar Wao*. Even as Díaz's characters are failing, they are affected by a utopian, passionate counternarrative, what he dubs a "zafa." One of the invigorating effects of Díaz's historias of failure concerns their literary forms and the characters' everyday poetic rhythms. His prose has a powerful vitality, even when treating apocalyptic end-of-the-world themes.

In short, my book responds to the question posed by its title, *Junot Díaz: On the Half-Life of Love*. Who is Junot Díaz, and what is this "half-life of love" that permeates his fiction, most centrally in his short story "The Cheater's Guide to Love"? Do his characters' passions triumph over experience? Are Yunior de Las Casas and Oscar de León wise when they fall in love? Or when they experience the radioactive-like decay of heartbreak? Díaz suggests that love is itself not only a specific kind of relationship between human subjects and objects of desire but also a means of decolonial knowledge production.[22] Do Díaz's male and female characters find out who they are by loving? The book addresses the first part of the titular question with a straightforward answer: Díaz is still one of the leading American writers of his generation, capable of reaching both a global mainstream audience and more professionalized readers and writers like President Obama. The answer to the second part of the question—what Díaz's sense of (decolonial) love is and why the half-life of love lasts forever—is less straightforward, less portable, and more arabesque.

Acknowledgments

My debts, stretching back over a ten-year period, are too numerous to acknowledge fully.

When I began research in 2010, I received much generous help from the eminent Díaz scholars Paula M. L. Moya, who had attended graduate school with Díaz at Cornell, and Arlene Dávila and Silvio Torres-Saillant, who had been Díaz's colleagues at Syracuse University. Since then, I have accumulated many further debts to such notable Díaz scholars as H. Samy Alim, Glenda R. Carpio, Evelyn Nien-Ming Ch'ien, Edwidge Danticat, Yomaira Figueroa-Vásquez, Lorgia García Peña, Lyn Di Irio, Monica Hanna, Jennifer Harford Vargas, Ylce Irizarry, Claudia Millan, Julie Avril Minich, Richard Pérez, Sarah Quesada, Ramón Saldívar, and Deborah R. Vargas. Marina De Chiara, Ilan Stavans, Lisa Surwillo, and Gerald Torres read early drafts of the manuscript and made many invaluable suggestions. I am also deeply indebted to those who kindly supplied me with material on Díaz, including Deborah Chasman, Junot Díaz, and Jaime Hernandez; to those who materially assisted in the completion of this book; and to my research assistants at Stanford University, Jonathan Leal and Joseph Wager, whose devoted help in the later stages of copyediting and proofreading saved me from innumerable errors of expression or fact.

In Santo Domingo, Dominican Republic, I thank Miguel Yarrul, short-story writer and the screenplay writer of the iconic film *La Gungua*, who was my guide and took me on an extended neighborhood walk around Villa Juana on Calle Sumner Wells, where Díaz grew up, and who gave me an understanding of Díaz's unique relationship with the capital city. His expert networking skills as an engineer and writer gave me advantages and resources invaluable to a US researcher. I also want to thank Luisa de Peña, the director of the Museo Memorial de la Resistencia, who gave me a tour of the museum and contributed to my understanding of the Trujillato and to the anarchy of US empire; not only would this have been a different book without their help and advice, but the research and preparation would have been much less interesting.

Nelson Maldonado Torres of Rutgers has always been helpful and welcoming, as was his colleague Andrew Parker, who showed me the Rutgers campus via the very same bus route that Yunior, Lola, and Oscar used to travel to school. A big thank-you to Emmanuel Martinez and Rafael Vizcaino for taking me to see Demarest Hall at Rutgers.

Worldwide, others to whom I am grateful for inviting me to lecture on Díaz include Danuta Fjellestad at the University of Uppsala, Sweden; Bo G. Ekelund at the University of Stockholm, Sweden; Mónica García González at the Pontificia Universidad Católica de Valparaíso, Chile; Antonio Aja and Ana Niria Alba Díaz at the Programa de estudios sobre Latinos en los Estados Unidos, Casa de las Américas, Havana, Cuba; Tim Lanzendorfer and Oliver Scheiding at the Johannes Guttenberg University of Mainz; Mary Pat Brady, Lamar Herrin, Stephanie Vaughn, and Helena María Viramontes at Cornell University; Astrid Fellner and Yiorgas Kalogeras (organizers of the 2014 MESEA international conference) at Saarland University, Saarbrucken, Germany; Tobias Jochum and Ulla Hasselstein (organizers of the 2015 graduate conference Alliances) at the John F. Kennedy Graduate School for North American Studies, Free University, Berlin; and Aítor Ibarrola-Armendariz and Jesús Benito (organizers of the 2020 SAAS international conference) at the University of Duesto, Bilbao, Spain. I also want to single out Ulla Hasselstein, deputy director at the John F. Kennedy Graduate School for North American Studies, Free University in Berlin, who invited me to co-teach a graduate seminar with her on the aesthetics of reading and Díaz's fiction.

Parts of this book evolved in my undergraduate and graduate seminars at Stanford University. I have learned a tremendous amount by co-teaching with Patricia Valderrama, Alexis Marie Pearce, Chiara Giovanni, Ellis Schriefer, and Joseph Wager.

This book could not have been written without the loving support and good cheer of Laura, David X, and Gabriel Saldívar. Gabo, during his undergraduate and graduate studies at Stanford, was a perfect research assistant, especially on matters relating to his own high-tech fields of symbolic systems and academic technology.

The team at Duke University Press—my editor Ken Wissoker and editorial associate Ryan Kendall—were crucial; the book is much the better for their efforts. I am also particularly grateful to the two anonymous readers for their insightful comments on the book manuscript.

Portions of the present text have appeared earlier in the following journals and books: "Conjectures on 'Americanity' and Junot Díaz's 'Fukú Americanus' in *The Brief Wondrous Life of Oscar Wao*," *Global South*, 5, no. 1 (Spring 2011): 120–36; "Conjecturas sobre amor descolonial, transamericanidad y el 'Fukú Americanus' de Junot Díaz," *Revista Casa de las Américas* 297 (octubre deciembre 2014), 85–91; and "Junot Díaz's Search for Decolonial Aesthetics and Love," in *Junot Díaz and the Decolonial Imagination*, ed. Monica Hanna, Jennifer Harford Vargas, and José David Saldívar (Durham, NC: Duke University Press, 2016), 321–50.

Introduction

This book explores Junot Díaz's imaginative work and the diasporic and immigrant world he lives in, showing how his influences converged in his fiction and how his work—especially his Pulitzer Prize–winning novel *The Brief Wondrous Life of Oscar Wao*—radically changed the course of US Latinx literature and created a new way of viewing the decolonial world.

Díaz's fictional work is rich and diverse both in its inheritances from the author's past in Santo Domingo and New Jersey and in its reactions to the life of its own time. Although I have not written an intellectual biography, the opening chapter and each subsequent chapter of *Junot Díaz: On the Half-Life of Love* begins with a section about Díaz's life during the composition of his books. However, the main emphases are literary and critical.

In taking up such matters as Díaz's vexed relationship to the literary aesthetics of Whiteness that dominated his MFA experience in the English Department at Cornell University; his critiques of the colonialities of power, race, and gender in the cultures and societies of the Dominican Republic, the US, and the Américas; and his use of the science-fiction imaginary to explore the capitalist zombification of our planet, I show how Díaz's works stand in relation both to the literary currents of the early twenty-first century and to what we now call the transmodernist movement.

The author's personal perspective is closely connected with the social and the historical. Partly, perhaps, because US critics have not been interested in trans-American literary, cultural, and intellectual history, or in what I call trans-Americanity[1] writ large, these aspects of Díaz's imaginative work have not received very much attention. Díaz certainly raises especially difficult problems for the literary scholar; however, these difficulties arise because his trans-American inheritances from Santo Domingo and New Jersey are so rich, diverse, and unique. Indeed, scholars such as Eric Paul Roorda, Lauren Derby, Raymundo González, Yolanda Martínez-San Miguel, and Dixa Ramírez have argued that the Dominican Republic (Díaz's birthplace) is a historical oddity in the hemisphere, for racial mixture has been the norm rather than exception. There, buccaneering prospered, and a society-wide plantation system did not exist as it did in Haiti, Cuba, Puerto Rico, and Martinique, for slavery ended with national sovereignty in the early nineteenth century.[2] If, from 1492 to the present, Santo Domingo has been the "ground zero" of the New World's doom, the cursed "ghosts" of coloniality in Díaz's fiction—unleashed by Columbus— refuse to stay put in its port of entry. Díaz uses the Dominican Republic and the Dominican Afro-Latinx diaspora in the United States to redefine the notion of coloniality, and, in his novel, *The Brief Wondrous Life of Oscar Wao*, he uses coloniality to rearticulate the condition of coloniality in the broader context of what Yolanda Martínez-San Miguel calls the "intra-coloniality of diasporas."[3]

Through an interpretative literary commentary that restricts itself to the repertoire of meanings, or the aesthetics of reception, that the imagination can discover in detailed readings of Díaz's fictions—"Negocios," *Drown*, *The Brief Wondrous Life of Oscar Wao*, *This Is How You Lose Her*, *Islandborn*, and "Monstro"— Díaz's works, I suggest, expose the unattested deficiencies of hegemonic systems of thought.[4] By examining Díaz's decolonial turn and the negative aesthetics in his texts, I explore how the role of the imagination is crucial to the functioning of his fictions in allowing us the experience of a negative aesthetics: something not literally represented. Texts like Díaz's *The Brief Wondrous Life of Oscar Wao*[5] compel readers to bridge the many gaps, blanks, and páginas en blanco created by the author's intentional suspension of relations between meaningful segments of the work. Moreover, these textual gaps, black holes, and silences allow Díaz, as I argue in chapter 4, to call attention to the history of erased genocides, traumas, and tortures in the Dominican Republic, the Caribbean, and the New World Américas in his novel.

As I write this, I remember vividly the evening at the University of California, in the Berkeley Dwinelle Hall auditorium in April 2003, when I first met the then thirty-five-year-old Junot Díaz, who was sharing the podium as a keynote speaker along with his longtime friend and fellow writer Edwidge Danticat and me at a small conference on the Hispanic and Francophone Caribbean diaspora organized by some graduate students in the departments of comparative literature and history. At the event, Danticat spoke passionately about the Dominican Republic's war on Haitian immigrants and the deportations that had been happening on the border that separates the Dominican Republic from Haiti since the early 1990s on the island of Hispaniola. And Díaz, true to form, read an extraordinary historia about a young Dominican American romantic bungler who had committed the sin of making his novia unhappy.

During the Q&A, Díaz and Danticat eviscerated anti-Black and anti-Haitian politics, criticized past Dominican presidents for ordering the deportations of Haitians and Haitian Dominicans, and spoke of the lasting legacy of Rafael Molina Trujillo's genocidal massacres of thousands of Haitian immigrants along the border.[6]

The next day, I went to Moe's Books on Telegraph Avenue, a favorite haunt of mine at the time, and bought every Danticat title and every present and back issue of the *New Yorker* I could find featuring Díaz's short stories (I already owned and had taught Díaz's *Drown* in my Latinx literature classes), and I have been bingeing on their historias ever since. I was especially impressed by their carefully rendered Hispaniola historias of apocalyptic doom and hope. Díaz, it seemed to me, was attempting to look at the US Latinx cultural milieu with profoundly unsettled and unsettling eyes. He was captivating readers not only with his mesmerizing prose but also with his mind. He was designing the imaginary (or constructed) worlds in his fiction by drawing upon and subverting the political, aesthetic, and generic power of role-playing games, films, comics, video games, and literary texts to build his fiction. And his goal as a writer, it occurred to me, was to create imaginary (alternative) multimundos: ultimately, all his efforts to date serve that higher purpose.

This book endeavors to chart Díaz's improbable literary career as he fights off the trauma of his childhood rape, his writer's block, the trauma of September 11, 2001, and the farragoes of nonsense and miserable botches in the text's drafts to emerge with what many see as the best novel written at the start of the twenty-first century, *The Brief Wondrous Life of Oscar Wao*.[7] With this book I hope to cast new light on what Díaz's fiction is and to show how it was that he came to invent it.

In my opinion, Díaz's novel radically revamps our understanding of US Latinx literary culture. US Latinx literature, as Ilan Stavans suggests in his monumental *Norton Anthology of Latino Literature*, is a hemisphere of great dreams, vast immigrant mirages, and shattering odysseys and curses, with "double attachments to place, language, and to identity."[8] Díaz begins his novel by taking us back to the first colonial usurper, who he simply calls throughout the text the "Admiral." Almirante Colón, of course, was the first writer of lo real maravilloso americano because when he crossed the Atlantic in 1492, he did not so much discover Hispaniola (now Haiti and the Dominican Republic) and the New World Américas as invent them, exaggerating their marvels and wonders, giving Europeanized names to everything he saw, and classifying, like a future mad Linnaeus, races, flora, and fauna. Although the almirante's journals were fanciful leaps of the imagination, he ended up, as Díaz's Dominican American narrator, Yunior de Las Casas, opines, "miserable and syphilitic, hearing (dique) divine voices." Thus envisaged, although the almirante's journals were full of marvels, his true tale of the New World was a bitter historia of failure and doom, opening the "nightmare door that cracked open" the processes of Americanity, or what Díaz refers to throughout the novel as the "fukú americanus," the monumental curse and the "Doom of the New World."⁹ Four hundred and seventy-five years after Almirante Colón's ethnographic-like realist tale of the New World's failure, the Colombian Nobel Prize–winning writer Gabriel García Márquez offered his own discovery tale of solitude and fukú-like curses in *Cien años de soledad* (*One Hundred Years of Solitude*) by narrating how after leading twenty-one unsuccessful civil wars against Macondo's conservative regime, the novel's revolutionary colonel Aureliano Buendía sees his grandiose vision of creating a unified federation of emancipated American states—from the Patagonia to Alaska—come to nothing, and the Colonel dies miserably, declaring that he who spends his life fighting ends up "jodido" (fucked).

For Junot Díaz, the United States of America, Latin America, and the Caribbean island of Hispaniola had precise dates of birth with Almirante Colón's first landfall on October 12, 1492, and most of the republics of the Américas also shared birthdays when they achieved revolutionary emancipation from the British, Dutch, French, and Spanish colonial rule some centuries later. Inevitably, the history of Caribbean Hispaniola, Latin America, and the United States has followed, for Díaz, the rhythms and logic of European coloniality. In *The Brief Wondrous Life of Oscar Wao*, Díaz expertly surveys this whole erratic and doomed history, and he memorializes his hero's native island by setting Oscar de León's brief and tragic life's ending on the land that the almirante and he loved best. At the end of his life, Díaz's Oscar de León calls Santo Domingo "the Ground Zero of the New World."¹⁰

The Brief Wondrous Life of Oscar Wao is a sweeping family narrative about the violent sins and curses that haunt the literary Caribbean, Hispaniola, the continent, and its African diasporic children through centuries after centuries—conquest, murder, rape, expropriation, dictatorship, the cultures of US imperial invasion (the fukú americanus)—countered by the redemptive quest (or counterspell zafa) for legitimacy and the politics of identity and the struggle for emancipation, inevitably involving a raising of consciousness, further discrimination from within and without for "the most oppressed of the oppressed," and a new round of doom and despair. I assert that US Latinx América can be said to exist in large part because novels like Díaz's *The Brief Wondrous Life of Oscar*

Wao give rise to and unify, in the most material way imaginable, that historically constructed, riven, fragmented space we call América. Indeed, novels like Díaz's confirm the existence of the fukú americanus as the legacy of coloniality and the sepulchral hand of global capital.

Díaz wrote *The Brief Wondrous Life of Oscar Wao* over an eleven-year period: first in seclusion on a Guggenheim Fellowship in Mexico City; later in Syracuse and Harlem, New York; and still later in Cambridge, Massachusetts. The repertoire of Díaz's text, as I will elaborate in chapter 4, not only is derived from a great number of different systems but is also presented in such density that first-time readers find themselves being constantly disoriented. The problem lies not so much in the unfamiliarity of the novel's allusive elements, for these in themselves are not difficult to identify—Jack Kirby and Stan Lee's *The Fantastic Four*, J. R. R. Tolkien's *The Lord of the Rings*, Flaubert's *Sentimental Education*, Homer's and Derek Walcott's *Odyssey* and *Omeros*, Aimé Césaire and Édouard Glissant's Greater Antillean poetics, Sandra Cisneros's and Toni Morrison's novels—but in the intermingling and the sheer mass (some 150 allusions to sci-fi books, characters, films, and TV series) that cause the repertoire to become, depending on your reaction, noise or symphony. As Díaz suggests about his work's repertoire, "I tried to stuff as many books as I could into *Oscar Wao*. I mean, shit, even the title refers to Oscar Wilde and 'The Short Happy Life of Francis Macomber' simultaneously."[11] Further, each chapter of *The Brief Wondrous Life of Oscar Wao* stretches backward and forward in time from the dictator Trujillo's 1930s to Reagan's dark 1980s and follows the arcs of Díaz's various immigrant characters' (mis)adventures and their inability to change the "hurricane winds of history." The novel is the history of these common winds of doom that surround the upper-class Cabrals in the Dominican Republic and the diasporic and working-class de Leóns in New Jersey. The dictator Trujillo imprisoned their family's patriarch, Dr. Abelard Cabral, over trumped-up charges, an act that sets off some of the curses on Oscar de León and his family. An initial chapter deals with the nerdy Oscar's misadventures in love as a child and adolescent in Paterson, New Jersey, and focuses on how his early life "goes down the tubes": as Yunior de las Casas explains, Oscar is a "pariguayo" with "no hustle" and "no G" who finds sanctuary in the "world of magic and mystery" to which he is transported as he reads "the more speculative genres."[12]

The next chapter of Díaz's novel shifts to Oscar's sister, Lola, who tells her own autohistoria, or feminist historia of coming to consciousness,[13] and offers its own possibilities of connection between the text's diverse elements. Like many Latinx feminist-of-color's autohistorias, Lola's chapter tells of her tussles with her Black Dominican immigrant mother, Belicia. One day she "punches" her mother's hand away from her in a failed attempt to defeat Belicia's rage, which "fill[s] the House." This mother-daughter tussling foreshadows Lola's "coraje" and her suffering with a spiritualized "bruja feeling" that consumes all of the de León family. With a return to Yunior's narrative, *The Brief Wondrous Life of Oscar Wao* moves back in time from Reagan's América oscuro (dark America) to the 1940s Dominican Republic's fukú americanus as we read of Oscar and Lola's Belicia's doomed affair with a monstrous character simply called "the Gangster," a sadistic man she loves "atomically" and who inflicts love's "heaviest radiations" on her. Like everyone else in this story, Yunior explains that Belicia "underestimated the shit she was in," for the Gangster was not only a married Dominicano but also married to the dictator Rafael Trujillo's sister, known as La Fea—"una mujer bien cruel . . . who ate girls like Beli like they were pan de agua." "If this was Dickens,"—Yunior ironizes—"La Fea would also run an orphanage."[14] With the teenage Belicia's near-fatal beating in the Dominican Republic's sugarcane fields in 1961 on orders from La Fea, and her eventual diasporic escape to the sanctuary of Paterson, New Jersey, the trans-American novel and science-fiction tale turns again from a near Dickens-like British realism to the form of the bildungsroman as Yunior, the Flaubertian sentimental hero, continues to fill in the text's numerous gaps, páginas en blanco, and literal blanks between the text's different elements and Oscar's misadventures in love, sentimental education, and attempted suicide at Rutgers University.

One Halloween, the nearly three-hundred-pound Rutgers freshman Oscar de León makes "a mistake" and dresses up like the British science-fiction television character Dr. Who, a time lord and time-traveling humanoid alien. (As Yunior remembers crudely, "[I] couldn't believe how much he looked like that fat homo Oscar Wilde.") One of their Dominicano undergraduate friends, Melvin, fully corrupts Oscar's new name by asking, "Oscar Wao, quien es Oscar Wao?"[15] Yunior's historia takes another historical turn with the story of the failed attempts of Oscar's grandfather, Dr. Abelard Cabral, to save his daughters and wife from rape and murder at the hands of the "pig-eyed" dictator Rafael Molina Trujillo in the 1940s Dominican Republic, a place of "implacable ruthless brutality" that was run by the dictator "like it was a Marine boot camp."[16] The final chapters of Díaz's novel return from the modes of the bildungsroman and the historical novel to complete the doomed ending of Oscar and Yunior's misadventures in love. Through this repertoire and sequence, linking the de Léon family's dark "fukú americanus" to the doomish savagery brought about by the Trujillo regime, the narrative attempts to show that Oscar's postcontemporary misadventures in love had, if not their beginnings, at least their type in Abelard's doomed attempt to protect his familia from Trujillo's potent "mixture of violence, intimidation, massacre, rape, co-optation and terror'"[17] and in the afterlife of Beli's tragic affair with the Gangster, a brother-in-law of the dictator. A final element in the text's repertoire returns readers to speculative, heroic fantasy by way of Yunior de Las Casas, who offers a contrapuntal remedy to the dark fukú or doom of the Américas by telling of Oscar's police beating and murder in a sugarcane field in the Dominican Republic.

The story of how Junot Díaz's *The Brief Wondrous Life of Oscar Wao* and its title came to be is in itself an improbable historia. Eleven years had passed after the publication of his first book, *Drown*. After winning a Guggenheim award in 1999, Díaz spent a year living in Mexico City writing a failed "Akira-like" science-fiction novel in progress, constructing what was to become his Pulitzer Prize–winning novel, and trying to improve his Spanish. Díaz lived next door to his longtime Guatemalan American friend Francisco Goldman, a novelist and journalist. One night after carousing the streets of Mexico City with Goldman, Díaz picked up a copy of Oscar Wilde's *The Importance of Being Earnest*, and someone said Oscar Wilde's name in a thick Spanish accent—a "quick joke," Díaz notes—but the incredible name Oscar Wao took on life. In his Mexico City epiphany, Díaz had a "vision of a poor, doomed ghetto nerd ... dashing the first part [of the novel] out in a couple of weeks."[18] The novel went on to win the Pulitzer Prize and nab almost every other prize available. With Díaz now included, one can count on two hands the number of first-time novelists who have won a Pulitzer Prize, not to mention that he is only the second Latinx writer to win one.[19]

The novel's Pulitzer Prize helped Díaz skyrocket into the broader public consciousness, giving US Latinx fiction an unprecedented visibility in the Américas and across the planet, and altering the landscapes of American literature and culture.[20] My reading and writing about *The Brief Wondrous Life of Oscar Wao* has certainly gotten me to rethink my approach to literature, prompting me to better understand the DNA of literary fiction through Díaz's novel: how it works, why it matters, why readers from all over the planet read and identify with Díaz's imaginative texts, and what the profound connection between Díaz's characters and imaginative transference is all about. As I've traveled all over the world lecturing on Díaz's work—to La Habana, Cuba; Santo Domingo, Dominican Republic; San Juan, Puerto Rico; Berlin, Germany; Stockholm and Uppsala, Sweden; as well as through many college and university towns across the United States, including Díaz's alma maters Rutgers and Cornell—I've always had my copies of Díaz's novel and creolized short stories nearby. It's clear that Díaz has been searching for new ways of conveying the plural and contradictory (speculative) realities of what the almirante had

Figure I.1 Santo Domingo, Dominican Republic, panorama. Wikipedia Commons.

"cracked open" in 1492, which is why *The Brief Wondrous Life of Oscar Wao*—like Gabriel García Márquez's *Cien años de soledad*, Toni Morrison's *Beloved*, Roberto Bolaño's *2666*, and Zadie Smith's *White Teeth*—is a decolonial narrative with world-systemic, global perspectives. In other words, the works I study by Díaz in this book are exemplary of the postcontemporary worlding of US Latinx literature—texts that contribute to the consolidation of both our world and US Latinx/Latin America as their chamber of resonance.[21]

Junot Díaz's Life, or, Becoming Junot Díaz: Santo Domingo, New Jersey

Every life tells a story, and this is what we know about Díaz's. He was born in Santo Domingo, Dominican Republic, on December 31, 1968, and was raised there until he was six years old (see figure I.1). His father, Rafael, was from Baitoa, some seventy-five miles from La Capital, where Dominicanos are proud of their cattle, their merengue, and their national parks, and where Rafael learned the value systems of a stern patriarchy, militarism, and love of bulls. In Santiago, Rafael became a cobbler and later moved to Santo Domingo, where he joined the notorious military police of the post-but-pro-Trujillo regime of President Joaquin Balaguer. Díaz's mother, Virtudes, was originally from Estebanía (near Azua) and migrated to La Capital, where she worked long hours in a chocolate factory. Rafael and Virtudes met in Villa Juana in the 1950s, married, and had a daughter, Marisabela, and a son, Rafael, after which Junot and his younger siblings, Maritza and Paul, were born. (The youngest brother, Paul, would be born in New Jersey.) Díaz recalls that "he loved his teachers" in the Santo Domingo neighborhood schools and that his early schooling (in Spanish) was often "chaotic and fun."[22] The Díaz family lived in various working-class sections of Santo Domingo and eventually settled in Villa Juana, where they lived in a small wooden house without plumbing on 53 Calle Sumner Wells—also known as Calle 21.

As it stands today, the house on Calle Sumner Wells is not, properly speaking, the original wooden house (without plumbing) where Díaz was raised but instead the total reconstruction of the dwelling Díaz helped pay for in 2007 (fig-

Figure I.2 53 Calle Sumner Wells, Villa Juana, Santo Domingo. Photograph by the author.

ure I.2). The stark effect of the reconstructed, hyperurban new house, with its barbed-wire gates and iron-barred windows, is the mark of modern Santo Domingo, where some of Díaz's relatives reside. Symbolically, the house on 53 Calle Sumner Wells anchors itself in Villa Juana, where it is surrounded by colmados (general barrio stores); bars; vast high-rise working-class housing projects; and the Caribbean sonics of the masses speaking to one another in the kinetic vernaculars of La Capital. As Díaz recalls, it is the very "polyrhythms of Santo Domingo in which I grew up all my life which were in people's body language, in the music they listened to and in the words they spoke. These rhythms infiltrated all my writing. I think a really good sentence, a really good piece of writing a certain attention should be paid to its rhythm."[23]

Here on Calle Sumner Wells, Junot Díaz and his siblings grew up without their father, who had emigrated to the United States. Díaz had met his father only a few times during his infrequent visits to the island. But Rafael, Díaz says, "was a total pro-Trujillo fanatic."[24] He loved having his picture taken in his military attire (like his hero Trujillo), but for Díaz his father's military uniform would become an emblem of "terror" for him. For instance, one of Díaz's "scariest" and traumatic moments he experienced as a young boy in Santo Domingo was when his father Rafael "jokingly" locked him into one of the prison cells in the "cuartel" where he worked. These were the very "same cells," Díaz recalls, "where the Trujillo regime used to torture its victims." It was not "a real swell dad-son moment" for the young Díaz.[25] Although Díaz does not like to go into details about his father's fascist-like military ethic, he has noted in his interviews how his father's harsh disciplinary code of conduct and influence shaped his and his siblings' diasporic lives in the United States. All of his brothers, for example, signed up for the US military, although his older brother was rejected for medical reasons. His sister married a US army soldier, and they spent the 1980s together on a tank base in Germany.[26]

American journalists and literary scholars have familiarized themselves with Díaz's immigrant life in New Jersey, Nueva York, and Cambridge, Massachusetts, but few have explored in any depth Díaz's world in Santo Domingo, where he was born and spent the first six years of his life. I have embarked on this sketch of Díaz's early life in Santo Domingo, and Parlin, New Jersey, in the immediate aftermath of Edwidge Danticat and Díaz's critique of the Dominican Republic's continuing deportation of Haitian "illegal aliens."

Before I traveled to Santo Domingo, I was warned by Díaz and several Dominican American friends not to announce too publicly that I was writing a book on him because the hard-core nationalists and right-wing fanatics of La Capital were incensed by his public criticism of their government's immigration policy. As Díaz wrote to me, "honestly right now the attacks from the right and the nationalist are insane. I'd be careful in the DR about being too public about what you're doing."[27] As I arrived in Santo Domingo, I was told by some of his more activist and vocal supporters, especially the award-winning screenplay writer Miguel Yarrul and the human-rights activist and curator Luisa de Peña, that although they love all of Díaz's books and that his Pulitzer and MacArthur honors have made them feel immensely proud as Dominicans, they were nevertheless deeply disappointed, saddened, and heartbroken by his very public criticism of their country's government plan to deport the thousands of Haitians living in the country without papers. Even in the midst of what we might call *Junotpalooza* in Santo Domingo—partying with people like there's no tomorrow—the intellectuals from La Capital I met were not shy about presenting their local analytical and critical views of Díaz's life, work, and career in the United States. The primary criticism of Díaz was twofold: first, he had not attempted to meet with local activists such as themselves, who had long been openly opposed to their government's policies on Haitian migrants; and second, Díaz had not been in Santo Domingo to see for himself what was actually happening on the ground. However, as newspapers such as the *Miami Herald* and the *Guardian* reported, Díaz had in fact been in La Capital and had witnessed for himself the events of the country's anti-Haitian racism in June 2015.

At a Miami press conference on June 24, 2015, Díaz and Danticat participated in a panel calling for protests against the deportations of Black Haitian migrants living in the Dominican Republic. Together with more than 150 US-based activists and Latinx community members, they asked for more political pressure to strip power from the country's government and from corporations benefiting, they argued, from a racist policy that targeted Black Haitians. Having just returned from Santo Domingo that week, Díaz, according to the *Miami Herald*, reported that "there's a state of terror" in La Capital, referring to the country's humanitarian crisis: the Dominican government's plan to deport hundreds of thousands of Dominicans of Haitian descent and undocumented immigrants from Haiti. "If you're not concerned you should be," said Danticat, "especially when we live in a town where most of us came from somewhere else. . . . A lot of people are in hiding and are afraid to go out since the deadline passed."[28]

Maria Rodriguez, executive director of the Florida Immigrant Coalition, led the Miami panel discussion and called the actions of the Dominican Republic's government a "globalized anti-black expression." The goal of the panel was not to call for a boycott of the Dominican Republic but rather to shed light on the quarter-century-long clash between Haitians and Dominicans on the island of Hispaniola. According to the *Herald*, another panelist, Edilberto Roman, a professor of law at Florida International University, noted that the tensions between the two countries had escalated when the Dominican government "re-interpreted" its constitution and announced that Haitians and Dominicans with Haitian blood who came and worked after 1929 would be denied citizenship. "What the court in the Dominican Republic did in 2013, was that it said the [Haitian] people there were 'in transit' since 1929," Roman explained. "These are repeated efforts where the Dominican Republic has tried to alienate its people."[29]

Díaz added that "in Santo Domingo, citizenship is a commodity," for "even under the best circumstances, folks who are rural and poor would be incredibly hard-pressed to meet any of the criteria [for citizenship]."[30] Although the Dominican Republic and Haiti share the island of Hispaniola, the countries have long had an uneasy borderlands relationship, particularly regarding migrant workers. According to the *Guardian*, an estimated 500,000 Haitian stateless migrants presently live in the Dominican Republic, but Dominican government officials said that just 10,000 had provided the documents required by an immigration registration program aimed at regulating the flow of migrants across its border. The Dominican government claimed it would deport the noncitizens who did not submit applications to establish legal residency before a June 17, 2015, deadline. At the Miami press conference, Díaz and Danticat, like many advocates for migratory human rights from all over the world, decried this registration program because it was discriminatory.

Whereas Díaz characterized what he found in the Dominican Republic's capital of Santo Domingo as "a state of terror" just as the June 2015 deadline passed, with the government's critics (including Díaz himself) receiving death threats and taking their families into hiding, Danticat worried about images of women and young children who had nowhere to go after being deported to Haiti. Together, they linked the Dominican Republic's announced deportations to the violence against African Americans in the United States, including the mass shooting of nine people in June 2015 at a South Carolina church, as well as migrant surges at Mexico's US border, across the Mediterranean into Europe, and in Asia. At fault, Díaz noted, is an indifference to racial and political tensions that exploit migrant workers and their countries' resources while stripping humanity from people "who are attempting to save themselves from the ruin inflicted by other people."[31] But the Dominican Republic's government is vulnerable to political pressure from travel boycotts and protests wherever Dominican officials make trade trips. "I've been working on targeting all the intellectual authors of this, not only identifying them but also boycotting and finding that way to interrupt their access to their easy privilege here in the United States," Díaz told the Associated Press. "There's a lot of us who are putting a lot of money in these corrupt human beings' pockets, and questions have to be raised at a personal level and at an organizational level."[32]

It was within this long-racialized history of tensions and mistrusts about Haitian migrants in the Dominican Republic that I was lucky enough in 2015 to travel to Santo Domingo to begin to measure for myself the incredible sum of the early biographical experiences and places that Díaz had accumulated in the first six years of his life in Santo Domingo, places and experiences that he later fully (re)imagined in his MFA thesis, "Negocios" (1995), and in his first book, *Drown* (1996). I not only visited Díaz's Santo Domingo childhood home on Calle Sumner Wells to get a feel for his nabe, but also talked with numerous writers, filmmakers, and human-rights activists about Díaz's imaginative work and social-justice activism. One of the highlights of my trip was seeing firsthand the energetic barrios of La Capital, or Santo Domingo, where many of Díaz's short stories and sections of *The Brief Wondrous Life of Oscar Wao* are set, in all their mixtures of cultures and surreal polyrhythmic vibrancy. At the center of the oldest of America's New World cities is Zona Colonial, where some 525 years later, one can still visit—as I did—some of the oldest surviving Catholic churches and European fortresses in the Américas, and the Colón monument.

In many of his early historias, as well as in sections of *The Brief Wondrous Life of Oscar Wao*, amid its geography of cobblestoned streets and colonial architecture, Díaz paints an intensely urban Caribbean city of ruins, home not only to its surviving colonial-era architecture but also to its vibrancy in our current decolonial era. Late in the novel, for instance, Díaz's Oscar writes in one of his notebooks that Santo Domingo's "tropical fecund smell" was for him "more evocative than any madeleine . . . like a whole new country was materializing atop the ruins of old ones."[33] In the Zona Colonial, for instance, one immediately sees the Catedral Primada de América, where the stones of the cathedral were first set in 1514 by Diego Columbus, Almirante Colón's son. One morning, I searched unsuccessfully for the ashes of both the almirante and his son—ashes rumored to have been laid in the chapel's crypt. Towering over the Catedral Primada is the Museo Alcazár, the citadel that was the chief home of Diego during the early sixteenth century. One can look through the Alcazár's Gothic-Mudejar windows, gaze out to the sea, and imagine Colón's perfect view of what was to become the Spanish Caribbean empire.

Near the Parque Colón is the iconic statue of Almirante Colón (figure I.3). This statue of the Genovese Colón, like the grandiose Columbus Lighthouse public monument that President Balaguer completed in 1992, as Dixa Ramírez suggests, is a "totem" that celebrates the beginnings of the world history of Colón's colonial modernity—its genealogy of a Hispanophilic past—and inaugurates the Hegelian-like world spirit of great men like Colón and his heirs monumentalized by Trujillo and Balaguer in the Dominican Republic, and figures like Kennedy and Reagan in the United States.[34] The park is one of the primary meeting places for Santo Domingo's local citizens, and it is vibrant with tourists and their guides, taxi drivers, shoeshine boys, and members of the national police. It is here, between the Colón park and Santo Domingo's iconic bridge on the Ozama River, where one of Díaz's best early short stories, "Aguantando," is haunted by the 1965 invasion of the Dominican Republic by the US military. As I elaborate in chapter 2, "Aguantando" is a series of anecdotes from when Díaz's primary narrator, an adolescent Yunior de Las Casas, was living in Santo Domingo. For the first six years of his life, Yunior lives in Santo Domingo without his father, who has migrated to Miami and then Nueva York to provide for the family. During these years Yunior's mother, Virta, tells her sons that their father had sent her letters telling her that he was coming to bring them back to the United States. After the first few letters, after Papi

Figure I.3 Christopher Columbus, Zona Colonial, Santo Domingo. Photograph by the author.

doesn't show up, they stop believing him. To provide for Rafa and Yunior, their mother works long hours at a chocolate factory; when she cannot afford to feed or clothe them, they stay at relatives' houses. During one period, shortly after receiving a letter from their father promising that he is coming home, Mami disappears for many weeks. She returns distraught, inconsolable, and distant from the boys, having relapsed into the deep depression and trauma she had suffered from her wounding when the US military had invaded the Dominican Republic, entering Santo Domingo via the Ozama River bridge.

Another major highlight of my Santo Domingo trip was visiting, alongside Dominicano screenwriter Miguel Yarrul, the Museo de la Resistencia on Calle Arzobispo Nouel, Número 210, in the Zona Colonial. The museo was inaugurated in May 2011, the fiftieth anniversary of the assassination of the dictator Rafael Leónidas Trujillo Molina. Since its opening, the museo's mission has been to collect, organize, catalog, and exhibit the struggles of several generations of Dominicans subjected to Trujillo's reign of terror. And during my visit, the cofounder and director of the museum, Luisa de Peña, gave Yarrul and me a personal tour. "It's an exhibition," de Peña told me in English, "to commemorate the fallen in the struggle for democracy, but more than anything it is an educational institution devoted to educating new generations of citizens about the value of life and fundamental human rights."[35] We spent several hours poring over photographs, films, books, videos, and objects belonging to those who resisted not only the Trujillo dictatorship between 1930 and 1961 but also the three presidential terms of his political heir, Joaquín Balaguer: 1960-62, 1966-78, and 1986-96. De Peña proudly tells me that the Museo de la Resistencia was recently accepted as a member of the International Coalition of Historic Sites of Museums of Conscience, a network of museums around the world dedicated to covering topics such as genocide, human trafficking, state terrorism, and totalitarianism. Thus envisaged, the Museo de la Resistencia documents the disastrous effects of the leadership of Trujillo and Balaguer on the collective bodies and the psyches of Dominicans.

After showing me the bloodied shirts of one of Trujillo's assassins and an animated hologram reanimating the iconic Mirabal sisters—dissidents whose 1960 murders by Trujillo's military forces galvanized global opposition to him[36]—de Peña ended our tour by stopping at one of the museo's dioramas, a piece highlighting the Dominican resistance to the cultures of US imperialism. She then asked one of her staff assistants to escort me down into the museum's chilly basement. There they have re-created a model of one of Trujillo's torture centers, complete with a replica of one of Trujillo's horrific electric chairs, a small bulb on the armrest, a wire snaking from handle to socket.

I couldn't help but freeze at the sight of this electric chair (figure I.4). It reminded me of the horrific scenes in Díaz's *The Brief Wondrous Life of Oscar Wao* set in Santo Domingo's torture chamber, where Díaz depicts Oscar de León's grandfather Dr. Abelard Cabral with eyes bulging, mouth flung open in terror as he endures routine torture. Both de Peña's Museo de la Resistencia and Díaz's celebrated novel bring into stark relief the thirty years of Trujillo's repressive rule, considered by historians among the bloodiest in the Américas. They are shocks to our conscience, reminding us of an all-too-human tendency to bury bloody chapters rather than measure traumatic legacies.

Before asking one of the museo's associate directors to show me the electric chair, Luisa de Peña stopped in front of a poster presentation that rescues the memory of her father, Luis, who was killed in 1967 as he plotted an insurrection against the dictatorial Balaguer. When de Peña tells me that our tour is over, she reminds me in her despedida that I am visiting the Museum of Resistance

Figure I.4 Electric chair, Museo de la Resistencia, Santo Domingo. Photograph by the author.

on September 3, 2015, the fiftieth anniversary of the US military invasion of the Dominican Republic. This call to "never forget" stays with me for the remainder of my time in Santo Domingo. The United States, as we know, has always imagined its national-identity politics to be somehow insulated from violent imperial interventions abroad: Díaz's imaginative work set in Santo Domingo, like de Peña's museo, argues that such a view of the United States is illusory. How can we ever forget the war with Mexico in 1848? With the former parts of the Spanish Empire in Cuba, Puerto Rico, and the Philippines in 1898? The invasions of Haiti and the Dominican Republic in the twentieth century? In parts of chapter 3 I fold these questions into a reading of Díaz's debut short-story collection, tracing how President Johnson's efforts to fan the anarchy of empire in the Dominican Republic helped engender the eruption of anarchy.

Junot Díaz, his mother, and his siblings emigrated from the Dominican Republic to Parlin, New Jersey, in December 1974. Joining Díaz's father, Rafael, who had moved to New Jersey years before, the diasporic family settled in a working-class New Jersey neighborhood. His mother cared for the five children and later worked on an assembly line; his father drove a forklift. Shifting worlds from an island in the global South to the empire of the global North was akin to living out a time-traveling science-fiction text, a cultural and linguistic shock of truly fantastical dimensions. As a young, poor Afro-Atlantic Dominican, Díaz found that his only access to the world outside his Parlin neighborhood was through film, literature, and television. While he was attending Madison Park Elementary School, his teachers thought something was wrong with him because he would not speak English, so they assigned him work with a speech therapist. At this time, he recalls, he became an inveterate reader of such popular sci-fi and heroic-fantasy writers as Ray Bradbury, Victor Appleton (author of the Tom Swift series), J. R. R. Tolkien, and later Stephen King, partly "to compensate for my lack of control of spoken English."[37] Aptly, he learned to read and write in English by poring over a novel of colonial revenge, the children's illustrated version of Sir Arthur Conan Doyle's *The Sign of the Four*. At eleven, Díaz started working his first job: a paper route in Parlin to pay for tickets to Hollywood movies, which became his "first narrative love."[38] From 1974 to 1989, Díaz and his family lived in Parlin's London Terrace apartments, an industrial red-orange-brick complex (figures I.5 and I.6). New Jersey's malls, crumbling streets, and monumental garbage heaps and toxic landfills were his first glimpse into the underside of América oscura. There, Díaz began writing fiction at thirteen when his older brother Rafa contracted leukemia in 1981: a disease likely caused by the carcinogenic dump near their London Terrace apartments. As Díaz revealed to Evelyn Ch'ien, he wrote his first short historias "to amuse Rafa during his hospital confinement" and to make sense of what had changed after his brother's slow recovery.[39] In my examination of Díaz's MFA thesis, "Negocios," in chapter 2, I analyze one of the work's central short stories ("London Terrace"), which is about social death and the toxic Global Landfill that surrounds the de Las Casas family.

Both Santo Domingo and Parlin—the American cities from the global South and global North in which Díaz grew up—shaped his worldview, his polyrhythmic Caribbean and New Jersey language, and his decolonial imagination. As an unpublished graduate student at Cornell, he conceived as early as the 1990s that his unfolding fictions would find form in an American cosmos—or in the

Figure I.5 London Terrace Apartments, Parlin, New Jersey. Screenshot. *New York Times Sunday Magazine.*

Figure I.6 Photographic collage of adolescent Junot Díaz with his mother and older brother. Screenshot. *New York Times Sunday Magazine.*

multimundo of New Jersey and the Dominican Republic. The majority of his fiction is set in the working-class suburbs of New Jersey, the island a haunting overlay; as I noted above, several of the stories from *Drown* and *This Is How You Lose Her*, as well as half of *The Brief Wondrous Life of Oscar Wao*, take place in the Dominican Republic. Furthermore, Díaz's language testifies to the polyrhythms and body languages of these dual locations; his imaginative literature is marked by a creolized vernacular: equal parts New Jersey and Santo Domingo urban slang that slides seamlessly between English and Spanish. As Ch'ien suggests in *Weird English*, "Díaz invests language with the power to influence political and social vision. He forcefully incorporates Spanish into his mainly English texts, showing concretely the linguistic violence that Spanish inflicts on English and vice versa. Instead of contorting English to fit Spanish, he demonstrates the inadequacy of English by substitution rather than metonymy or metaphor."[40]

After graduating from Cedar Ridge High School in Old Bridge, New Jersey, in 1987, Díaz attended Kean College in Union for a year before transferring to Rutgers, the State University of New Jersey in New Brunswick, where he completed his BA in English in 1992.[41] At Rutgers, Díaz read for the first time the two feminist writers of color who would inspire him to become a writer: Toni Morrison and Sandra Cisneros.

Years later, Díaz confessed to Morrison while interviewing her that when he read her novel *Song of Solomon* his first semester at Rutgers, "the axis of my world shifted and it has never returned."[42] And more recently, Díaz spoke about the poem "One Last Poem for Richard" by Sandra Cisneros, from which he takes his epigraph for *This Is How You Lose Her*. Discussing Cisneros's influence, Díaz raved about the revolutionary character of literature portraying intimacy between people of color:

> There was something really revolutionary about Sandra Cisneros's [works] when I encountered them as a young artist.... There's a part of me that just recognized that in a history like ours, in a country like ours which does everything to convince people of color that they're ugly and not valuable, to convince people of color that there's another body that is more aesthetically beautiful that you should desire more, I always felt like that poem for me that for two people of color to actually like each other in a country that tells you that you are a despised body is a fucking revolution. It's like a revolution, man, and I felt that that was very important because I grew up in that regime. I grew up in a world where all things white were more beautiful than all things black. I grew up in a world where you were being taught that there was a sexual economy where you

weren't on the winning side, and I read that poem and I felt that that was important. For many of us in what we would call a post-colonial situation, intimacy has been a profoundly difficult challenge when you live in a world that tells you to think of yourself as somehow out of order already always.[43]

These celebrated women-of-color artists gave him a formative education not only in feminist praxis but also in the aesthetics of decolonization.

After Rutgers, Díaz went on to pursue an MFA in creative writing at Cornell, where he fashioned a beautiful thesis titled "Negocios" (1995), developed an activist consciousness, and began crafting a racialized (decolonial) aesthetic. "Negocios" is a gritty realist and postminimalist work comprising seven stories equally set in Santo Domingo and Parlin: the stories introduce his central character and principal narrator, Yunior de Las Casas, who has appeared in all of his subsequent work.[44] While writing his MFA thesis, Díaz published his first story, "Ysrael" (1995), in the now-defunct *Story* magazine. Two other short stories—"How to Date a Brown Girl (Black Girl, White Girl, or Halfie)" (1995) and "Drown" (1996)—were published in the *New Yorker* under the editorship of Bill Buford. These publications paved the way for Díaz's literary agent, Nicole Aragi, to place his first book, *Drown*, with Riverhead Books.

The interconnected stories in *Drown* center on the experiences of diasporic Dominicano and Dominicana characters and are relayed in powerful, creatively wrought Dominican Afro-Atlantic vernaculars. On the whole, *Drown* introduced some of Díaz's enduring preoccupations with Afro-Dominicanidad, hypermasculinity, and the ravages of internalized racism and transnational poverty on individuals, families, and communities. Published to critical acclaim, the book was a remarkable beginning for an Afro-Dominican writer in his mid-twenties. But, as Aragi recalls, when she first attempted to place Díaz's stories, "it was difficult to get anyone interested," for publishing is always "about matchmaking." "You have to find just one other person who gets it."[45] Indeed, since then, Díaz's publishers, award committees, and readers have "gotten it."

In 2007 Díaz published *The Brief Wondrous Life of Oscar Wao*. Five years later, he published a second short-story collection, *This Is How You Lose Her* (2012), as well as a part of a science-fiction novel then in progress titled "Monstro": an apocalyptic zombie story (what he might now dub a "critical, global dystopia"[46]) set in the Dominican Republic and Haiti. *This Is How You Lose Her* generated considerable buzz: the book garnered a National Book Award short-listing, and Díaz received a prestigious MacArthur Fellowship in that same year. With this book, Díaz again reworks the genre of the short-story cycle by dispersing the narratological locus of enunciation among first-, second-, and third-person narratological perspectives, generating a complex and sustained critique of racism, White supremacy, machismo, and poverty. One of Díaz's goals, I argue, is to decolonize intimacy, affect, and love.

At a time when US Latinx politicians' responses to the Republican Party's (Trumpist) anti-immigrant, anti-Latinx, and extreme masculinist agenda were "tepid," as the National Institute of Latino Policy put it,[47] and at a time when Latinx speakers were nearly erased on national media, prevented from speaking out against Trumpist policies affecting the futures of our communities on health care, immigration, and the wall he proposed to build on the US-Mexico borderlands, Díaz provided timely critiques that rebuked the nation's White supremacy. He theorized in person and in print why so many White voters embraced the class fears and racial fantasies that Trump sowed to push a normalizing national brand and to "de-democratize" an already-ailing nation. As Díaz proclaimed, Latinx people need to connect with the fear and vulnerability that Trump's 2016 victory inflicted on our communities to resist the pull of utter despair and thus make recovery possible: "I grew up a poor immigrant of African descent from a parent who came over illegally—who was undocumented—and I have experienced precarity. I've always written about what it means to be in a country which depends on immigrant exploitation but demonizes and victimizes them all the same. I have been vaulted into middle-class comforts, but this time, this election, for many people has underscored their sense of how vulnerable they are. I do feel an urgency to write a little more, a little faster. All our voices, all our interventions are sorely needed."[48] Facing the abyss of Republican Party Trumpolandia, Díaz turned his literary writing into a doctrine of critiquing the tumultuous normalization of our times. He made a point to call allies into action.

Not since the publication of the Latin American writer Roberto Bolaño's *The Savage Detectives* has there been such a considerable critical reaction of a Hemispheric American author in the US, Latin America, and Europe. In a conversation with Díaz in *Document* magazine, Toni Morrison described her first reading of Díaz's work as a life-affirming, rhapsodic experience:

> I believe I read your short stories first. What attracted me to those stories or whatever I read—I have short-term memory loss, you have to understand, I'm 86, so I get to forget things—was how startled I was by the language. It was so real and intelligent and wild. There was the wildness as well as some deep intelligence, and I didn't think the combination of the two was possible in recent literature. Yours struck quite immedi-

ately and it wasn't just the combination of words from Santo Domingo or curse words or grammatical [uniqueness]. It was provocative but there was something so human in the nostalgia and in the knowing of human beings. I don't know anybody who writes like that, the way you do, but it's very fetching, and I look forward to more, and more, and more.[49]

Morrison suggests that through Díaz's "deeply intelligent" and "wild" literary language readers can rediscover what it means to be in the presence of the "knowing" of human beings. In other words, Díaz's imaginative work, as Morrison suggests, does not strip humanity of its futurities and its utopian possibilities, nor does it negate the ethical imperatives of human survivance.

Tracing the becoming of Junot Díaz as writer and activist intellectual, the chapters in this book take us from his activist years as a graduate student at Cornell in the 1990s to his rapid success with the publications of *Drown*, *The Brief Wondrous Life of Oscar Wao*, and *This Is How You Lose Her*, as well as the dawn of his current activism.[50]

Díaz has not only been an outspoken critic of White supremacy in our culture and institutions of higher education, but also, more recently, he has taken on Dominican Republic governmental officials who have orchestrated the "state of terror" and fear in the Dominican Republic in which most Haitian residents now live. From the *Miami Herald* to the *Guardian* and the *Nation*, Díaz has been featured as one of our country's most outspoken critics of the anti-Haitian "pogrom" in his home island of the Dominican Republic. "The last time something like this happened," Díaz said, "was Nazi Germany, and yet people are like, shrugging about it."[51] In addition to appearing on panel discussions to criticize the anti-Haitian policies in the Dominican Republic, Danticat and Díaz have met with US senators, representatives, and their staffs to urge Congress to condemn the Dominican Republic's taking away the nationality and citizenship of Dominicans of Haitian descent.

However, Díaz's activism has come with a price. A cultural hero of the Dominican Republic, Díaz had been granted the Order of Merit by Eduardo Selman, the general consul of the Dominican Republic in New York, for his "talent, creativity, and professional trajectory of our most accomplished Dominicans, who symbolize the most genuine values and principles of la dominicanidad" or Dominican-ness.[52] But Selman audaciously took back the Order of Merit from Díaz after the government saw his condemnations as anti-Dominicano. One wonders: will Selman revoke Díaz's citizenship too?

When I was in Santo Domingo, I heard and felt how Díaz was passionately detested by the Dominican Republic's hard-core nationalists and right-wing zealots because of his vocal insistence that rising White supremacy and its related xenophobias are largely driven by the nation's elites. Selman's position as general consul of the Dominican Republic in New York is mainly to conduct damage control against the planetary condemnation of his country's policies against Dominicans of Haitian descent, but going after the Dominican American writer Díaz and stripping him of his Order of Merit surely backfired by drawing even more global attention to the "civil genocide" of Dominicans of Haitian descent in the Dominican Republic.

Sometimes losing an award isn't such a bad thing.[53]

Overview and Form of This Book

Divided as it is into three parts and five chapters, this book is more traditional and symmetrical than any other work I have written. To discuss the improbable rise of Díaz's literary career and his decolonial imagination in the chapters that follow, I have provided critical and decolonial, literary readings of his MFA thesis, "Negocios"; his first book, *Drown*; *The Brief Wondrous Life of Oscar Wao*; and *This Is How You Lose Her*. Chapter 1 provides a genealogy of Díaz's activism and his lifelong wrestling with J. R. R. Tolkien's states of fantasy and world building. Part I is then divided into two overlapping chapters. Chapter 2 deals with some of the key stories that Díaz wrote in Ithaca, New York, as an MFA student in the English Department at Cornell: "Aurora," "Negocios," and "London Terrace." These spare short stories showcase Díaz's central consciousness, Yunior de Las Casas, attempting to make sense of his diasporic adolescence, diasporic belonging, and survival in Parlin's multimundo of London Terrace. Their dystopian tone should not disguise their practical purposes. For the teenaged Yunior, "belonging" in "Aurora," "Negocios," and "London Terrace" is largely articulated with appeals to his different "translocal" solidarities: feelings born of estrangement, truancy, and diasporic rootings in Central New Jersey. In chapter 3 I track the transformation of Díaz's MFA thesis into his first book, *Drown*, by focusing on seven central stories: "Ysrael," "Fiesta, 1980," "Aguantando," "Drown," "Boyfriend," "No Face," and "How to Date a Browngirl, Blackgirl, Whitegirl, or Halfie."

In my novella-length chapter 4, "Becoming Oscar Wao," I grapple with Díaz's eleven-year battle that produced *The Brief Wondrous Life of Oscar Wao*. By following Díaz's life in Mexico City, Syracuse, and Cambridge, where he first wrote a long short story titled "The Brief Wondrous Life of Oscar Wao," which was published in the *New Yorker*, I attempt to unpack how Díaz's novel, building on the version of the text that appeared in magazine, used blanks, gaps, and páginas en blanco to create a productive oscillation between determinacy and indeterminacy. Díaz's blanks are not merely gaps or omissions. Rather, following the literary-reception works by Wolfgang Iser and Winfried Fluck, I suggest that they are carefully crafted interruptions of relations—and relations of interruption—that enjoin readers to provide links between the novel's discontinuities. His blanks and páginas en blanco compel us to set up relations between the text and our own imaginary constructs. Díaz's textual "negativity"—his literal blanks and páginas en blanco—generate his aesthetic experience by enticing his readers to articulate something that is absent in the text.[54] To supply, in other words, their own light in the dark.

Finally, I turn to Díaz's theory of the fukú americanus and how it originated in colonial modernity with Almirante Colón and how it was then carried into the present by homegrown figures such as Rafael Leónidas Trujillo Molina and Ronald Reagan. To chart the full dimensions of Díaz's narratological compass in the global South, I analyze the attempt of the sociologists Immanuel Wallerstein and Aníbal Quijano to recover the complexity of what they call "Americanity." My aim here is to illustrate the complexity of Americanity's history and afterlife by analyzing it in relation to Díaz's decolonial theory of the fukú americanus. By introducing Fluck's "negative aesthetics" and Quijano and Wallerstein's "Americanity," I attempt to bring about a shift in the framework and the perspective as well as the object of analysis of Díaz's novel.

Bearing in mind Paula M. L. Moya's endorsement of Junot Díaz's "search for decolonial love" in his three books of fiction as well as her revelation that Díaz had informed her that his central consciousness Yunior's "ideas about women and the actions of these ideas [about them] always [left] him more alone, more thwarted, more disconnected from his community and himself,"[55] I make some claims in the fifth and final chapter of this book for the value of searching for decolonial aesthetics and love in his work. I begin first by analyzing a paratextual passage—a footnote[56]—from Díaz's *The Brief Wondrous Life of Oscar Wao* in which Yunior de Las Casas critically reflects on his friend's spectacularly closeted reading of science-fiction and fantasy books and the effects that Oscar's reading in the closet has on Oscar's mother, on community friends, and on Yunior as the text's "faithful watcher."[57] The whole point of Yunior's observation and the allegory of Oscar's reading in the closet, I suggest, is for us to start thinking about what happens to US Latinx "immigrant-rising" barrio kids of color like Oscar, Yunior, and Lola when they read imaginative literature and, more importantly, what goes on in their complex inner lives. Whereas Yunior throughout the course of his narrating of Oscar's brief and wondrous life highlights and occasionally critiques Oscar's developing identity politics (who he really is), he also champions Oscar's and his own changing politics of subjectivity (how they feel) as humans, their evolving dialectics of difference, and their ethics of convivencia and coexistence. I conclude by focusing on the last section on Yunior's forty-something fulsome search for decolonial love in "The Cheater's Guide to Love," the concluding story of *This Is How You Lose Her*. Here Díaz's Yunior de Las Casas, now a fully professionalized assistant professor of creative writing within what literary historian Mark McGurl has called the "program era" in US creative writing,[58] offers us much more than a lowbrow "guide" of his series of thwarted attempts to make human intimacy for himself and his series of lovers. I want to view both of Díaz's linked texts as extended exercises in dissident antihomophobic inquiry and racial hermeneutics that have had important effects on the author's provocative theories about the coloniality of power and gender, identity, sexuality, and their interrelations. Formally speaking, the role of the decolonial imagination is crucial to an understanding of Díaz's search for love. Díaz's negative aesthetics—his literature's potential to expose the hegemonic deficiencies of our world's accepted systems of thought and to provide readers with a new theory of justice—is crucial for an understanding of his fiction.

What do Díaz's writings offer in our (post)pandemic age? Why do his latest historias—"Monstro," a 2012 sci-fi text about the zombification of global capitalism, and *Islandborn*, a 2018 children's book—add to our thinking about diasporic history? What do they indicate about his future work? The conclusion and the coda trace answers to these questions by synthesizing arguments built up in previous chapters: Díaz's historically informed futurity might be key to recuperating communities and decolonizing, at long last, bodies, hearts, and almas. Díaz's poetics of indeterminacy and his signature use of negative aesthetics are brought to bear on a catastrophic ecological collapse that, in an objective and prophetic form, conveys the sense of our planet's doom. For its part, *Islandborn* develops the disjunctions between his Afro-Atlantic Dominican American characters' individual double consciousnesses and the role of the decolonial imagination in understanding Díaz's search for love.

1

"Wrestling with J. R. R. Tolkien's *Lord of the Rings*"

How Junot Díaz Thinks about Coloniality, Power, and the Speculative Genres

Some years ago, Monica Hanna, Jennifer Harford Vargas, and I coordinated a literary and cultural event at Stanford University called "Junot Díaz: A Symposium," which led to the publication of *Junot Díaz and the Decolonial Imagination* (2016).[1] The first evening of the two-day symposium featured Pulitzer Prize–winning author Díaz, whom we had invited to deliver the Stanford Center for Comparative Studies in Race and Ethnicity (CCSRE) annual Anne and Loren Kieve Distinguished Lecture.[2] That evening, after taking a moment to underscore the importance of the Kieve Distinguished Lecture and the great honor that the symposium organizers and panelists had bestowed upon him, Díaz, in his opening riffs, identified the force fields of race, racism, and immi-

Figure 1.1 Junot Díaz, "Junot Díaz Symposium," May 18, 2012, Stanford University. Photograph by the author.

gration that he worked hard to capture in his fictions. He then stepped away from the podium, unexpectedly, and addressed a packed house without any written notes whatsoever. Dressed in dark jeans, an Ivy League pullover with white collar, and running shoes, he surprised everyone with an impromptu announcement: "Guess what? No fucking lecture."[3]

Walking to the front of an auditorium packed with undergraduates, graduate students, faculty, and scholars attending the symposium (figure 1.1), Díaz delivered a brilliant off-the-cuff analysis of J. R. R. Tolkien's *The Lord of the Rings* (1954–55), his all-time favorite modernist novel, where he illustrated how—ever since he was a young immigrant Afro-Dominicano boy growing up in the impoverished barrioscapes of New Jersey—he saw Tolkien's work as primarily centered on race, power, and magic. During his hour-long performance, Díaz demonstrated why he is so highly regarded in cultural circles: not only does he write rescriptable stories, essays, and novels, but he also possesses unique bilanguaging skills, enormous gifts of the ear and eye, pristine phrasing and timing in English and Spanglish, and even some occasional "nerdspeak" thrown into the mix that even the most indolent, refined masters of mainstream US culture covet.

I start this chapter with Díaz's 2012 lecture not only because it elucidates his recent, urgent uses of speculative (realist) fantasy to critique White supremacy but also because it attests to his sharp wit, polymathic intelligence, and penchant for unorthodox insights—a constellation unusual among literary authors and public intellectuals. Moreover, in Díaz's fiction, criticism, and speaking engagements, we see these capacities interfacing with his deeply rooted activist sensibility: an unwavering sense that things could be otherwise. With this in mind, I end the chapter with a coda in which I explore the presidential lecture he delivered at Stanford in May 2017, in which he encouraged student-activists of color in the audience to offer one another strength and security in our turbulent political climate. Both of Díaz's Stanford lectures give us an invaluable sense of how his thinking about literature, fantasy, race, and his lifelong Dominicano activism has been developing since the early 1990s.

This chapter is thus an exercise in the history of the present, an effort to track the growth of Díaz's literary and activist thinking. Whereas Díaz has directly recognized the celebrated Nuyorican writers Piri Thomas, Nicholasa Mohr, Tato Laviera, and Edward Vega as influences who helped him develop an Afro-Dominicano voice, this chapter grapples with Tolkien's states of fantasy, unpacking how Díaz "wrestled" with him to imagine a world-making otherwise.[4]

In the 2012 lecture, Díaz spoke about J. K. Rowling, about H. P. Lovecraft, and most of all about Tolkien. Tolkien, he said, was a writer he "grew up on," and *The Lord of the Rings* "fed" his near insatiable hunger for "other worlds"; he was a young fan of everything Middle-earth, yet even as an adult he continues "to wrestle with Tolkien" for reasons that had as much to do with his growing up in the shadow of his own dark lord in Santo Domingo: what some dictators really become "in the imagination of the nations they afflict." Just as the *Beowulf* writer used a dragon to personify fully the evils and "waifs" of his world, so Díaz's dark lord, Trujillo, is an emblem of malice, sexual abuse, and militarism equal to his and our times. As the "architect" of power and history in *The Brief Wondrous Life of Oscar Wao*, Trujillo and his "mixture of violence, intimidation, rape, and terror" afflict the Dominican Republic with many agonies.[5]

For the first part of his address, Díaz spoke about race. "I write about race—by extension, I write about White supremacy," he said, cutting to what I had asked him to address. He noted how agitated he feels about "the rhetorical legerdemain" of "deforming our silences to fit in with larger silences of [US] society." He emphasized that it's a betrayal, especially, of the people (like him) who lived "at the racially sharp end of the stick." Speaking directly to the crowd of Stanford undergraduates and faculty, Díaz discussed how "our privileges exacerbate the horrors of others."

He also discussed how the hegemonic idea of the United States as a postracial society and culture is a "happy delusion": "We are as hyper-racial today as we were two hundred years ago." He said that describing oneself as somehow "beyond race" was as delusional as a man saying he isn't sexist: "These languages never go away." The coloniality of power and the coloniality of gender's privilege also "never go away," he said. He reported how many of the young undergraduates he teaches at MIT and other college campuses, including Syracuse University and New York University, often tell him that they "have never experienced racism" and, as result, that's "why they can't write about race." Saying that one has never experienced racism, he quipped, is "like saying I never experienced dying." Moreover, his students lament about the melancholy of their racial politics of identity: they ask him why they can't "just be a writer." Why do college students always "appeal to the universal"? Díaz asked. "Believe you me," he said, "when I remember the people I grew up with in Santo Domingo and in New Jersey—they'd find that this postracial obfuscating way of speaking about race and racism holds no currency whatsoever . . . They'd call you n***** in a second, and that meant that you were Black as shit."

Partly as result of his Dominican Republic upbringing in the late 1960s and his diasporic emigration to New Jersey, Díaz felt it was entirely possible to "create a new kind of art" that would not shy away from representing all of the "complex layers of race." In what he described as his "hybrid" and "creolized" books, for example, he desired to "create a kind of art that would be ethically responsible to the friends" he grew up with: "the friends who would call bullshit at the ways we talked about race in the academy." He recalled how another friend he grew up with, "an Asian American," once confided to him that "I don't want to write anything that's Asian American." When Díaz reported this anecdote of how we negotiate the tensions of talking about race to one of his friends, who had never attended college, his friend said, "Like, damn! I thought we had enough White writers."

He urged his audience to measure how deep our denial is about racism. He recalled observing of a group of Northeastern male peers that they were all dating White women or women lighter skinned than themselves. Their predictable response, he noted, was "Oh, but that was love . . . !" "We just met." "It was random." No one could "fess up" to the fact that "I date who I date because I was told people who are light-skinned are better." Looking at the sea of undergraduate and graduate students at Stanford's Levinthal Hall, he asked: "Who wants to embrace that?" Under such circumstances of coloniality and White supremacy in present-day América, "How do we bear witness to ourselves?"

He addressed other timely topics, including his own thoughts about art and decolonial aesthetics, feelings, affect, and the monotopical Kantian idea of "universality": why is "the default setting of universality" always "White"? Does Kant's reason have a color? Are our aesthetic categories of the sublime racist?[6] Although many writers of color often resist this categorization of Kantian universality, he noted how he had never encountered a "White writer who said, 'You know what? I don't want to be a White writer.'" In fact, he argued, people outside that "dominant default setting" live in what he called "a delusional space" in which race can be seen but not heard—or what Stephanie Li calls "signifying without specifying."[7] He illustrated this problematic by referring to what he sees as President Barack Obama's double message on race: "I'm not Black, but I will code some shit so you know I'm Black." But he was asked to "signify without specifying" in his work, and he resisted: "I ran from that as hard as I could." He often asks himself whether or not it is really possible to capture in writing all the nuances of denial and truth to avoid the writer's deadliest pitfall: "I'm not going to blind myself so no one notices I'm not noticing."

His aspiration as a writer was to "figure out a way to represent more honestly the way people variously talk about race, its discourses, its silences, its logics, its reality—that is, figure out a way that the actual material did not endorse that reality—that one could actually represent our insane racial logic without endorsing that insane logic." He said that unlike Rowling's witches and wizards (including Harry Potter), he wants us to "not be afraid of saying Voldemort's name." Almost no one wants to say political race and racism's name; instead, we refer to them by epithets: "universalism," "colorblindness," "postrace."

Commenting on the seemingly homogeneous sphere of the US English Department he was interpellated in during his undergraduate years at Rutgers and his graduate studies at Cornell, Díaz briefly addressed the deep schism that he has resisted between creative writing—Planet MFA—and literary and cultural scholarship—Planet PhD—disciplines that often differ in their canonical and noncanonical points of reference (*Beowulf* versus *Mango Street*), their rhetorical ideologies (symptomatic versus nonsymptomatic and close versus distant readings), and their perceived objects of inquiry (literature versus fiction).[8] Because US English departments in general and creative-writing programs in particular have exercised perhaps the single most important influence on postwar US literary production—and because any convincing interpretation of the imaginative literary works themselves has to take their role into account—Díaz criticized the way he was instructed not to write about either politics or race in his fiction: "The basic tool in creative writing was don't be political."[9] But then, as now, Díaz disagreed. As a writer, he was "the concretization of everything you should not be": "You should not be too raced; you should not be too specific—you should always go universal—signifying without specifying—and you should not be too political." In the US academy's program era, he was a walking personification of the negative.

He ended the first part of his Kieve Lecture by turning increasingly autobiographical/circumfessional and by showcasing his razor-sharp, decolonial litcrit acumen. His panoramic novel, *The Brief Wondrous Life of Oscar Wao*, was his attempt to use all of Tolkien and science fiction's "nerd stuff" to paint "the hemispheric madness" through his home island of the Dominican Republic. "Science fiction, gothic fantasy, and speculative genres of magic were obvious sources of inspiration" for him. After winning a Guggenheim award in 1999,

Díaz went on sabbatical leave from Syracuse and spent a year living in Mexico City writing an apocalyptic novel, "Akira," about the destruction of New York City, and what was to become his Pulitzer Prize–winning novel, *The Brief Wondrous Life of Oscar Wao*. Here in Mexico's Distrito Federal (DF), Díaz had an epiphany: a "vision of a poor, doomed ghetto nerd." As he recalled, he "dash[ed] the first part" of his first novel "out in a couple of weeks."

He then shifted gears and explained how he "wanted to have a simple conversation." He had earlier started that morning "with the folks at the Junot Díaz Symposium" about his celebrated novel. "It's like opening the studio doors," he told his audience, and saying "Here are the paints I used"—something he is often reluctant to do as an artist. The literary and cultural scholars and theorists "will say 'blue,' and I'll say OK, you say that." Díaz also elaborated on how as a writer he is always working narratologically, on the structure of his texts. It's one of these "formal problems" that delights him. For example, the narrative structure of *The Brief Wondrous Life of Oscar Wao* slowly pushes readers forward into its own "silences," the silences it creates even as it "exposes other" all-important components. And Díaz honed in on the novel's two basic narratological threads: Oscar de León's wondrous life told in a linear fashion and Oscar's family's life told in the reverse. Once readers "braid these two strands together," he explained, "they have the novel's basic form."

Díaz, of course, elaborated on other threads in his novel—what he called the "nerd stuff" in *Oscar Wao*: "comic books, role-playing games, and the importance of science fiction," narratives that his Dominican American hero Oscar de León calls "the speculative genres." Juxtaposed contrapuntally to this "nerd stuff," Díaz emphasized that the other foundational narratological thread in the novel—what he referred to as the "decolonial turn" in *Oscar Wao*—was "the history of hemispheric life in the Américas as seen through the lens of the Dominican Republic."

Looking at the intertextual books that loom behind *The Brief Wondrous Life of Oscar Wao*'s "nerdish side," the writer critically commented on Tolkien's *The Lord of the Rings*, Wagner's *Rheingold*, Lovecraft's gothic fantasies, and Rowling's *Harry Potter*. Astute readers of *Oscar Wao*, he said, have readily picked up on his references to Rowling, Tolkien, and Wagner, but Lovecraft's early twentieth-century work, which "shows up repeatedly in the text," goes largely unnoticed because most of his readers blur over "this 'nerd shit' because they are too busy figuring out if I am fucking talking about them when I write in Spanish in *Oscar Wao*. They say, 'What the fuck, Yo!' I go, 'Negro, I'm talking about you in nerdish.'"

Díaz "raised this nerd stuff" in his address because what "dawned on him" as a young novelist was "that these speculative genres" have immense significance for our planet's "sub-zeitgeist," for if "Victoria Nelson in her monumental book *The Secret Life of Puppets* (2001) can argue that in our sub-zeitgeist (all the pop cultural crap that exists in our culture's comic books, role-playing games, and movies), that is, all our impulses toward the supernatural, all of the impulses toward the transcendent, and the impulses toward religiosity—all of these impulses were displaced from people by the Enlightenment." The Enlightenment, in other words, displaced our impulses for wonder and magic. In the West the Enlightenment "knocked the shit out of wonder," and then these very impulses "began to express" themselves in and "find a home" in "the sub-sub-zeitgeist in comic books, movies, and the speculative genres."

If Nelson could make this persuasive argument in her text, Díaz suggested he could reasonably argue that what made *The Brief Wondrous Life of Oscar Wao* "possible" was that "science fiction" for his characters Oscar and Yunior "is dark consciousness"—that is, "it's the dark unconscious of our time." Moreover, by combining Nelson's philosophical ideas about the Enlightenment with Quijano's iconic insights about the coloniality of power's planetary genesis in 1492, he could theorize that "coloniality is the dark subconscious of the speculative genres."[10]

When we think about Tolkien's *The Lord of the Rings*, Díaz explained, "we do not usually think about the genealogies" that this modernist work "comes out of," say, the great "Nordic tradition"—out of the fantastic violences among the dragons and Elves. But we need to ask ourselves about the innovation Tolkien makes to this tradition. Before we get Tolkien, "we get fantasy stories, we get stories of the marvelous and magic and wonder, all the time." But "we never get a dark lord." If there were demon presences, these haunting and spectral presences were "standard Christian ones." Moreover, "what we find in the Nordic tradition are the dragon figures" that largely function as "great disrupting figures." Thus envisaged, "when one thinks about the curses," in Tolkien's work, said Díaz—when one hears the echo of Wagner's *Das Rheingold* in the dwarf's desire for the cursed ring—one can understand Tolkien's achievement: "the totalizing thematization of slavery." For in *Das Rheingold* the ring "doesn't have the maligned intelligence—the ring just makes shit go bad for you." It thus operates like objects in many fairy tales: "it exacerbate[s] whatever your vice is," just as in *Rheingold* greed exacerbates people's greed.

In the remainder of his performance address, Díaz focused on the vastly different treatment of the ring in *Rheingold* and *The Lord of the Rings*. In contrast to Wagner's ring "just making stuff go bad for you," in Tolkien's innovative work "the ring produces slavery" and functions, Díaz argued, "racially." "The fear that everyone has in the Middle-earth is not that [they are] going to be conquered; rather, it is that Lord Sauron is going to enslave [them]—'a slavery without limits,' Tolkien writes." Every group in Middle-earth that "talks about Sauron says there is going to be a total enslavement." The huge impact that *The Lord of the Rings* has staged in our culture is that Tolkien took "coloniality" seriously. "Coloniality"—as Quijano has theorized it and as Díaz explained—is "the rendering of the world into races." That is "the absolutely primary artifact," Díaz said. In Tolkien, "We see that the fantasy world was rendered into races." As an aside, Díaz quipped, "We can see that one of the potent things" that Tolkien has bequeathed to us is "the precarious way that race has been adapted into our 'video' and 'role-playing games,' that the 'creative world'—the subdivided world that Tolkien writes about—is divided into races. . . . Tolkien had the great idea that there are Elves, dwarfs, hobbits, and these are races for him. 'OK, guys—What's the big deal?' he asked."

To illustrate his decolonial reading, Díaz asked us to think about the function of Tolkien's character Sauron. Just as we might ask what would Shakespeare's *King Lear* look like without the character Lear, he asked what would Tolkien's novels look like without the dark lord: "For me, Sauron, the dark lord, is more than just an archetypal bad guy. Let's think for a moment that Sauron is a being that comes from outside the Middle-earth, and that his realm in the novel, both Mordor and his own realm in the North, Angband—these were Sauron's settler colonies," for he "occupies these spaces and holds them against the struggling Indigenous people who live there." And this is precisely "when Sauron devises the way that he's going to enslave Middle-earth—that the very rings that he creates function racially." He creates "nine rings for men, three for Elves, and one for himself." And "the one ring he creates for himself," he explained, "controls and dominates all of them." "I think there is much to be said about this [dominance]," for "this is not something usually talked about in Tolkien, in gothic fantasy, or in science fiction." But at the heart of what Díaz called "classic heroic fantasy" is what—after Quijano—he characterized as "the coloniality of power."

Thus, in thinking about "the speculative genres," the one core definition that has been "left out"—the one typology that has been silenced or not fully described or adequately theorized—is how the speculative genres, including gothic fantasy, are absolutely predicated on something we know very well. *The Lord of the Rings* works and resonates powerfully within our decolonial theory of the coloniality of power. Moreover, we know about the systemic formation and classification of the division of the races:

We feel this in our bones—even if we don't want to talk about it. We certainly know that the terror Tolkien places at the very heart of *The Lord of the Rings* is the terror at the heart of gothic fantasies—all of the forms of repressed and forced enslavement.... For me, what I attempted to do in *Oscar Wao* was to align the "nerd stuff" with the Dominican coloniality of power because I saw them sharing a discourse or vocabulary.... As an artist, I recognized that these discourses were not being theorized.... And I saw very clearly how Quijano's coloniality of power is the secret, animating force that gives all things in fantasy life.... This is what gives Tolkien his real power.

All things considered, Tolkien was a survivor and a witness of World War I, and his Middle-earth is a mesmerizing postapocalyptic world. The dark lord Sauron is "a being that comes from outside the Middle-earth," from a "race that dominates Middle-earth." If the *Harry Potter* series thematizes "bad guys versus good guys, my power versus your power," Tolkien's focus thus offers a radically different interpretative horizon: "Fighting power with power you lose. Power breeds corruption," Díaz said. Michel Foucault, of course, hypothesized in *The History of Sexuality* that "power is everywhere"[11] and that as a result it robbed everyone of his or her freedom and made political resistance less a quantum of force and something immanent in every sort of social relations. "Power never destroys power," Díaz argued—echoing and advancing Foucault's hypothesis—because power seemingly comes from everywhere.

It is Oscar de León's familiarity and fluency in "nerdishness" that allows him to begin to see the stark operations of the coloniality of power working in his mundane and deracinated life in New Jersey. It is, in fact, "the nerdishness" of Oscar's "role-playing games, the way that race gets broken up, and the way that Oscar feels his ultimate enslavement: this opens his eyes to see the erasures in the Caribbean," the "erasures in these spaces of his Cabral-de León family." In chapter 4, "Becoming Oscar Wao," I will analyze the narratological work that his erasures and blanks, or negative aesthetics, perform in Díaz's novel.

Briefly, *The Lord of the Rings* is undoubtedly one of the most influential heroic-fantasy novels. More than previous writers, Tolkien had constructed an elaborate history, geography, linguistics, mythology, and racial formation for his invented world, and he fit his narrative into that. Of course, fantasy and world building had gone on before—as Díaz's own MIT syllabus on world building and the digital humanities suggests—but Tolkien saw the building of an internally consistent secondary world as central to the project of what he called "fairy stories" and what we would now call heroic fantasy.[12] Moreover, Tolkien's obsessive focus on the secondary world was a precursor of the post-1960s countercultural fantasy craze. It is easy to mock Middle-earth—as the utopian Marxist writers Darko Suvin and Fredric Jameson have done in their essays on the poetics and history of the literary genre of science fiction—but Díaz in his lecture responded to Tolkien's critics by suggesting that Tolkien's unique fantasy can be an interesting kind of project for imaginative decolonial writers like himself who think about race, power, and culture in their world-building books.[13] The Lord of the Rings not only involved great creativity and inventiveness, but also, for Díaz, it grappled with a very powerful way of effecting the kind of suspension of disbelief unique to the speculative genres.

Tolkien's worldview is, to be sure, resolutely rural, petty-bourgeois, conservative, antimodernist, misanthropically Christian, and, for both Suvin and Jameson, anti-utopian. That comes across stridently in Tolkien's fiction and nonfiction. For instance, Suvin has written on this in his iconic *Metamorphoses of Science Fiction*: "[In *The Lord of the Rings*, there is] the total shutting out of labor, scarcity of women figures as well as sexuality and erotics in general which feeds into the sharp allotment of black vs white moral evaluation to separate species—as in the Morlock-like Orcs, proletarians seen as sex-maniac and antheap ogres. Goodies are beautiful and tall Northerners—though the cast is redeemed by Hobbits, Elves, Dwarves and Ents—and the baddies are swarthy skulkers."[14] In opposition to what he called the Robot Age, Tolkien presented a past that never existed. Although no one can reasonably argue that he had a systematic opposition to modernity—just a terrified ranting about "better days," a chaos to be met with moderation—his revolt was not a totally escapist endeavor, for he encouraged readers and imaginative writers like Díaz to conjure alternatives to his condition, remedies for world problems such as racism and the coloniality of power. As Robert Tally Jr. suggests, even though Tolkien's world is not "homologous to our own," it is figured fantastically as a place where, as Aragon put it in his speech during the Council of Elrond, "the stars are strange."[15] Like Tally's interpretation, Díaz's decolonial reading of *The Lord of the Rings* outlined a world of clear-cut ethics that clarified his own racist New Jersey world.

When the symposium address was opened to questions from the audience, the tone remained largely in the keys of literary reflection, our (post)apocalyptic world, and the ideologies of precarity. Some of the undergraduates sitting in the front rows of the auditorium were active in the Bay Area's Occupy Art movement, and they asked about the radical possibilities of disrupting the terms of the conversation in the academy and, more specifically, about the challenges of being an activist and intellectual. Díaz was graceful in his responses. He said that he was perplexed about the tendencies he witnessed among young college activists to criticize themselves for not changing the world, rather than giving themselves credit for all of the work they do as students, scholars, and movement activists. He was very excited about how many of his students at MIT, as well as many others he had met across the country, rejected abandoning what we might call a materialist project, and he was energized by those who believed that postindustrial neoliberalism demanded an affirmation of the primacy of activism and a critique of the planet's economy.

Although it was indeed rare to have a celebrated living, thinking, and feeling writer in the very space of a symposium where panelists deconstructed and reconstructed his fiction, for the panelists and the audience having Junot Díaz participate in the event was energizing. How often can literary and cultural discussions turn to questions such as the following: Do writers of color have a life? Can scholars think about a writer's imaginative work without engaging with the writer's biography and intellectual formation in our program era? Is Díaz's biography something external to the literary and cultural exegesis of his fiction? The philosopher Jacques Derrida once playfully asked: "What was Heidegger's life?" Well, Derrida quipped, "He was born, he thought, and he died."[16] However, this was not Díaz's position at the symposium. By attending every session of the symposium and engaging us as a writer, activist-scholar, literary critic, and historian, Díaz was calling for the invention of a new literary and cultural problematic of the biographical in general and of the biography of the living, thinking, feeling writer in particular: a rigorous rethinking of the borders between "corpus" and the "body" (*carne, corps*). Shortly after the publication of *The Brief Wondrous Life of Oscar Wao*, Díaz spelled out the nuanced etymological relationships between *carne* and *carnality* in his imaginative fiction:

> What I do think is very present in [my novel] is the root of the word "carnality," which is *carne*. Bodies are extremely present in this book. Because there is no Caribbean-African diasporic experience that doesn't in some ways revolve around the question of these bodies—these bodies that guaranteed us for a certain period of time that we were going to be slaves, that we were going to be bred. And the problematics around those bodies, how those bodies work. Given the history of the Caribbean and the Americas, if you're a person of African descent, that kind of discussion of what role the body plays not only in organizing identity, but in organizing a quest for home—it just couldn't be avoided. It felt too rich.[17]

As we will see in the chapters that follow, what is often at stake with Díaz's characters in *Drown*, *The Brief Wondrous Life of Oscar Wao*, and *This Is How You Lose Her* is how masculinity gets performed in his texts and what Díaz often thematizes in his texts as a "disconnect" between the masculinity that characters such as Oscar and Yunior seem to perform: their "discourse-around-masculinity versus your practice [of masculinity] versus what-lies-beneath-the-masks."[18] What is fascinating and alluring about Díaz's character Oscar de León is that—unlike Yunior de Las Casas—he does not seem to have any masks. The person that he performs is the person who lies beneath the masks. For Díaz, there's a much more direct relationship between the Oscar that we see on the outside and the Oscar who lives inside. Perhaps this is why Lola de León laments more critically about Afro-Dominican survival that "the only way out is in."[19]

Coda: "Stealing Fire"—The Making of the Activist Writer

The political implications of Díaz's approach to carnality, the body, the coloniality of power, writing as a form of action, and activism have not been lost on Latinx and other student-activists of color, who have long been the objects rather than the subjects of Latinidad: they have been denied institutional validation of embodied knowledges, and they have been the objects of criminalizing and pathologizing discourses by the US Republican hegemony. Therefore, it is not surprising that a number of Latinx activists and critical theorists have attempted to emulate Díaz's activist role. As we know, student-activism around the struggle for Latinx studies at Cornell was Díaz's primary social politicization from 1993 to 1995. In 1993—as anthropologist Arlene Dávila has documented in her portrait of the artist—Díaz was one of the student-activists who "occupied" the central administration building, Day Hall, to protest the vandalization of an art installation by a visiting Chicano artist.[20] The student-activists called on the Ivy League administration not only to address the hostile anti-Latinx environment on campus but also to hire and tenure more Latinx faculty, to diversify the university undergraduate curriculum by offering more courses on and by Latinx, and to provide them with a major (or field imaginary) in Latinx studies. After the four-day protest ended, the students' demands led to the founding of a Latinx Living Center on campus, to the hiring of faculty such as the renowned writer Helena María Viramontes, and to the creation of a Latinx studies "minor." It was also not Díaz's sole preoccupation.

After Díaz had earned his MFA in 1995 (and before he joined the creative-writing faculty at Syracuse), he seemed to be everywhere in New York City at once, working with community organizations from the ProLibertad social movement (a group in support of Puerto Rican political prisoners), the Partido de los Trabajadores Dominicanos, and the Dominican Youth Union.

Díaz could also be found working with other community organizations such as the Committee against Anti-Asian Violence and helping organize national conferences on the Dominican diaspora. As a result of his activism and advocacy with ProLibertad, Díaz began working in New York City with Dominicans 2000, a grassroots group that campaigned for the electing of more Dominican American politicians at the city council level.

More recently, Díaz, like many Latinx activists, was also involved in one of the paradigmatic manifestations of local politics: the signing of petitions, especially on Facebook, and letters in support of antiracist and anti-immigrant campaigns, including (as I emphasized in the introduction) his critique of racist immigration policies against Haitians in the Dominican Republic. Díaz has some 195,000 followers on his personal Facebook page. He has not only showcased news articles condemning Trump as a White supremacist but has also posted op-ed pieces he has cowritten with Edwidge Danticat and Julia Alvarez[21] in which they criticize the Dominican Republic's Ruling 168, which revoked the citizenship of all Dominicans born after 1929 to undocumented parents. Many years earlier, on December 20, 1999, Díaz and Danticat had published an op-ed titled "The Dominican Republic's War on Haitian Workers" in the *New York Times*. In the essay they condemn the illegal deportation of Haitians and Haitian Dominicans by the Dominican government.[22]

To be sure, signing petitions in favor of local community organizations' call for political reform and writing op-ed pieces on Hispaniola are not superficial operations for young Latinx writers like Díaz. Although there is the real possibility of Díaz signing too many petitions and being charged as supporting too many heterogeneous activist causes, Díaz defends himself by arguing that "the real question is not what happens at the individual level. . . . What matters is what happens at the collective level."[23] This is why, even after so many national and international awards and prizes, he continues to work as a Latinx activist: he is the current honorary chairman of the DREAM project, a nonprofit education initiative in the Dominican Republic.

For all of his literary works' influence on new social Latinx student movements, it is fair to say much of Díaz's activist insights owe more to the Latinx student movements than they owe to him. At least some of Díaz's reflections on what Arlene Davila sees as a "progressive antimarketable Latinidad that challenges the whitening impulse of most Latinx pundits, writers, and intellectuals"[24] were inspired by struggles he saw all around him: political struggles waged by the Latinx student movements advocating their campuses to hire more Latinx faculty, to protect first-generation DREAMers on university campuses from US Immigration and Customs Enforcement and possible deportation, and to create antiracist departments and centers of education. Whatever relations of causality may obtain between Díaz's literary works and the Latinx student social movements, it is noteworthy that his imaginative fictional texts about young Latinx immigrants, about the pains of decolonial love, about homophobia and severe masculinism, and about the pressures of liberal "normalization"[25] on his literary characters like Yunior, Lola, and Oscar seem to have found their most passionate and receptive audience among young student-of-color activists, participants in various social movements with connections to US universities and to youth culture in general.

I conclude here by highlighting Díaz's mature thinking about activism, immigration, and antiracism: I reflect on why his 2017 national lecture tour, presidential addresses, and book readings—at Grinnell College, the University of Iowa, Cal Arts, Princeton, Emory, the University of Hawaii-Manoa, Stanford University, and the international Openair Literatur Festival in Zurich—have aroused so much interest among students, faculty, and local communities alike. What do young university students, especially activists of color, see in Junot Díaz? That is the final question of this chapter.

A number of plausible answers suggest themselves, and I will review a few of them before diving into the one I wish to emphasize. The most significant impetus for Latinx activists to find political and aesthetic inspiration from Díaz comes, I believe, from his refusal after winning the Pulitzer Prize to become what he himself has called the tokenized, abstract, "discursive" Latinx in US society. He has no desire—as I suggested in the introduction to this book—to signify without specifying: "I have no interest in being a 'writer,' shorn from all my communities' connections. I'm a Dominican writer, a writer of African descent, whether or not anyone else wants to admit it."[26] Students I have informally polled in Britain, Germany, Spain, Sweden, and across the Hemispheric Américas see something genuine in Díaz's resistance to being cast by the mainstream literary culture as the exceptional proto-American immigrant success story. They admire him when he critiques the gatekeeping literary canon and when he asserts that he is not a token discursive Latinx: Díaz never tires of explaining that he can "safely say that [he's] seen the US from the bottom up . . . and [that although he's] a success story," it's only "an individual story." He goes on: "But if you adjust the knob and just take it back one more setting to the family unit, I would say my family tells a more complicated story. It tells the story of two kids in prison. It tells the story of enormous poverty, of enormous difficulty."[27]

Díaz's activism—since his time as a graduate student at Cornell to his present position—has taken its distinctive and indicatively decolonial shape from the university campus and social struggles with which marginalized first-generation Latinx students have had to grapple. At their collective best, Latinx student-activists at universities across the nation have had to challenge our hegemonic modes of legitimizing knowledge and power at the heart of the university. They have had to attain knowledge of the multiple ways that power and, more specifically, the coloniality of power are everywhere around them: they have also had to learn how to undo the hierarchies of power and the power of the experts so that they can intervene in an age in which Trump's strategists have advocated that "darkness is good" and a moment in which Trump wretchedly caricatures unauthorized Mexican male workers as criminals and rapists. At a time when Trump's White supremacy rules, when his shamelessness is schematized into a grating, volatile fearlessness, and when charlatanism is somehow synonymous with charisma, Latinx student-activists are looking for inspiration and guidance from activist writers and public intellectuals like Díaz.

Finally, as I argue in chapters 4 and 5, nothing more eloquently and persuasively communicates Díaz's deconstruction of normalization and the relationality of power—the sense that young Latinx youths need to conform not only to the desires of becoming a discursive Latinx but also to rigid sexual and gender masculinist formations—than Díaz's descriptions of Oscar de León's experiences of reading science-fiction books in the barrio closet. For queer theorists such as Eve Kosofsky Sedgwick, the closet allegorizes and emblematizes the production of the complex relations of power. I linger on a central question Díaz asks in *The Brief Wondrous Life of Oscar Wao*: why is Oscar reading science-fiction novels in the closet? The main reason, Díaz suggests, is that the closet helps Oscar protect himself from the various wretched sorts of social, gendered, and ethno-racial disqualifications imposed on him by his family unit, his New Jersey schooling, and his community. The closet is hardly a space of freedom for Díaz's Oscar de León, although it dramatically affords him a space from which to imagine a better world for himself and his family; it affords him a liminal space to think about his Latinx world otherwise.

There are doubtless other factors that may explain the enormous appeal that Díaz and his literary works have among Latinx student-activists. For the purpose of this coda, however, I have concentrated on only one of the central motives for the Latinx activists' willingness to appropriate Díaz and his imaginative works for themselves. I believe that Díaz's approach to Latinx student activists' problems with the power of the university, with how they and other students have been marginalized, with the creep of the alt right's hallucinatory reality, and with the proliferation of millions of US Republican soldiers waging apocalyptic battles has enabled student-activists and Díaz's readers in general to devise effective strategies for confronting and resisting the vile world of White supremacy, anti-immigrant hate, and Latinxphobia.

In his May 2017 Stanford presidential lecture, Díaz spoke to his largely student and Bay Area community audience about Trump's grifteresque persona, the slogans of hatred, and all of Trump's put-downs of women, Latinx, Muslims, and the Left directly: "I was drawn and motivated and passionate about intervening in this new political climate."[28] He emphasized that "we really need to fight in ways that we have never fought before. These are not easy times, and it requires tremendous courage." He went on: "Fortunately, most of the young people involved in these fights are the greatest things I have ever seen." (See figure 1.2.)

Díaz then offered advice for the Latinx and other student-of-color activists in the audience, speaking directly to the unique circumstances that they face. The first step in fighting their marginalization is to seek university seminars and lecture courses that allow them to understand how the modern university functions as a matrix of the power-knowledge couplet: "Get yourself a definition of neoliberalism. Get yourself a definition of patriarchy. Get yourself a definition of Orientalism. Get yourself a definition of White supremacy. And you certainly need a definition of feminism." In other words, Díaz advocated that the students must educate themselves in the "system they inhabit."

Next, he suggested that students in the audience continue building collectivities and allying with other students around them: he stressed the political importance of forming initiatives on and off the university campus: "Get in the business of fighting for each other's freedom," for US White supremacy "is out in ways that I haven't seen before, and [believe me] I've seen it all."

Near the end of his lecture, he reminded his largely student audience to commit themselves to changing our society's problems, encouraging them to help others in times of distress: "Helping others will give you more perspective than anything else in your education."

"You are here to steal fire," Díaz concluded. "That is your goal. That is your mission. And that's what will hold you to this difficult task. We must steal fire because we must transform the world."

His Stanford presidential lecture called us to analyze our world strategically not only in terms of what the world's elites and their strategies of normalization say but also in terms of what they do. To put it plainly, it is clear to Díaz

Figure 1.2 Junot Díaz delivering the 2017 Stanford Presidential Lecture. Used with permission of Steven Castillo.

that what we are up against in our struggles to survive is the history of the present. The discourse and propositions of Trump's White supremacy cannot simply be refuted by the enlightenment of reason: they can be resisted only with a Promethean spirit, "our ancestors' courage." "They gave us so much. They will give us more, if we let them. When we bang with them our perspective will shift—it will no longer be in this dark moment.... In their presence and with their guidance, the long arc of our historical struggle for liberation is revealed. You will see our genius, you will see our joy, you will see our supernatural resistance."

When he asked Latinx and students of color to remember and honor their ancestors—to cherish and champion their ancestors, their sacrifices—Díaz reminded his audience that "every breath our ancestors" took was "a condemnation of colonialism," patriarchy, and colonialism's logic, the coloniality of power: "Each breath is the sound of chains breaking. Each breath is, in its own way, a revolution." This shift of perspective, his insistence on our ancestors' breaths as revolts against tyranny, is a part of a larger dispositif (apparatus) that connects new forms of knowledge with new subjects, objects, and new domains. For Díaz, our ancestors' bodies—their pleasures and pains—are linked to the strengthening of resistance. Together: a continuity, a lifeline, a flame.

Junot Díaz's MFA Program Era at Cornell University and Beyond

2

Díaz's Planet MFA

"Negocios"

Lots I could tell you about my time at Cornell, good, bad, crazy—and one day if I get a chance I'll try to write some of it down but for now I'll keep it simple and say only this: I didn't have a good workshop experience....
So what was the problem?
Oh just the standard problem of MFA programs.
That shit was just *too white*.

JUNOT DÍAZ, introduction to *Dismantle*, 1–2

Place seems to be everything to Junot Díaz. Throughout his short stories he mines his own urban place of ruins—diasporic, transnational, multidirectional, and avowedly Dominicano—to forge his literary materials. His linked cuentos' (stories') patterns and themes, their hearts and movements—from his Cornell University MFA thesis, "Negocios," to the ten stories he fully developed in his first book, *Drown*—are obsessed with what the anthropologist Jorge Duany once referred to as transnationalism's "colonial" soil: the multidirectional transnational flow of people, ideas, goods, and cultural forms of expression in the Américas.¹ As Díaz renders his largely Afro-Dominicano characters—through their dispersals, observations, and routes across aesthetic, familial, and geographical contexts throughout the Hispanophone Caribbean and the United States—the external features of Díaz's own emplotments become inner truths. For Díaz, place—at once transnational, ever changing, and urban—is, in short, a spiritual location from which he examines a truth deeper than anything like globalization.² Díaz sees himself as participating in a great migratory process, moving through history's practical past³ and through transculturation, and, in his own wondrous way, creating a new narrative counterhistoria.

How does Díaz compose short stories that maintain multiple social, aesthetic, and cultural ties across the global South and the global North? What do his early stories from his MFA thesis and his first book tell us about the postcontemporary nature of migration? About the uniqueness, similarities, and differences among, say, Dominican American, Puerto Rican, Cuban American, and other US Latinx immigrants crowding his fiction? Unlike contemporary and historical sociologists who have focused on the Hispanic Caribbean migrants from Cuba, Puerto Rico, or the Dominican Republic to the United States, Díaz does not assume that his immigrant characters' identities in "Negocios" and *Drown* are hybrid; he does not believe that his Dominican American characters—such as Yunior de Las Casas, who was born in Santo Domingo and educated in Central New Jersey—have a stable center or a unitary national identity, nor does he believe that his Greater Antillean immigrant characters somehow brought a core identity with them and blended it with the practices and forms of their destinations.⁴ As we will see below, Díaz shows us how his characters' identifications and racial formations are highly contested projects: what is considered to be from aquí (here) or allá (there) has more to do with his characters' communities and imaginary constructions of popular Dominicanidad.⁵ What holds, then, in Díaz's diasporic fiction is an aesthetics of "aquí" and "más allá."⁶ As the early stories in "Negocios" and *Drown* suggest, the relationships of place between the Hispanic Caribbean and the United States have been historically fluid, multidimensional, multidirectional, and imperially intertwined.

Díaz focuses in his early stories on a parallel world based on the "real" universes of Santo Domingo, Dominican Republic, and Parlin, New Jersey, urban spaces that he has characterized as "elsewhere" nonsites as opposed to "somewhere" sites.⁷ Of the eleven stories written in Ithaca, New York, between 1992 and 1996, six take place in and are named after an actual urban neighborhood and apartment complex called London Terrace in Parlin, as well as an adjacent monumental toxic mound named the Global Landfill. The other five stories take place in Santo Domingo and its surrounding campos (countryside). As we know, the Dominican Republic and Haiti share an island that Christopher Columbus baptized in 1492 as Hispaniola—an island that the avaricious, tyrannical Columbus chose as an ideal site for the Iberian colony.[8] The Dominican Republic's Santo Domingo is thus the oldest of the "Old World" societies chiseled in the Américas. The transculturation of all materially Indigenous, European, and African things, which is largely the history of the Américas, began with Díaz's Caribbean nation.[9]

In Díaz's stories and his novel, *The Brief Wondrous Life of Oscar Wao*, his Dominican American characters often allude to their own historical sense of "coloniality," a sense anchored in the arrival of the admiral and climaxing centuries later, with the US military occupations of the island nation. These US military invasions—first in 1916–24, second in 1965—laid the groundwork for the thirty-year dictatorship known by historians as the "Trujillo Era" as well as for the rise and fall of populist leaders Juan Bosch and José Francisco Peña.[10]

As Díaz's Pulitzer Prize–winning novel highlights in many of its shifting scenes and in several of its thirty-three paratextual footnotes, Trujillo, once a Marine acolyte, seized power in the 1930s and ruled for three decades. Some of Díaz's stories and a portion of his novel shed light on Trujillo's caudillo-like ambition, his masculinized sexual depravity, his intense megalomania.[11] The aftershocks of the US culture of imperialism reverberated not only through the decades of the twentieth century but also in the life histories of Díaz's central characters—especially Ramón and Virta de Las Casas in the early stories, such as "Negocios" and "Aguantando." Indeed, Díaz envisioned Ramón and Virta de Las Casas as survivors of the Trujillato's traumas and of the 1965 military invasion by the United States; these events are often unspoken, absorbed, and displaced onto Ramón and Virta's children, Rafa, Yunior, and Madai. All of Yunior's—as well as Oscar de León's—transnational clan relive these traumas of the coloniality of power and the coloniality of gender in Díaz's imaginative work.[12]

Is it in the nature of the history of coloniality and trauma for violent things to repeat themselves? For Díaz's central consciousness, Yunior de Las Casas, is the practical past a Joycean nightmare from which he is trying to escape? In many ways, Díaz's early Cornell MFA fiction is about his uncovering these hidden, nightmarish sources of disruption: it is about his subtle, intertextual, postcolonial conceits of "drowning" in the nightmares of history, about the echoes and reenactments of coloniality along the mean streets of US latinidad. Indeed, throughout his fictions—from "Negocios" to *This Is How You Lose Her*—Díaz charts Yunior's tortured diasporic journey from adolescence through the darker side of midlife; along the way, Díaz's prose illuminates a series of spiritual and bodily crises from which Yunior emerges, if not "cleansed," at least closer to achieving a bona fide human self. These crises—abandonment, immigrant poverty, disability—are the measure of the half-life of love.

Part I of this book is divided into two overlapping chapters. This chapter deals with some of the key stories Díaz wrote in Ithaca, New York, as a graduate student at Cornell: "Aurora," "Negocios," and "London Terrace." These stories showcase Díaz's central consciousness, Yunior de Las Casas, attempting to make sense of his diasporic belonging, adolescence, and survival in the elsewhere spaces of Parlin, New Jersey, that he calls London Terrace. They have a dystopian tone and narrative tension, although this should not miscast their philosophical and literary purposes. The modes of belonging for the teenage Yunior in these stories are largely articulated with appeals to powers of different "translocal" solidarities that have been shaped by his experiences of truancy and estrangement, belonging and dispersal, and rooting and alienation in Central New Jersey. As a counterpart to the densely populated New York City, Díaz's imagined New Jersey is full of "holes": monumental abysses in which its waste dumps and shabby suburbs are memory traces of a set of abandoned futures. The monuments he identifies are not tributes to a glorious past but monumental ruins in crisis: New Jersey areas marked by toxic wastelands, areas undergoing construction, or urban decay. But rather than dismiss a New Jersey increasingly marked by toxic dumps and banal housing developments, Díaz shows in his early stories how these ruined "holes" reflected real life and a battle against entropy, constantly falling apart at the same time that they were in the process of being rebuilt.[13] In chapter 3 I will conclude the first part of the book by focusing on the full development of Díaz's MFA thesis—"Negocios"—into his first book—*Drown*. In particular, I highlight these works' central stories: "Ysrael," "Fiesta, 1980," "Aguantando," "Drown," "Boyfriend," "No Face," and "How to Date a Browngirl, Blackgirl, Whitegirl, or Halfie."

London Terrace as Díaz's Metamundo

London Terrace is an unremarkable apartment complex and neighborhood on Ernston Road in Parlin, New Jersey, yet it is here where Díaz has grounded his literary universe,[14] where largely Dominicano characters, however edgy and impoverished, live undramatically and instill wisdom, maravillas (wonders), and tragedy in one another. For most of his writing career, London Terrace has been Díaz's Ithaca, the place to which he is always returning in his fiction, in spite of or perhaps because of the other Ithaca in his life. That one is in New York,

Figure 2.1 London Terrace Apartments, Parlin, New Jersey. Screenshot. PBS.

where he attended Cornell and where he struggled to establish his voice. As Díaz lamented in his 2014 autobiographical essay "MFA vs. POC," published online in the *New Yorker*, his largely White MFA cohort at Cornell frequently misunderstood his Afro-Latinx literary-political vision. Why did he consistently write about race, urban poverty, and gendered hypermasculinity in his short stories? Why did he use Spanish and hip-hop idiolects in his stories? Wasn't he supposed to be writing literature (in English) in an Ivy League MFA program? Surely, as some of his early workshop readers assumed, he must be attempting Raymond Carver minimalism.[15] How else could he justify those vernaculars?

In such an environment, it is notable that Díaz, as a graduate student, fought for his passionate attachments through economically struggling immigrant Dominicano characters—through, among others, triste teenagers like Yunior and Aurora so "blunted" on New Jersey "superweed" they couldn't see straight. It is notable that he crafted his own fictional London Terrace, populating it with characters who sit at or beneath the late-1990s US census poverty threshold.[16] (See figure 2.1.) Díaz's characters are in fact part of the large-scale migration from the Dominican Republic to the United States that began in the 1960s, in the face of the political turmoil that occurred after Trujillo was killed in 1961. The Dominican diasporic population in the United States, which numbered 12,000 in 1960, grew to more than 879,000 in 2010 and was largely concentrated in New York, New Jersey, and Florida. The major urban areas where Dominican Republic immigrants resided included the greater New York–New Jersey, Boston, and Miami metropolitan areas.[17]

Díaz's great discovery as a young writer at Cornell was that the ordinary is often the extraordinary. Culture and race—for Díaz's everyday people—are ordinary. To come to this conclusion, Díaz had to unite what many others kept separate: his Afro-Dominicano characters, though hardened by urban squalor and a "vulnerability to a premature death,"[18] have a capacity for bodily affects and an artistic imagining for a better life. His impossible teenage characters' bodies remorselessly stick to one another in their New Jersey social habitus of decay.

At Cornell, Díaz dedicated himself to reading and writing about the narrative tension in the short-story (cuento) form. He is "a true believer" in cuentos, and as a professor of writing he has taught the short story every year. Not only is he in "awe" of the cuento's formal "beauty," he says, but ever since his program-era schooling, he has been "bowled over" by its extraordinary "mutability and generativity": its "spooky effects," the power that extends from its "brevity and restraint" and its atavism of historia tellings. This is not to say that Díaz's stories fall into traditional patterns and emplotments that come straight from, say, Aristotle's *Poetics*. Díaz's cuentos are rowdy and rebellious in their structures, as in their hyperurban, implicitly hip-hop attitudes. Yet in what he has described as the short story's "disdainful" kinship to, say, the novel and in its "perennial underdog" status, he has championed the cuento's "atomic compound of economy plus power" in holding the reader's interest, in generating its "unforgiving" and "demanding" narrative tension.[19]

Narrative tension, as Chris Andrews has argued in his study of Roberto Bolaño's stories, is often a neglected subject of literary study for the following reasons. First, it is too normalized and canonical. Second, literary critics often think that it can be grappled with in a straightforward manner. As with Bolaño's cuentos, I argue, Díaz cultivates in his early cuentos what Andrews saw in Bolaño's: he offers "suspense more than curiosity and surprises the reader by confounding expectations rather than by revealing withheld information."[20]

So from where does the narrative tension arise in Díaz's stories? Does it arise from uncertainty about the kind of historia that is being told? A paradigm of the modern cuento developed by the Argentine writer and critic Ricardo Piglia is useful here in locating the cuento's paradigmatic form. Piglia's thesis is simple. As he suggests in his essay "Theses on the Short Story," "A cuento (short story) always tells two historias (stories/histories)." According to Piglia, there is a visible cuento in whose interstices a secret story is inscribed. At the cuento's end, a secret historia comes to the surface, producing the element of surprise. Thus, the two historias, for Piglia, are governed by two different logics, or what he calls "systems of causality." Each of the cuento's logics has a dual function, and the logics function simultaneously. Briefly, for Piglia the modern cuento works the tension between the two historias "without ever resolving it." The cuento tells two historias "as if they were one."[21]

In his MFA thesis, "Negocios," and later in his subsequent collections of cuentos, *Drown* and *This Is How You Lose Her*, Díaz works the tension between what Piglia has called the two historias encoded in the cuento without ever resolving it. In this chapter, on "Negocios," and in the following one, on *Drown*, I am interested in the variety of forms of the cuento's two historias and their simultaneity. Almost all of Díaz's cuentos present themselves as autoethnographic extracts from his fictionalized life. As he has noted, it is precisely in the cuento cycle that he has been able to put the reader "in touch with life's fleeting, inexorable rhythm." An immigrant, diasporic life like Díaz's—with its multiplicity, "its embeddedness" in the elsewhere multimundo of Santo Domingo and Central New Jersey—works better, he suggests, "when understood not as a novel" but as a "collection" of historias. Like the very historias themselves, he finds his life history there in the collection story cycle in all "these strange pieces that do not assemble into anything coherent." Díaz concludes his theoretical riffs on the cuento by saying that it is almost impossible for him to "square the kid in Santo Domingo, climbing an avocado tree with the teen in Central New Jersey bringing a gun to school with the professional writer" writing cuentos at MIT.[22]

It was during those very "first September weeks at Cornell," in 1994, Díaz recalls, when he started to "churn out" his very first graduate-student short stories, only to have them "gutted" and workshopped "to death" by his peers and professors alike. He says it was like a Jersey "beatdown" that forced him to "lick his wounds." For instance, he remembers that one classmate wrote a three-page typed response to his workshop cuento, detailing "everything that was wrong with it." Neither whimpering from the beatdown from his writing-workshop seminar nor giving up, Díaz says he "locked himself up" at Cornell's Olin Library "every morning" with a promise to himself that he would read "at least one hundred pages of short stories minimum." In other words, like an NFL running back he decided to go "beast mode" at Cornell, and he began to "attack the cuento's form with a fury." In retrospect, it paid off. He developed in his Ivy League workshops what he called a "new aesthetic standard"[23] found in the cuento's narrative tension.

For example, in "Aurora," written in Ithaca in 1994, Díaz writes a story in the first person about a young, impossible, truant Dominicano teenager accompanying his partner in crime, Cut. With piratical street swagger, acumen, and care, he pursues young clients seeking to score drugs, from the scaled-down "superweed" to the scaled-up crack and heroin. All the while he cagily eludes the police and the menacing drug dealers from nearby New York City who are moving in on London Terrace, the narrator's turf. For much of that time the narrator is addicted to cocaine and heroin, and he is moving among a semi-criminal demimonde that characterizes the urban Central Jersey scene. The narrator indulges in appetites and learns to live without too much guilt. As readers, we sense how skilled and entrepreneurial the unnamed narrator is on the magically urban, mean streets and trailer parks near Route 9: "We're still making mad paper but it's harder now." Although the narrator sleeps with many London Terrace young women, he is tormented, charmed, and doomed by his thick love for Aurora, a nineteen-year-old Latina opioid addict who aspires to be an artist. When he sees Aurora, she has just served six months in a New Jersey juvie "justice" detention prison. During her incarceration, Aurora and the narrator had occasionally exchanged letters. Díaz does not narrate the story "Aurora" linearly or chronologically. Instead, the story includes flashbacks to a time when the young lovers were "tighter"[24] and hooked up to have sex in abandoned buildings surrounding London Terrace, and also flash-forwards to a time when the narrator receives Aurora's anguished letters from prison. When Aurora is released, she has been "clean" of hard drugs for months but is eager to score again.

Upon spotting the narrator we know is Yunior, she hails him: "Hey macho." This interpellation immediately gets his attention. She's dressed fashionably, all in black, but Díaz's narrator notices only that she has lost weight in the juvie prison. The nineteen-year-old Aurora is so emaciated and triste that she looks as if she is only twelve years old. Her body shakes because she is experiencing withdrawal from crack and shot heroin. "Hard to kiss anyone like that, hard even to touch them," Yunior thinks to himself, because "the flesh moves like it's on rollers." But kiss her he does—bringing his lips to her "hand."[25]

However, the narrator's drug boss, Cut, wants nothing to do with Aurora's mixed bag of charms and warns his partner: "I'm surprised the AIDS ain't bit off your dick yet." Díaz's narrator, with teenage bravado, replies, "I'm immune." But when Aurora and Yunior have sex, he worries about "the mouth sized bruises" on her neck. "Don't worry about them," she tells him. "They ain't contagious."[26] Still, he worries over who gave them to his Afro-Roman lover.

As we start to read Díaz's graduate-student cuento "Aurora," the story's commonsense logic (story one, as Piglia would say) is one of the narrator waiting for Aurora to show up so that they enjoy their "superweed" and hook up. Around midnight, she taps on the abandoned building's basement windows—they haven't seen each other for a week. She's got the shakes, and the narrator does not inquire about the causes of her drug relapse (New Jersey superweed and alcohol and heroin are brute intensities in Díaz's urban multimundo), but the reader can see the logic of misery, poverty, hopelessness, and diasporic melancholy that might explain Aurora's shakes. The narrator, too, is "blunted." Eventually they have sex in the dilapidated building, and afterward they feel as if they have "pulled" too hard on each other's bodies—like they are trying "to open" them up. The narrator wonders why "there's no feeling positive" in their lovemaking.[27]

On other occasions, Aurora and the narrator "jig," drink a whole case of Budweiser, and chase it with some "H." Whereas Aurora once tried to "jam a pen in [his] thigh," all she is now interested in is kissing Yunior's "face" and "the skin that's rarely touched." Eventually the lovers pass out, and when the narrator awakens the following day, Aurora's gone—crack pipe and all. "Twice a month" they see each other, and in the nights when he is alone, the narrator recalls that before Aurora was locked up in the juvie, they had once been so much "tighter."

Díaz's fictional logic (story two) is suggested by a series of allusions to real love and by Aurora's desire to be an artist and for the narrator "to promise her" a "love that's never been seen anywhere." This story's fictional logic begins to recede, and the story's commonsense logic asserts itself but without dissolving the melancholic story of the failure of desire. A series of questions remain unanswered: Why can't the lovers be "tighter"? Why was Aurora in juvie? Why is the narrator the only one in London Terrace who sees in the ex-juvie Aurora the possibilities of a higher state of mind and aesthetic conocimientos (knowledge) that have now been diminished in prison? And why is he so haunted by Aurora's aesthetic praxis and creative sensibilities—her habit of painting on the walls of the broken-down, abandoned apartments they break in to to have sex? "Aurora would color the walls, draw pictures with crayons, splatter the red wax from the candles into patterns, beautiful patterns. You got talent, I told her and she laughed. I used to be real good at art. Real good." Díaz's narrator sees Aurora's inert art object as a symbolic act in its own right: a barriological practice, an aesthetic production they both confront. For Díaz, these raw materials are to be grasped simply as the whole object world of London Terrace's misery: its urban blight and the whole, rudimentary world of barrio underdevelopment reduced to its menacing but aesthetically beautiful patterns. Díaz's narrator wonders how Aurora's painting on the apartment walls explodes into a hallucinatory surface of crayon color while its patterns are garishly overlaid with hues of red candle wax. Why is Díaz's narrator haunted by Aurora's materializations of pure color? Is this the abject's act of aesthetic compensation through which the artist produces a new magically urban realm of the senses? A reconstitution of some semiautonomous space in its own right? He suggests this idea when he ponders Aurora's art in all of its raw colors and materials—crayons and the red wax from the candles that she brings with her. It is at this time in his wooing her that he tells her that he "love[s] her name": "You're named after a star, do you know that?"[28] Yunior thus informs her that her airy and bright name, Aurora, truly fits her: she is a goddess of light.

At the story's end, the narrator is heartbroken when, after he meets up with Aurora, she asks him to take her to the Hacienda, a down-and-out drug house where young Black and Brown addicts sell their hard bodies and commit all sorts of "beasting" with clients in return for drugs, as one "abuelo type" addict tells him. He then recalls how Aurora suffered when she was put in solitary confinement for twenty-five straight days at the New Jersey prison. She survived, she told him, by keeping her wits about her and imagining what their lives might have been without London Terrace's pernicious underdevelopment and poverty: "like we were normal people." She confesses to him that she "made up this whole new life in [solitary confinement]. . . . You should have seen it. The two of us had kids, a big blue house, hobbies, the whole fucking thing."[29]

One of the unexpected fusings represented in "Aurora"—the cuento's two simultaneous logics—takes place between Díaz's notion of aesthetic beauty and displeasure. To Díaz, the antinomies of abjection and pleasure, juxtaposed here in a hyperreal style—the lovers' tristeza and melancholia on the one hand and the lovers' heightened bodily states of affect (sexual pleasure and drug intensities) on the other—are easy to conjure in his MFA program-era writing. Just as the New Jersey neighborhood is dear and impoverished, so are the teenage lovers' bodies. If we go to his MFA thesis thinking that Díaz may be an apostle of brotherly Afro-Latinidad, he shows us instead the brothers Rafa and Yunior de Las Casas in a violent quarrel. If we go to his MFA thesis looking for the romanticized, mythic Latinx unity of la familia, he instead presents a cheating Dominican father, Ramón—a former post-Trujillo guardista—a character bordering on fascism, a megalomaniacal polygamist who abandons his island wife and children and marries a Puerto Rican entrepreneur in Brooklyn to attain his legal US citizenship and fulfill some misguided grand plan. If we go to his MFA thesis looking for stories of conviviality and the successful incorporation of Hispanic Caribbean immigrants into the American Dream, he introduces us instead to the dead end of consumer capitalism via the Global Landfill of carcinogenic waste. However, Yunior and the other characters are not without flaws. Is Diaz's MFA thesis the original cheater's guide for decolonial love and hypermasculinity? Read on one level, it glorifies Yunior and Rafa's piratical swagger, which they have not yet already put behind them. On the other hand, like the former opioid and sex addict sharing his stories, it comes from that therapeutic necessity to testify, accept responsibility, apologize, and be held accountable to everyone he has hurt. But there was more to Díaz's representation of Yunior in "Negocios" than just being what he called himself in "The Silence": un "loco maldito."[30]

As Díaz explained in a New Jersey PBS feature video on his New Jersey roots, Parlin's London Terrace is a "strange place." It is "actually a neighborhood name in Parlin, on Route 9," he notes, "on Ernston Road, basically squeezed in between Old Bridge and Sayreville. It is the kind of space one would have had to make up—it is so kooky." Díaz's allegiance to the "kookiness" of his London Terrace world is not only central to the seven linked short stories of "Negocios" but also to *Drown* and to the stories of his 2012 best-selling book *This Is How You Lose Her*. In Díaz's imaginative fiction, London Terrace is striking because it was the real community he grew up in—"the kind of community we never thought was going to collapse." But collapse it did. And "once [the New Jersey EPA] closed the toxic Global Landfill . . . in the 1980s," the Díaz's family's multimundo changed forever. "Though the Landfill was less than a mile from" where the Díaz family lived when they first arrived from the Dominican Republic in 1974, it was precisely because the London Terrace apartment complex sat so close to the toxic mounds of putrid waste that they could afford to live there. "The prices," Díaz recalled, "were so low."[31]

"As soon as the Global Landfill [was] shut down" by the New Jersey Department of Environmental Protection Agency, rental "prices" at the London Terrace apartments "rocketed up where the kind of community that I belonged to was suddenly no longer affordable to the immigrants who lived there." Ironically for Díaz, "the strange thing" about growing up in the multimundo of London Terrace was that "the thing that bothered [them] the most"—the Global Landfill's noise, smell, and excess of waste—was also the urban glue that "held" the immigrant Díaz family "together." "As soon as [Global Landfill] was gone, we were gone. We never imagined this—we cursed that Landfill—but little did we know that it held our universe together."[32]

In my following analysis of the linked cuentos about London Terrace and Global Landfill in "Negocios" and *Drown*, I am concerned with the multiple ways that Díaz organizes, breaks up, and represents nature's monumentality as well as urban space. What are the social, political, environmental, and literary-aesthetic implications of this ordering in Díaz's fiction?[33] Why does Díaz attend to the vibrant materials, the substances, and the Dominican American and other US Latinx immigrants who have been relegated and positioned as marginal and out of place? This focus on Díaz's real urban place of London

Terrace and its nearby Global Landfill demands an interdisciplinary focus combining the social scientific inquiry, literary critical studies of affect and states of consciousness, and landscape studies of waste in the United States.

In his MFA thesis Díaz examines, among other things, issues of immigrant survival in an urban region falling somewhere between a geography of waste and a geography of underdevelopment. These unhappy geographies of "elsewheres," in Díaz's early fictions, intersect with his understanding of history as doom and urban exhaustion, producing a sense of biological citizenship. Some background: when Global Landfill opened in 1968, the approximately sixty-acre dump was licensed by the New Jersey Environmental Protection Agency to accept tons of waste. After heavy rains in 1984, two high tides occurred in the nearby wetlands. A portion of the Global Landfill collapsed, sliding into the adjoining wetland and contaminating it. The accident forced the New Jersey EPA to close the facility.[34]

There is always a risk in making too legible the connections between a writer's raw materials and his imaginative re-creations of that material. Díaz did not in his MFA thesis simply reproduce the underdeveloped-neighborhood multimundo London Terrace—which was heavily African American, Dominican American, and Latino and Latina—and the nearby Global Landfill in a documentary fashion. Rather, Díaz tends to focus mostly on the Hispanic Caribbean Dominican Americans and Puerto Ricans, although he does confront the cross-racial question quite boldly at times—especially in the short story "How to Date a Browngirl, Blackgirl, Whitegirl, or Halfie," which he published in the *New Yorker* when he was just out of graduate school and later included in *Drown*. The idea of Díaz's central consciousness, Yunior, beginning to present cross-sections of differently raced urban immigrants from across the Black and Brown Atlantic at different times in history absorbed him, but he can hardly be said to have represented a straightforward history of his beloved regions—New Jersey and the hyperurban Santo Domingo—because his stories often jump back to earlier days or flash-forward in time. The elements of his imaginary mundo—London Terrace, its nearby Global Landfill, and Santo Domingo—become places related to the real world but not always in reliable ways.

In other words, there is a real distinction between Díaz and Yunior de Las Casas. It is not only that Díaz has a cognitive superiority over Yunior but also that he has a richer and increased creativity. Indeed, Díaz often has his character-narrator Yunior fail throughout the linked historia, and he deliberately makes it clear to readers that he is doing so. Quite consciously, Díaz places a distance throughout "Negocios," *Drown*, *The Brief Wondrous Life of Oscar Wao*, and *This Is How You Lose Her* between himself, protagonist, and narrator alike.[35]

Surprisingly, few critics of Díaz's emerging short stories and novel have spent any time linking up the real Santo Domingo neighborhood of Villa Juana, the London Terrace apartment complex, and the Global Landfill geographies with the imaginative ones in Díaz's early fiction. Although I think that this type of analysis will be quite productive for his future biographers, who will probably chisel more doggedly into the past for clues about key people and events behind his fiction, this chapter is not a biography of Díaz's life and times. Rather, I am interested in highlighting that in Díaz's early MFA work we can see a writer who is an artful reviser of his New Jersey and Dominican Republic realities. Santo Domingo, London Terrace, and the nearby Global Landfill's geographies of waste and space are, for Díaz, places of the imagination and its decolonial worlds, a revision of reality that captures the fiction writer's sense of historia's truth.

Díaz's life narrative is also a place where his imaginative revisions seemed necessary. He understands in "Negocios"—the last and longest story he wrote at Cornell in 1995—that we must construct a story of our lives: the tortured transnational tales that the young narrator often repeats, after dark, to his older brother, who shares a room with him, just before they both fall asleep. For example, in "Ysrael," one of the first short stories Díaz wrote as a graduate student in Ithaca, Yunior tells Rafa an Antillean Island story that his brother no longer remembers: "We talked a lot about growing up on the Island but most of my stories make him shake his head. Ysrael was a long time ago, I say. He looks hard at me and then smiles, like it's nothing. He's beautiful and you wouldn't think us brothers, you wouldn't think he lived anywhere but the softest neighborhoods. You got *an imagination*, he says. I'll give you that."[36] From the very start, Díaz's Rafa knows that his younger brother, Yunior, loves to embellish and recreate their shared Dominican Republic and diasporic New Jersey lives, reporting and sometimes inventing all kinds of details, shaping and reshaping the personae of Rafa, of his parents, Ramón and Virta, and of himself to suit him. As I argue in chapter 5, sometimes Yunior reinvents the same origin story about his Dominican family's odyssey twice: in "Negocios," for instance, and in *This Is How You Lose Her*'s "Otravida, Otravez." But the characters in Díaz's MFA thesis bring into relief the nature of his own family; indeed, he works hard to invent and deepen both, looking for the realities of his diasporic, Black Atlantic life through the lenses that art affords.

Implicit in this chapter is an analysis of what Rafa de Las Casas sees as Yunior's terrific gift of a diasporic imagination—a constitutive feature of his transnational Afro-Dominican subjectivity. What are the sources of Yunior's experimentations with the family's self making in Santo Domingo and Parlin's London Terrace? What scripts do the de Las Casas family's diasporic ruptures allow him to invent? Yunior's history of migration is juxtaposed with the mass-mediated images of comic books and graphic novels—with a new ordering of (in)stability in the production of subjectivity and Afro-Atlantic latinidad. Whereas Rafa lovingly and mockingly chides Yunior for his powers of the imagination, Yunior is committed to the production of what the anthropologist Arjun Appadurai has called the "diasporic public sphere": phenomena that "confound theories that depend on the continual salience of the nation-state as the key arbiter of important social change."[37] These historical and migratory oral and textual mediations compel Yunior's diasporic imagination.

Lives are lived in overlapping historical halos—as Marina De Chiara suggests, "with meaningful parts of ourselves cut off"—and involve perceptions not only of the historical past but also of its practical pasts and present.[38] One of the main ideas in Díaz's books is that his characters must comprehend what many (trans)modernist writers from James Joyce and William Faulkner to Toni Morrison, Édouard Glissant, Derek Walcott, Patrick Chamoiseau, and Edwidge Danticat called "the pastness of the past."[39] There is just no way in which the past can be easily abolished from the present. Past and present—their jagged edges, longings, and silences rising up from the gaps of space and time—inform each other in Yunior's linked historias in "Negocios," *Drown*, *The Brief Wondrous Life of Oscar Wao*, and *This Is How You Lose Her*. Díaz's Yunior is hopelessly fascinated by the realities he assembles out of the fragments and by the bridges he builds across the past's páginas en blanco.

In "Negocios," the title story of his MFA thesis, the graduate student Díaz writes one of the longest and best historias of the linked narratives in the collection. (It makes up nearly a third of the entire thesis.) The story is Yunior's dynamic and dialectical metahistoria of the mythic journey of economic migration of his father from the Dominican Republic to Virginia and to his epic arrival in Nueva York. As we come to learn, "My father, Ramón de Las Casas, left Santo Domingo just before my first birthday."[40] Yunior's historia thus spans the five years that his father Ramón was absent from his Dominican island's family life: from the moment he steps off the airplane in Miami until he returns, many years later, to scoop up his family and take them on to their diasporic journey to New Jersey, where he has found work at the Reynolds Aluminum factory. Díaz's story is about historia and power. It deals with the many overlapping ways in which the production of history as well as historia involves how the competing members of the de Las Casas family—including Yunior, the writer of the tale—have varied means and degrees of access to the production of historia. "Negocios" dramatizes this tussle, stitching together competing stories within a story with a brilliance unique to Díaz's Yunior. Last, just as in his cuento "Aurora," here in "Negocios" there are two logics in this short story: an initial logic of common sense and the logic of metahistorical fiction of what happens. There is a tacit pact between the reader and writer, according to which something is going to happen.

Initially, Yunior writes about how Ramón, his twenty-four-year-old father, survived in Miami by finding two dishwashing jobs in a Cubano sandwich shop[41] in the Calle Ocho section of Miami. He moves in with three struggling Guatemalan immigrants and pays the leader of the group rent to sleep on a roach-infested living-room couch. On the breaks between his two jobs, Ramón passes his time by either washing his aprons or reading "the Western dreadfuls he was fond of"[42] and could read in an hour or so. Díaz's Yunior thus chronicles how his father eventually moved al Norte, for after losing one of his dishwashing jobs he realizes that at the low wages he was earning he would never have been able to earn enough money to bring Virta, Rafa, Yunior, and Yajira over from the Dominican Republic to the United States.

"Negocios" gestures toward the epic when Yunior—relying almost exclusively on his role as the Telemachian son—writes that one winter, to save money, his father literally walked in "his bad shoes" some "three hundred and eighty miles" from Miami to Virginia on his way north to Nueva York's Washington Heights, for "Nueva York was the city of jobs, the city that had first called the cubanos and their cigar industry, then the Bootstrap puertoricans and now called him."[43] However, what Díaz's Yunior does in this passage from "Negocios" is something more extraordinary than migratory description and emplotment. In these two sentences, Díaz summarizes the complex, layered history of Cuban and Puerto Rican migration to the United States, which Yunior's Dominicano father supplements in his tale. Between 1898 and the early 1930s, the US military occupation of the Caribbean island nations compelled thousands of Cubans and Puerto Ricans to move to New York City. In the first two decades of the twentieth century, scores of skilled Puerto Rican and Cuban workers, especially tobacco workers who made cigars, arrived in the capital of globalization. Puerto Ricans, as Díaz's Ramón suggests, settled in New York City neighborhoods such as East Harlem and the Lower East Side.[44] These Hispanic Caribbean colonias developed alongside the diasporic African American communities. Through an impressive feat of compression, Díaz not only links these historical migrations with the Dominicano Ramón's arrival in Nueva York but also highlights the great migration of Puerto Ricans and Dominicans to New York City.[45] No small feat for two short sentences.

Once Ramón reaches Virginia, he lucks out when two sheriff's deputies driving a convicted murderer from the Deep South to Trenton, New Jersey, offer him a ride. From there, he easily travels to Nueva York. But Yunior suspects that his father's versions of history include silences and absences and that not all of his father's historias were created equal. If Ramón's version of his life history fills in the landscape of the first half of the story and thus leaves little room for the historia of his abandoned wife in "Negocios," Yunior humbly notes that because "no photos exist of his father's mustached days in the United States," they are "easily imagined." In "Negocios," Díaz's Yunior informs his readers that "there are two stories about what happened . . . one from Papi and one from Mami."[46] If his father's version is largely self-serving and leaves crucial things out, his mother's version passes on to him something else. Even as he tries to become an ideal family chronicler, Díaz's Yunior necessarily creates meaning and occasionally silences the past. Thus envisaged, Yunior participates in the history of the de Las Casas family both as actor and as narrator. As Michel-Rolph Trouillot argues in his iconic book on power and the production of history, *Silencing the Past*, the "inherent ambivalence of the word 'history' in many modern languages, suggests this dual participation. In vernacular use, history means both the facts of the matter and a narrative of those facts, both 'what happened' and 'that which is said to have happened.' The first places the emphasis on the sociohistorical process, the second on the knowledge of that process or on a story about that process."[47] Díaz's historia "Negocios," I argue, grapples with the dialectical overlapping and migrating tension between the sociohistorical processes and Yunior's knowledge of them. Historia for Yunior can mean either the sociohistorical processes or his knowledge about them, but it can also underscore the boundary between the two meanings as fluid, liminal, and migratory.

As Yunior imagines his father heroically negotiating the sociohistorical processes of becoming a legal citizen of the United States and his various "negocios" in Miami and Nueva York, Yunior the chronicler also narrates his own knowledge about how his father's "business" plan simultaneously included the abandoning and repudiation of his mother, his brother, his sister, and him in Santo Domingo. Ramón leaves them when Yunior is five years old and then again when the father arrives in Nueva York and hatches his "plan" to acquire legal citizenship. Ramón does so by first befriending and then wooing a middle-aged Puerto Rican widow and entrepreneur, Nilda, who owns a restaurant, a successful negocio of her own. Yunior also narrates his father's design as a performative scheming and imagines his father "deliver[ing] some of his most polished performances" to convince Nilda that he loves her and not his economically underdeveloped island family that he had abandoned in the Caribe. Within a month of his wooing Nilda, Yunior writes that his "Papi moved out of his apartment to her house in Brooklyn. They were married in March."[48]

Having acquired a place and legal citizenship papers through his polygamous marriage with Nilda, Yunior's father is advised by his business mentor, Jo-Jo, to "save some money and buy yourself a little business." To be sure, Ramón's plan also means a carefully formulated design, a plan that he conceives and tries to carry out. But this plan, as Yunior envisions it in "Negocios," means something more: "Papi wanted a negocios of his own, that was his dream, but he balked at starting at the bottom. . . . His aspirations required minimally a business as shiny and lucrative as Jo-Jo's grocery store. While most of the men around were two-times broke, he had seen a few, fresh off the boat, shake the water from their backs and jump right into the lowest branches of the American establishment. That leap was what he envisioned for himself, not some slow upward crawl through the mud."[49] For Yunior, his father's grand plan is not only to establish a business and leap into the American entrepreneurial establishment but also to achieve psychic rewards and thus surpass Nilda and Jo-Jo's small-time business powers. Yunior thus narrates how, having formed his plan, his father moves with remarkable speed to carry it out. If the young Yunior constructs an idealized version of his Papi's absence from them, Yunior the chronicler freely invents in his assemblage—in the linked story "Aguantando"—a version of his Papi, who "was a cloud of cigar smoke . . . he was pieces of my friends' fathers, of the dominos players on the corner, pieces of Mami and Abuelo. I didn't know him at all. I didn't know that he's abandoned us."[50]

In the remainder of "Negocios," Yunior reconstructs how his father had repudiated them and how his mother had learned of her husband's polygamy and repudiation through the chisme (gossip) relayed to her by the diasporic chain of family and friends that stretched from New York to the island. By thus "reaching back across . . . a chain of immigrants"[51] from the global North to the global South, Virta de Las Casas "locates" the truth of what her husband's business in Nueva York was really about. Virta's archive of "gossip and tales" thus functions as a feminist project in Díaz's story. Gossip interrupts and displaces what Lisa Lowe calls "official represented regimes."[52] Virta's archive of chisme—an archive fiebre (fever) perhaps—allows Yunior to deconstruct his father's epic, patriarchal historia and mission in the global North. Gossip relays and exaggerates a counterdiscourse that undoes the logics of the private and public, of legitimate and illegitimate discourse. Moreover, in the letters she composes to her husband and shares with Yunior, Virta "detailed how his children were suffering; how his little girl was so anemic that the people thought she was a corpse brought back to life. She told him about his sons playing in the barrio." Thus, through the double optic of his father and mother's vernacular chronicling of the transnational events, Yunior's frame narrative contrapuntally plays off the idealized, heroic, epic-like version of his father's patriarchal history of migration against the deconstructed critique offered by his mother's devastatingly blunt letters: she "called Papi a desgraciado and a puto of the highest order for abandoning them, a traitor worm, an eater of public lice, a cockless, ball-less cabrón."[53]

"Negocios" ends with Yunior's recounting how his father "landed a union job with Reynolds Aluminum in West New York (which happens to be a city in New Jersey) that paid him triple" of what he had previously earned in Nueva York. One night, Ramón and a fellow Latino traveler, Chuito, drive south into New Jersey "to a small town outside of Perth Amboy." This is one of the first dystopian visions we have of Yunior's future multimundo of the London Terrace and its abutting Global Landfill: "Huge rents had been gorged into the earth and towering ziggurats of tan bricks stood ready to be organized into buildings. New pipes were being laid by the mile and the air was tart with the smell of chemicals." The next steps in Ramón's plan stir doubts about what his design really is: "Here was the place to move his familia if it came from the Island. Quiet and close to his job. Most important the neighbors would not know him or the wife he had in the States."[54] In other words, Ramón cares only about concealing from the rest of the London Terrace world his repudiation of Virta and his family.

Yunior concludes the story by narrating and embellishing how his now "legal" father returns to Santo Domingo to complete his plan only partially: "For nearly four years, he'd not spoken the Spanish loudly in front of the Northamericans and now he was hearing it bellowed and flung from every mouth." He imagines his father in Villa Juana taking a guagua "down Sumner Wells, as Calle XXI had been renamed," and cruising to be reunited with the family. Yunior's conjuring is his own making entirely: "Maybe Papi stopped at the local grocers; maybe he even stopped in front of the house." Alas, the father "never visits" his island family, and his "absence" remains "a seamless thing." Having come close to reuniting himself with his island family, Ramón abandons them again, returning to Brooklyn and his second family. After an accident at Reynolds Aluminum, the father convalesces at Nilda's home. In an epiphany, Ramón—as Yunior explains it—sees that his "first family was his [life's] destination." The island family in fact constitutes what Yunior calls his father's salvation: "saviors" and a "regenerative force that could redeem his fortunes." Ramón sees his future Fortuna in the London Terrace apartments, "formerly delayed because they'd been built on a chemical dump site,"⁵⁵ finally completed and opening.

Ramón's change of heart seems somewhat puzzling. Why had he decided to leave his Brooklyn family and return to Santo Domingo to scoop up his island family and fly them to New York's JFK? To move them into Parlin's London Terrace neighborhood and the nearby Global Landfill? And most puzzling of all to Nilda, his Nueva York wife, why had Ramón abandoned her and their newborn son, also named Ramón?

Many years later, Yunior, now a fledgling writer, visits (with his mother's mixed blessings) Nilda in Brooklyn: his chronicle, "Negocios," does not silence her and his stepbrother's past. Nilda tells him how his father had schemed and adjusted his grand plan or design by surreptitiously moving his clothes out of the Brooklyn home he shared with her, his stepdaughter, Milagra, and their new baby, Ramón. "I thought I would never stop hurting," Nilda reports to Yunior. "I knew what it must have felt like for your mother. Tell her that."⁵⁶ Yunior the chronicler then calls on his younger self to take the witness stand, to faithfully witness and explain his father's business plan:

> December. He had left [his Brooklyn family]. The company had given him a two week vacation, which Nilda knew nothing about. . . . I doubt if he was crying or even anxious. He lit a cigarette, tossed the match on the kitchen table and headed out into the angular winds that were blowing long and cold from the south. . . . The first subway station on Bond would have taken him to the airport and I like to think that he grabbed that first train, instead of what was most likely true, that he had gone out to Chuito's first, before flying south to get us.⁵⁷

Ramón's grand plan had required hard work, polygamy to get his legal papers in the United States, and a desire for business and the American Dream. If Yunior's narrative does anything at all, it demonstrates how his father's ruthless grand plan—like his own story within a story—is a triumph of the imagination. His father's single-minded efforts to carry the plan out are an impressively monomaniacal act of immigrant determination and desperation. If Nilda looks at the events of Ramón's "negocios" not only in puzzlement but also with awe, Virta rightly continues to object to her husband having used other people, including his familia, as mere objects to be placed, abandoned, and betrayed.

Yunior, the metahistorian, offers readers of "Negocios" a theory of the production of historia that acknowledges both the distinction and the overlap between process and narrative. Thus, although many of the stories that make up Díaz's MFA thesis are about historia as power, knowledge, and narrative, they fully embrace the narratological ambivalence inherent in the cuento's two logics of causality and in the cuento's two sides of the historia's historicity. Writing as a double major in history and creative writing, Yunior is always opening up a way of thinking history outside and against the very disciplinary norms that shape history's official presentation. Yunior insists that history endures as a set of more practical presentations: they are known to us only through imagination, dreams, and fantasies, accessible by literary and rhetorical (figurative) means. In other words, Yunior is interested in what Hayden White called "the practical past" rather than the historical past composed by historians, anthropologists, and archaeologists.[58]

Trying to write fiction in new, transmodernist ways was not a goal unique to the young Junot Díaz. Since at least the modernist 1950s, young writers training in MFA programs and their writing professors had been thematizing authorship in their work. In short stories such as "Aurora," "Negocios," and those he included in *Drown*, Díaz was developing what it seems fair to call a singular Afro-Atlantic Dominican authorial persona—a persona with rhythmically syncopated aesthetics that shift contrapuntally between autoethnographic transparency and metahistorical fictional opacity, between diasporic exclusion and an illusion of acculturated inclusion, between defiance and decolonial desire. Moreover, Díaz was developing in such stories an unmistakably beautiful and invariant writing style: he energetically flavors his English with healthy doses of the idioms of hip-hop, the lilt of our magically urban drug culture, and, as in "Negocios," an academic sense of the production of history and metahistoria. And let's not forget Díaz's profound permutations of swear words in Spanglish and English: turbocharged, wryly torqued, freaky real.

Indeed, Díaz's conjoining of historia (in both senses of the word), confession, denunciation, pedagogy, the philosophy of history, and popular hip-hop languages and sonics is matched in his MFA thesis with a dynamic constellation of patently autoethnographic themes: masculinity, Dominicanness, latinidad, betrayal, abandonment, estrangement, and authorship itself. As I will underscore in the following chapters on Díaz's *The Brief Wondrous Life of Oscar Wao* and his linked story collection *This Is How You Lose Her*—even beyond his explicitly interrelated Yunior de Las Casas historias—there is an internal stylistic consistency and serial metahistorical narrative coherence within this emerging autoethnographic-poetic enterprise.

In the stories of his MFA thesis, Díaz was, of course, experimenting with the long and the short of the short-story form[59]—concentrating his prose and, with attitude and swagger, giving CPR to an exhausted, America-centric minimalism. His simple yet syncopated sentences in the stories "Aurora" and "Negocios" weigh down heavily on his central consciousness Yunior de Las Casas; Díaz's declarative sentences in "Aurora" attempt to give great meaning to the triste nineteen-year-old drug addict, telegraphing to his readers the vulnerability to misery, premature death, and blighted economic opportunity for the Auroras of London Terrace.

As Díaz entered his Ivy League program at Cornell in 1992, creative-writing graduate students in the United States were writing short-story collections in hegemonically White-voiced minimalist styles or in trendy postmodernist postures, affecting a Kmart misery and a Brat Pack Neiman Marcus fetishization toward a US literary world they knew mostly from other MFA-trained program-era teachers and writers like them.[60] Díaz's thesis, "Negocios," and his first book, *Drown*, are, in my opinion, by turns endlessly more inventive and narratologically complex than either the Carver-inspired minimalists or the Pynchon-like postmodernists, for he acutely finds new ways to manipulate his Yunior de Las Casas's multimundo of Parlin's London Terrace and Santo Domingo. The Afro-Atlantic Dominicano artist, writing at Cornell University, pursued his truth beyond a hall of mirrors.

Unlike these minimalists or postmodernists crowding the top MFA programs in the 1990s, Díaz's transnational decolonial fiction opens a small window through which readers can see the states of racial double consciousness, sufferings, and the affects of tristeza that will become the signature Díaz subject: from "Negocios" and *Drown* to *The Brief Wondrous Life of Oscar Wao* to *This Is How You Lose Her*, he reveals what it means to him to belong to an Afro-Atlantic Latinx diaspora and what it means to live out the possibilities and liminalities of transculturated Hispanic Caribbean status. And Díaz's subject and perspective is on full display in "London Terrace."

"London Terrace" is the only story from the original seven in "Negocios" that Díaz decided to drop from his first book, *Drown*, and then, years later, included in the linked stories of *This Is How You Lose Her*, albeit under a new title, "Invierno."[61] "London Terrace" is one of the most devastating stories in Díaz's thesis, and it unfurls a finely wrought portrait of New Jersey's magical urbanism and the subsequent alienation that Virta, Rafa, and Yunior experience as non-English-speaking immigrants. Six-year-old Yunior, along with his eight-year-old brother and their thirty-something mother, has just arrived in New York—and later, Parlin, New Jersey—from Santo Domingo: they have been relocated from their Hispanophone Caribbean island by Ramón, their father, whom Yunior barely knows. It's winter in Parlin's London Terrace. Papi will not allow his wife or his sons out of their newly opened apartment complex, ostensibly because of the bitter cold and snow, but "really," Yunior learns in retrospect, because there was no reason other than that's what his Papi wanted. While their acculturating and domineering father is off at his Reynolds Aluminum factory job, the adolescents Yunior and Rafa spend their days cooped up inside their new apartment and looking out at the unfamiliar snowstorms or at the television as they mimic the English lessons they hear on PBS's *Sesame Street*, repeating the foreign English words deliberately and slowly for their monolingual mother Virta's benefit, like "huge, lazy soap bubbles of sound."[62]

Yunior is himself imprisoned within a kind of bubble—triply underdeveloped in his London Terrace multimundo—separated from his new environs by his father's rigidity, by his mother's lack of familiarity with the English language, and by the frozen un-green landscape beyond his London Terrace's windowpanes, on which "a bead of water gathered . . . like bees,"[63] obscuring the view. Even Yunior's "pelo malo"[64]—having too much of the Black Atlantic in it—cuts him off from his lighter-complexioned and straighter-haired brother and the rest of the family. In a striking scene in "London Terrace," Papi thus hauls Yunior off to a special Boricua (Puerto Rican) barber in nearby Perth Amboy because his Papi knows exactly "what to do with" Yunior's "pelo malo." But Yunior's curly hair defies all of the hairstylist's straightening creams and acumen. In the end, the unfeeling Papi commands the Puerto Rican barber to shave off Yunior's locks. Yunior is mortified.

These highly stylized and raced topoi (themes) alone in "London Terrace" would have made for a remarkable Cornell graduate-school short story. Yet in the story's phenomenologically reduced final pages, Díaz takes his "London Terrace" historia to another dialectical level. Gusting snow becomes the tropological medium or figural image through which Mami, Rafa, and Yunior finally venture out and cross over from their neighborhood's "plane of ice" into the wider magically urban world and see for the first time the nearby toxic garbage landfill. Díaz paints the landfill as a surreal geography of waste: "Rubbish fires burned all over it like sores and the dump trucks and bulldozers slept quietly and reverently at its base."[65] Even Yunior's de-Africanized head becomes a surprising symbolic instrument of perception, a means of communing with lo real and the marvelous urbanism.

How does Díaz tell the story of London Terrace and its Global Landfill multimundo, given that his story was based on his real London Terrace and Global Landfill world he grew up in, a world so toxic that in 1984 the New Jersey Department of Environmental Protection Agency closed it because it discovered "buried drums containing hazardous waste"[66] and other chemicals in "leachate" seeping from the site? How does Díaz's story provide readers with clear boundaries we can wrap our minds around? Like the Global Landfill itself—some sixty

Figure 2.2 Global Landfill, Parlin, New Jersey. Screenshot. PBS

acres—Díaz's MFA thesis in general and "London Terrace" in particular are the dustbin of a larger story of consumer late capitalism and waste (figure 2.2). How does Díaz manage all of the Global Landfill's unruly toxic mess? Does "London Terrace" signal Díaz's attempt to represent aesthetically how marginalized hyperurban nature is organized, partitioned, and arrayed in New Jersey? Does the writer attend to the materials and the working-class Latinx+ immigrants who are deemed by the state to be so disposable?

"London Terrace" is a fascinating memory era and an ecological reconfiguration of the ways that deadly monumental waste is stored near the poorest of immigrant communities.[67] It is also Díaz's aesthetic act of remembering his magically urban space of Parlin, in which he (re)configures his metamundo spatially and temporally. Díaz's Yunior does not invent images in his story that are cut off from the natural environment he lives in: "Each day the trucks would roll into our neighborhood with garbage. The landfill stood two miles out, but the mechanics of winter air conducted its sounds and odors to us undiluted. When we opened a window we could hear and smell the bulldozers spreading the garbage out in thick, putrid layers across the top of the landfill. We could see the gulls attending the mound, thousands of them, wheeling."[68]

Díaz's remembrance of how the garbage trucks "roll[ed]" into his London Terrace world falls into a long history of ordering urban space, of the state reshaping nature's periphery. As Díaz provocatively suggests in "London Terrace," it is not surprising at all that Global Landfill is located along the edges of his impoverished neighborhood, at a distance deemed "safe" from and manageable by the dominant center. The location of toxic matter from the inside to the outside within the boundaries of capitalism's waste and consumer accumulation is at the heart of Díaz's historia because it allows him to show the nation's transportation of waste and the processes of the center's decay at London Terrace's periphery. As landscape designer Mira Engler argues, "Waste is always marginal, and margins almost always include waste; in fact, they invite waste. Waste is often put in marginal areas to await further transaction.... The act of disposal is an act of sorting and placing rejected material into rejected marginal spaces."[69] "London Terrace" thus redefines for us what it really means for those on the planet's margins, like the ostensibly disposable de Las Casas family, to have to grapple with waste and ecological death.

In Díaz's reinvention and remembrance of place—Parlin's London Terrace and its abutting Global Landfill—he unveils one of the many layered contradictions of the geographies of late capitalism. Just as the urban centers have had to expand, so also have the borderlands between center and margin had to be carved outward. In Díaz's short story, waste must be defined by its very peripherality. Whether or not he aesthetically reclaims nature's materiality through his beautifully crafted "majestic landscapes," it is clear that his artistic vision of London Terrace's vibrant materiality sanctions a specific use of a spatial cognitive "fix," to use Fredric Jameson's term, to define the uneven quantum leaps of late-capitalist expansion.[70] Díaz's appeal to the notions of planetary nature in "London Terrace" is an appeal, as Bruno Latour suggests in *The Politics of Nature*, to "the assemblage that [nature] authorizes." It "counts for infinitely more than the ontological quality of 'naturalness,' whose origins it would guarantee."[71] The representation of our urbanscape's "naturalness" morphs in "London Terrace" into a new representation of an entire planetary ontological ecosystem. Thus, Global Landfill, in its peripheral place next to Díaz's London Terrace, is not only an aesthetic image for structuring the iconography of Díaz's urban sense of place: it is also a vibrant "image" that he sees as having an agency of its own. At stake in Díaz's MFA thesis is a politics—one that I think deepens throughout his entire work's corpus—of defining where and how lifescapes exist within our planet's landscapes. A sense of urban place, again, is everything to Junot Díaz.

"London Terrace" ends with the television's news announcement of an impending snowstorm. Ramón telephones his wife to inform her that he will not be able to get back to their home from his work at Reynolds Aluminum; he will instead be staying over at a coworker's home—but, given his past serial cheating, we sense that he is spending the night with a lover. Thus, Ramón leaves his family to fend for themselves and face the travails of their first blizzard alone.

We also sense that Ramón and Virta de Las Casas have reached the dissolution of their marriage. Although Yunior and Rafa are too young to realize the stakes of the failure of their parents' marriage, Díaz ends the story by showing us the weight of the consequences that have fallen on the mother's shoulders. Virta, "depressed" and triste, is here truly alone and estranged. Díaz makes us dramatically feel this estrangement as he shows us Virta walking and stumbling in the black ice, with Rafa and Yunior helping her stand up as they make their way from the London Terrace apartment complex to the ravaged and frigid Global Landfill dump. It is the denouement of the story. For Yunior, Rafa, and Virta, Parlin's Global Landfill is a place of last gasps—it is the place in which the patriarch, Ramón, has literally made them into disposable subjects. Global Landfill, Yunior writes, "smelled like something the river had tossed from its floor, something moist and heaving. . . . Mami was crying but we pretended not to notice. We threw snowballs at the sliding cars and once I removed my cap just to feel the snowflakes scatter across my cold scalp."[72] Díaz's Global Landfill's monumental waste mound is alive, "moist" and "heaving"; it stands for late modernity's monumentality but also symbolizes death; it conceals for Yunior and Rafa hidden baubles but discloses a picture of late capitalism's deadly consumer culture. It is Díaz's ritual site in his MFA thesis and the one he returns to years later in *This Is How You Lose Her*. It distills and sharpens our visions. Its high, putrid mounds provide a ground from which to see ourselves.

From the moment Díaz submitted "Negocios" in January 1995 to Stephanie Vaughn and Lamar Herrin—his creative-writing faculty committee members—and received the imprimatur of Cornell University, it was a foregone conclusion that he would receive his MFA. It is not only the overall audaciousness of his urban elsewheres of Santo Domingo and London Terrace that convinces but also the lyrical details that display Díaz's startlingly new approach to his wondrous world making. In the "Negocios" short stories, Díaz had already sketched out in great detail his diasporic Dominicano world building long before he wrote his books of stories, *Drown* and *This Is How You Lose Her*, and his novel, *The Brief Wondrous Life of Oscar Wao*, which occur in this world. In developing languages, describing his culture of Afro-Atlantic Latinidad, drawing new transnational cognitive maps, and writing his family historias in the cuento's two logics and urban mythologies, Díaz was interested in trying to create a fully realized transnational place. The stories in "Negocios" capitalized upon this world making and were a means of presenting it. World-building stories like "Aurora," "London Terrace," and "Negocios" hold the sea, the sun, the moon, the sky, the barrioscapes, the smoldering landfill, the earth, and all in it.[73] In comparing the graduate-student stories Díaz had composed in Ithaca with the versions of these stories he later published in *Drown*, I am struck by the mosaic-like craftsmanship of his texts. The stories he wrote for "Negocios" and then published in *Drown*, with some very minor copyediting, are meticulous and exacting. Although Díaz could never be satisfied with anything he wrote, one of the most instructive experiences afforded by reading his MFA thesis is the spectacle of a writer moving with steadily developing confidence to found his own artistic domain—to hone his Black and Brown Latinx voice despite a world of institutions that rushes to stifle it.

3

Díaz's Planet POC (People of Color)

Drown

My apartment [where I moved to after completing my MFA thesis] on State Street [in Brooklyn] was slumlord shitty and had no insulation, and when it got cold, winter came right through me and my roommate's big front windows, like a SkyWalker, and we had to use our coats indoors if we wanted to live.

JUNOT DÍAZ, "Junot Díaz Writes about Moving to Brooklyn"

[I] remember finding my voice while I was writing a page that got thrown out of *Drown*. That was the guiding spirit of it, and it'll go back in if I ever write another book.... I remember writing that page, and remember that this was so different. ... [As] soon as I had that scene written down, I knew I had nailed my New Jersey moment, where we were black and Latino.

JUNOT DÍAZ cited in Als, "Junot Díaz"

As he was completing his MFA thesis, "Negocios," in Ithaca, New York, Díaz had been sending out his short stories to magazines for publication for months. And then, in 1994, Lois Rosenthal, editor of *Story* magazine, accepted "Ysrael," the short story that opens his thesis, and, later, "Fiesta, 1980." "Junot just leaped out of the mail pile," Rosenthal recalled in a *New York Times* feature article on Díaz. "His voice was so incredibly fresh and so powerful. I called [him] immediately. I said who are you?"[1] In this chapter I will attempt to answer Rosenthal's existentially complex question.

But before that, some additional background. What happened was that after the publication of "Ysrael," Nicole Aragi wrote Díaz, and after meeting her once in New York City, he signed on with her as his agent. It was she who a year later sold his collection of stories to Julie Grau. In 1996 Díaz hit pay dirt again: the *Paris Review* accepted Díaz's "Edison, New Jersey," a short story from his MFA thesis, and the *New Yorker* accepted "Drown" and "How to Date a Browngirl, Blackgirl, Whitegirl, or Halfie." With three stories accepted for publication in major magazines, Díaz, "dead broke," moved to State Street in Brooklyn and worked at Pfizer Pharmaceuticals in Manhattan, making "photocopies by the millions." He then pitched an idea to Julie Grau, the founding editor of Riverhead Books, a new imprint of Penguin: a collection of ten linked stories based on the seven original stories of his MFA thesis. Although short-story collections do not sell as well as novels, Grau offered Díaz a spectacular advance of $150,000 and a book contract, which was "like winning the lottery."[2] The agreement not only covered *Drown* but also a book that, years later, turned out to be *This Is How You Lose Her*.[3] This was incredible news to Díaz, confirming what the short stories in his thesis had accomplished and what they still had to do: make him a young, internationally published writer. And the elation was palpable: "Yo!," he told a *New York Times* reporter, "Somebody [wants] to buy my book."[4]

As *Drown* was beginning to take shape for Riverhead, Díaz knew he needed other major magazines to publish some of the stories first. With "Ysrael," "Edison, New Jersey," "Drown," and "How to Date a Browngirl, Blackgirl, Whitegirl, or Halfie" scheduled for publication, Díaz was creating tremendous buzz in the New York publishing world. He was practically an overnight sensation: a twenty-seven-year-old Dominicano (Latinx) writer whose taut, linked, necessarily incomplete stories about Yunior de Las Casas's Dominican odyssey—written from the Telemachus point of view of the son left behind while the father journeyed abroad—were poised to revise the realism and minimalism that dominated US literary magazines. It is easy to see why Rosenthal and Bill

Buford—the fiction editor at the *New Yorker*—were drawn to Díaz's imaginative work.

"Ysrael" takes place in the Dominican Republic. A nine-year-old Yunior and his twelve-year-old brother, Rafa, are sent by their mother, Virta, to live in the campos with their uncle for the summer; Virta is working long hours in a local Santo Domingo chocolate factory and does not have the time to care for them. Their father, Ramón, had abandoned his family in the Dominican Republic to find work in the United States. During this time, Yunior recalls how Rafa, the more "handsome" sibling, would spend his hot afternoons wooing campo girls by taking them to the "dams to swim and if he was lucky they let him put it in their mouths or their asses." Most nights, Rafa's toxic masculinist and ribald tales about "tetas and chochas" enthrall Yunior—tales about the half-Haitian girl he had sex with or the campo girl who miraculously "believed she wouldn't get pregnant if she drank a Coca-Cola backwards."[5] It is not until the story's middle section that "Ysrael" dramatically shifts its logic of causality from a traditional story of adolescent brotherly rivalry to the different logic of the haunting tale of sexual violence and trauma—of the existential human face and the face of the other. It is during their stay with their uncle that the brothers first hear about Ysrael.

What follows is a story in which the face of a young boy, Ysrael, is disfigured after a pig attacks him when he is an infant, "skinn[ing]" him "like an orange." Ysrael's father, who is ashamed of his son's disfigurement and disability, forces him to wear a "mask" that has been "handsewn" by his wife "from thin blue cotton fabric." Ysrael then becomes famous all over the campos: all of the island hooligans itch to see what is behind Ysrael's "twitch[ing] mask."[6] Díaz disturbs and undermines the commonsense logic of the mask by simultaneously embedding a logic of philosophical fictionality in the remainder of the story.

One afternoon, Tío Miguel sends his nephews on an errand to the colmado to buy beer for him: Rafa, determined to ambush Ysrael and perversely see the face that is behind the mask, concocts a plan after Yunior informs him that the boys who had unmasked Ysrael "howled" with disgust when seeing his disfigured face. As Yunior puts it, Ysrael's face was not only "ugly" but horrifyingly so, and seeing his face "would make you sick." Yunior also incorporates a Caribbean folk sensibility, explaining that his tía "said that if we were to look on his face we would be sad for the rest of our lives." Rafa, obsessed and plotting, wonders "how much of Ysrael's face is gone." The next day, he enacts his plan: they will take the bus to Barbacoa, where Ysrael lives, and unmask him. In an attempt to distract the bus driver and get a free ride, Rafa pretends to help others get on the bus and instructs Yunior to sit near the back by an older man. When a pastelito that Yunior stuffed into his pockets begins to stain his trousers, the older stranger offers to help him by spitting on his fingers and rubbing "at the stain but then pinching at the tip of my pinga through the fabric of my shorts. He was smiling." The stranger's inappropriate sexual groping shocks Yunior, and he is powerless to stop the "big"-toothed man, "ropy with muscles." The stranger then "squeezes" Yunior's "biceps, quietly, hard the way my friends would sneak me into church," causing him to "whimper." Rafa is oblivious to what has happened. After they get off the bus, Rafa finally notices that the abused Yunior is crying, and instead of comforting him, he belittles him: "You have to get tougher. Crying all the time. Do you think our papi is crying [in Nueva York]?"[7] Here an out-of-nowhere historia becomes a hauntology of Papi's absence.

When they finally encounter Ysrael, Yunior, unaware of his brother Rafa's plan to attack and unmask the disabled boy, begins to see how much alike they really are: both are boys whose fathers have symbolically orphaned them by leaving the Dominican Republic to seek work in Nueva York. Both boys also cherish the small gifts that their absent fathers have sent them from the United States. However, Rafa cannot see the reflection and has little sympathy for Ysrael. After Ysrael confesses to the brothers that he hopes one day to travel to the global North—to Canada—where doctors can operate on his face so he will not have to hide behind his blue cotton mask, the story's denouement explodes at the very moment Yunior and Ysrael are starting to bond: "The mask twitched. I realized he was smiling and then my brother brought his arm around and smashed the bottle on top of [Ysrael's] head. It exploded, the thick bottom spinning away like a crazed eyeglass and I said, Holy fucking shit." Ysrael stumbles and slams into a fence post, glass crumbling "off his mask." As Ysrael lays unconscious on the campo ground, Rafa tears off the mask: "His left ear was a nub and you could see the thick veined slab of his tongue through a hole in his cheek. He had no lips. His head was tipped back and his eyes had gone white and the cords were out on his neck. He'd been an infant when the pig had come into the house. The damage looked old but still I jumped back and said, Please Rafa, let's go. Rafa crouched and using only two of his fingers, turned Ysrael's head from side to side."[8]

Ysrael's (unmasked) face assumes immense meaning in this short story. It can be said that Díaz writes an ethic of ethics, a striking exploration of the meaning of face-to-face intersubjectivity and lived immediacy in light of his characters' Caribbean existence and the human other. At the core of Díaz's story are descriptions of Rafa and Yunior's encounters with others. These encounters dramatize particular features: the way that others affect Rafa and Yunior unlike any worldly object or force. Yunior, in particular, attempts to constitute the other Ysrael cognitively on the basis of human empathy and vision as an alter ego.[9] He struggles to see that Ysrael is not only like him, not only acts like him in Santo Domingo, but is also the master of his conscious life. The two constitute each other within the shared social universe of their shared island.

Thus envisaged, "Ysrael" grapples poetically with the core elements of what the philosophers call the intersubjective life: Ysrael, the other, addresses Yunior, calling to him. Ysrael does not even have to speak for Rafa and Yunior to *feel* the summons. It is this encounter between Rafa, Yunior, and Ysrael that Díaz presents as fully as it is possible: he not only introduces a profound, affective event into the everyday language of literature but also avoids the pitfall of turning it into an intellectual theme. Beyond any other ethical concerns, the fundamental intuition of the story is the nonreciprocal relation of responsibility.

Can the phenomenological descriptions of intersubjective responsibility be built into an analysis of living in the world? By situating "Ysrael" as a series of unmaskings and face-to-face encounters, Díaz chooses to begin his story by starting from an interpretive phenomenology. He strips away accumulated layers of conceptualization to reveal experience as it comes to light for Yunior de Las Casas. For Díaz, this intersubjective experience proves "ethical" in the sense that Yunior's "I" discovers its own particularity when it is singled out by Ysrael, who embodies the gaze of the other. This gaze is interrogative and imperative: Ysrael's human face says to Yunior and Rafa "Do not kill me." This face also implores the "I." The command and supplication occur because human faces affect us as affective moments: the face of the other is expressive because it is a force. The unmasked face opens the primordial discourse whose first word is obligation, which no "interiority" permits avoiding. Like Díaz's "Aurora," "Negocios," and "London Terrace," everything in "Ysrael" exemplifies the narrative tension between the visible cuento's logic and the logic of the secret historia embedded within it.

Further, everything I have suggested above about the complex philosophical meanings of Ysrael's face are, of course, inspired by the philosopher Emmanuel Levinas's reflections in *Alterity and Transcendence* on the face of the other. According to Levinas, "the face of the other" is the "original locus of the meaningful.... It is precisely in that recalling of me of my responsibility by the face that summons me, that demands me, that requires me—it is in that calling into question—that the other is my neighbor."[10] For me, these are the central issues thematized in Díaz's story. As Richard Pérez noted in one of the best essays on Díaz's "Ysrael," one of the central preoccupations in "Ysrael" is how the figure of the Levinasian face "communicates a promise of legibility followed by a realization that, in fact [Díaz's portrait of Ysrael's face] hides as much as it displays." For Pérez, this inability thus "gives the face . . . a destabilizing aspect, combining, at once, an intentionality of appearance with an unwitting capacity to veil a complex inner life."[11]

It is thus easy, in retrospect, to understand why Rosenthal was so moved and amazed by the sheer literary and philosophical power of Díaz's text when she first read "Ysrael" over the transom—why it compelled her to call Díaz immediately and ask "Who are you?"[12] The epiphany of Ysrael's face reveals a philosophical answer to her question: Díaz is an Afro-Atlantic Dominicano writer who grapples in his fiction with the complex, individual, and familial diasporic mutations of coloniality in Santo Domingo and New Jersey, compelling readers of his stories to see new parts of themselves and their relations to others in the world. "Ysrael" expertly manages the narrative tension, yet it also keeps the reader wondering what kind of short story it will turn out to be in the end.

Like "Ysrael," another story in *Drown*, "Fiesta, 1980," was first published in *Story* magazine. Set in Parlin's London Terrace and the Bronx, "Fiesta, 1980" presents a preteen Yunior who has emigrated with Rafa and Virta from Santo Domingo to Parlin. The precocious Yunior sneers at his relatives who live in an apartment "furnished in contemporary Dominican Tacky."[13] Yunior's father, Ramón—whom we saw memorialized as a plotting and scheming twenty-four-year-old newly arrived economic migrant in Díaz's story "Negocios"—is here in "Fiesta, 1980," far from his earlier immigrant and undocumented status. By 1980, Ramón is a legal citizen well on his way to being acculturated and incorporated in the United States. And the story begins there in the de Las Casas's modest London Terrace home as they dress for a fiesta to be held at Virta's sister's home in the Bronx. At the story's beginning, Yunior makes a confession: Papi is having an affair with a "sucia" Puerto Rican woman, and while everyone in the family knows about it, the subject is avoided, the truth disavowed.

Yunior has a reputation in the family for getting carsick in his father's "bought to impress" bright lime-green VW van: Papi thus scolds Mami for allowing their son to eat before the car ride to the Bronx. He fears that food in Yunior's stomach will make him "vomit" in his prized automobile. Yunior feels mortified about this affliction, and his father and Rafa belittle him about it, making him feel worse. Mami defends Yunior, saying it is not his fault he gets sick. As we know from Díaz's previous representations of the father, Papi is a believer in harsh corporal punishment: he threatens Yunior with a beating if he gets sick in the van. Once at the family fiesta, Yunior observes his mother in the crowd of relatives. He is unable to understand her complex feelings for him, especially considering his father's toxic masculinity and his serial philandering: the afternoon of the party Papi had come home, stormed his way past the family, and jumped straight into the shower. Rafa and Yunior both "knew" that their father "had been with the Puerto Rican woman he was seeing and wanted to wash off the evidence quick."[14]

As readers arrive at the story's taut denouement, its many fragments—the father's infidelity, Yunior's carsickness, the mother's suffering—all converge for Yunior, painting a portrait of his family's acute estrangement. Unlike in "London Terrace," the father's cheating in "Fiesta, 1980," though repugnant to Yunior, his mother, and all of the relatives attending the fiesta, is not catastrophic; it is routine. For Yunior, his father's all-encompassing patriarchal power, duplicity, and cruelty make him want to "imagine" a different "Mami before Papi" and to comfort his mother: "Later I would think, maybe if I had told her [about the Puerto Rican "sucia"], she would have confronted him, would have done something, but who can know such things."[15] The story ends with Mami putting "her hand on [Yunior's] shoulders" and lovingly comforting him. By shifting the perspective and tone in "Fiesta, 1980," Díaz defamiliarizes a commonplace story about his everyday people. And although the short story contains little dramatic action, its logic of common sense chronicles the family's ritual preparation for driving to, participating in, and returning from a fiesta. It not only ends where it began—the London Terrace apartment—but also delivers on its early promise: Yunior pukes in his father's brand-new lime-green van. Formally, if not materially, the story is one of Díaz's neatest.

Whereas "Fiesta, 1980" is anchored in Yunior's growing up in Parlin's London Terrace, "Aguantando" takes place earlier, in hyperurban Santo Domingo's Calle Sumner Wells (figure 3.1), just after Ramón has first abandoned Virta, Rafa, and Yunior to a life of poverty and a state of suspension. More than a series of anecdotes of life in Santo Domingo, this striking story is one of the central pieces in *Drown*: Díaz describes in the cuento's secret story how the US military invasion of the Dominican Republic in 1965 traumatized Yunior's mother, Virta. During these years Virta tells her sons that their absent father had sent her letters promising he would soon return to whisk the family away to the United States. When Ramón fails to show up, they stop believing him.

To provide for Rafa and Yunior, their mother works long hours at a chocolate factory, as Díaz chronicles in "Ysrael." And when she cannot afford to feed them, she tries to console them, as Yunior recalls: "We were poor. The only way we could have been poorer was to have lived in the campo or to have been Haitian immigrants, and Mami regularly offered these to us as brutal consolation."[16]

Still, the family cannot afford meat or beans, instead living off of boiled yucca, boiled platano, pieces of cheese, and shreds of bacalao. When Virta can

Figure 3.1 Calle Sumner Wells, Díaz's Santo Domingo neighborhood. Photograph by the author.

no longer clothe or care for her sons, she sends them away to stay at their tío Miguel's house. During this period, shortly after receiving a letter from her husband promising that he is coming home, Mami leaves, disappearing for many weeks. Virta's disappearance creates suspense in the story, raising the implicit questions of why. As the cuento goes on, this logic of suspense gains urgency. When Virta returns home, she is distraught, inconsolable, and distant from the boys. Yunior is an eyewitness to his mother's island travails and breakdown: "I remember the heaviness of that month, thicker than almost anything. When Abuelito tried to reach our father on the phone number he'd left none of the men who lived with him knew anything about where he had gone. . . . She did not call me her Prieto or bring me chocolates from her work."[17]

But what other constellation of forces contributed to Virta's feeling so distant and distraught? Díaz's Yunior provides some provocative historical answers, detailing how the US's Cold War military invasion of the Dominican Republic and its anarchy of empire affected his mother's physical and mental well-being. His mother, he emphasizes, "had been pregnant with my first never-born brother" and suffered "across her stomach and back the scars from the recent attack she's survived in 1965."[18] Although Virta's scars and the de Las Casas family's lost baby are direct *physical* manifestations of US military invasion, "Aguantando" goes further, thematizing the *psychic* damages the US Cold War invasion has wrought on the family.

While Papi is working in Nueva York, Yunior chronicles how "many fulanos" were "drawn" to his mother. "From my porch," he continues, "I'd watched more than one Porfirio Rubirosos say see you tomorrow."[19] To fully understand Virta's Cold War–era injuries—the aborted birth of the "first never-born" son, as well as her psychic injuries and her mental breakdown—readers have to fill in the larger historical context of the Dominican Republic's political culture: Yunior only begins to outline this, calling on readers to do more. To that end: following the 1961 assassination of the dictator Rafael Leónidas Trujillo Molina, the island nation's politics plunged into chaos. The election of the leftist writer-intellectual Juan Bosch to the presidency in 1962 did not bring the order that some envisioned. Seven months after Bosch's inauguration, a military coup, backed politically and militarily by the United States, ousted the democratic leftist and installed a nominally democratic civilian regime. As historian Abraham Lowenthal explains in *The Dominican Intervention*, by early 1965, US ambassador W. Tapley Bennett Jr. stood as the purportedly independent president Donald Reid Cabral's lone powerful ally.[20]

On April 24, 1965, army officers rebelled, and a battle for power on the island nation began. The US Embassy supported a military junta to replace President Reid, fearing that chaos would not only lead to communist gains in the Caribbean—where Fidel Castro's Cuba served as a model of resistance to US hegemony—but would also endanger US citizens. When it appeared that pro-Bosch forces would triumph, rival anti-Bosch generals united to launch an air attack on the rebels. If Lowenthal claimed that US officials did not propose the assault, as Bosch and others have alleged, he suggests "that the general US approval of their course encouraged [the anti-Bosch forces] to undertake that specific tactic at this particular juncture." Rather than resolving matters, that is, the anti-rebel offensive fanned the flames of civil war on the island nation. US policy makers backed the anti-Bosch contingent. Boschists interpreted this as proof of their suspicions about Washington. A "self-reinforcing cycle of mutual distrust . . . set in," Lowenthal notes, making a compromise less likely and making US military intervention more likely.[21]

As military attacks on pro-Bosch forces stalled, US worry about the communist menace in Santo Domingo surged. On April 28 the anticommunist leaders asked for US troops to invade the island. Twenty-two thousand US Marines began to land, Lowenthal explains, even before President Johnson approved the action. The White House first insisted—as it has done often—that these US troops had been deployed to protect American lives, and it later claimed to have struck against Greater Antillean (read: Cuban) communist expansion. Regardless of the rationale, US policy during the first days of the intervention was anticommunist. By the morning of May 3, 1965, an overwhelming US military presence flexed its military might. Lowenthal completes the book with a chapter critiquing the US literature on the cultures of US imperialism. He identifies, and finds lacking, two "fundamentally distinct approaches." First, the "official line" praises the goals and results of White House policies, but "is obviously wrong" because the administration was never neutral, as its supporters claim.[22] Second, the anti-hegemonic view condemns the military intervention as a classic example of flawed US foreign policy. Lowenthal admits that Washington's incredible attempts to justify its actions make the anti-hegemonic framework believable. In place of these inadequate interpretations, I propose we read Junot Díaz's short story "Aguantando" together with his critique of the thirty-some-year "Trujillato" in *The Brief Wondrous Life of Oscar Wao* to construct a fuller picture of how the US anticommunism war in the Dominican Republic affected families such as the de Las Casas and the Cabral-de Leóns.[23] In his short-story cycles chronicling Virta de Las Casas's bodily wounding in 1965 and of the Cabral-de León family's experiences of imprisonment and death on the island, Díaz's narratives and their constitutive "character matrices" paint a more personal portrait: they depict how the forty-plus years of US military intervention in Haiti and the Dominican Republic rippled through individuals and their communities.

Aware of the complex personal and sociopolitical forces tearing apart his family, Díaz's Yunior fantasizes, at the end of "Aguantando," about his father's coming home from Nueva York to awaken them from their nightmarish history: "He'd have gold on his fingers, cologne on his neck, a silk shirt, good leather shoes. The whole barrio would come out to greet him."[24]

In "Drown," the title story and the emotional center of Junot Díaz's first Riverhead book, the author returns the reader to Yunior's disordered world of Parlin's London Terrace. It begins with events that had occurred two years earlier when Yunior's mother made an announcement: Beto, Yunior's best friend, was home for the summer and had been asking for him. After informing Yunior, Virta is surprised by her son's cavalier avoidance of his old friend: the two once were so close that Beto would typically "walk into the apartment without knocking." As becomes clear as the story progresses, the root of Yunior's response is circumstantial. Yunior and his mother, now a housecleaner, are living alone in their London Terrace apartment: Ramón has left the family for a second and final time. Yunior is finishing high school, though not without struggle. Routinely, one of his wealthy New Jersey high school teachers, "whose family had two grammar schools named after it," tells him that kids in his school will never amount to anything notable. Even though he fears his fate, Yunior does little to prevent it, spending time skipping classes, shoplifting with Beto, and carousing in nearby New Brunswick college-town bars like the Roxy. Recalling his teacher's comparison of students to space shuttles, Yunior believes he'll "burn out": "A few of you are going to make it. Those are the orbiters. But the majority of you are going to burn out, going nowhere." With these words, Yunior drops his head on his school desk and imagines himself "losing altitude, fading, the earth spread out beneath me, hard and bright."[25] Díaz mixes this loss of "altitude"—this sense of abandonment and intellectual failure—with what Yunior remembers of his high school days with Beto, ultimately capturing the teenage protagonist's angst, yearning, and unexpected withdrawal. As well, Yunior's sense of responsibility for his mother, who has become a ghost of herself—a "shadow warrior," "dreaming of being with a man who betrayed her"—blends beautifully into Yunior's longing to escape the neighborhood and its suffocating entrapment. (Rafa is not mentioned: his absence will not be explained until *This Is How You Lose Her*, when we learn that the oldest brother had died of cancer.)

Years earlier, Yunior and Beto had loved the right time of London Terrace's nighttime. They enjoyed escaping their apartments' "heat that was like something heavy that had come home to die. Families arranged on their porches, the glow from their TVs washing blue against the brick." After staying out late at local bars and hitting on "the sucias we con into joining us," Yunior comes home alone, walking through the surrounding London Terrace fields: "In the distance you can see the Raritan, as shiny as an earthworm. . . . The dump has long since shut down, and grass has spread over it like a sickly fuzz . . . the landfill might be the top of a blond head, square and old."[26]

When Yunior isn't making do as a stickball player, small-time drug dealer, and increasingly expert truant, he recalls how Beto and he would steal off to the local community center, jump its fences, and leap "into the pool." Beto and Yunior loved what this pool provided: an escape from their urban London Terrace "racket"—a special underwater solace: "While everything above is loud and bright, everything below whispers."[27] And there, one day, Beto, "stronger than" Yunior, "holds" him "down until water flooded" his "nose and throat."[28]

If Yunior feels himself losing "altitude," becoming a "burned out" loser at his high school, this scene at the pool suggests acute sensations of drowning in Beto's company. These combined memories trigger Yunior's recollections of his sexual encounters with Beto: "Twice, that's it." The first time was in summertime, when they went to Beto's apartment after swimming, and they "watch a porn video." An hour into the movie, Beto reached into Yunior's trunks. "What the fuck are you doing? I asked, but he didn't stop . . . I kept my eyes on the television, too scared to watch. I came right away, smearing the plastic covers." Yunior recalls the resulting silence, awkwardness, and homosocial panic: he felt "terrified" that he would "end up abnormal, a fucking pato [homosexual]."[29] Although Yunior is not homophobic, he does say he does not want to be a "pato" or pasivo like Beto: the male recipient of anal penetration, on the one hand, and the one who performs fellatio on other males, on the other.

Sensing Yunior's anxiety, Virta "pesters" him about his ugly feelings, and the teenager tells her to leave him "the fuck alone," retreating to his basement room. When Beto calls to smooth things over, Yunior is "cool" but initially refuses to meet up with him at the mall. He remembers changing his mind, for he realizes Beto was his "bestfriend and back then that mattered to me more than anything." Yunior then seeks Beto out at the pool, ending again up at his friend's apartment: "We sat in front of the television, in our towels, his hands bracing against my abdomen and thighs. I'll stop if you want, but I didn't respond. I wasn't asleep or awake, but caught somewhere in between, rocked slowly back and forth, the way the surf holds junk against the shore, rolling it over and over."[30] A complex embedding of questions ensures that the cuento's narrative tension is maintained.

For example, why does Díaz represent Yunior's fears as sensations of drowning or being rocked back and forth "the way the surf holds junk against the shore"? The answer may lie in the story's form. "Drown," like many of Díaz's other stories, ends in perfect symmetry: he and his mother are alone in their London Terrace apartment watching a Hollywood blockbuster (probably *Bonnie and Clyde*). Virta and Yunior comfort each other, her hands gently touching his, until she falls asleep, dreaming of strolling along the Boca Raton jacarandas with her marido (husband), Ramón. Yunior remembers his college-bound friend, Beto, advising him that he should prepare for a better future: "You can't be anywhere forever."[31] He remembers the parting gift Beto gave him—a book, personally inscribed—that in the end he never reads. To catch his breath—to keep from drowning—Yunior flings it into the garbage.

Readers of *Drown* have naturally tended to associate the linked collection of stories with its title story—with Yunior's feelings of suffocation and drowning by Parlin's London Terrace's toxicants: its Global Landfill, bad public schools, deflating teachers, aggressive cops, homosocial encounters, and scarce jobs. One of the best readers of Díaz's *Drown*—Ylce Irizarry—suggests that the very title of the book "is the dominant metaphor for the struggle the characters experience. They drown—economically and culturally—and are well aware of their failure to arrive."[32] Although these meanings of economic and cultural drowning are immediately palpable in Díaz's book and title story, I suggest that an intertextual reading of *Drown* evinces a more extended postcolonial literary impetus behind Yunior's "drowning," adding both subjective and philosophical dimensions to his Joycean contention that history is a nightmare from which he is trying to awake. And just as this intertextual reading has an autobiographical dimension—a dimension in which Díaz strives to transcend his own literary precursors (Homer, Derek Walcott, Toni Morrison, and James Joyce), it also has implications for Díaz's motivic characters, Yunior de Las Casas and Oscar de León.

Even one who has not read *The Brief Wondrous Life of Oscar Wao* may have heard of Yunior and Lola de León's famous assessments of the novel's young hero, Oscar: that he is working to become the Dominican Tolkien or that he may become New Jersey's Dominican James Joyce.[33] Such an individual may also have heard that Díaz's Yunior, in "Flaca," from *This Is How You Lose Her*, falls in love with Veronica Hardrada when he sees her during an undergraduate seminar on James Joyce. Indeed, a rather cursory examination of these moments might suggest a relationship between Joyce's Stephen Dedalus, on the one hand, and Díaz's Oscar de León and Yunior de Las Casas, on the other hand: all three exiled writers-characters desire a decolonial liberation from the snares of nationalism, language, and empire.[34] Such a view would frame Joyce's famous line about history in *Ulysses* as central to Díaz's historia in *Drown*. Both Stephen Dedalus and Yunior de Las Casas's notion of their island histories would thus be rooted in existential and decolonial conceptions of history. And this, ultimately, would beget questions: what are the crucial, metatextual implications of Joyce and Díaz's heroes "awakening" from their nightmares of history? If readers applied this Joycean motif and conceit of the "drowning man" in *Ulysses* to an extended reading of Díaz's "drowning" Yunior, would we better see the hermeneutic implications for a reading of Díaz's *Drown*?

I suggest that tarrying with these questions is instructive. For instance, one of the earliest images of drowning to appear in Joyce's *Ulysses* occurs when Stephen concedes his lack of social permeability to his roommate, Buck Mulligan: "You saved men from drowning. I'm not a hero, however." When this drowning motif/image later appears in the novel's "Proteus" episode, it takes on more political and melancholy hues: "A drowning man. His human eyes scream out to me in horror of his death. I . . . with him together down . . . I could not save her. Waters: bitter death: lost."[35] Stephen's inability to save drowning men evokes his failure to absolve his mother at death. Through repeated images of drowning, in concert with the other novel's leitmotifs, Joyce fetishizes Stephen's notion of history. Rather than awakening Stephen from his nightmare, Joyce's *Ulysses* awakens readers to the nightmare itself.

Díaz's nuanced references to Yunior's drowning in his London Terrace metamundo are complementary to the story's two logics of causality. They not only highlight Yunior's homosocial feelings of drowning at the pool with Beto but also illuminate how his mother is doubly "drowned out": on the one hand, by the US invasion of her island nation in 1965, and on the other, by her husband's abandonment, misogyny, and serial cheating in Nueva York and Boca Raton. The Joycean image of drowning, coupled with Stephen's inability to save his mother in *Ulysses*, clarifies Yunior's inability to protect his mother from poverty and his abusive papi. If Joyce's *Ulysses*, *Portrait of the Artist as a Young Man*, and *Stephen Hero* are always autobiographical, are Díaz's *Drown*, *The Brief Wondrous Life of Oscar Wao*, and *This Is How You Lose Her* always autobiographical, too? As this intertextual approach suggests, we might argue as much: the textual fragments in Joyce's oeuvre and in Díaz's historia not only possess a nightmarish quality for audiences but also for Joyce and Díaz themselves.

Moreover, if the schemas of Joyce's Bloom and Díaz's Ramón are intended to parallel the "Ithaca" episode in the *Odyssey*—if they imply that Bloom and Ramón are, to some extent, Odyssean themselves—are we to interpret this as suggesting that the sons Stephen and Yunior are iterations of Odysseus's son Telemachus? A few more intertextual questions arise: considering that these pairs—Stephen and Joyce, on the one hand, and Yunior and Díaz, on the other—seem to be hyperaware of their attempts to escape their personal, world-historical nightmares of coloniality, is this awareness enough to explain their related visions of history and fears of the drowning? Are Joyce's Stephen and Díaz's Yunior on an epistemological quest (otherwise) for truth in their historias? Is this how Díaz creates narrative tension in his cuentos? And more specifically for my reading of Díaz's MFA thesis and *Drown*, will Yunior learn to overcome the nightmare of his histories in Santo Domingo and Parlin's London Terrace?

Again, it is instructive to read Díaz's use of the drowning man image in his MFA thesis and in *Drown* as an allusion, per Joyce, to Odysseus's many drowned companions in Homer's epic. As Díaz frames it in his fictions, Santo Domingo nightmares—its ghosts of the (socially) dead—oppress Díaz's London Terrace, the world of the living. This oppression shapes Yunior's youth, imprinting it, as we saw in "Negocios" and *Drown*, through the forms of the bildungsroman and the historical metatext on his way to his sentimental education at Rutgers University. And as Díaz's aesthetic choices remind us, we do not have to decide whether a later Yunior (fallen from grace) will fail in his literary ambitions and university teaching career; we do not have to decide, on the contrary, if Yunior will one day become, like Díaz himself, a creative-writing professor in Cambridge, Massachusetts. We only have to recognize that Díaz unifies subgenres by imposing a mythic New World (New Word) structure to unite his odyssey's diasporic multiplicities. We only have to recognize the bildungsroman by way of a transnational Greater Antillean perspective—a diasporic perspective that radically counters with the Eurocentric geotemporality of the older form and cancels it, leaving behind only its negation as a trace.

Just as Fredric Jameson suggests in James Joyce's *Ulysses*, that "genre is itself hypostasized and projected outside the novel by the *Odyssey* parallels,"[36] so, too, do I argue that Díaz's linked historia projects its subgenres outward. That is, the *Odyssey* parallel preserves the diachrony of the interpersonal de Las Casas situations, as if it were from memory that we read and decode, in a quite different dimension. One can therefore read Yunior de Las Casas's stories in *Drown* and *This Is How You Lose Her*—as I attempt to do in chapter 5—not only as linked, rescripted short stories that work perfectly well on their own terms but also as a collective cycle of historias that chronicle, bolster, and make trouble for one another, producing an arresting surplus of feeling and affect that exceeds the ordinary sum of their parts. This is the wonderful patch of liminality that Díaz in his own Afro-Atlantic Dominicano odyssey spins out in his linked-story collections of a son abandoned on his island by his father and in the novel *The Brief Wondrous Life of Oscar Wao*, texts in which he depicts his endured and enacted abandonments, relays his historia of Oscar Wao, and chronicles that difficult, necessary search for decolonial love.

In addition to "Aguantando," Díaz also wrote two new stories for *Drown*: "Boyfriend" and "How to Date a Browngirl, Blackgirl, Whitegirl, or Halfie." "Boyfriend," originally published in *Time Out*, is the briefest of Díaz's stories:

it is five-and-a-half-pages long, filled with a variety of colloquial idiolects. In its friction and propulsiveness, it is one of Díaz's small masterpieces. One night Yunior—stoned out of his mind on New Jersey "superweed"—finds that he has been sleepwalking and has somehow ended up in the hallway of his flat. When he wakes, he overhears a Hispanic Caribbean machista boyfriend fighting with his girlfriend (with world-class "model looks") in their apartment directly beneath his flat. "It would have broken my heart," Yunior confesses, "if it hadn't been so damn familiar. I guess I'd gotten numb to that sort of story."[37]

Although initially Yunior's creepy snooping is what he calls "accidental," he eventually becomes fascinated by the lovers' heartbreaks and travails. He tries to convince himself that his spying on the couple—hearing "the Spanish they shared" with one another—gives him an immense pleasure. He simultaneously notes a distance—a "numb[ness] and scene so damn familiar"—that complicates this pleasure, lacing it with heartache and traces of the "superweed." Thus envisaged, the lovers' heartbreak becomes the tenor and vehicle for Yunior to work through his own pain as a certified "sucio," misogynist, and a loser of love:

> Boyfriend came around a couple of times that week for his things, and I guess to finish the job. . . . He listened to what she had to say, arguments that had taken her hours to put together, and then he would sigh and say it didn't matter, he needed his space, punto. She let him fuck her every time, maybe hoping that it would make him stay but you know, once somebody gets a little escape velocity going, ain't no play in the world that will keep him from leaving. Damn, ain't nothing more shabby than those farewell fucks.[38]

"Boyfriend," then, allows Díaz to open a small window on the tortured pains of breaking up. It helps measure, like the quiet, contemplative Yunior, the half-life of love.

When Junot Díaz was in his mid-twenties, "worn out" from delivering luxury pool tables, an experience that he fictionalized in his story "Edison, New Jersey," he decided to apply to several MFA creative-writing programs. He was starting to write short stories, and the work was coming along slowly. One of his undergraduate writing advisers at Rutgers had told him about the possibilities of applying to graduate school in creative writing, but as he explained in his 2014 *New Yorker* online essay, "MFA vs. POC," "No one could really tell you what MFA programs really are."[39] You had to experience them for yourself.

When I gave the Distinguished Cornell University Lecture in April 2014 on Junot Díaz's "The Cheater's Guide to Love," I made it a point before and after my presentation to meet with Díaz's creative-writing advisers, Stephanie Vaughn and Lamar Herrin. I wanted to discuss the genesis of Díaz's speculative realist, imaginative writing in Ithaca. I met first with Professor Vaughn, affirming at the start of our conversation that I was not writing a biography of Díaz but rather a critical literary study of his work. Vaughn had signed off on Díaz's thesis in January 1995, and she recalled during our meeting that when he had applied to Cornell's program as a fiction writer in 1991, his creative-writing sample, though raw, was significantly better than the polished submissions of the published fiction writers who were competing with Díaz for the four spots in the Cornell MFA fiction cohort.[40] We also chatted more informally about our respective graduate-school formations. She had come to Cornell as a Mellon postdoctoral Fellow, and she had then served as the director of creative writing three different times. Vaughn had received her MFA at the Iowa Creative Writing Program and had completed additional postgraduate work as a Stegner Fellow at Stanford University. We ended our discussion by sharing our mutual interests in Willa Cather's *My Ántonia*, and I informed her that my graduate PhD mentor at Stanford University, Arturo Islas, had also worked with Wallace Stegner and was, in all ways, a terrific creative writer and literary critic. Because her time was limited—she had squeezed me in during her office hours—I thanked her for sharing with me her memories of Díaz and the workshopped stories that he produced for his MFA thesis. That day, Vaughn attended my presentation on Díaz and later commented that she enjoyed my presentation and loved one of the slides that featured Díaz's family photos: one of a young Díaz with his mother and brother, another of an adolescent Díaz cutting a birthday cake at a party hosted by his mother. The photographs, she said, reminded her that Díaz had always been close to his mother. When he worked as a graduate student on *Epoch*, the program's creative-writing journal, Vaughn said that Díaz sent the extra money he earned as an assistant editor home to New Jersey to help his mother make do.

The following day the novelist and professor Lamar Herrin, who had received his PhD in English at the University of Kentucky and then served on Díaz's MFA committee, took me to lunch in downtown Ithaca. We spent several hours discussing our interests in writers from the global South, especially William Faulkner, Gabriel García Márquez, and Junot Díaz himself. Herrin informed me that after twenty-nine years of teaching creative writing at Cornell, he had discovered a terrific metaphor for writing a novel he had passed on to his graduate students, including Díaz. Because I did not take any notes at our Ithaca lunch, I am relying here on Lamar Herrin's written words on writing:

> Say you are in Cincinnati, Ohio (where I once lived) and want to go by river to Louisville, Kentucky, approximately one hundred miles downstream. You know where you want to go, that is, you have an ending for your novel in mind, but you have never been on the river before. A glance at a map will tell you the names of the major tributaries between the two cities and the larger towns located on the banks (that is, the novel's main events and characters), but you do not know the river's currents, its snags, its smaller islands, its minor tributaries, and any number of other pertinent factors. You don't know the thrill of catching a swift current or the drudgery of day to day paddling (you are self-, not motor-propelled). You know the river will take you to Louisville if you navigate its currents successfully and if you don't give up after days and weeks of dispiriting monotony.... If you do get to Louisville, of course, it may be Louisville in name only and bear little resemblance to the city you have carried around for so long in your head. But at least you're somewhere, you can be said to have arrived. At which point, a second trip down a now more familiar river, that is the revision, can begin.[41]

One can glean from Herrin's complex metaphor that even if his graduate student Díaz was not yet writing a novel, the linked stories of his MFA thesis, "Negocios," with its intricate "snags" and cognitive mappings of London Terrace, its abutting Global Landfill, the Raritan River, the names of the calles in Santo Domingo, and its inimitable campos, are indeed some of his stories' main events—events constitutive of his elaborate character matrix. For Herrin and Díaz, the movement and the lived experience of somebody traveling "by river" is similar, as Herrin suggests, to the structure of any narrative or historia. The lived experience of traveling on the river forces travelers to focus on the changing perceptions on which their consciousness focuses during the stretch of time, say, from Cincinnati to Louisville. But for Herrin it isn't only that a novel or story resembles a river road or river path and that the river road leads to an endpoint or "arrival": rather, the river road and its currents and countercurrents—its "snags" and tributaries—between Cincinnati and Louisville are "the novel's main events and characters" that constitute the character-driven matrix that is the novel. Once you arrive, Herrin argues, the second trip "down a more familiar river" begins: revising the narrative or historia.

Herrin thus associates the concept of the river road with the basic temporal structure of the novel, though without thematizing it as such. The different structures of the river road lead to encounters and events that reflect what Hans Ulrich Gumbrecht suggests are "indicative of different layers in the history of social knowledge and of the *mentalités* that surround and accompany the history of the genre."[42]

In my conversations with Vaughn and Herrin, I informed them that I was interested in grappling with how Díaz's fiction writing could be properly understood in relation to and as a critique of higher education and the creative-writing program. How had Cornell University's MFA program and its writing faculty (re)organized Díaz's own literary productions at Cornell? Could we take into account the intimacy of creative-writing instruction in a reading of Díaz's oeuvre? What insights would emerge from entwining a reading and schooling in a reading of Díaz's fiction and creativity with a reading of the Cornell program itself? The Iowa Writers' Workshop, where Vaughn had gone to receive her own MFA training, had been founded in 1936, and educators such as Paul Engle, who directed the program from the early 1940s to the mid-1960s, enthusiastically believed that creative writing *could* be taught—that native talent could be nurtured and disciplined under the gaze of one's peers and mentors. Control and tone were important for the graduate-student creative writer, and close editing was weighted much more than simple expression. Good poets and novelists, Engle had famously quipped, were like "good hybrid corn": "both born and made."[43] By 1945, Wallace Stegner, my Stanford adviser's mentor, had followed Engle's University of Iowa lead by founding Stanford's MFA program, and other programs emerged at Boston University, the universities of Indiana, Florida, and Denver, as well as Cornell and Johns Hopkins.

As Mark McGurl's iconic literary history *The Program Era* suggests, after the success of these first MFA programs, the number of degree-granting creative-writing programs across the country began to grow exponentially. The handful of creative-writing programs that existed in the 1940s had, by 1975, increased to fifty-two. By 1984, there were some 150 graduate degree programs (offering the MA, MFA, or PhD), and as of 2004, there were more than 350 creative-writing programs in the United States, all of them staffed by practicing writers like Díaz's teachers at Cornell, most of whom held an advanced degree in creative writing or in English. More than anything else, McGurl's *The Program Era* is a sweeping history of the MFA program and of the MFA program's relation to US higher education throughout the second half of the twentieth century. "Creative writing," McGurl argues, "is in sum, as American as baseball, apple pie, and homicide. And yet there is evidence that after fifty years of standing more or less alone, this is beginning to change—evidence that writing programs are, like fast food and nuclear weapons and (perhaps more relevantly) mass higher education, beginning to proliferate abroad."[44] With his focus on the institutional history of "the program era," however, McGurl does not devote any space to discussing how Planet MFA and Planet PhD routinely subalternized underrepresented men and women of color through what Díaz characterizes as the MFA and PhD's narrow ideology of Whiteness in the training and work of both the writing instructors and the cohorts of MFA graduate students.

In his 2014 essay "MFA vs. POC," Díaz recalls that like many first-generation students of color, he had "never visited Cornell" or the other MFA programs to which he had applied. Nor had he pragmatically or systematically "looked up" the publications of writing faculty he wanted to work with, contacted them, or communicated with their students. "I went after [the Cornell University MFA] with about the same amount of foresight that my parents brought to their immigration—which from my perspective seemed to be none." Díaz originally planned to "spend two years in [Cornell's] workshops" learning all he "could about fiction" in what he assumed was going to "be a supportive environment."[45]

Like many of us first-generation graduate students of color in MFA and PhD programs in English departments, Díaz did not have an immediately gratifying or "great workshop experience." By the start of his second year, in 1993, he embraced a new goal: "get me the fuck out of here." As Díaz understood it, the problem at Cornell was not just that the majority of his teachers were championing postmodernism or literary minimalism; rather, it was that, as he wrote in the *New Yorker*: "that [MFA] shit was too white."[46]

Elaborating on his call for more racial and ethnic diversity in US workshops and MFA programs, Díaz explained that his Cornell MFA program "had almost no POC—people of color" writing teachers or graduate students. His MFA program was "too white"—"no faculty of color in the fiction program—and neither the faculty nor the administration saw that lack of color as a big problem." Díaz lamented how this situation had affected his emerging writing career: "My workshop experience reproduced exactly the dominant culture's blind spots and assumptions about race and racism (and sexism and heteronormativity, etc)." If his creative-writing teachers at Cornell preferred to have their MFA graduate students read and model their writing on "William Gaddis, Francine Prose, or Alice Munro," why didn't they also choose to examine the literary works of writers of color Díaz had been forced to read on his own—"Toni Morrison, Cherríe Moraga, Maxine Hong Kingston, Arundhati Roy"? Why weren't his Cornell MFA teachers, he recalls, interested in the tradition of POC writers—writers focused on the way that complex narratives swept up and held readers' attention, acknowledging all the while important issues on race, diaspora, and immigration? At Cornell University, he was programmed with "straight white" male focalizations. "No way,"[47] he stated.

It is thus no wonder why Díaz was so unhappy with his program-era MFA at Cornell. He was, as he recalls, "a person of color in a workshop whose theory of reality did not include" his "most fundamental experiences as a person of color": it did not include or teach worldview writers like him. The few "Calibans" and "Sycoraxes" in his cohort thus "talked constantly about the workshops' problems, about the shit our peers said to us: Why is there even Spanish in the stories? Or, I don't want to write about race. I want to write about real literature."[48] To see what real American literature meant for Díaz, one merely has to read his MFA thesis, "Negocios," and his first book, *Drown*. Stories for Díaz were "real" when readers knew what they were reading about and why the events of the stories mattered so much to them. All of the short stories he wrote at Cornell, as I have argued above, are character driven and embedded in narrative tension; they have taut arcs and terrific denouements, and many of them have moments of human crisis ending in Joycean epiphanies.

With this in mind, I conclude here by examining one more representative narrative: Díaz's 1995 processual "How to Date a Browngirl, Blackgirl, Whitegirl, or Halfie," first published in the *New Yorker* and later included in *Drown*. To be sure, this story straddles a delicate balance between narrative and vernacular prose poetry. It also begs a question: should "how-to" stories, written in the imperative, have been retired, say, after the Argentine Julio Cortázar's 1962 story "Instructions on How to Wind a Watch"? After all, Cortázar had written a minimalist one-page killer story that somehow thematized the mission of all world literature: "Hold the watch down with one hand, take the stem in two fingers, and rotate it smoothly. Now another style of time opens, trees spread their leaves, boats run their races . . . like the shadow of a woman, the smell of bread." Then "strap it on your wrist . . . imitate it quietly. And death is there in the background."[49] One might indeed fault the Argentine's story as suffering from an excess of artifice, but I really doubt that Cortázar's comparing the human condition to winding a watch by processually pointing out our longing for life without fear wasn't a brilliant thing to do in the short-story form.

Díaz's Yunior, like Cortázar's narrator, writes in "How to Date a Browngirl, Blackgirl, Whitegirl, or Halfie" a processual short story. A process, as we know, is a series of actions, changes, functions, steps, or operations that bring about a particular end or result. Process, for both Díaz and Cortázar, suggests ongoing movement and continuous action. But the emphasis in a process story is on the *how* rather than the *what*. As a topic of invention, process stories answer the basic questions: How did it happen? How does it work? What are the stages, phases, steps, or operations? Process stories and analyses are special forms of exposition in which you present a step-by-step description of *how* of a process takes place: how to wind a watch in Cortázar's story or how to date Brown, Black, White, or Halfie girls in Díaz's text.

Díaz's processual dating guide for the Afro-Atlantic Dominican teenage male takes on the authority of experience by employing a narrator speaking in the second person. The story centers on a naive teenage Yunior giving instructions to the reader about and the hows and whats of dating in Parlin's London Terrace. Yunior begins by instructing the reader to remove obvious signs of working-class Dominicanness from the home such as the "government cheese"[50] from the refrigerator; then he reminds the reader that approaching possible dates depending on whether or not they are ethno-racial "insiders" or "outsiders" is a very tricky thing. As the short story progresses, one sees how the narrator's words and mannerisms change according to the ethnicity of the potential teenage girl. These locations determine Yunior's speech and his physical approaches to them. Díaz's narrator constantly shifts descriptions of both the women and their ethno-racial formations and social classes. And by the end of the short story, one (dis)identifies with the struggle of Yunior's shifting positionality—with the way that he feels he must manipulate himself to woo the girls he is tending to in his London Terrace apartment.

Right from the start, "How to Date a Browngirl, Blackgirl, Whitegirl, or Halfie" hails us as readers. In her terrific reading of this story, Paula M. L. Moya is absolutely right when she suggests that Díaz's how-to story is a story of radical racial interpellation.[51] Thirteen-year-old Yunior narrates how he imagines—in near phantasmatic fashion—how an Afro-Latinx teenage boy can successfully date his London Terrace teenage classmates. Moreover, in an ingeniously robust form, Díaz's present-tense, second-person story wittily showcases how the contradictory, knucklehead Yunior blinds himself to the processes of racial interpellation—of "doing race"—that are at work in London Terrace culture and society. How does one precisely date girls given their gendered, raced, and classed formations? And given all of this mingling of race, class, and gender, how do these girls in turn regard Yunior as a diasporic Afro-Atlantic Dominicano male subject?

Yunior lives in a colonial world system of race not of his own making. But throughout the story we feel that somehow Yunior is aware of his raced and gendered conocimientos—aware that his double consciousness helps him understand what differently raced and classed girls may want from him. Step one: "Clear the government cheese from the refrigerator." Steps two and three: "Take down any embarrassing photos of your family in the campo.... Hide the pictures of yourself with an Afro." Because Yunior, all of thirteen, is already hyperaware of his Parlin surroundings, he constantly worries that his insider London Terrace homeboys and homegirls might shock his "outsider" dates. Give these outsiders directions, he tells himself—make sure that their parents drop the date at his apartment's doorsteps. At other moments, when one of his outsider dates is late for their hooking up, he wonders whether or not he should go out and ask one of his London Terrace homeboys if he has seen the date: "Give one of your boys a shout out and when he says, are you still waiting on that bitch? say, Hell yeah."[52]

When I read Díaz's representations of his teenage boys' naive hip-hop–like bantering in London Terrace, I can't help but laugh out loud. On the one hand, Díaz loves to regale his readers with antiphonal call-and-response hip-hop humor: his pacing and timing are always on target, and he loves to zing his readers with his characters' piratical boyish swagger. On the other hand, throughout the story Díaz's language drips with inappropriate and unfiltered masculine, racialized cultural meanings. What to make of this emblematic narrative tension?

The scene depicting Yunior "still waiting" for a girl is more than an example of hip-hop swagger, Yunior's developing misogyny, and unchecked hypermasculinity; it verges on Díaz giving readers a joke within a joke. Díaz's literary language mimics the very speech making, signifying, and testifying of his everyday people. And on the whole, this story about Yunior's dating in our epoch of what Claudia Rankine and colleagues call "the racial imaginary"[53] is also a primer on the protocols and rhetoric of Afro-Atlantic Latinx teenage boys: their complex and contradictory idiolects and meanings. This story, like others in Díaz's oeuvre, features not only what Yunior and his peers say about their world but also *how* those things are said: the spirit of a processual story enacted at the level of language. As a writer with a global hip-hop worldview, Díaz, as sociolinguist Samy Alim, along with Awad Ibrahim and Alastair Pennycook, has written of hip-hop's verse, captures language as it is "flexed, created, and sometimes (often intentionally) bent up beyond recognition."[54]

More directly: how Díaz's Afro-Atlantic Dominican youths are heard and represented makes a critical difference in how they are perceived. No matter how high Yunior wants to ascend in London Terrace, Díaz's language always helps him bring Yunior, as his central consciousness, and the other London Terrace characters to the inescapable fact of their Blackness and Brownness—to their everyday ways of speaking and being heard in the world.

The very cues provided by the girls Yunior is hoping to date often force him to misread the forces of the coloniality of race and gender that hail him: "She might," Yunior imagines, "kiss you and then go, or she might, if she's reckless, give it up. Don't stop her. . . . Tell her that you love her skin, her lips, because in truth, you love them more than you love your own."⁵⁵ As Moya suggests, "Having Yunior admit his preference for European-origin features over his own African-origin features is thus Díaz's fictional way of pushing Yunior (and the reader) forward in the journey toward epistemic and emotional decolonization."⁵⁶ With this in mind, a truth of this story becomes evident: in this story Díaz is making loud and boisterous the very diversity work that his Cornell University teachers and graduate-student classmates criticized him for.

In January 1996, Riverhead Books published Junot Díaz's *Drown*. The ten short stories from the very "barrios of the Dominican Republic to the struggling urban communities of New Jersey," Grau's Riverhead Books catalog stated, veer "off" the "traveled road of contemporary fiction" and capture a range of experiences heretofore uncharted, and now emphatically his own.⁵⁷ These words perfectly sum up the hope that Díaz had for his first book. However, *New York Times* reviewer David Gates found the stories from *Drown* occasionally "suffering from an excess of artifice."⁵⁸ On the plus side, in a later piece in the *Times*, the novelist Barbara Stewart gave Díaz and *Drown* a splashy review and a terrific authorial introduction. Hers was the first positive notice of Díaz and *Drown*. She praised Díaz's uncanny talent for writing "in the language of immigrant teenagers, a mix of English and Spanish and street slang." Moreover, she gave Díaz a platform to announce to the newspaper's audience and the world that he writes "for the people I grew up with. . . . I took extreme pains for my book to not be a native informant. Not: 'This is Dominican food. This is a Spanish word.'" Díaz's *Drown*—not just the individual stories but the book as a whole—is where he found his "Black and Brown" literary voice. It opened a door to a new kind of contemporary American literature and introduced us to a writer departing from the Program Era's possessive, hegemonic investment in Whiteness and White culture. It reinvested in what he saw as the writer's responsibility, arguing that "the information we people of color have about the world is necessary to all of us. To think, to be, to survive. Information without which no better future is possible. And without which literature too is not possible."⁵⁹

Understanding Imaginary Transference and the Colonial Difference

4

Becoming "Oscar Wao"

Actually the title came first! One day in Mexico City I was at a party. Someone there said "Oscar Wao" but with a Chilango accent. He had said "Oscar Wilde" but it sounded like "Oscar Wao." As soon as he said that, "the brief, wondrous life of Oscar Wao" jumped into my head.

  JUNOT DÍAZ, quoted in Charney, "Junot Díaz: How I Write"

Cultural identity . . . is a matter of "becoming" as well as "being." It belongs to the future as much as to the past. It is not something which already exists, transcending place, time, history and culture. Cultural identities come from somewhere, have histories. But like everything which is historical, they undergo constant transformation. Far from being eternally fixed in some essentialised past, they are subject to the continuous "play" of history, culture and power.

  STUART HALL, "Cultural Identity and Diaspora," 260

Díaz's story of Oscar de León's cultural identity is a matter of "being" and "becoming"—a story recounted by Yunior de Las Casas and Lola de León, who as the primary narrators piece together the proliferating fragments of Oscar's life and death to produce a unified portrait. But Oscar's story remains largely unfinished; it is, as its triply iterated DC Comics–informed finalities suggest, unending—a making and remaking by Díaz's narrators, who have different stakes in Oscar's future and legacy.[1] To highlight this process, as Díaz does—to focus on one's "becoming," as Stuart Hall suggests—is to emphasize discontinuity as a hallmark of identity formation.[2] Díaz uses Oscar's cultural identity of "being" to explain why the first kind of Dominicano identity is necessary but why the second one—of "becoming"—is truer to Oscar's decolonial condition. And through Yunior's fragments, blanks, enormous gaps, and páginas en blanco, which are traumatic traces and silences that, like the New World's historia of genocide, call for more versions, symbologies, and endings, Díaz does precisely this, committing to form what his characters experience in full: the pain and possibility of absence and articulation. In this chapter I focus on this pain and possibility; I follow the fragmented, redacted interpretations of Oscar's Dominicano historia, tracking the play of history and power indexed by Díaz's *The Brief Wondrous Life of Oscar Wao*.

The Brief Wondrous Life of Oscar Wao has been called one of the early twenty-first century's "greatest" novels. It ranks above or alongside Jonathan Franzen's *The Corrections*, Chimamanda Ngozi Adichie's *Half of a Yellow Sun*, Zadie Smith's *White Teeth*, and Roberto Bolaño's *2666*, and it is a tour de force of planetary aesthetics and decolonial design.[3] It has inspired alternative theater in San Francisco and in New York,[4] and it has been championed for its formulations on the philosophy of decolonial love—on the reclaiming of nerdy, counterhegemonic identifications.[5] From another angle, however, our interpretations of this book may benefit from some healthy reorientation: what has been almost forgotten about its long, tortuous genesis is that Díaz began scripting his "Oscar Wao" text as a "long" short story or "short" novella in Mexico City in 1999, publishing it a year later in the January 2000 issue of the *New Yorker*.[6] Some seven years afterward, in 2007, Díaz released his transformation of that *New Yorker* story into the prize-winning novel we recognize today—a novel that, after all, may well be a speculative fantasy. This twin history of text and author underscores that in addition to a reworking of the novelistic form—from Cervantes's *Don Quixote* and Flaubert's bildungsroman *Sentimental Education* to J. R. R. Tolkien's modernist novel *The Lord of the Rings* and Sandra Cisneros's Chicana-encyclopedic *Caramelo*—Díaz's novel also has a substantial contribution to make to the global South's poetics of the fukú americanus: the doom of the New World Américas. Why was its twisting, turning road to global canonization, to its status as one of the seminal books of our century, not more immediate?

It is thus worth the effort to reestablish the terrific formal innovations Díaz made between his initial, paratext-free *New Yorker* story and the epic novel he rescripted about Oscar Wao. Did the short-story version of "The Brief Wondrous Life of Oscar Wao" do justice to what Díaz's cold, coldhearted narrator and character Yunior de Las Casas says about his subject Oscar de León and his family's Afro-Dominicano doom? Was Díaz's story able to create the desires and distortions that it imposes serially on Oscar's immigrant Dominicano experience? Why did Díaz's arrangements and strategies in *The Brief Wondrous Life of Oscar Wao*—its now famous páginas en blanco, its gaps, blanks, and thirty-three paratextual footnotes—take so many long years of writing, rescripting, and conjuring to finally open itself up to not only what the "callous"[7] Gen-Y narrator Yunior says about Oscar and his family? To what the narrator's negative aesthetics of gaps and blanks fail to say about himself and his subjects?

Important work has been done analyzing Díaz's craftsmanship—his wrestling American English into his own ethnically mixed medium of decolonized compositions, his art of showing us in language what it means to be Black, Latinx, and an immigrant in the United States.[8] His novel's core arrangements reside in its insight into the creation of literary forms suited to the historia of torture, injustice, and death that so characterizes Dominican and Caribbean histories in general and the history of the de León-Cabral family in particular;[9] in its treatment of nerd genres' shattered histories and Tolkien-esque heroic fantasy;[10] in its thematization of the decolonialist's guide to disability;[11] in its dissection of the slippery similarities between dictators and narrative controllers or writers;[12] in its relationships to masks, jurones (mongooses), and the Anthropocene;[13] in the ways that Díaz's novel allegorizes both the "repressive" and the "productive" forms of Foucauldian biopolitical power and thus elaborates "a non-emancipatory version of decolonization";[14] in its treatment of how island and diasporic Dominican men—most of them nonwhite—resist the persistence of nationalist and imperialist violence that the Columbus Lighthouse Memorial in Santo Domingo represents through distinctly hypermasculinist performances known as "tigueraje";[15] or in its part-comedic "Chiste Apocalyptus," a cunning, half-tragic, and half-redemptive play with jokes, the unconscious, and the hero Oscar's laughing "through a broken mouth."[16]

And yet despite these revelations, large gaps remain. These may one day be addressed in retrospect by Junot Díaz's intellectual biographers—by those who wish in earnest to link the fictional events of the text to the original, untranslatable episodes of Díaz's life. And although important discoveries of the kind have recently been made by Silvio Torres-Saillant, Lorgia García-Peña, and Yomaira Figueroa-Vásquez—discoveries of how the Dominican diasporic society that Díaz painted in his novel is a "possessed text" or a "texto montado" in the cradle of Blackness in the Américas and how a profound "decolonial witnessing" in Díaz's fiction opens up a chronotope thematizing "the ethics of bearing witness" that unveils "the machinations of coloniality and gendered violence"—still, Díaz's rescripted novel has many untapped registers and cores.[17] There is much still to be gained from analyzing its tumultuous history and heterogeneous strands.

Building on the work of decolonial Caribbean-Latinx scholars such as Ramón Grosfoguel, Agustín Lao-Montes, Vanessa Pérez-Rosario, Yolanda Martínez-San Miguel, and Figueroa-Vásquez, I suggest that what is most remarkable in *The Brief Wondrous Life of Oscar Wao* is the central role of the decolonial imagination in the author's construction of diasporic personhood and the self.[18] It is a role so politically momentous that, as I explored in the book's first chapter, Díaz himself has credited sociologist Aníbal Quijano's theory of the coloniality of power—and by extension, the decolonial imagination—as central to his novel. As I have explained elsewhere, Díaz's decolonial imagination entails a critique of the coloniality of power matrix that the Iberians and Almirant Colón brought with them when they first landed on the island that is Díaz's birthplace, Hispaniola, instituting the oldest system of colonial domination in the West.[19] It is, of course, not easy to explore in full the idea of Díaz's island of the Dominican Republic outside of the celebratory rhetoric of Columbus's "discovery" and the subsequent arrival of a pitiless modernity in the Américas, to dive headlong into the coloniality of power that his novel robustly and creatively unravels and deconstructs.[20] Yet as I argue here, the logic of coloniality—the conflictual beliefs, sensibilities, and processes forming what Díaz dubs the "fukú americanus"—is the very thread that he pulls to reveal and dismantle the American colonial fabric. Some two years before Díaz was to confess about his own experience of being raped in his essay "The Silence," in an iconic interview with Paula M. L. Moya he discussed how his novel revealed male reactions to rape cultures in colonial situations, state-sponsored institutionalized rape, and the effects on boys and men whose mothers, as well as other women in their lives, had been raped. Thus envisaged, Díaz's fukú americanus can also provide his readers an account of the ways in which sexual subjectivity is formed for men under these circumstances of coloniality: "In the novel [*The Brief Wondrous Life of Oscar Wao*] you see the horror of rape closes in on all of [the characters]. The whole family is in this circuit of rape. And you know, the point the book keeps making again and again is that, in the Dominican Republic, which is to say, in the world that the DR built, if you are Beli, a Lola, a Yunior—if you are anybody—rape is never going to be far."[21] My point here is that the "fukú" embodies for Díaz "an intergenerational transfer of trauma from mothers who are rape victims to their daughters, [and] there is also intergenerational transfer of rape trauma between mothers and their sons."[22] The effects of this is thematized in the novel as Yunior's, Oscar's, Lola's, and Beli's retreat from the vulnerability that accompanies intimacy.

The fukú americanus's origins are in 1492, but it was spectacularly visible under the US-supported Trujillo dictatorship from the 1930s to the 1960s, it continued in the haunting afterlife of the Trujillato on the island, and it persisted in the 1980s–1990s Reagan and Clinton neoliberal United States of Oscar's and Lola's youth. To read Díaz's text as a deep engagement with the colonial matrix of power is to think from the perspective of his subjugated de León-Cabral characters and their own traumatic, transgenerational memories of rape, torture, violence, and domination that his texts render visible and central. And to consider Díaz's Hemispheric Américas from the perspectives of his characters, letting their decolonial perspectives take center stage, is to reveal a vibrant, vital historia. This, indeed, is one of the larger takeaways of my reading: the decolonial imagination plays a central, commanding, and constitutive role in Díaz's novel.

In my book's previous chapters on Díaz's program-era experience at Cornell University and in his post-Cornell years in New York City, I showed how he quickly penned and then transformed his thesis, "Negocios," into his first book, *Drown*. Díaz's *Drown* remains vital because in it he strived valiantly for an idiosyncratic form of expression despite the aesthetic climate of Cornell's MFA Program; in it, he worked doggedly to craft an urban, creolized language intrinsic to the story he wanted to tell about Santo Domingo and Parlin, New Jersey, and his young protagonist, Yunior de Las Casas.

In the pages that follow I maintain this trajectory, extending my intellectual biographical historia to document how Díaz struggled over the next eleven years—and in the wake of 9/11—to compose his Pulitzer Prize–winning novel. Whereas *Drown*'s urban mood holds it together as a book of short stories, *The Brief Wondrous Life of Oscar Wao* swells with linguistic registers, gleeful experimentation, and supercharged inventiveness, establishing it as one of the most remarkable literary achievements at the dawn of the twenty-first century.

After the groundbreaking debut of Díaz's *Drown*, the twenty-eight-year-old writer continued to publish a few short stories in the *New Yorker*, although he was spending most of his time teaching creative writing at Syracuse University, up in the snow-covered farmlands of New York. Although he had loved being in the mix and working at Pfizer in New York City, honing his political grassroots activism, and polishing and supplementing his MFA thesis with new stories, he was now almost entirely alone, working as an untenured assistant professor in a postindustrial city full of warping clapboard houses and semi-kept lawns.[23] Accolades began piling up after the publication of *Drown*: *Newsweek*, for instance, picked Díaz as "one of the new faces of 1996." He had "the dispassionate eye of a journalist," the magazine waxed lyrically, "and the heart of a poet."[24] Not to be outdone by a national rival, the *New Yorker* selected and lionized Díaz as one of the best writers ("20 under 40") of the new millennium.[25]

However, Díaz was having hardly any success at writing his follow-up novel to *Drown*. He was writing, to be sure, but the pages did not meet his own spectacularly high standards. Nothing was working, nothing brewing. According to Frank Brues, Díaz could not even find anything that he had scribbled in his notebooks "that would make his follow-up bigger than his debut."[26] His Guatemalan American *camarada* (comrade) and acclaimed fellow writer Francisco Goldman, who had years earlier glowingly endorsed *Drown* for Riverhead Books, noticed that Díaz had almost stopped publishing, and he worried what in the world the young Afro-Dominicano writer was doing at Syracuse. Goldman—hoping to jump-start his friend's promising writing career—invited Díaz to join him and to write in Mexico City. Díaz recalls exactly what Goldman said to him: "You're up at Syracuse falling on your sword. You need to get away from there, come to Mexico City. It's an amazing city. It's problematic and beautiful. It's exactly the thing you'll love."[27] And love it he did.

With the support of a Guggenheim Fellowship—another major award after the publication of *Drown*—Díaz took a yearlong sabbatical leave from Syracuse and readily accepted Goldman's invitation to live and write in Mexico City. At the time, Díaz was working on a sci-fi novel in progress provisionally titled "Akira," inspired by the Japanese classic manga series and the 1989 blockbuster anime film *Akira*. Like Katsuhiro Otomo's cryptic story set in Neo Tokyo, Díaz's big follow-up book to *Drown* was to be about the apocalypse of (Neo) New York City. According to Brues, Díaz worked long and hard on the "Akira novel" in his spartan and sunny Mexico City apartment. To keep the sun out, Díaz daily taped "garbage bags over the windows" and blasted hip-hop mixtapes out into the mean streets of Mexico City. In the evenings, Díaz and Goldman spent their time walking those streets, sharing dinners together at neighborhood restaurants, and watching loads of "bad Belgian sci-fi movies."[28]

In the first months of his Mexico City sojourn, Díaz worked diligently on his sci-fi novel. If "Akira," the Japanese anime, depicted with cyberpunk panache a dystopian *Blade Runner*-esque vision of Tokyo in the year 2919, Díaz's "Akira novel," by contrast, was set in New York City. He wanted his book to focus on the ugly feelings of a nuclear sublime that he had always felt as an immigrant boy growing in the late 1970s and early 1980s tristate area. As he explains, "I was one of those children who persistently dreamed about a nuclear blast." It was Ronald Reagan's America Oscuro (Dark America). "I was always haunted by the radial map of New York with the concentric rings of destruction. Where I lived [in Parlin, New Jersey], was the third ring." There was so much of Reagan's apocalypse "in the air," Díaz recalls, "in the culture, in the writing, in the movies. The comic books were filled with it."[29] Desperate to complete his second book in Mexico City, he kept writing and filling up countless notebooks. Altogether, he would spend years trying to create his "Akira novel," but without success.

As Díaz recalls, he really cannot remember the precise date when he quit working on his sci-fi text "Akira" and how his literary character Oscar Wao, in an uncanny epiphany, appeared (wondrously) one day to him in Mexico City. Nor does he remember the specific month when Oscar de León was spawned. However, what Díaz vividly recalls was the number of tortuous years it took him to complete *The Brief Wondrous Life of Oscar Wao*: eleven. In an autoethnographic piece he wrote for the *Guardian*, he explained why this was so; before the publication of *Drown*, "writing was something I did—now it's who I am."[30] This realization about how he had come to be defined by others was overwhelming.

Eventually, though, Díaz killed off his "Akira novel" and began work on a killer text about the beleaguered, lovable, "queered," "closeted," melancholic, super-"ghettonerd" Oscar de León. After some astonishingly productive months in Mexico City, "The Brief Wondrous Life of Oscar Wao" was ready for publication in the January 1, 2000, issue of the *New Yorker*.

The Long and Short of "Oscar Wao"

Four years after the debut of *Drown*, Díaz published a story that ran to fifteen printed pages of the *New Yorker*. Beautifully illustrated by the Chicanx graphic artist Jaime Hernandez (figure 4.1), the story focused, as the title suggests, on the brief life of a super-"ghettonerdy" Dominicano kid from Paterson, New Jersey—a kid Díaz "could not get out of his head" because, like Díaz himself, Oscar was a "devoted reader" who "had this imagination that no one had any use for, but which gave him so much enjoyment and sense of purpose."[31] Díaz's story, "The Brief Wondrous Life of Oscar Wao," like Ernest Hemingway's "The Short Happy Life of Francis Macomber," collapsed the paired correspondences between literary

Figure 4.1 Illustration of "The Brief Wondrous Life of Oscar Wao," by Jaime Hernandez, *New Yorker*, January 1, 2000. Used with permission of the artist.

genres—the short story's moment of truth and the novel's linear life chronicle—into each other: Oscar de León's wondrous life, as opposed to his whole life, lasts only a few years, and corresponds to his moment of truth. Brief life, wondrous story.

Furthermore, as Díaz himself has remarked about his text's rich, dense intertextuality—as the text's many-layered title suggests—he tried "to stuff as many books" as he could "into Oscar Wao." "I mean, shit, even the title refers to Oscar Wilde," as well as to Hemingway's short story.³² As I will explain in chapter 5 (in which I analyze why Oscar reads science-fiction books in the closet), Díaz's title alludes not only to the meanings of the playwright Oscar Wilde's sex scandal in

Victorian Britain but also to the range of what "maleness" means and the continuum of what forms of masculine desire are possible for the hero, Oscar Wao. Oscar Wilde and Oscar Wao not only share a name but also articulate a male sexuality that for Díaz evokes asymmetrical power relationships.[33] Like Michel Foucault's analysis of the ways that sex supports the regimes of power, Díaz concerns himself in *The Brief Wondrous Life of Oscar Wao* less with refuting the homophobia and toxic masculinism that Oscar de León encounters in his short, everyday life than with describing how the discourses and practices of the masculinism he grapples with have been constituted—and, more importantly, how they compel him to participate in the legitimation of oppressive social practices.[34] Oscar de León is simultaneously cast by his family, public-school peers, and his surly "sucio" college roommate, Yunior, as a super-"ghettonerd" dork: a "fat loser," a social misfit, an unnatural "monster," "Caliban," and "freak."[35] Díaz is interested in how this parade of names and attributes, rather than canceling out one another in practice, work together to produce Oscar's abjection.

To sharpen the contrast in genres between the surprising economical beauty of Díaz's *New Yorker* story "The Brief Wondrous Life of Oscar Wao" and the novel it would become, I will begin this academic novella-length chapter by presenting a traditional explication of the text.[36] I then address the historia's complex and ingenious narratological threads and textual repertoire, focusing on the variety of linguistic registers, paratextual devices, gaps, blanks, and páginas en blanco that Díaz invented for his novel.

Díaz's *New Yorker* story is divided into fourteen sections. The first section, "The Golden Age," focuses on the life of seven-year-old Oscar de León in Paterson; he "dates" two Latinx girls, Maritza and Olga, at the same time. However, the triangle soon collapses "when they dump him," and Oscar's life shoots "straight down the tubes" from then on. He is bullied by his classmates—called a "gordo asqueroso [fat, disgusting person]"—and early adolescence, as Yunior de Las Casas unsympathetically notes, "scrambles his face into nothing you'd call cute." Sections two through four, "The Moronic Inferno," "Oscar Is Brave," and "Oscar Comes Close," jump some ten years ahead to Oscar's senior year at Don Bosco Tech High School, where we find him "bloated, dyspeptic, and most cruelly alone"—like a tumescent Dominican Bartleby. Oscar's nerdy interests in comic books, heroic fantasy, and role-playing games—what he calls the speculative genres—make him even more undesirable to his classmates, and his only "nerd" friends are the "completely normal"-looking South Asian immigrants Al and Miggs, the "freak[s]" "with a retard's laugh." When Al and Miggs find girlfriends and cruelly leave Oscar out of the picture, he realizes that even they (the ethnically minoritized outré outcasts of Paterson, New Jersey) "were em-

Figure 4.2 Rutgers University, New Brunswick, New Jersey. Screenshot. PBS.

barrassed by him." One December, while Oscar is applying to his dream school, New York University, and other, safer local colleges, he meets a Latinx girl named Ana Obregón in his SAT prep class and falls "totally and irrevocably" in love with her. Ana and Oscar become close friends, and although he "comes close" romantically with her, they are never physically intimate. Eventually, Ana's hyper-alpha male boyfriend, Manny, returns from the US Army and compels his novia to stop spending her time with the nerd; meanwhile, Oscar begins dreaming "about nuclear annihilation." Soon thereafter, he goes to the public university at Rutgers-New Brunswick (figure 4.2), and he envisions that his love life in college will be entirely different. While at Rutgers, though, he realizes that he is still buried "in what amounted to the college version of what he'd majored in throughout high school: getting no ass."[37]

Section five, "Sentimental Education," takes place at Rutgers, where Oscar attends college and meets his roommate Yunior de Las Casas, a fellow Dominican American, at the artsy dormitory Demarest Hall (figure 4.3). This section of the *New Yorker* story contains the preliminary analysis of the institutional social space in which the author Díaz was himself located as an undergraduate, giving readers the instruments needed for analysis. And the sentimental education that Díaz is primarily interested in is Yunior's, for, like Flaubert's protagonist, the student Frédéric Moreau, Yunior's education is nothing other

Figure 4.3 Demarest Hall, Rutgers University, New Brunswick, New Jersey. Photograph by the author.

than a progressive apprenticeship in the impossibility of reconciling two discrepant worlds: art and passion, on the one hand, and venal sexual affection and program-era creative writing, on the other. Further, like Flaubert's *L'Éducation sentimentale* (1869), Díaz's "The Brief Wondrous Life of Oscar Wao" is nothing other than the enumeration of those coincidences when the two discrepant worlds of Santo Domingo and Paterson become entangled with each other. What readers initially understood as Díaz's standard omniscient narrator in the historia is actually a specific person readers had previously met years earlier in *Drown*. Díaz asserts that he was doing nothing new in this *New Yorker* story, for he wanted his readers to understand why Yunior de Las Casas was telling this story about the "ghettonerd" Oscar de León. Díaz asks: What is Yunior's stake in telling the story he tells? Why this particular story? Was Yunior's telling an "act of contrition"? Díaz, of course, thinks this confessionalist reading of the historia is too incomplete, and I agree completely.

If Oscar and Yunior, like Cervantes's Don Quixote and Sancho Panza, are unlikely friends, they mostly get along. By the end of the second semester, Yunior starts to like the kid a little, for "wasn't it Turgenev," the bookish English major Yunior asks himself, "who said, Whom you laugh at you forgive and come near to loving?"[38] Of course, Díaz doesn't let his callous "sucio" player Yunior off the hook so easily. Throughout, he details how hard-hearted and conniving

Yunior truly is—he befriends Oscar at Rutgers more for the sake of inducing the gratitude of Oscar's sister, Lola, than out of any compassion and pity for what will, in the end, prove to be Oscar's doomed life.

In both the short story and later in the novel, Díaz shows us how his characters, especially Yunior and Oscar, laugh differently, reflecting their varied perspectives: power (or lack thereof), social standing, and psychology. As Lyn Di Iorio Sandín suggests about Díaz's magnetic duo, "Sometimes they laugh in counter-hegemonic protest, sometimes from a stance of superiority over those less powerful whom they find ridiculous, sometimes from a wretchedly sadistic jokesterism, and once towards the end, which is certainly not often enough, from joy and self-affirmation."[39]

Meanwhile, Yunior recalls that it was during the spring semester at Rutgers when he saw Oscar fall deeply in love with a Puerto Rican Goth girl named Catalyn Sangre de Toro Luperón. They spend a lot of time chitchatting and holding hands on the Rutgers campus, but they are never physically intimate. Alas, when Oscar finds his would-be novia entertaining "some Goth kid," both naked and "probably covered in blood," he acts out violently, tearing the posters off her dorm-room walls and yelling obscenities at her in Spanglish. Soon after, in the sixth section, "The Dark Age," Oscar is forced by university officials to take anger-management classes and attend therapy sessions; eventually, he moves back to Paterson to live with his mom, Belicia, and his tío, Rodolfo, a Vietnam veteran and heroin addict. "[L]eft a virgin, returned one," Yunior says. Oscar gets a job subbing and gradually attains a full-time position at his old haunt Don Bosco Tech, becoming a depressed high school teacher and sinking into what Yunior sensationally calls "the Darkness." Soon after, Oscar tries to commit suicide by going into his tío Rodolfo's closet and putting "the Colt between his eyes."[40] The epistemology of the closet (as I argue in chapter 5) looms large in Díaz's historia.

After three years of this melancholy "darkness," miserably teaching part-time at Don Bosco Tech and living at home with his tío and mom, Oscar decides one summer—in section seven ("Oscar Takes a Vacation")—that he will travel to his home island's La Capital, or Santo Domingo, with his mom, tío, and sister Lola. In sections eight and nine ("Return to a Native Land" and "The Girl from Sabana Iglesia"), Oscar meets his island Dulcinea and falls in love with a semiretired sex worker named Ybón Pimentel. He becomes Ybón's best friend, but like all of his relationships in "The Brief Wondrous Life of Oscar Wao," Ybón and he get "close" but are not physically intimate. In section nine, "Oscar at the Rubicon," we discover that Ybón has an alpha-male boyfriend, a tiguerre capitán, and that he is in the Dominican Republic's notoriously brutal and violent national police force. One night, when Oscar is driving Ybón home from a local bar, Ybón's boyfriend-capitán pulls them over. As soon as they are collared, the capitán finds Ybón passed out next to Oscar. On the capitán's orders, Oscar is taken to a cane field by the national-police goons, Grundy and Grood, and they severely beat him "with their pistol butts," but he survives. Ybón is violently beaten by the capitán as well; the next day she comes to visit Oscar with "two black eyes" to let him know she "could never be with him again."[41] Oscar's mother books a flight for him to leave Santo Domingo, and in section twelve ("P-Town Blues"), he returns to Paterson, New Jersey.

Díaz's *New Yorker* story ends with the sections "P-Town Blues," "The Last Days," and "The End of the Story." When Oscar returns to Paterson, he visits his former college roommate Yunior in New York City's neighborhood of Washington Heights and borrows money from him. Unbeknownst to anyone, Oscar uses the money to fly back to the Dominican Republic and pursues Ybón in La Capital. He spends twenty-seven days there in pursuit of his Dominican Dulcinea, all the while researching and drafting an encyclopedic science-fiction space opera. At the end of the twenty-seven days,[42] Oscar is kidnapped by the police capitán's henchmen, taken to a cane field, and shot by two men who work with the National Police capitán.

Eight weeks after twenty-three-year-old Oscar is murdered at the hands of the national police, a package "arrive[s] [at the de León] house in Paterson" containing two manuscripts. One has a few chapters "of [Oscar's] never-to-be completed opus": a Dominicano space opera called "Starscourge." The other is a long letter to his sister, Lola, in which he reveals that he was able to go on a trip alone with Ybón, where he had sex with her and enjoyed the intimacies of a romantic relationship: "So this is what everybody's always talking about! Diablo! If only I'd known. The beauty! The beauty!"[43] If Joseph Conrad's iconic colonialist and ivory trader Kurtz in *Heart of Darkness* ends his life exploiting Africans and sees only the horror of imperialism and racism in the Congo, Díaz's Oscar de León ends his letter to Lola by experiencing the beauty of his intimacy with Ybón and Santo Domingo.[44]

But was Díaz's *New Yorker* story about Oscar de León inherently too brief to tell the whole incredible life? Was he enamored of the text's form of "surpassing [economical] beauty, where 'the small is large'?[45] All his life, Díaz's Oscar thinks, he had been X until one day Y happened, and for the rest of his life he was Z. Thus envisaged, Díaz's *New Yorker* story was nevertheless able to achieve some of the plentitude and totality of his future Pulitzer Prize–winning novel. What Díaz realized, as Hemingway's work had revealed to him in workshop seminars (as I argue in my previous chapters on "Negocios" and *Drown*) was that it was indeed possible to convey in a story (or a novel) a great many things on paper without stating them all. At Cornell, the dedicated MFA student Díaz had mastered the art of implication by making his sentences say many things at once. As we know, "Big Two-Hearted River," one of Hemingway's paradigmatic stories, encodes two stories simultaneously: one story records the traumatic effects of the war on Nick Adams to such an extent that the short story seems to be a trivial description of a fishing trip. Hemingway puts all his craft into the hermetic narration of the second story—what the Argentine writer and literary theorist Ricardo Piglia calls the cuento's "secret story."[46] Like Hemingway, Díaz thus employs the art of ellipsis and gaps with such mastery that he succeeds in making us notice the absence of the other story.

Further, it needs emphasizing that Díaz's steady craftsmanship as a writer of both short stories and the novel (like Hemingway and Bolaño) is conjunctural. In Díaz's best work—already evident in his MFA thesis—form and discourse (the cuento's two distinct logics of causality) destabilize the reader's encounter with his world-building metamundo. *Drown*, *The Brief Wondrous Life of Oscar Wao* (the *New Yorker* story and the novel), *This Is How You Lose Her*, and *Islandborn* play off the same edges of Díaz's metahistoria's double logics; when read together as a chronicle in progress, they set into motion readings and rereadings of his changing same historias. In overturning his imaginative works' script, Díaz rescripts them. As I mentioned in the preface, Díaz's fiction-making system, like Bolaño's, involves processes of expansion and circulating characters. He revisits previously written and published texts and, as Chris Andrews says of Bolaño's work, "expand[s] them from within,"[47] scaling up and down Yunior's metahistoria in his short stories, children's book, and novel.

Unlike Díaz's Dominicano male characters in "Negocios" and *Drown*— Ysrael, Beto, Ramón, and his sons Rafa and Yunior de Las Casas—Oscar de León is a totally new character for Díaz, the end point of what he recalls as a "larger, almost invisible historical moment." In the crónica-historia he was writing, Oscar is the child of the Dominican Republic's dictatorship of Rafael Leonidas Trujillo and Americanity's five-hundred-year-old apocalypse that for Díaz is the New World.[48] Whereas the *New Yorker* story only partially scripts this, the epic novel achieves it in full: a sense of how the young Oscar de León is utterly unaware of his family's abysmal travails during the Trujillo dictatorship and is yet so thoroughly dominated by them. Moreover, Díaz's rescriptable novel focuses in on how Oscar personifies one of the "weirdest out-riders"[49] in postcontemporary American literature, for he is not anything like the male characters that his fellow male (Latinx and White) writers were conjuring at the time.[50]

Díaz's *New Yorker* story was a compressed version of what he would spend the next seven years working on—an epic novel that spans the course of many decades, from the trying 1930s to the Reagan 1980s. The novel tells the sharp-edged stories of not just Oscar de León—as the *New Yorker* historia did—but also the haunted stories of several family members and friends related to him. Unlike the *New Yorker* story's telling of the brief and wondrous life of Oscar Wao, Díaz's novel captures the complex historia of the coloniality of power in our "fragmented world," for space in Díaz's novel is "open," "exploded," and "rent," an irruption into (trans)modernity. If readers look at the structure of Díaz's text, they can begin to see that the structure is more in keeping with what Díaz remembers as the "reality" of this long Dominican Republic history rather than with its most popular national myths: that of the unity and continuity of the nation. As he was mulling over the "exploded" form of the book, it occurred to him that *The Brief Wondrous Life of Oscar Wao* would "take the shape of an archipelago," for the novel was "supposed to be a textual Caribbean,"[51] an ambitious attempt to read the Caribbean and the New World (including New Jersey) experience, not as a response to easy univocal meanings imposed by the past but as a varied and inexhaustible postcontemporary text. The effect Díaz envisioned for his readers was that of fragmentation rather than linear progression: a shattered and rent historia rather than the extended short story's unity of effect "somehow holding [itself] together."[52] Like a Black Dominicano Orpheus, Oscar de León descends into the underworld of Santo Domingo, its mongooses and cane fields. Díaz, in tracing this descent, draws from Édouard Glissant's cross-cultural poetics and critiques how Western totalizations of history had relegated the Caribbean to the nonhistorical periphery—"la face cachée de la Terre" (the Earth's hidden face). Moreover, he references the poet Aimé Césaire's "Notebook of a Return to the Native Land" (1939), a journey from "ex-isle" to a coming to consciousness in the native land.

In Mexico City, however, a new clarity was beginning to emerge in Díaz's attempt to wrest into controllable form such central concerns in his novel as ghettonerdiness, Afro-Atlantic Dominicano self-consciousness, cross-cultural Caribbean poetics, Latinx masculinity, heroic fantasy, and laughter. The prose style that would later separate Díaz's writing from that of his celebrated peers was also taking shape during the time of the *New Yorker* story, for it owed something to the Hemingway-esque plainspokenness evident in the title of the short story as well as to Díaz's turning to Yunior's hyperurban superbent and stretched hip-hop idiom.

It combined an informal Spanglish diction—"Oscar was a carajito who was into girls mad young"—with recondite allusions to hyperurban Black and Latinx musical styles—"The only thing that changed in those years" were the sonics "volting out of the car's speakers. First freestyle, then Special Ed-era hip hop, and right at the end . . . Hector Lavoe and the boys."[53] This mixture hinted at the ways Black and Afro-Latinx high and low cultures were flourishing and jumbled in Yunior's mind. On the page, Díaz was opening a portal into Spanglished hyperspace. And his effort had a track record: Díaz's short stories "How to Date a Browngirl, Blackgirl, Whitegirl, or Halfie" and "The Brief Wondrous Life of Oscar Wao"—stories originally published in the *New Yorker*—probably did more than any other US writer's imaginative work to create an alternative sense of what was proper American prose and what was not, what was stylistically possible and what was not.[54]

Díaz's "The Brief Wondrous Life of Oscar Wao" was written for the changing tastes of literary magazine cultures in the northeastern United States. In fact, Díaz's *New Yorker* stories had been published under Tina Brown's editorial regime, from 1992 to 1998, when she ideologically shifted the classic, stodgy, and White-male dominant style of the magazine to what Ben Yagoda hyperbolically called Brown's "up to the minute cocktail of glitz, hype, and topicality."[55] I maintain that Diaz's "long" short story about Oscar de León is far from "topical" or "glitzy"; instead, it is strong, original, true. Díaz, undoubtedly, took cash from the *New Yorker*, but doing so represented a benefit whose significance was limited in terms of its impact on the organization of his critical and imaginative thinking. In his words, "it is the way" he processes things when he is "doing a piece" and begins "to understand the subject."[56] In other words: Díaz did not simply write a typical story about a dork and ghettonerd to make a buck; he flipped the script of an Afro-Atlantic Dominican masculinity and deployed the languages of Yunior's New Jersey geekdom to tell the story about Oscar in "nerdish."

A partial catalog of the various nerdy sci-fi and academic registers in Díaz's text reveals this: "Her Jedi mind tricks did not, however, work on Oscar." "Throughout high school he did the usual ghettonerd things: he collected comic books, he played role-playing games, he worked at a hardware store to save money for an outdated Apple IIe. . . . He watched shows like Doctor Who and Blake 7, and could tell you the difference between a Veritech fighter and a Zentraedi battle pod. . . ." "After a couple of Fridays alone he joined the university's geek organization, R. U. Gamers." "What is it about us niggers and our bodies? Not even Fanon can explain it to me."[57] There is very little that is glitzy about Oscar's existence; his is a nerd's life, cast in glyphs, silicon, and polyhedral dice. As Evelyn Ch'ien suggests, "Nerds are [in Díaz's text] the emblems of unintelligibility, jargon-laden creatures who roll for initiative (a term from Dungeons and Dragons) and are caught up in the tangled suppression of desire."[58]

A mighty Melvillean-like novel with the mighty theme of migratory displacement was what Díaz really wanted to write, but like his attempt at writing

"Akira," here he was having less luck. Some piece of him still felt too fragile to attempt an effort that turned out to be so key to his professional writing career and well-being. As he recalls, "The thing with me was that I was a nerd supreme: a smart kid in a poor ass community." Moreover, as I explained in the book's previous chapters, Díaz's fragility was related to his embeddedness "in a dictatorial military family where the boys had to fight all the time, where we were smacked around by our father (to toughen us up), where we shot guns every weekend . . . [and] where you were only a human being if you were an aggressive violent hombre."[59] The problem was not putting words on the page; it was not that he had somehow lost confidence in his ability to write fiction. Rather, it was a need to write perfectly well-wrought and compelling prose suited to the scope of his vision.

Díaz went on: "So I was a nerd who had all of this 'man' training, for lack of a better term. I was a nerd with a special passport that allowed me to hang with the non-nerd boys. So I grew up with this whole group of smart kids of color, was one of them and yet wasn't, and that's how Oscar came to be. Oscar was a composite of all of the nerds that I grew up with who didn't have the special reservoir of male privilege. Oscar was who I would have been if it had not been for my father or brother or my own inability to fit into any category easily."[60]

Díaz's self-portrait as "supreme ghettonerd" helped him conjure the life and times of his character Oscar de León: "He emerged," he remembers, "like Athena, almost fully formed out of my skull."[61] The *New Yorker* short story—so centrally about Oscar de León—was the "easiest" part of the historia for Díaz to compose in Mexico City. But "it was the rest of it" that "took [seven more years]" for Díaz to write. Why so many years, and why such a tortuous genesis? In the following sections, I offer a few answers.

"This Shit Was a Pain in the Ass until the Very End"

After finishing "The Brief Wondrous Life of Oscar Wao" for the *New Yorker*, Díaz returned to working on "Akira," his sci-fi novel in progress, but it still was not gelling. This would not be the first time—or the last—for Díaz to encounter what he has called his own "very difficult relationship to writing." He once casually told me over dinner in Monterey, California, that he had slain "Akira" and that he had some five drafts of novels he had completed about Yunior de Las Casas but lacked the "courage" to publish them. "I know I put a lot of pressure on myself. . . . I know these things. But at the same time, despite all the difficulties, sometimes writing comes and sometimes it doesn't."[62]

Then one day, on September 11, 2001, Al-Qaeda coordinated four horrific attacks on the World Trade Towers and three other socially symbolic landmarks. The United States responded to these attacks by launching George W. Bush's war on terror, invading Afghanistan in an attempt to defeat the Taliban, which had harbored Al-Qaeda. For Díaz, the real crumbling and burning of parts of New York City affected the fictional apocalyptic destruction he had envisioned in "Akira": "The reality of 9/11 was devouring my invented reality. It wasn't that the city was destroyed; it was the consequences which I misread. I actually thought it would send the country's efforts not outward, but inward. Instead of launching an opportunistic pogrom against Iraq, I thought it would launch an opportunistic pogrom against internal enemies and the country would begin to eat itself."[63]

When Díaz's Nostradamus-like prophecy did not materialize, he had to radically rethink "Akira." However, in the aftermath of September 11 he could not stop thinking about his supreme ghettonerd, the loveless, heartbroken Oscar de León, who had been "desaparecido" from the world's consumer newsstands as soon as the *New Yorker* magazine's weeklong shelf life had run its course, one issue giving way to the next. But "The Brief Wondrous Life of Oscar Wao" "infected" Díaz "in the brain," he recalls. "It just kept going after I wrote it. Even after it was published. In my mind, it just kept saying, 'Stay with this, stay with this, stay with this.'"[64]

Over the next seven years—leaving Mexico City, returning to his assistant professor position at Syracuse, and then in 2003 joining the writing faculty at the Massachusetts Institute of Technology (MIT), where he currently holds an endowed professorship teaching writing—Díaz through sheer will and perseverance "stayed with this" Oscar Wao historia. Although he initially worked on both "Akira" and "The Brief Wondrous Life of Oscar Wao" at the same time and had high hopes for completing "Akira," in the end, *The Brief Wondrous Life of Oscar Wao* won out. From 2000 through 2007, he wrote and revised his new novel: "The best way to look at it is that for one year, my 'Oscar' book didn't generate anything. In the second year 'Oscar' generated fourteen pages and the 'Akira' one didn't generate any." In the end, Díaz quipped, using a sports analogy, "It's like one of those slow wrestling matches—just by the accumulation of pages, the other book ['Akira'] got slain."[65]

Although his MFA thesis, "Negocios," and his first book, *Drown*, had taken Díaz only three years to write, *The Brief Wondrous Life of Oscar Wao* stretched into eleven long years. He recalls, for instance, that the second chapter of his novel filled out into some 309 pages, and even after so many words, the chapter, he confessed, "had [no] idea of itself." The rest of the novel would fare no better:

"I don't want to sound too grandiose, but I must have thrown away forty or fifty versions of each of those shitty chapters. The last five pages ... I wrote at least ninety to a hundred pages before the last five pages developed. This shit was a pain in the ass to the very end." Through sheer hard work and battling despair and writer's block, Díaz finished writing *The Brief Wondrous Life of Oscar Wao* in 2007. "The amount of despair it took me to finish it is so ironic," he noted, "because that book is about anything but despair. In some ways, there is so much joy in the book, that it belies the difficulties of construction."[66]

Several areas of discussion about the novel's "difficulties of construction" emerge from all this. The first concerns the type of formal framing, intertextual registers, and sheer joyful inventiveness that Díaz pursued in the making of his epic novel. As some Díaz scholars have crisply characterized the work, without the comic and fantasy books allegorizing the Trujillo dictatorship's repression and its impact on Oscar de León and his family, there is no epic Díaz novel.[67] Here I will simply say that we have a lot to learn from Díaz's political project in *The Brief Wondrous Life of Oscar Wao*: his use of what Winfried Fluck calls "negative aesthetics" and "imaginary transference"[68] in the text, which have been overlooked so far by his readers. I contend that they are foundational for a critical comprehension of the way that Díaz positions his readers to criticize the hegemonic "thought systems" of our time. Can evil—personified in Díaz's dark lord Trujillo—ever imagine anything but itself? Would Oscar's and Yunior's Afro-Dominicano families have become "wraiths" under the dominion of their dark lord, the dictator Trujillo? How does Díaz, in other words, insert the political into his world of heroic speculative fantasy? This is, of course, an old question: are the proper objects of the speculative genres—including heroic fantasy, a subcategory of sci-fi—individual cases or ideologically complex abstract models? In the following pages I argue at some length why I believe it is the latter.

Díaz's Paratexts as the Halo That Encloses
The Brief Wondrous Life of Oscar Wao

Now the paratext is neither on the interior nor on the exterior: it is both; it is on the threshold; and it is on this very site that we must study it.
GÉRARD GENETTE, *Paratexts*, Kindle edition

Without losing any sight of the great joys and aesthetic affirmations that Díaz incorporated in his revisions, here I argue that the multidimensional paratextual framing of his dream book—"its difficulties of construction"—helped him radically transform his partial *New Yorker* story of Oscar Wao into a fulsome novel. His epigraphs, his thirty-three footnotes that enrich the narrative with a sense of Trujillo as an "an architect of history," and his added prologue about Almirante Colón midwifing the doom of the New World all function not only ideologically but also aesthetically. In brief, they permit Díaz to introduce ellipses, páginas en blanco of all varieties. And this is to say nothing of the additional chapters set on the Jersey shore and told by Oscar's feminist sister, Lola, or of those set in Santo Domingo that recount the travails and horrifying torture of Oscar's mother, Belicia, and his grandfather, Dr. Abelard Cabral, under the Trujillato, that near-endless "silence and blood, machete and perejil [parsley], darkness, and denial."[69] These gaps and erasures, I argue, helped Díaz enormously as he worked to incorporate elements of mystery, elision, and uncertainty into his epic novel *The Brief Wondrous Life of Oscar Wao*—paratextual elements with an illocutionary force that were far greater than those in the *New Yorker* version. Moreover, these textual gaps, black holes, and silences allowed Díaz to call attention to the history of erased genocides, traumas, and tortures in the Dominican Republic, the Caribbean, and the New World Américas in his novel.

Díaz eloquently expanded on this idea in an interview (conducted in Spanish) with Rita De Maeseneer: "si la novela pudiera decir las cosas que no dice, en el corazón de la novela se encuentra de la manera más inmediata el genocidio del siglo veinte contra los haitianos y los haitiano-dominicanos, pero de manera general también se encuentra allí el genocidio de la República Dominicana, que crea el Caribe, que crea el Nuevo Mundo. [*La maravillosa vida breve de Oscar Wao*] trata de eso de manera directa, porque el Nuevo Mundo trata de eso de manera indirecta" (if the novel could say the things it does not say, at the heart of the novel the twentieth-century genocide against Haitians and Haitian Dominicans is most immediately found, but there too, generally speaking, is the genocide of the Dominican Republic, which creates the Caribbean, which creates the New World. [*The Brief Wondrous Life of Oscar Wao*] deals with that directly, because the New World deals with it indirectly).[70] Throughout his text, Díaz masterfully outlines what can and what cannot be said about Haiti's and the Dominican Republic's historical traumas—their blood and violence, "darkness and perejil"—by using "indirection" and blanked-out (negative) aesthetics.

As we know, the paratext is a relatively new concept in literary interpretation. Books are rarely presented—as Gérard Genette argued—in an unadorned state, unaccompanied by other material supplied by editors, publishers, and printers, which is known as the paratext. These added elements form a master frame for the main text and can change the reader's reception or interpretation.

Footnotes to the main text also fall into the category of the paratext. According to Díaz, his paratextual footnotes constitute a kind of zone of crude contact between text and off-text, a zone not only of historical transition but also of transaction: the footnotes sit "in the lower frequencies" and "challenge the main text, which is the higher narrative."[71] The concept of the paratext is closely related to the concept of a threshold, a vestibule that offers readers the possibility of stepping in or turning back. Genette defined paratextual devices as those things in a published work that accompany the text—the author's name, the title, the preface or introduction, and/or the illustrations. "More than a boundary or a sealed border," Genette argues, "the paratext is, rather, a threshold." It is "a privileged place of pragmatics and a strategy, of an influence on the public, an influence that . . . is at the service of a better reception for the text and a more pertinent reading of it."[72] In other words, the paratext is a fringe of the printed text that shapes the reader's experience of it.

To track the development of *The Brief Wondrous Life of Oscar Wao* is not only to examine some of the generic asymmetries in the relation between Díaz's *New Yorker* version and the author's epic novel version but also to map the work's vast (para)textual Caribbean territory, noting the dizzying array of paratextual patterns, horizons, and meanings in and around the novel's main body. In the following sections I will first explore the initial paratexts to Díaz's novel, then hone in on the major narratological juxtapositional threads that he added to the story of Oscar Wao, particularly those rendering the novel a historia of Belicia's, Lola's, and Yunior's survival and solidarity.

As Yunior's reconfigured text suggests, Belicia and her children are the last remaining members of the Cabral family to have survived Trujillo's killings by fleeing into the diaspora. Belicia's, Lola's, and Oscar's stories of joy and survival are strategically pieced together by Yunior de Las Casas through a repertoire of gaps, blanks, ellipses, and páginas en blanco. As Glenda R. Carpio suggests, Yunior not only constructs his historia by "collect[ing] and intertwin[ing]" Belicia's coming-of-age story via Lola's cuentos about her dark mother—not only by reading Oscar's notebooks and space operas (often, creepily, without his permission), and personally interviewing Belicia herself as she lies dying in Paterson, New Jersey—but also by highlighting the fukú americanus curse looming over the entire Cabral-de León family and conjuring his own, complex, metanarrative commentary: "the zafa . . . or counterspell." Thus envisaged, Yunior's novel is a self-reflexive act of Dominicano historical recuperation—a restitution for Belicia; her father, Abelard; and her children, Lola and Oscar. As Carpio suggests, Díaz's epic novel—in contradistinction to his *New Yorker* story, which is about Oscar de León—is centrally "an act of reclaiming a mother figure" in

Belicia, "who is part Kali, part Rekha, [and] part Indian: it itself is [like Toni Morrison's *Beloved*] an act of love."⁷³ Indeed, Díaz's shape-shifting woman-centric vision in his novel—a feminist vision he cobbled together from carefully reading women-of-color writers such as Julia Alvarez, Sandra Cisneros, Audre Lorde, and Toni Morrison—helped texture the historia he began writing in Mexico City. With its focus on Oscar's and Lola's Black mother, Belicia, and on her figurative mother signifying Indigeneity, La Inca, this vision helped him forge connections across the Américas that highlight the unique African and Native American cultural heritages of Latinx in the United States.

Like the Dominican American novelist Julia Alvarez before him, Díaz not only aligned himself with Hispaniola's Blackness and Indigeneity—evidence, perhaps, of what Alvarez called, after José Martí: "two wings of a bird that can fly together"⁷⁴—but he also used his character universe of women such as Belicia, La Inca, and Lola to challenge the legal, political, and gender authority of the hypermasculinism and obscene patriarchy wrought by the Trujillo dictatorship. For example, Alvarez's *In the Time of the Butterflies* not only hones in on how three young Dominican women who had joined the revolutionary movement to overthrow the Trujillo regime were ambushed and assassinated as they drove back from visiting their jailed husbands; the work also deconstructs how these mythical figures—Patria, Minerva, and María Teresa Mirabal—were known in the Dominican Republic: "las mariposas," the butterflies. Both Díaz and Alvarez's Dominican American novels capture the terrorizing atmosphere of Trujillo's brutal police state by using an alternative Dominican lens; specifically, they turned to Dominican women characters whose courage, resilience, and desperation were emblematic of larger social, political, and historical tensions. In the process, Díaz and Alvarez provided readers with alternative historias of trauma—vital testimonies bearing witness to Trujillo's murders, rapes, and assassinations—told not from within the nation's imaginary planes but instead from carved-out, transnational spaces in the diaspora.⁷⁵

Díaz begins *The Brief Wondrous Life of Oscar Wao* with two extraordinary epigraphs that trace out the novel's earliest "halo." The first epigraph is from Stan Lee and Jack Kirby's *Fantastic Four* comic-book series. It immediately and simultaneously conveys both fantasy and speculative realism, especially as it refers to stories of "brief, nameless lives": "Of what import are brief, nameless lives . . . to Galactus?" Lee and Kirby asked in the opening volume of the *Fantastic Four* in April 1966. Here Díaz's paratextual epigraph functions aesthetically, allowing images from the unconscious mind to fuel our reading of the novel; it also, importantly, indexes what sci-fi fantasy accomplishes as a genre and form: a dramatized link between imagination and desire. The value of Díaz's *Fantastic Four* epigraph is, as Ramón Saldívar has astutely asserted in his reading of the novel's "historical fantasy," to reside "in its 'free-floating' and escapist qualities and its propensity to inhabit the space between reality and dream." In other words, we can freely read Díaz's character universe in *The Brief Wondrous Life of Oscar Wao*'s character spaces as inhabited not only by the more "realistic" characters Díaz invents but also, fantastically, by Afro-Latinx superheroes: Mr. Fantastic, Sue Storm, Monstrous Thing, and Hannah Torch. "With respect to the imagination," Ramón Saldívar suggests, "the products of fantasy gain power from appearing 'to be "free"' from many of the conventions and restraints of more realistic texts: they have refused to observe unities of time, space, and character, doing away with chronology and three-dimensionality."[76]

Joining the works of J. R. R. Tolkien and other fabulists of heroic fantasy, Díaz's novel supplements a literary tradition that claims the transcending of reality, the possibility of escaping the human condition, and constructing (utopian) alternate realities that recapture and revivify lost moral and social hierarchy. Like Tolkien's fantasy heroes—Frodo and Sam in *The Lord of the Rings*—Díaz's Oscar and Yunior suffer countless bewilderments, infatuations, and a profound sense of being lost in the cane fields; all of the heroes are abandoned, orphaned. "If these hobbits understood the danger," Gandalf says to Elrond, surely "they would dare not go." Díaz's New Jersey, Santo Domingo, is thus nearly "calqued" onto Tolkien's Middle-earth, and his elements of a composed world are translated bit by bit to make a new world in another language. Like the Elves and many of the human nations of Middle-earth, Oscar's and Yunior's families are in exile, living in the shadows of Trujillo's afterlife— looking up even at the starlight from which they are excluded. One can almost hear the forlorn Oscar telling Yunior and his extended family: "All that is gold does not glitter, not all who wander are lost," or "too long I have dwelt upon this hither [Jersey] shore."[77] Both Tolkien's and Díaz's novels blend together the melancholic histories of race and culture. Although pleasure is surely dissipating in the stories they tell, it is also squeezed out from disaster and doom. In both Tolkien's *Lord of the Rings* and Díaz's *The Brief Wondrous Life of Oscar Wao*, an aesthetics of sonics—the phonetics of Old English and Finnish, or Elvish, Spanglish, and hip-hop—reigns supreme, for Tolkien too had taught Díaz that readers can feel history in the style or in the reception or imagination of a word form.[78]

Thus envisaged, through Díaz's initial paratext his novel absorbs Tolkien's heroic fantasy, as Tim Lanzendorfer rightly suggests, "in order to understand the marvelous nature of its heritage and thus to arrive at a new idea of Caribbean history."[79] Although Oscar repeatedly insists that Caribbean history is best apprehended through the intertextual genre of Tolkien's heroic fantasy (he has read *The Lord of the Rings* hundreds of times), Yunior claims that Tolkien's fantasy texts go only so far in evoking their doomed and cursed island nation, for Trujillo surpasses Middle-earth's dark lord Sauron: Yunior's theory of coloniality, the fukú americanus, is likened to "Morgoth's bane." Through his allusive references to Tolkien's heroic fantasy, Yunior thus uses metaphor to help readers of his novel to see with absolute clarity the hidden similarities between two ideas: Tolkien's Sauron and Yunior's Trujillo. Elsewhere, Yunior typically notes that his "homeboy" Trujillo "dominated Santo Domingo like it was his very own private Mordor."[80] Neither entirely Tolkien's "ringwraith" nor Sauron, Yunior's Trujillo is surely something else, for he rules over his terrain with an "implacable ruthless brutality" that outdoes Tolkien's fantastic antagonists. As I outline, Yunior uses Tolkien's modes of emplotment like the quest to tell us how Oscar's family, especially Belicia and Jacquelyn, are linked with the figure of Tolkien's singular ring. Like Frodo's, Gollum's, and Sauron's desire to possess the One Ring, Yunior's Trujillo is blinded by the allure of sexually possessing and raping Belicia and Jacquelyn. Lanzendorfer perhaps puts it best when he argues that Yunior's and Oscar's familiarity with Tolkien's heroic fantasy allows them to explain through metaphor and allegory "the nature of Dominican reality."[81]

The second paratextual epigraph in Díaz's book comes from Derek Walcott's poem "The Schooner Flight": "I had a sound colonial education / I have Dutch, nigger, and English in me, / and either I'm nobody, or I'm a nation."[82] If Walcott's words are not an exaltation of the unconstrained identity politics of postmodernism—bereft of history and politics, though also, in its juxtaposition between "nobody" and "a nation," a decolonial New World reflection on the anxieties of being and belonging—Walcott's poem does not imagine any redemption in the dispersal of its identity. Rather, Walcott's poetic voice, Shabine, adduces that "I had no nation now but the imagination." As Ramón Saldívar suggests, the name "Shabine," which is "the Antillean creole word for *mulatto, mestizo*, signals hybridity as the answer to the dispersal of identity, but it does so only as an effect of the imaginary."[83]

From the first paratextual epigraphs in *The Brief Wondrous Life of Oscar Wao* we have entered Díaz's metamundo with quotations from *The Fantastic Four* and a Caribbean poetics of relation by Walcott, both poignant and calculated windows into the novel. Like other Anglophone and Hispanophone Caribbean writers, Díaz uses the novel to demonstrate that the catastrophe of coloniality besetting his Caribbean island of Hispaniola helps provide him with a key vantage point from which to elucidate the histories of empire in the Américas.[84]

Díaz's paratextual framing thus also begins with notions of namelessness—with the idea of brief lives and the ways that individuals and nations disrupt and end them. If his *New Yorker* story about Oscar Wao is a story that can be swallowed whole in one sitting, his novel shifts gears by moving from a historia about a protagonist immediately named in the title to one rescued from this very namelessness. Moreover, Díaz's main narrators—Yunior, Oscar, and Lola—explore the erased and elided structures of coloniality and power, for their diasporic homelands are ruled by the dark afterlives of imperial men, including Colón, Trujillo, John F. Kennedy, and Ronald Reagan.[85]

As Díaz explains, he consciously built his novel around a character, the nerdy Oscar de León, for he was the furthest thing away from the type of character

> one wants to build the image of a nation around.... I wanted to start [the novel] with a different kind of erasure, a smaller one but one that to me felt equally horrible. In the Dominican culture that I know, a character like Oscar was not going to be anyone's notion of the ideal Dominican boy ... someone like Oscar would not be labeled Dominican, no matter what his actual background was. So that's what really attracted me to him. His compassion, his outré interests, his dearth of traditional masculine markers—these were the things that defined Oscar in my head but that also guaranteed that no one would ever happily connect him to the nation he grew up out of and the nation, that I thought he was representative of.[86]

It is for all these reasons that in this book I stand with Oscar.

"Coloniality Is the Dark Subconscious of the Speculative Genres"

Ingeniously, Díaz juxtaposed Oscar's "nerd stuff," one of the focuses of his *New Yorker* story, with newer theoretical threads and registers in the novel that were entirely absent in the short story: foundational historical and sociological threads that he described in his Stanford Distinguished Lecture as the "decolonial turn in *Oscar Wao*—that is, 'the [epic] history of hemispheric life in the Américas as seen through the lens of the Dominican Republic.'" By asking his audience to look at the intertextual books that loom behind his novel's "nerdish side," Díaz hinted at the secret plot of his epic novel, a plot that took him eleven years to figure out or unravel, a narrative built on imaginative, speculative works such as Tolkien's *The Lord of the Rings*, Wagner's *Rheingold*, Lovecraft's Gothic fantasies, and Rowling's *Harry Potter*. Astute readers of his novel had readily picked up on his references to Tolkien's classic modernist work, yet Díaz's references to Wagner,

Rowling, and Lovecraft repeatedly went unnoticed by readers. Most "blur[red] over his nerd shit" because "they were too busy figuring out if I am fucking talking about them when I write in Spanish in *Oscar Wao*. They say, 'What the fuck, Yo!' I go, 'Negro, I'm talking about you in nerdish.'"[87]

In his 2012 Stanford lecture, as I argued in chapter 1, Díaz focused on what he called this "nerd stuff" because what "dawned on him"—as he was transforming his story of Oscar Wao into an epic novel—was "that these speculative genres" have had immense significance for our planet's "sub-zeitgeist," for if "Nelson in her book *The Secret Life of Puppets* (2001) had argued that in our sub-zeitgeist (all the pop cultural crap that exists in our culture's comic books, role-playing games, and movies), that is, all our impulses towards the supernatural, all of the impulses toward the transcendent, and the impulses toward religiosity—all of these impulses were displaced from people by the Enlightenment."[88]

Indeed, what made his novel become "possible," Díaz argued, was that Tolkien's heroic fantasy embodied for him what he called our planet's "'dark consciousness': the dark unconscious of our space and time."[89] Furthermore, by combining Nelson's philosophical ideas about the Enlightenment with Quijano's iconic insights about the coloniality of power's planetary genesis in 1492, Díaz was able to theorize, against Tolkien's Marxist Eurocentered critics, that "coloniality is the dark subconscious of the speculative genres."[90]

What Díaz attempted to do in *Oscar Wao* was to align what he terms the "nerd stuff" with the Dominican coloniality of power because he saw the two sharing a discourse or vocabulary. "As an artist," he explained, "these discourses were not being theorized." And he saw very clearly how fundamental Quijano's coloniality of power was to what he termed "the secret, animating force that gives all things in fantasy life. This is what gives Tolkien his real power."[91] For Tolkien, ever the philologist, the speakers of a particular language formed some kind of unity, and his speakers in *Lords of the Rings* tended to be a "nation," "culture," or "race." For example, in his classification of the "races" (or kindreds) of Middle-earth, Tolkien—as Díaz emphasized—established a hierarchy of racial formations and power: Elves are at the top, divided by their relationship to the light of the Trees. Then, with Men, the Three Houses of the Edain, whose descendants are given gifts of wisdom and longevity as the Númenóreans, seem to be a "high" group. The matter of Orcs is more difficult: as Dimitra Fimi argues, they bear a disturbing resemblance to John Longdon Downs's nineteenth-century description of those who suffered from the syndrome that came to bear his name.[92]

It was precisely Oscar de León's familiarity with and fluency in "nerdishness," Díaz suggests, that "allowed him to begin to see the stark operations of the coloniality of power working in his mundane and deracinated life in New Jersey." It is, in fact, "the nerdishness" of Oscar's "role playing games, the way that race gets broken up, and the way that Oscar feels his ultimate enslavement: this opens his eyes to see the erasures in the Caribbean," the "erasures in these spaces of his Cabral-de León family."[93] In this sense, Díaz's erasures, gaps, and blanks are not only "empty spaces"; they are also vital illocutionary propellants for initiating communication.

We can see this near the end of *Oscar Wao*, where Díaz's Yunior incorporates the following empty spaces or literal blanks into the text. The first involves Oscar after his initial beating in the cane fields and his encounter with the otherworldly, vibrant Mongoose,[94] a feminized apparition with its "golden lion eyes" that years earlier had appeared at the side of Oscar's mother, Belicia, during her near-fatal beating by La Fea's henchmen, pulling her away from death:

> Oscar remembers having a dream where a mongoose was chatting with him. Except the mongoose was the Mongoose. What will it be, muchacho? It demanded. More or less. And for a moment he almost said less. So tired, and so much pain—Less! Less! Less! —but then in the back of his head he remembered his family. Lola and his mother and Nena Inca. Remembered how he used to be when he was younger and more optimistic.
>
> The lunch box next to his bed, the first thing he saw in the morning. Planet of the Apes.
>
> More, he croaked.
>
> ____ _____ _____, said the Mongoose, and then the wind swept him back into darkness.[95]

The second incorporation of blanks grapples with Díaz's theory of decolonial love by way of Yunior's nightmarish erasure of the final words about his own sexual abuse (an abuse he alluded to in *Drown*) that might have saved Lola and his relationship:

> Lola's hair is long now and never straightened; she's heavier and less guileless, but she's still the ciguapa of my dreams. Always happy to see me, no bad feelings, entiendes. None at all.
>
> Yunior, how are you?
>
> I'm fine. How are you.
>
> Before all hope died I used to have this stupid dream that shit could be saved, that we would be in bed together like the old times, with the fan on, the smoke from our weed drifting above us, and I'd finally try to say words that could have saved us.

———— ———— ————.
But before I can shape the vowels I wake up.⁹⁶

To be sure, blanks are literalized here, concretized materially in the text. Throughout the novel, however, they also have clearly taken on different structural and ideological qualities. Perhaps it's too much, but it's my contention that thinking through such blanks and erasures—searching for and sitting with them—is our greatest chance to get at the profound negative aesthetics at work in Díaz's epic text. Each unnamed silence is a call for readers to create their own referential field—to fill in the blanks, to act upon them, and so speak what the novel leaves unsaid. Each blank, as Díaz has said of good writing in general, literally and experientially "creates space" for the reader to participate.

And this is precisely the point of *The Brief Wondrous Life of Oscar Wao*, that it is not only a textual object but also the presentation of a monumental problem screaming for a new critical matrix: the problem of the coloniality of power's horrifying history of blood, conquest, rape, and genocide in the New World. Díaz's theory of aesthetics, of the changing functions of the colonial difference encapsulated by gaps, blanks, and open wounds, is thus always a spur to participate, a call to action, and of power needing a leap to get started.

Negative Aesthetics and Imaginary Transference in *Oscar Wao*

In addition to the series of erasures, gaps, and blanks that Díaz's Oscar sees in the Dominican Republic, there are countless places of indeterminacy in *The Brief Wondrous Life of Oscar Wao*—Oscar's talking to the baká-like Mongoose, Yunior's blanked-out words to Lola. Sometimes these are to be filled in, other times to be left open, and still other times to be passed over by the reader. The attention that Díaz pays to the actual experience of reading a novel—to the very "time flow" of a reader's engagement—renders these indeterminacies vital. As readers, we must grapple with his epic novel's continual interplay between modified expectations and transformed memories; we must find an order amid the wandering focalizations, mediated by Yunior and Lola; we must find our way through shifting points of view and the sequence of events that either confirm or refute these perspectives. Often we build up "images" of Díaz's central characters and events—of what they seem to mean—and then must correct them as Yunior, Lola, or Belicia provides new information. For instance, this active dialogue between reader and text speaks to one of the novel's developing portraits of an awkward, supernerdy young man. As we proceed through the chapters, our initial image of Oscar de León begs modification when, late in the novel, Oscar claims he is Dominicano: "I am Dominican, I am."[97] That image again warrants refashioning when, nearing the novel's explosive resolution, we learn that Oscar can't see through his murderers' motivations and bad jokes. Unable to help himself, Oscar gives the capitán's goons the word *fuego* (fire), which they use to kill him. What many readers experience while reading a novel like Díaz's is the shifting sequence of points of view from the narrators (Yunior, Belicia, and Lola) to what Wolfgang Iser has called the "implied reader's"[98] point of view as well as shifting the sequence of events that either confirm or disconfirm these outlooks.

What makes reading *The Brief Wondrous Life of Oscar Wao* an active, constructive process is the fact that Díaz does not provide all the necessary links between points of view and the historical train of events. What Díaz's novel ingeniously provides instead are "blanks" of all sorts, including apparent inconsistencies and contradictions that the reader must fill in or explain. For instance, Yunior occasionally laughs at his own shortcomings as the novel's primary storyteller when he realizes he must add footnotes to clarify his inconsistency.[99] In being forced to grapple with Díaz's text's major blanks, gaps, and páginas en blanco, driven as they are by the search for consistency, readers must both construct and experience their own meanings. As we discover, for example, the deficiencies of the various points of view in *Oscar Wao*, each of which represents a late-capitalist or postcontemporary view of human nature, we simultaneously construct one of the central meanings of the novel: that there is a gulf between the rigid confines of principle and the endless fluidity of human experience. The significance of this meaning is whatever it reveals to the readers about themselves: readers should see themselves reflected in the literary text's characters and so should come to a better understanding of themselves.[100]

These brief theoretical reflections on the nature of aesthetic experience (in the widest sense of the term) have been thoroughly influenced by my experience when I taught at Berlin's Free University in 2018 and encountered Germany's "Konstance School of Reception Aesthetics"—not to be confused with the so-called US-centric reader-response criticism—and especially Iser's *The Act of Reading* and Fluck's theories of negative aesthetics and imaginary transference in his *Romance with America?*, in which the question of why we need literature remains the foundational question of all the work currently being done in literary studies.

How might Iser and Fluck's basic phenomenological approach—an approach in which indeterminacy is the nourishing ground of our aesthetic experience—illuminate the palpable gaps and blanks present in Díaz's novel? One of the peculiar features of *The Act of Reading*, given its stress on the discovery of the meanings of novels, is its initial exposé of the "traditional expository style of interpretation," whereby the work is "reduced" to a "single hidden meaning." Iser makes use of Henry James's "The Figure in the Carpet" to discredit such reductions, but he proceeds to enunciate "that meaning is no longer an object to be defined, but is an effect to be experienced."[101] In other words, works of art are no longer autonomous but rely on readers for their meaning to be experienced or actualized. Literary texts thus anticipate the presence of their audience.

For our purposes, what Iser suggests about how imaginative writers use textual "gaps" or "blanks" to stimulate readers' active engagements with texts is utterly useful, for it is the literary text's very gaps and blanks that invite the reader's projections. Often we encounter these vacancies and "erasures," as Díaz refers to them, both in terms of *what* is said—at the thematic level—and *how* it is said—at the level of textual strategies, registers, or repertoires. Moreover, the interaction between the text and the reader, as Iser and Fluck suggest, is a closed feedback loop of instruction giving and meaning assembly. Thus envisaged, the reader's task is to pay close attention to the literary text's "network of response-inviting structures" laid for her in the text and to accomplish a structural act, or the "act of comprehension." To grasp this significance of the text and reader interaction is to keep in mind that Iser posits another kind of interaction that precedes the reading experience, namely the one "between the text and . . . the social historical norms of its environment." For Iser and, as we will see, for Fluck, literary texts are acts of communication whose purpose is the reformulation of existing thought systems in order to bring about "the imaginary corrections of deficient realities." A novel like Díaz's *The Brief Wondrous Life of Oscar Wao* thus offers various perspectives that refer readers to a selection of social, ideological, historical, or cultural processes and phenomena, or, more succinctly, the text's repertoires. By creating and presenting slices of reality in a unique and provocative combination—as opposed to aspiring to represent "everything everywhere," as it were—readers are invited to scrutinize these manageable slices of the real, articulating their own relationships to the material represented. For Iser, the conception of literature as a recodification and transformation of existing "thought systems" meant to engender new answers to large problems illuminates the entire discussion of textual strategies. With these ideas in mind, the primary function of the text's repertoire is to pave the way for new understanding by "defamiliarizing the familiar."[102]

The role of the reader emerges for Iser from the text's "interplay of perspectives." Because the links or connections between perspectives are either withheld or, in the case of *Oscar Wao*, deliberately "erased," it is up to the reader to bridge the gap by filling in the blanks with possible connections. How this is done, though, is explained by Iser in his concept of "theme and horizon": "As perspectives are continually interweaving and interacting, it is not possible for the reader to embrace all of the perspectives at once, and so the view he is involved with at any particular one moment is what constitutes . . . the 'theme.' This, however, always stands before the 'horizon' of the other perspective segments in which he had previously been situated."[103] For Iser, this is the first step of the text-reader interactive process that sets in motion the imaginative faculties of the reader. Then, while the reader is thus "positioned" or situated inside the text, or the reader processes "wandering perspectives" between textual information, slowly, eventually, the reader synthesizes this information and arrives at comprehension. In the process of constituting and appropriating the meaning of the text, the reader reaches the level of "significance" through a self-structured interpretive process.

Like Díaz's very own making of *Oscar Wao*, reading is a "becoming conscious process." Reading allows us to formulate ourselves and to "discover an inner world of which we had hitherto not been conscious."[104] This "becoming conscious process" directly leads readers to a radically critical stance toward the world because the "negation" of social and cultural norms in the text's repertoire prompts readers to question their validity. So Díaz's point is not only to have readers interpret the world but also to change it. The repertoire of *Oscar Wao*—as I have analyzed in this chapter—is not only derived from a great number of different systems but is also presented in such density that first-time readers find themselves being constantly disoriented. The problem lies not so much in the unfamiliarity of the novel's allusions, for these in themselves are not difficult to identify—Kirby and Lee's *The Fantastic Four*, Tolkien's *The Lord of the Rings*, Flaubert's *Sentimental Education*, Homer and Walcott's *Odyssey* and *Omeros*, Césaire and Glissant's Greater Antillean poetics—but in the intermingling and the sheer mass of allusions to some 150 sci-fi and heroic-fantasy texts, films, and comic books, causing the repertoire to become amorphous.

Fluck supplements and builds on Iser's act of reading by arguing that because a literary text and its meanings are "never identical," it follows that reading can be characterized by the concept of "non-identity": to acquire any meaning, the "text must be actualized by a reader who has to translate the words on the page by his or her own imagination."[105] Moreover, the "aesthetic experience," Fluck suggests, does not rest on direct identification but is based on what he argues is an "imaginary transfer" that "opens up" a field of "analogies." Said differently, if the meaning of literary representation is not a form of mimesis but a performative act—what Iser called a "happening"—the text creates an object that is never "stable and identical with it."[106]

It is precisely this "non-identity" that is an important source of the aesthetic experience for Fluck because it allows readers of literary texts to "articulate imaginary elements" and "to look at them from the outside." As a result of this "doubling structure" of fictionality, we are "ourselves" and "someone else at the same time."[107] Staging oneself as someone else is not only a source of our aesthetic pleasure but also the means by which the happening of meaning is "transferred" from the literary text to the reader. As Fluck argues, this imaginary transfer should not be confused with the "projection of our desire into the text,"[108] for the reading experience remains tied to the text's social norms, ideology, and literary conventions—the text's repertoire—and what this repertoire offers.

For example, when Díaz provides a characterization of the Dominicano Oscar de León, his sister, or his mother, our imagining them will be "shaped" by the repertoire and description of Díaz's text. One of the joys of reading Díaz's novel *The Brief Wondrous Life of Oscar Wao* through Fluck's concept of imaginary transference is that we can be both "inside" and "outside" a Dominicano character like Oscar at once, for the "expansive (doubled) version of ourselves" is in Fluck's theory "an extension of our own interiority over a whole made up world"[109]—a world, a metamundo, I might add, after the Zapatista dictum "donde quepan muchos mundos."[110]

By turning to Iser and Fluck's theory of aesthetic experience and imaginary transfer, we can better see what analogies Chicanx and Latinx literatures have offered to world literature and to its mainline, largely White readerships engaging texts from the "outside." What a novel like *The Brief Wondrous Life of Oscar Wao* foregrounds is an opportunity for profound imaginary transference—transformations of his characters' ethno-racialized inferiority into a wondrous ethical superiority, of their protracted suffering into promising, energizing empowerment. This is why, I would argue, Latinx and ethnic US literary works have been so especially attractive to readers from around the world; as Fluck argues, they collectively "dramatize exemplary scenes of misrecognition"[111] and, through their attendant frictions, possibility.

These scenes of misrecognition through transference are thus taken out of the text's repertoire or context and function as analogies for readers—particularly those who consider the experience of hypervisibility to be one of the major injustices they experience under their own, ostensibly democratic conditions. The search for recognition in *The Brief Wondrous Life of Oscar Wao* becomes the "host" for articulating the reader's own imaginary longing for justice and recognition.

In the following section I will examine how, as Díaz began the historia of Oscar de León's "brief" and "wondrous" life, he turned to the forms of the global South's outernational poetics of planetary coloniality and wonder, discovery and conquest: his own Caribbean and New Jersey poetics of relation. Oscar de León's experiences of diaspora, structures of underdevelopment, exuberant raciology, Jersey-Dominicano double and maybe triple consciousness, and navigation of the world of the damnés all outline what Díaz describes as the fukú americanus: that "Great American doom"[112] aggrieving a great, weathered many. Here I examine Díaz's theory of the fukú americanus: how it originated in colonial modernity with the almirante and how it was then carried into the present decolonial period by homegrown world-historical male figures such as Rafael Leónidas Trujillo Molina, John F. Kennedy, Ronald Reagan, and William Jefferson Clinton. To chart the full dimensions of Díaz's narratological compass in the global South, I analyze the attempt by the sociologists Immanuel Wallerstein and Aníbal Quijano to recover the complexity of Americanity's history and afterlife by seeing their concept of Americanity in relation to Díaz's decolonial theory of the fukú americanus. And by introducing the vocabularies of "negative aesthetics" and Americanity into the conversation, I attempt to shift the framework, perspective, and object of analysis in studies of world-system literature and the US Latinx novel.

Conjectures on "Americanity," the "Fukú Americanus," and the Colonial Difference in *Oscar Wao*

To embrace Americanity is to dwell in the erasures of coloniality.
  WALTER MIGNOLO, *The Idea of Latin America*, 48

How do we begin studying Díaz's *The Brief Wondrous Life of Oscar Wao* as his major contribution to the world-(colonial)-system literatures of the global South?[113] Does his text suggest that the planetary literature all around us now is unmistakably global and simultaneously unequal? As Franco Moretti suggests in his essay on world literature, "reading more"[114] hardly seems to be the solution in mapping the geographical scope of the world-system literatures around us because we have just started rediscovering what Margaret Cohen calls the "great unread"[115] in the archive of literature. Perhaps tackling the world-colonial system of what Quijano and Wallerstein call "Americanity"[116] is the way to go.

If reading more (always a great thing) is not the entire solution for conceptualizing world-(colonial)-system literatures, our task as literary historians of the global South needs to be different. Moretti pleads that "the categories" and our units of analysis also need to be different, for it isn't what he sees as "the actual interconnection of things" that matter in our reading of world-system literatures but—quoting Max Weber—the "conceptual interconnection of problems which define the scope"[117] of the various idiographic and nomothetic sciences and of world-system literatures. Here I am interested in the consequences for the global South's literary history of one kind of archive that gets lost in world-system literatures: the archive of Americanity's literatures. Specifically, I discuss how the invention of Americanity makes it possible for us to see why Díaz begins *The Brief Wondrous Life of Oscar Wao* not with his hero, Oscar de León, but instead with the Genovese almirante in 1492 unleashing a great planetary curse on the New World Américas, as well as with the afterlife of dictator Rafael Leónidas Trujillo Molina, who ruled the island from 1931 to 1960. As Yunior tells us in the prologue, the almirante's advent in the Américas unleashed a "Great American doom" or "curse" into the world. For all of its Dominican Republic and New Jersey shore particularity, Díaz's postcontemporary US Latinx novel aims to represent the entire imperium of what Quijano and Wallerstein called "Americanity" and what he named the "fukú americanus"[118] as the almirante's desire to have dominion over the entire globe. Why is Americanity's invention so crucial in understanding Díaz's wide compass of the fukú americanus in *The Brief Wondrous Life of Oscar Wao*?

As I have argued elsewhere, for Quijano and Wallerstein, Americanity's "invention" was a fourfold process, and each part was closely linked to the other.[119] Quijano and Wallerstein intended their concept of Americanity to accomplish and perform a number of disparate and related functions: it would look at the cross-genealogy of the Américas as involved in an ongoing conflict with the provincialism of Europe (and Eurocentrism and coloniality), for European hegemony (especially the Iberian and British) created and crafted "a rank order" of social classification in the modern world system and with this new dominant rank of order enabled a "new set of rules"[120] for the interaction of the planet's cultures, societies, and states with one another. With the invention and so-called discovery of the Américas in 1492, Quijano and Wallerstein suggest that an essential boundary line was powerfully put in place for the first time: that of empire vis-à-vis other metropolitan empires.

The European hierarchy of coloniality manifested itself, as Quijano and Wallerstein suggest, "in all domains—political, economic, and not least of all cultural." Over the centuries, they argue, Americanity's coloniality of power "reproduced itself" over and over again. However, "when [the] formal colonial states ended" through the wars of independence and what we today call decolonization, the coloniality of power, the authors suggest, did not end. Instead, Americanity's coloniality of power continued "in the form of a socio-cultural hierarchy of European and non-European."[121]

Like Díaz's theory of the fukú americanus, Quijano and Wallerstein's concept of Americanity critiques visions of history as a linear temporal process, instead suggesting that the history of Americanity is an "historico-structural heterogeneity," a space and place where multiple paradigms are at war with one another.[122] Instead of envisioning the so-called discovery of the New World by Columbus as the enactment of a coherent Eurocentric modernity, Quijano and Wallerstein conceptualize it from the logic of Americanity's newness, racism, capitalist estrangement, and death. In Americanity's and the fukú americanus's spatiotemporal logic, there is no triumphal process of modernity, only doom, domination, and the death of coloniality and its power. Díaz's theory of the fukú americanus gets us out of the belief that history is a progression of events culminating in modernity by incorporating into his historia the multiple spatialities and violences of coloniality. His historia, I argue, grapples from the very start with the copresence of historical times, structural fragments, and varying forms of geocultural insights that shape the roots and routes of all societies.

Díaz's novel presents the "true account"[123] or history of Oscar Wao's sexual (mis)adventures and his trying quest for true decolonial love: it also, importantly, presents a supplementary story with a different set of characters and something of a development of its own. This is the historia of how Oscar de León's adventures came to be known and written up, a record that traces how Yunior de Las Casas came to archive, read, and interpret the various manuscripts Oscar leaves behind: unfinished books, letters, composition notebooks, and a quartet of space operas. In this supplementary narrative, Yunior's actions underscore how gaps and fragments often become raw materials for complex stories. And in the novel as a whole, Yunior's efforts as archivist, writer, and historian/chronicler emerge as integral to the postcontemporary US Latinx novel. Indeed, this secondary tale, as it unfolds in the margins of Oscar's search for decolonial love, develops its own planetary entanglements.[124]

The characters in this corollary tale all help transmit a preamble to stories of unrequited love: they also, importantly, foreshadow Oscar's unhappy and tragic Antillean ending. Their adventures in decolonial love and compassion are recorded in the search for and recovery of the source materials Yunior finds in the Dominican Republic—materials he later archives in the "four refrigerators" in the basement of his New Jersey home. In them are Oscar's "books, his games, his manuscripts, his comic books and his papers."[125] As we learn, the continuous narrative we are reading is actually an arrangement of fragmentary and even overlapping sources; their arranger, far from detached, routinely interjects Black English-Spanglish signifying commentary and paratexts—Yunior the watcher, ever the jester.

Whereas Yunior's paratextual footnotes form a distinctive part of his negative aesthetics, openly challenging thought systems in the main text, they also add an immense power to his writing, a power theorized by historian Anthony Grafton. In *The Footnote* he not only gives us an engrossing account of how footnotes to history gave way to footnotes *as* history, recounting in their subtle way the curious story of the progress of knowledge in written form, but he also treats the development of the footnote—the one form of proof normally supplied by historians in support of their assertions—as writers on science have long treated the development of laboratory equipment, statistical arguments, and reports on experiments: a complex story, rich in human interest, that sheds light on the status of history as art, as science, and as institution. Grafton starts in the Berlin of the brilliant nineteenth-century historian Leopold von Ranke, who is often credited with inventing documented history in its modern form. Casting back to antiquity and forward to the twentieth century, Grafton's investigation exposes Ranke's position as a far more ambiguous one and offers us a rich vision of the true origins and gradual triumph of the footnote. For our purposes, Grafton argues that the footnote is conjured to indicate how scholarly history writing does really differ from imaginative fiction. The footnote provides evidence that a text rests on a strict social science investigative or nomothetic discipline. Footnotes, Grafton suggests, are the only guarantee that statements about the past derive from identifiable sources. His conclusions about the footnote are especially crucial for Yunior as writer/chronicler of the practical past: the contingent footnote holds intrigue and buzz, for footnotes "make it possible to resist the efforts of modern governments . . . to conceal the compromises they have made, the deaths they have caused, the tortures they . . . have inflicted": footnotes are enemies of "the enemy of truth," Grafton concludes.[126] Through footnotes—and Yunior's footnotes are full of sound and fury—it is possible for him to resist the governments of the Dominican Republic and the United States; it is possible for him to comment on the compromises these institutions have made: the deaths and genocides pursued, the terrors and tortures inflicted. In a novel on the evil magics of dark lords—Colón, Trujillo, Balaguer, Kennedy, Reagan, Bush, and Clinton—it is not surprising that Yunior's initial footnotes connect the doom of the New World not only to the almirante but also to President John F. Kennedy, the man who "green-lighted the assassination of Trujillo in 1961, [and] who ordered the CIA to deliver arms to the Island."[127]

Yunior is at times playfully lyrical as a storyteller and chronicler, but he is indeed guided by serious concerns. He begins and ends his narrative about survival by confessing that, like Oscar, he has been infected by the hero's "adolescent nerdiness," which "vaporiz[ed] any iota of a chance they had for young [decolonial] love."[128] He also narrates how for some ten years after Oscar's death by the military police in Santo Domingo, he has been haunted by Oscar and the story he leaves behind—his notebooks, letters, marginal notes to *Watchmen*, and unfinished science-fiction manuscripts. The joy that Yunior takes in chronicling how Belicia and her son Oscar survived the Trujillato and its afterlife is the joy of his storytelling. "¿Quien es Oscar Wao?" is the question at the center of Yunior's novel: to answer it, Yunior has to figure out why Oscar defied death for his faith in decolonial love. Part of that answer lies in the story of the damnés of Santo Domingo and Paterson. Why were the Cabral-de Leóns so cursed and doomed?

A true Gen-Y blogger and near-expert Greater Antillean and US Latinx philologist, Yunior de Las Casas recalls at the novel's beginning that "a couple of weeks ago while I was finishing this book, I posted the thread *fukú* on the DRI forum.... These days I'm nerdy like that. The talkback blew the fuck up. You should see how many responses that I've gotten. They just keep coming in."[129] Díaz's choice of naming his narrator de Las Casas is but one example of his extended metaphoric system (and by extension his negative aesthetics), which purports to unify the elements of the galaxy under one aesthetic system full of holes, blanks, gaps, and fragments of independent parts. By naming his storyteller Yunior de Las Casas, Díaz asks us to recall the Spanish chronicler Bartolóme de Las Casas as a writer who not only evangelized the Indigenous peoples of the New World but also advocated for the repeal of the laws of colonial modernity that allowed the Indigenous people to be used as slaves. No doubt there is great portent here: another mediation in Díaz's imaginative literature on the fantastic, historical, and political dimensions of writing, storytelling, and historia.

After collecting and sorting through the DRI "talkback" on his neologism and keyword, *fukú*, as well as interviewing all of his Dominican family and friends, Yunior conceptualizes the entire history of the Dominican Republic and the Greater Antilles as a long process of what he dubs the fukú americanus. It is a binominal nomenclature: genus, fukú; species, americanus. And it condenses in the novel's opening dictum the stakes of the writing act itself: "generally a curse or doom of some kind; specifically, the Curse and the Doom of the New World. Also called the fukú of the Admiral [Colón] because the Admiral was both its midwife and one of its great European victims; despite 'discovering' the New World the Admiral died miserable and syphilitic, hearing (dique) divine voices."[130] Not only is Yunior interested in critically reflecting on Oscar de León's life history as he writes it as a fukú narrative (read doomed and damned) but also in "thinking from" such an experience. Thus envisaged, Yunior chooses to write Oscar's life story as a postcontemporary Joycean "nightmare" that is "cracked open" by the almirante's so-called discovery of the New World and the production of the coloniality of power.

With the arrival of the Iberians on Hispaniola, the Genovese almirante and the Iberians "unleashed the fukú on the world, and we've been in the shit ever since." Fukú americanus "ain't just ancient history," Yunior insists, for the fukú was in the postcontemporary "air" and throughout the centuries, he theorizes, and it moved easily from Almirante Colón to "our then dictator-for-life Rafael Leónidas Trujillo Molina."[131] What Wallerstein and Quijano refer to as "Americanity" was constituted—like Yunior's fukú americanus—together with and as a part of the Américas' matrix or coloniality of power that today prevails on a planetary scale.

It is here at the start of Yunior's imaginatively written "true account"[132] of Oscar de León's life of survival that the fukú americanus and the coloniality of power are conjuncturally configured as his units of analysis: it is here, in the opening gestures of this grand, wondrous novel, that Yunior establishes these terms descriptive of a new planetary coloniality of power. Such is Yunior's beginning point of departure of the historical process that came to define not only Oscar de León and his family's "doomed" and "cursed" diasporic story in the Greater Antilles (including the New Jersey shore), but also the historically doomed and damned processes that Frantz Fanon claimed defined the inhabitants of the Greater Antilles as the damnés de la terre.[133] For Yunior, it was in the very same movement—the almirante's unleashing of the fukú americanus—that best defined for him the material and subjective elements at the roots and routes of the de León-Cabral family's tragedy and "great doom." It was also the movement we call modernity: "As I'm sure you've guessed by now, I have a fukú story too. . . . Mine ain't the scariest, the clearest, the most painful or the most beautiful. . . . It just happens to be the one that's got its fingers around my throat."[134] Put differently, the Greater Antilles—Oscar and Yunior's birthplace—was the space and inaugural time of the historical period and the planet we now live in. Yunior's fukú americanus and the Greater Antilles (including the Dominican Republic) were defined at the point of the almirante's arrival from Europe in 1492: Yunior and Oscar's lives have experienced their tragic "destinies" within the matrix of the fukú and the coloniality of power. Yet more than blind Eurocentric arrogance is at issue here for Yunior. If "terminologies," as Michel-Rolph Trouillot argues in *Silencing the Past*, "demarcate a field [imaginary], politically and epistemologically,"[135] for Díaz and his narrators Yunior and Lola terms such as the *fukú americanus*—describing the unleashing of a great American doom—set up a field of overlapping coloniality and power in the novel. Is "the only way out" of power "in," as Lola suggests to Yunior?[136] Is there only a grappling with and surviving despite the coloniality of power for Díaz's narrators in *The Brief Wondrous Life of Oscar Wao*?

Although Yunior defines the fukú americanus mainly in terms of violent colonial contact—the ghastly horror, rape culture, and shattering genocide between people living in what we today call the global North and the global South—he also suggests that closer to his own historical time and space the fukú had its own "high priest" or "hypeman" in the Dominican Republic in the form of the "dictator-for-life" Trujillo, a tyrant he wryly dubs in the literary codes of the speculative genres as "our Sauron," "Arwen," and "our Darkseid." For those in subaltern circles, he was the fukú's "servant or its master." For Dominicans in the more "educated circles," Yunior writes, Trujillo's supernatural powers allowed him to incur an all-powerful "curse" and doom on those who "plotted against" him: a fukú "down to the seventh generation and beyond."[137]

Although Yunior transculturates in a true, social-science sense of the neologism (as articulated by Fernando Ortiz[138]) the origins and development of the fukú americanus by bringing together local Antillean folklore, Creole double consciousness, and planetary historical fantasy and science-fiction imaginative literature, thereby producing a diversalist knowledge in a geohistorical location so he can fully map and emplot Oscar de León's tumultuous life history in his novel, he's not certain whether or not his hero would entirely agree with his Greater Antillean theorizing of the fukú: "I'm not entirely sure Oscar would have liked this [Greater Antillean] designation. He was a hardcore sci-fi and fantasy man, believed that that was the kind of story we are all living in. He'd ask: What more sci-fi than Santo Domingo? What more fantasy than the Antilles?" But Yunior happily and partially trumps Oscar's literary science-fiction phantasmatics by championing his own global theory of the fukú americanus and by announcing his privileged retrospectively omniscient watcher-like powers as the author of the book we are reading: "But now that I know how it all turns out, I have to ask [Oscar] in turn, What more fukú?"[139] For Yunior, then, the fukú americanus is not only out there in the Greater Antillean sea and air but also in Oscar—our hero—and his loci of enunciations. In ways perhaps more powerful and rigorous than Oscar's science-fiction imaginary, Yunior's theorizing of the fukú allows him to think of knowledge and history in terms of dominant and subaltern positions in the field of knowledge (or epistemology), those doing imaginative writing from within colonial and imperial nations of the global North and those producing literature from the colonized and damned countries from the global South. But Yunior takes an authorial hint from Oscar's science-fiction phantasmatics and writes a transmodernist[140] US Latinx novel.

Yunior's weighty reflections on the fukú americanus validate a transmodernist perspective that he pieces together complete with a characteristic antiantiessentialist and fully decolonial gaze that accompanies his tale. His novel can thus be read as providing imaginative testimony of the almirante's unleashing the hegemony of Eurocentrism as a mode of both producing and controlling the global South's subjectivity and knowledge. As the novel progresses, Yunior follows the vexed historias of the Cabral-de León lives, desires, and inability to change the fukú that looms generationally over their everyday lives in the Dominican Republic and later on in the diasporic and urban New Jersey. After Yunior's self-reflexive prologue, in which he introduces his theory of the Greater Antilles' doom, he details Oscar's initial adolescent (mis)adventures in Paterson, New Jersey, and his "outsized" Dominican love for Ana and later Jenny.

Díaz then radically shifts narratological focalization by momentarily vaporizing Yunior and diegetically having Lola de León take the center stage by narrating from her own locus of enunciation as a US Latinx: first as a New Jersey shore "punk" runaway from her cruel and evil dying mother, Beli—à la Bon Jovi's pop sonics[141]—and then from her situated bitter exile to the Dominican Republic, where she is raised by her grandmother La Inca. Once she is rehabilitated by La Inca, Lola returns to Paterson to care for her mother, who is suffering from breast cancer, and to attend Rutgers University.

Oscar Wao then shifts gears again, and Yunior returns to narrate the Cabral-de León family historia. The tale moves geographically and temporally from New Jersey to Santo Domingo, La Capital of the Dominican Republic, where we learn of Belicia Cabral's cursed historia of Blackness and "the darkest character" in Yunior's character metamundo. Orphaned by the Trujillato that killed her parents and siblings, she is sold into slavery by her extended family and burned horribly by her new master and mistress (like Toni Morrison's iconic Sethe in *Beloved*) and must bear the terrible scar of "festering ruination" written on her back. This is how Yunior learns from Lola why Belicia came to be called "La Prieta Quemada or La Fea Quemada." Yunior also tells us about Belicia's brutal affair with a man known simply as the Gangster: a monstrous man who excels at the "binding, selling and degrading of women"[142] and who happens to be the island dictator Trujillo's brother-in-law. With Belicia's near-fatal beating in a cane field for having transgressed the rigid island love laws—she's openly rolled in the hay with the dictator Trujillo's sister's husband, Dionisio—she is exiled by her mother to New York and New Jersey, where she marries a Dominican man and then is quickly abandoned. Belicia's dark tale is an immigrant and diasporic survivor's story of a Black Dominicana in what US historian Mike Davis sees as the "exuberant" magical urbanism of the global North,[143] where she bravely makes do working three menial jobs to support her children.

Embedded in Díaz's social epic—in which he is largely sympathetic to Oscar and Yunior's "sentimental education"[144] in New Brunswick—is Yunior's simultaneous tale of Oscar's sexual misadventures in decolonial love and compassion, as well as a turn to the horrific story of Oscar's grandfather, Dr. Abelard Cabral, and his failure to keep his wife and daughters free from the dictator Trujillo's sexual perversions and domination, or fukú. The final chapters of *Oscar Wao* mix dizzyingly the literary modes of the bildungsroman—Oscar and Yunior's college education in love and the historical novel, Oscar's science-fiction phantasmatics, and Yunior's Greater Antillean story of the fukú americanus. Thus envisaged, within the central story of Oscar and Yunior's education Díaz gives us the transcultural interplay of historia, teller, and reader on smaller scales. As I noted in the preceding pages, Díaz accomplishes this by way of a wide variety of modes of emplotment.

Now I aim to examine two variations that provide the most vivid illustrations of Díaz's writing of Oscar's life history within his Greater Antillean and the global South's poetics. These are the sections late in the novel in which Yunior highlights the way Abelard Cabral incurs his island's fukú americanus and, many years later, when the Dominican American Oscar Wao "goes native" by returning to the Dominican Republic, falling totally in decolonial love with Ybón Pimental and transforming into "Mr. de León."[145] In both of these sections of the novel, Díaz probes superbly the Greater Antillean discourses of Fernando Ortiz, as well as Aimé Césaire's négritude poetry, which Dr. Cabral and his grandson Oscar respectively use to write their own antiauthoritarian texts.

As Yunior speculates, Dr. Cabral, who in addition to "being a brilliant doctor possessing one of the most remarkable minds" in the Dominican Republic, being widely read in Spanish, French, Latin, and Greek, is also one of the island's best collectors of rare books—"outlandish abstractions"—and a sharp theorist of the dictator Trujillo's "supernatural" powers. As Yunior suggests, Dr. Cabral provides them with one of the first scenes of anticolonial writing, for he is, like Yunior and Oscar, "a *todologos* of sorts." But in publicly defying Trujillo's pursuit of his wife and daughters—and in allegedly writing a book outlining

Trujillo's authoritative sins—Abelard, Yunior concludes, also brought the looming fukú or great doom on the entire Cabral-de León family line. Starting in 1945, instead of bringing his beautiful wife, Socorro (also a professional health worker), and his dazzling daughter, Jacquelyn, to the dictator's ritualized predatory soirées "as custom dictated," Abelard defied Trujillo's insatiable sexual cupidity by leaving them at home. Yunior symptomatically and summarily puts the Cabral family's tragedy this way: "Hiding your doe-eyed, large-breasted daughter from Trujillo . . . was anything but easy." Because of their distinctive class position as elites on the island, Abelard, Socorro, and Jacquelyn, tragically, "were as carefree as Hobbits,"[146] never once seeing the looming fukú that was to come down brutally on their heads.

Some four weeks after Abelard again refuses to capitulate to Trujillo's demands for him to bring Socorro and Jacquelyn to another island soirée—and thus allow the dictator free rein to rape his wife and daughter as the island "custom demanded"—Trujillo orders his military police to have the doctor arrested and charged with acts of "slander and gross calumny against the Person of the President." Once in prison, Abelard's tortured body cannot be separated from the (neo)fascist turn under the Trujillato because it was through the severe punishment of men and women that the military state imposed its projects of discipline, anticommunism, and antiqueerness: indeed, the doctor's "prison guards proceeded to inform the other [political] prisoners that Abelard was a homosexual and a Communist."[147] Within the ideological framing of the Cold War and US geopolitics in the region, Trujillo's secret agents tortured cosmopolitan citizens like Abelard to extract information from those the state labeled subversives and terrorists. In her acute analysis of the way Pinochet tortured Chileans in the age of neoliberalism, Macarena Gómez-Barris emphasizes in *Where Memory Dwells* that state torture was not only a contest over the physical body but also a contest over "the social imagination."[148]

In his effort to "taxonomize" the torture he is undergoing, Abelard learns from his prison guards that he'll experience ghastly electrical shocks to his body through an island contraption called the "pulpo." They spend the rest of the night showing him how it works. Yunior interrupts this painting of Abelard's torture and death as a kind of spatiotemporal fracturing by telling us how years later in his own ethnographic research on Oscar's grandfather, his island informants recalled the Cabral tale of torture as a fukú story with "a supernatural twist." Yunior records in his inimical style how the subaltern "folk" believed that "not only did Trujillo want Abelard's daughter, but when he couldn't snatch her, out of spite he put a fukú on the family's ass. Which is why all the terrible shit that happened happened."[149] The story of Trujillo's fukú on the Cabral-de León family is then embroidered by Yunior and narrated in the form of what M. H. Abrams called "natural-supernaturalism."[150] That is, before his fall in the Dominican Republic, Abelard followed a path largely in a state of political innocence or what Yunior dubs the doctor's simply "keeping his head down." When Trujillo's 1937 genocide of Haitians was in the making, Abelard kept his "eyes and nose safely tucked in his books." When Trujillo's survivors "staggered into his surgery with unspeakable machete wounds, he fixed them up as best as he could without making any comment as to the ghastliness of their wounds." Abelard's torture at the hands of Trujillo's secret police is as much about the emasculating torture and the mobilization of shame he experienced at the hands of the male guards. Yunior suggests that Abelard, even before his imprisonment, may have been at risk: by 1945, he was allegedly deep in the writing of what his island informants described as "an exposé of the supernatural roots of the Trujillo regime. A book about the Dark Powers of the President, a book in which Abelard argued that the tales the common people told about the president—that he was supernatural, that he was not human, may in some ways have been true."[151]

By bringing forth the atrocities and memories of the Trujillo regime, Dr. Abelard Cabral's book was written as a kind of Antillean textbook of magic or grimoire. Why does Díaz's Yunior, one of the novel's todologos, use the recondite term *grimoire*? As Yunior knows, the word derives from the Old French word *grammaire*, which had been used to refer to books written in Latin—that is to say, for all practical purposes during the early modern period, *all* books. By the end of the eighteenth century, however, the term had coined its more common usage to refer to books of magic. Yet as Ramón Saldívar suggests, the word *grimoire* also developed "into *a figure of speech* used to indicate something that was difficult or even impossible to understand. It was only in the 19th century, with the increasing interest in occultism in England following the publication of Frances Barrett's *The Magus* (1801), that the term entered the English language in reference to the specific mystery occasioned by books of magic."

In the Américas, grimoires came into contact with the natural philosophies and mystical beliefs of Indigenous peoples and thus intersected with structures of knowledge of other new populations brought to America from Africa. Saldívar concludes his exegesis by summing up the grammatological genealogy of the term *grimoire*: "From descriptions of a set of symbols and how to combine them to create well-formed sentences in Latin, and then, by extension and metonymy, to books of magic, a grimoire thus becomes the grammar of magic, the rhetoric of magic spells, the syntax of charms and divinations, as well as the form of books on how to summon or invoke supernatural entities such as angels, spirits, or demons, conveying the protocols of belief systems outside the pale of accepted patterns of belief. In time, the very books themselves, as mystical book objects, come to be imbued with magical powers."[152]

Into this history of the grimoire enters the history of Abelard. In Oscar and Yunior's discussion about their possibly finding the doctor's grimoire—all his books were destroyed after he was arrested—they conclude that this "shit would have been one wild motherfucking ride." In Abelard's imprisonment and his subsequent alleged writing of a book about the dictator's "supernatural powers,"[153] Díaz presents a Cabral-de León narrator who, before Oscar was born, believed that Santo Domingo's history was one affiliated with magic, fantasy, and the making-strange aesthetic. The Abelard tale of entanglement with Trujillo also allows Díaz to show his readers how the diverse social groups and family identities produced by the Trujillo dictatorship—the relatives of the tortured and murdered, surviving, and so on—exercised a form of brave cultural citizenship imbricated with the history of authoritarian brutality. Dr. Cabral's Greater Antillean magic—as opposed to the magic and reactionary nostalgia for Christianity and the medieval world found in, say, Tolkien's work—may be read as a figure for the enlargement of human powers and what Fredric Jameson sees in science fiction as a passage into the limit of the human: "an actualization of everything latent and virtual in the stunted human organism of the present."[154]

Oscar's journal writing in the Dominican Republic also presents an interesting case—an earnest attempt to fuse his fledgling science-fiction writings within the tradition of Césaire. After Oscar recovers from his suicide attempt at Rutgers, graduates from college, and makes do in Paterson by substitute teaching English and history at his former high school, Don Bosco Tech, he decides one summer to return with his mother, Beli, to Santo Domingo to visit his island family. There Oscar is amazed "at how incredibly beautiful Dominican women" really were, and he spends his leisure time reading Octavia Butler's science-fiction novels and painting in his journals what he characterizes as the "surreal whirligig that was life in La Capital."[155]

After one week of nonstop reading and writing, Oscar falls irrevocably in love with his grandmother's neighbor, Ybón Pimentel, a semiretired prostitute. When years later, Yunior recovers a portion of Oscar's prodigious summer writings, he dubs the journals as the hero's "THE CONDENSED NOTEBOOK OF A RETURN TO THE NATIVELAND," calling the trans-American reader's intertextual attention to Césaire's heteroglot and veering poem "Notebook of a Return to My Native Land" (1939). There Césaire defines *négritude* as "not stone . . . not liquid . . . neither tower nor cathedral" but as taking "root in the red flesh of the soil" and "in the ardent flesh of the sky."[156] Like Césaire's writing about the Greater Antilles, Oscar's journals are in Yunior's view largely about the hero's finding a poetic voice, about returning from the global North to the global South, and most importantly about Oscar's *creolizing* his science fiction-infused writings. All of Yunior and Oscar's Dominican American neologisms—the antiphonal counterpoints of *fukú* and *zafa, pariguayo* and *enamorao*—suggest Césaire's larger discursive and globally diversalist framework. If Oscar Wao, in the process of his reading and writing rediscovers his Afro-Atlantic Blackness—"dominicano soy yo"[157]—he finally transforms himself as Huáscar de León. This is a notable shift, for as Césaire mentions in his 1980 interview with René Depestre his neologism *négritude*—first used in his poem "Notebook of a Return to the Native Land"—was simply his way of concretizing "his coming to consciousness."[158] For Yunior, Oscar's double sciences—the global North's science fiction and Césaire's global South's new science or discipline of négritude—point him to a new positionality, a complex double register vis-à-vis Western scientific, disciplinary knowledge.

Thus envisaged, Dr. Abelard Cabral's black-magic book writing and Oscar's late Black science-fiction Creolist writings in the Dominican Republic are analogues to *The Brief Wondrous Life of Oscar Wao* as a whole: they reproduce on a miniature scale not only the basic relationships among his storytellers, histories, readers, and audience but also what decolonial philologist and theorist Walter Mignolo calls the "colonial difference."[159] All of these dynamics are discernible in the novel's overall epistemological and narratological scheme.

There are, finally, other striking similarities between the whole and the parts of Díaz's text. These have to do with Díaz's postcontemporary decolonial US Latinx novel. If Abelard Cabral's story of imprisonment, torture, and death at the hands of the dictator Trujillo is an historia of how the Trujillato addressed, managed, and obfuscated the violent excesses of the US-supported military junta during the Cold War, Díaz's interest in Dr. Cabral's harrowing tale helps him explain to his readers how the Dominican Republic's "spectacular state"[160]—to use the philosopher Giorgio Agamben's notion in *State of Exception*—became legitimized through ghastly spectacles of the state's erasure of violence. To be sure, *Oscar Wao* also examines what sociologist Macarena Gómez-Barris calls the "afterlife"[161] of the Latin American dictatorships in the cultural-symbolic arena. The representation of political state violence by Dr. Cabral's book of magic and Oscar de León's surrealist and creolized science-fiction notebooks contains significant ideas about the very afterlife and memory of Trujillo's bloodlust.

Yunior not only searches for Cabral's book (only to find out that it has been burned by the state) and collects the archives and expressions of the force of the past in the present in Oscar's notebooks; he also wants to produce his own "true account" of the hero Oscar Wao: to record, interpret, and rescue the productive sites of meanings where Oscar and his grandfather before him have attempted to engage, contest, survive, and struggle against Trujillo's hegemony. In this sense, Díaz's *Oscar Wao* contributes significantly to the emergent industry of the global South's scholarly books in the Caribbean, the United States, and Latin America that have analyzed and documented how neoliberalist states tend toward amnesia about their ghastly, violent pasts.[162]

Díaz's novel tells stories about the multiple sites of Americanity's ruptured history and the processes of possible retrieval, recovery, and transculturation of what fragments remain. Yunior thus views the Cabral-de León cultural representations as sites of the Greater Antillean fukú americanus and as ways to understand the persistence of state terror in people's lives, bodies, identifications, and subjectivities. Dr. Cabral's erased supernatural book and Oscar's unpublished manuscripts circulate quite differently, but they share what Díaz sees as essential qualities of decolonial imaginative texts about state terror—texts enunciated from the tortured, the oppressed, and the surviving. "Four times," Yunior writes, the de León "family hired lawyers but no charges were ever filed. The embassy didn't help and neither did the government." Lola swears that she will never return to the Dominican Republic, for "ten million Trujillos is all we are,"[163] thus returning to her earlier ideological critique that there isn't any "way out" of our planet's webs of coloniality of power and gender.

Many years later, when Yunior is close to completing his novel, he dreams of Oscar Wao. They are both back in the artsy Demarest dormitory rooms at Rutgers, and the "Dude is holding up a book for me to take a closer look—It takes me a while before I notice that Oscar's hands are seamless and all the book's pages are blank."[164] Does this book of blank pages, mediated by Yunior's dream, stand in for the spectacular state's erasing all of its past tortures and murders? Does the spectacular state, like the overdetermined dreamwork itself, function through a process of condensation and secondary revision, culminating in a process of exclusions? Even long after the Trujillo dictatorship in the Dominican Republic had ended in the 1960s, political democracy on the island, Díaz suggests, continued to exclude and "blank out" social subjects just as it fractured, beat, and abused those like La Inca, Belicia, Lola, and Oscar during its reign of spectacular authority. As I noted earlier, Díaz's páginas en blanco in *Oscar Wao* are examples of the author's "negative aesthetics" because they spectacularly dramatize the novel's potential to expose the ideological and hegemonic deficiencies of the state-sanctioned systems of thought.

Díaz's *The Brief Wondrous Life of Oscar Wao* joins other books from the human and social sciences that argue for the reader's contending with the spectral legacies of US-supported state torture—books that grapple with the unremembered disappeared, with the gratuitous rehearsals of violence reproduced and its effects. If Díaz's text ends with Yunior focusing on Oscar's spectacular representations of Santo Domingo, it is because he wants us to see his character's notebooks as socially symbolic sites of memory: representations that one can turn to for evidence of the relationship between collective violence and its devastating effects in the global South and global North.

Moreover, Yunior's theorizing of the fukú americanus in his novel's prologue allows his readers to comprehend the constitutive relationship between the historical a priori of Eurocentric genocide and of its hegemonic history of offshore activities. His remarkable framing of the fukú americanus as an alternative unit of analysis beyond the unit of the nation-state further allows him to think through the US-centric and Eurocentric structures of hegemonic thought and representations that continue to dominate the globe today. It also signals the planetary networks within which fukú Americanity, global capitalism, and modernity themselves all became possible. Thus, the fukú americanus operates at the text's very start to displace the teleological (Hegelian) and linear progression of modernity and even postmodernity, rendering even the crunchiest postmodernist traveling theory complicit, as Yunior suggests, with the temporal concepts of colonialism and imperialism, thus erasing the colonial difference.

Finally, Yunior intends his theory of the fukú americanus to displace the Eurocentric timetable that usually begins with the classical Greeks and Romans, continues with the so-called Renaissance age of discovery, and culminates with our late and pitiless modern world of camp thinking—from Hitler's World War II death camps to Bush's, Obama's, and Trump's combatant detainees Camps Delta and Camp Iguana in Guantanamo, Cuba, and the prison camps for children on the US-Mexico border. In its place, Yunior spatializes Oscar's temporal periodizings in which the whole planet (and possibly entire galaxies) are involved at every stage of his wondrous, tumultuous life. If colonial modernity—as Yunior envisions it in his critique of postmodernity at the novel's end—is usually imagined as Eurocentric and modern, he imagines the fukú americanus in the novel's prologue as transculturally transmodernist, with actors from all over the planet.

Transmodernity, as a form of Yunior's fukú americanus, signifies the global networks within which modernity became possible. If the Eurocentric imaginary of modernity has forgotten colonialism and imperialism, the task of Díaz's fukú americanus as analogous to the colonial difference is to reinscribe the novel's spatiotemporal simultaneity. To make the Greater Antilles, New Jersey, and Americanity no longer considered peripheral and behind the contemporaneity of all societies, Díaz ingeniously replaces hierarchical categories and field imaginaries such as the "discovery" and colonial "encounter" by the almirante with better ones such as his theory of Colón's unleashing the fukú on the planet. His concept of the fukú americanus is thus an attempt to reveal and displace the logic of coloniality by which Europeans have represented their others. By the logic of the fukú americanus, Díaz breaks out of this logic. He seeks both to reveal the ways in which the power-knowledge couplet has been at work in creating that difference as well as the ways in which colonial and imperial power represents difference. The fukú americanus in *The Brief Wondrous Life of Oscar Wao* thus imagines, hones in on, and critiques the colonial/imperial difference.

Standing with Oscar de León

From the barrioscapes of Mexico City—the heart and soul of Tenochtitlán—Oscar Wao reached out to Díaz in an epiphany: he did not let go until Díaz told his historia. From Mexico City to Syracuse, Cambridge to New York, Díaz wrote every day "at his desk, in bed, on the No. 6 train to Shea Stadium." He built a foundation with his *New Yorker* "Oscar Wao" and added some seventy new, worthy pages. His novel in progress on Oscar stalled, however, and Díaz entered a "No Writing Twilight Zone."[165]

This stint in the Twilight Zone was a painful parade of anxieties. Díaz did write when he returned from Mexico City—every day, for five straight years—although he felt like "a Pop Warner Edward Rivera" and a "minor league Ralph Ellison." He boxed up the hundreds of manuscript pages, exiling them to faraway lockups. His saved pages were always representative of a larger "mountain of loss."[166]

Until, that is, he finished.

As I've suggested in this chapter, decolonial writerly endurance is a process of becoming. In order to write *The Brief Wondrous Life of Oscar Wao*, Díaz had to become—as he explained in his acclaimed New York Public Library conversation with Toni Morrison—"the person he needed to become to write"[167] his book. However, this triumphalism leads us to wonder: What about Díaz's narrator Yunior de Las Casas? Why wasn't he so much "done" with Oscar de León? Although Yunior's historia about Oscar's incredible life and tragic death leads him to some measure of satisfaction at the novel's end—he tells us that he's happily domesticated and professionalized through marriage and a composition position at Middlesex Community College, a local institution—why is he so hard-hearted? Why at twenty-eight is he so full of guilt and regret? Why is he (as he says about Lola) as "cold as Saturn"?[168]

An answer: Yunior's triply iterated, DC Comics–infused, metafictional endings following Oscar's murder suggest that his text's attempted exorcism of Oscar's doom has failed: Oscar de León remains occluded by Yunior the writer, pieced together haphazardly in his favorite modes of fantasy, science fiction, and horror—in the very forms of the high-speculative "states of fantasy" in service of a (meta)historia gone awry.[169] Whereas Oscar de León's death and spectral presence throughout *The Brief Wondrous Life of Oscar Wao* allies him in solidarity with his mother, his grandfather, his sister, and his lover, his murder by the state police in Santo Domingo's cane fields yokes him to all the living and the dead who have fallen prey to the abyss of Hemispheric America's police forces, militias, (post)dictatorships, and cruel neoliberalisms. Yunior remains alienated, haunted by Oscar's ethical beliefs in the everyday beauties of life, intimacy, social justice, and struggle. Where Yunior remains unfinished, Oscar, by contrast, speaks with a hard-won certainty for life, willing a planet beset by erasure toward a campaign against silence and injustice.

A Legacy

In-formation

5

Junot Díaz's Search for Decolonial Love

In *Oscar Wao* we have a family that has fled, half-destroyed, from one of the rape incubators of the New World, and they are trying to find love. But not just any love. How can there be "just any love" given the history of rape and sexual violence that created the Caribbean—that Trujillo uses in the novel? The kind of love that I was interested in, that my characters long for intuitively, is the only kind of love that could liberate them from that horrible legacy of colonial violence. I am speaking about decolonial love.

JUNOT DÍAZ, quoted in Moya, "The Search for
Decolonial Love, Parts I and II"

I know this sounds completely ridiculous, but the persona who writes my books, is a writer writing my books. Yunior is a big liar, and he filters the whole thing. He's also smarter than I am, because one can write someone who is smarter than you. One of the things about Yunior is that he loves to destabilize a reader's sense of who he is, who his family is, and he loves breaking up any kind of authoritative narrative about his family or himself.

JUNOT DÍAZ, quoted in Als, "Junot Díaz"

As I have argued in this book, the emergence of an embodied, distinctly Dominican American voice like Junot Díaz's not only announces a new turn in the dialectic of our program-era fiction but also a shift in the interplay of reciprocity, liberation, and decolonial love. The literal and figurative developments of his voice—learning a new language after emigrating from Santo Domingo; working through a speech mutism in Parlin, New Jersey; claiming a distinctive Dominicano timbre at Rutgers, Cornell, and beyond—underscore a singular, hard-won vibrancy alive in each of Díaz's major works. As I hear it, his is a "Black and Brown" Latinx voice that resists the mark of mass production by the Ivy-fueled MFA machine; it rejects, in its bite and brio, the flashy, postmodernist displays of self-reflexive crunch and clang: longtime hallmarks of McOndo (read: MTV-crazed) fiction.[1] Rather, the voice Díaz forged—and continues to refine—has helped him resist homogenization. It has enabled him to craft cuentos straight out of Jersey's Afro-Dominicano London Terrace and fresh from Santo Domingo's Villa Juana (and, it could be argued, from the literary archive that was consumed inside these places). And this is truly one of the greatest imports of Díaz's pages: in them, the emotional and improvisational grain of his Dominican American experience and the related vitality of characters who live and dream in high-def.

Yet, as we notice via the scenarios Díaz invents for Yunior de Las Casas, even the hippest dreams can fail. Why, we might ask, does Díaz let this happen? Why inscribe failure into these fictions? Why does Díaz deliberately highlight Yunior's pitfalls, shortcomings, and missed opportunities in *Drown*, *The Brief Wondrous Life of Oscar Wao*, and *This Is How You Lose Her*? Does Yunior ever learn from his failure to practice love's dialectic of reciprocity and recognition? Why does Díaz deliberately distance himself from his central protagonist and narrator? Is the distinction between Junot Díaz and Yunior de Las Casas mostly one of cognitive superiority? Of Díaz understanding better than saturnine Yunior the arts of the decolonial imagination? Or is this separation one of increased creativity and human reciprocity? Of, as Díaz says, Yunior's world interpellations as largely based in writerly and historical process: registering, processing, analyzing, assembling, footnoting, "filter[ing] the whole thing," and "destabiliz[ing] a reader's sense of who he is"?[2] Let's not forget: Díaz invents all of this.[3]

These questions beg a firm clarification: Yunior's "filtered" views do not directly correspond to Díaz's artistic practice. Nor, further, does the decolonial kind of love Díaz is "interested in" apply only to Yunior; many of the characters in his texts, as he suggests, "long intuitively" for a kind of love that might "liberate them from" the New World's "horrible legacy of colonial violence."[4] This kind of love, for Díaz, is an event—a rupture of the social order. It is risky, though not irrational. It is, on the contrary, the very means by which Díaz's characters teach themselves that they *are* rational, free, and "liberated," as he says, from "their horrible legacy of colonial violence."[5] This is a decolonial love indeed, the half-life of which is beyond standard measure.

To approach this subject in earnest—to appreciate the forces at work in Díaz's texts and to comprehend their breath *and* depth—we must avoid the tremendous urge to take Yunior's "filtered" side. We must acknowledge that flaws, failures, and cover-ups always already mediate our experience of the worlds that Díaz invents.

Díaz, of course, agrees with much of what Yunior says about the fukú americanus, about his Afro-Dominicano metamundo, and about what his characters say over the course of "Negocios," *Drown*, *The Brief Wondrous Life of Oscar Wao*, and *This Is How You Lose Her*. Just as the beliefs overlap, so do Yunior's experiences bear close resemblances to Díaz's own. Both Yunior and Díaz become professional writers and professors of creative writing; both are ghettonerds and nervous sons of fanatical, Trujillo-aping military-police fathers who abandon them; both suffer, in their midlives, from physical disabilities caused by years of weight lifting and hauling heavy pool tables. Yunior and Díaz, further, are yoked to their single-parent-household Dominicana mothers and fascinated by the practice of world building in their art; both are born in Santo Domingo and emigrate at the age of six to Parlin, New Jersey; and both attend junior college before transferring to Rutgers University, New Brunswick. But as opposed to Yunior's writings, Díaz's works of fiction—as I suggested in chapters 2 and 3—are not glorified pieces of documentary realism. And as he makes plain, they need not be.

Again, a refrain: Yunior de Las Casas is not Junot Díaz. This distinction, simple as it may read, is vital to the entire enterprise of reading Díaz's fiction. To conflate the two figures, as happens regularly in social media, is to suggest that Díaz and his literary works are nakedly blunt and misogynistic, that his female characters are always beautiful diosas, or that many of his short stories, including "Miss Lora" and "The Cheater's Guide to Love," are attempts at autobiographical self-therapy.[6] (And to write about Díaz without addressing this conflation is to kick the towering hornet's nest.) Such readings, grounded as they may be in viscerality and nuance, present a number of difficulties. How should readers address these complaints?

In discussing *Drown*, Díaz himself noted that

> we have a book where racist shit happens—but it's not like at a thematic level the book is saying: Right on, racist shit! I was hoping that the book

would expose my characters' race craziness and that this craziness would strike readers, at the very minimum, as authentic. But exposing our racisms, etc., accurately has never seemed to be enough; the problem with faithful representations is that they run the risk of being mere titillation or sensationalism. In my books, I try to show how these oppressive paradigms work together with the social reality of the characters to undermine the very dreams the characters have for themselves. So, Yunior thinks X and Y about people and that logic is, in part, what fucks him up.[7]

Fucks him up, indeed.

For Díaz, the gulf between himself and Yunior turns out to be a *constitutive* distinction. And in hastily assuming that Díaz is writing documentary-realist texts, some readers overlook this important point: making Yunior de Las Casas the central persona and protagonist in his books is one of Díaz's long-game strategies; it allows him to introduce and tarry with key literary-philosophical issues, including the one animating this final chapter: decolonial love.[8]

As I suggest here, Díaz has long been fundamentally interested in how Yunior and his characters intuitively search for this kind of love, long motivated by the prospect of rehabilitating our most intimate and revealing modes of relation. Given the half-life of these concerns—their presence in each of Díaz's pages—we might be justified in asking: what has Díaz to say on the half-life of love?

A few days before the Junot Díaz Symposium at Stanford in May 2012, Nicole Aragi, Díaz's literary agent, sent me fifteen bound copies of the galley proofs to his much-awaited book of short stories, *This Is How You Lose Her*—copies the co-organizers and I immediately shared with the symposium speakers. Yunior de Las Casas, who appears as a young boy in Santo Domingo, a piratical swaggering and misogynist adolescent in New Jersey in *Drown*, and then as a fledgling young campus novelist in *The Brief Wondrous Life of Oscar Wao*, is featured in this book of short stories, although this time he takes center stage as a romantic bungler and sex addict, a writer suffering from spinal stenosis, and a forty-something creative-writing professor living in Cambridge, Massachusetts, composing a cheater's guide to love.

One should not, as I have argued, underestimate the polyrhythms of Díaz's central narrator, Yunior de Las Casas, or underestimate his own serious issues with what Díaz calls Yunior's toxic "masculinist sensibilities."[9] Neither should one underestimate the almost theatrical quality of Díaz's imaginative literary texts and his scores of interventions, readings, and keynote addresses, perform-

Figure 5.1 Díaz holding court on *Late Night with Seth Meyers*, October 10, 2015. Screenshot. NBC.

ing his masculinity. Sometimes, the Santo Domingo and New Jersey polyrhythms in his sentences slow down; other times, they speed up. Quotations in nerdspeak interrupt the erudite MIT creative-writing professor, and multiple languages (English and Spanish) mingle. *¡Olvídate!* Certain passages, though deadly serious about sexual abuse, sexual violence, coloniality, or political race, cause laughter by his highlighting repetition of certain words or aporias. What to make of these many densities?

For those who have not heard Junot Díaz read from his work (often from his cell phone) or listened to him speak in public—sometimes on late-night television talk shows such as NBC's *Late Night with Seth Meyers* (figure 5.1), other times on stately interview platforms such as PBS's *Moyers and Company*—one might miss how Díaz charms and plays with his audiences. On camera and in person, Díaz enchants not merely through the restless audacity of his aesthetic vision but also through his live performances of novelistic sensibilities: perfect diction, animated gestures, off-the-cuff erudition, infectious energy. With a sharp *lengua* (tongue) and cutting wit, Díaz exacts the best out of his interlocutors, occasionally even spurring bright hipsters like McSweeney's founder Dave Eggers—as I witnessed during a June 2009 Intersection for the Arts conversation at Glide Memorial Church in San Francisco—into tongue-tied befuddlement. As many can attest, Díaz has the capacity to speak eloquently, sans notes, for more than an hour, easily. As many have experienced, he can also answer

JUNOT DÍAZ'S SEARCH FOR DECOLONIAL LOVE · 155

Figure 5.2 View of the packed crowd at Barnes & Noble, Union Square, New York City, September 12, 2012. Used with permission of Díaz.

questions in demanding interviews, improvise in high-pressure situations, and address even the coarsest questions with admirable grit and grace.

Whether in public, on seemingly epic book tours, or in appearances at bookstores and festivals around the world, it was clear that by 2012, Díaz had moved center stage. A prime example: on September 11, 2012, at an appearance at a New York City bookstore where he read from *This Is How You Lose Her*, Díaz sparked a "near-riot in the Union Square Barnes and Noble."[10] More than a thousand Díaz fans showed up to meet the author in a space with capacity for only four hundred. To gain control, the bookstore's staff called in the NYPD for assistance—for a *reading of short stories*, we might remind ourselves (figure 5.2). This from a man who, as a young boy just arrived in Parlin, New Jersey, had been so unsure of himself that he refused to speak English.

On a personal level, years earlier, just as his novel *The Brief Wondrous Life of Oscar Wao* was about to be published, his engagement to his fiancée, a lawyer, imploded. Díaz recalls that in some ways those years were also the worst years of his life. "My female friends were fucking pissed," he confessed to reporters. "That was the one relationship they liked."[11]

Like Yunior de Las Casas, Díaz says that he once had a penchant for chasing sucia love.[12] And he never covered up his past relationships, for he freely admitted to having cheated on about half his girlfriends prior to the engagement. However, at the time of his finishing *Oscar Wao*, Díaz confessed that he "committed the most unpardonable sin," which was to make his fiancée "unhappy."[13] That tempestuous breakup (and its gossipy afterlife covered in the *New York Post*[14]) became the occasion for Díaz to begin piecing together a group of short stories he had published in the *New Yorker* in slightly different form: "The Sun, the Moon, the Stars," "Otravida, Otravez," "The Pura Principle," and "Nilda." He also included in the then book in progress a story titled "Flaca," a story about one of Yunior's "whitetrash" New Jersey lovers that had originally appeared in *Story*, and a version of a short story about Yunior's immigrant family's implosion and social death in Parlin, New Jersey, originally titled "London Terrace"—the very story that, as I explained in chapter 3, he wrote for his MFA thesis and then rescripted and retitled as "Invierno" for *Glimmer Train*.

Díaz's heartbreak stayed in him like poisonous radiation; it was also the catalyst for his return to an earlier, splendid literary failure titled "The Cheater's Guide." (The backstory: some twenty years earlier, when he had signed his first professional book contract for *Drown*, he had envisioned and signed a second book contract for a work provisionally titled "The Cheater's Guide to Love," an historia about a Dominicano lost dude's rise and fall as a serial cheater.)

Díaz, at the time nearing forty, was ready to take on not only Yunior de Las Casas's romantic offenses or peccadilloes but also his own brother Rafa's early struggle with leukemia. Although his real brother Rafael fully recovered from his cancer, Yunior's older brother Rafa did not fare so well in *This Is How You Lose Her*. And as if that weren't enough, in the midst of this book writing Díaz was also diagnosed with spinal stenosis—a condition that, during the 2012 Junot Díaz Symposium, he traced back to his years of weightlifting and his part-time gig delivering pool tables during his undergraduate years at Rutgers.

Just like Yunior's BFF (the married Dominicano Elvis) in "The Cheater's Guide to Love," who forces his mistakes on a new generation and neglects his wife and daughter, Díaz had witnessed what he calls the cycle of male "dumbasses" neglecting their familias. He wanted *This Is How You Lose Her* to shed critical light on this male dumbassery. As with his previous literary failures and successes, Díaz says that it took him "forever to get the . . . stories I needed to do this project."[15]

An early version of "Alma," for instance, was first written when he was an undergraduate at Rutgers and he had met his first love, "one of those Sonic Youth, comic book-reading alternlatinas without whom you might never have lost your virginity." Another campus story, simply titled "Flaca," focused on Veronica Hardrada, a "whitetrash from outside of Paterson" who Yunior meets and falls in love with during their postcolonial James Joyce seminar at Rutgers. *This*

Is How You Lose Her closes with "The Cheater's Guide to Love"—a story that, like two others in the book, uses the second-person present to blast off: "You," Yunior, the historia's bad guy. By then, Yunior—a (creative) writing professor at an Ivy League, elite STEM university in Cambridge, Massachusetts—botches a long-term relationship, grapples with disability (spinal stenosis and plantar fasciitis), and finally wills himself to turn heartbreak and bodily pain into a philosophical treatise on decolonial love—a treatise featuring one of the most memorable, encapsulating sentences in decades: "*The half-life of love is forever.*"[16]

Why is the half-life of love, for Díaz's Yunior, so irradiative, so contaminated? Why is heartbreak and radiation on the one hand and mourning and melancholia on the other hand so embedded in this cuento's two logics, as Ricardo Piglia might say?[17] Not only does Yunior's half-life of love decay by giving off energy and matter in his work, but it also decays throughout his texts at a rate that is characteristic to itself. For—as Díaz, the MIT professor, knows—just as the rate at which a radioactive isotope decays is scientifically measured in half-life, so too is the half-life of decolonial love. Díaz's term can thus be defined as the time it takes for one-half of the atoms of radioactive material—of the character's human attachments constituting love—to disintegrate.

As my book's title argues, Díaz's works are themselves extended philosophical meditations on the half-life of love. His writing not only allows him to create characters who are psychologically and philosophically alive to experiencing love as a historically transformative practice—a practice replete with a Fanonian, dialectical dynamic of reciprocity and liberation—but also demonstrates that (decolonial) love is implicit in the relationship between Díaz and his characters. Thus envisaged, the dialectical encounter of radioactively decaying heartbreak and potential reciprocity and freedom—the halo around love itself—is Díaz's literary signature.[18]

This is why, as I explained in chapter 4, the young Belicia loves the Gangster so "atomically" and destructively in *The Brief Wondrous Life of Oscar Wao*. This is why Yunior pegs all of his lovers as radiated "sucias": dirty, unpure, impoverished, contaminated. This is why Yunior's historias often take the loser's side of love. But are Yunior's "sucias" conscious of their own contaminated aberrance? Can Yunior de Las Casas, unlike his father, Ramón, or his brother, Rafa, ever transcend his immigrant, working-class positionality as a sucio—his oscuro suciality,[19] if you will—and begin to address his socially acquired toxic masculinist deficiencies? Like Deborah R. Vargas and Paula M. L. Moya, who have explored in their work Díaz's sucios' and sucias' figurations of decolonial love, here I am interested in analyzing how Díaz's racialized masculinities and femininities emerge in his fiction.

Decolonizing Sucio and Sucia Love

Vargas's "Sucia Love: Losing, Lying, and Leaving in *This Is How You Lose Her*" suggests that a racialized, classed politics of "la sucia" and "lo sucio"—the unclean, the filthy, the imperfect—is at the center of Díaz's imaginative work. Both "lo sucio" and "la sucia" operate as a decolonial analytic or logic that explains many of the constructions of racialized, classed masculinities and femininities in his texts. Moreover, Díaz's vernacular uses of the sucios and sucias function for Vargas "as a structural metonym" for his "non-normative constructions of intimacy, sexual desire, and kinship." In other words, the sucias and sucios represented in *This Is How You Lose Her* inhabit racialized genders and sexualities that represent the "deficit citizenry of institutional regimes of normative love and intimacy, including marriage, monogamy, biological reproduction, fidelity, and commitment." By analyzing Díaz's Latinx female characters, including Magdalena, Alma, Cassandra, Flaca, Pura, and Yasmin, Vargas shows how they love not only aggressively and occasionally cynically in Yunior's historias but also without any "commitments to a life promised by the American dream." The sucias, in short, are Latinx working-class, Spanglish-speaking, racialized women who persistently have "to be cleaned up by projects of neoliberal capitalism." However, these projects fail. Díaz's sucias thus represent, as Vargas says, "the obscure manner in which Yunior goes about losing love as well as the accumulated wasted matter marking his lost loves." If Yunior's sucia lovers opt out in Díaz's fiction from what Vargas sees as the "heteronormative temporality of love"[20]—a love without guarantees—do they teach Yunior anything about his own self-representations as a "sucio"? Do his sucia lovers teach him that love is wise or unwise?

Bearing in mind Moya's endorsement of Díaz's "search for decolonial love" in his three books of fiction—as well as her revelation that, according to Díaz's own comments, Yunior de Las Casas's "ideas about women and the actions of these ideas [about them] always [left] him more alone, more thwarted, more disconnected from his community and himself"[21]—I conclude my study of Díaz's fiction by answering the questions I have posed about sucia and sucio love. In particular, I aim to underscore the value of searching for decolonial love in *The Brief Wondrous Life of Oscar Wao* and *This Is How You Lose Her*. To that end, in the following pages I analyze a paratextual passage (a footnote)[22] from Díaz's *The Brief Wondrous Life of Oscar Wao* in which Yunior, as chronicler/novelist, critically reflects on and queers Oscar de León's spectacularly closeted reading of the science fiction and fantasy books he loves; relatedly, I also unpack the effects of Oscar's closeted reading on his mother, Belicia, his community friends, and Yunior, the novel's "faithful watcher."²³ In the process I suggest that Yunior's paratextual observations and incomparable allegorizing—Oscar's closeted reading—call readers to consider what happens to US Latinx "immigrant-rising" barrio kids of color when they read imaginative literature and, more importantly, what goes on in their complex inner lives.²⁴ Ultimately, I aim to extend the work of the previous chapter—tracing the decolonial process of becoming Oscar Wao—by writing at a different angle.

Although Yunior occasionally critiques Oscar's developing identity politics, he also champions Oscar's and his own changing subjectivities: their developing structures of feeling, their evolving dialectics of difference, their ethics of convivencia and coexistence. As I argue here, this resonates with Yunior's fulsome, forty-something search for decolonial love in "The Cheater's Guide to Love." In that story Yunior, now a fully professionalized assistant professor of creative writing within US academia's "program era,"²⁵ offers us much more than a lowbrow catalog of thwarted attempts at human intimacy. Indeed, when we read *The Brief Wondrous Life of Oscar Wao* and "The Cheater's Guide to Love" as linked texts, we instead encounter decolonial exercises in dissident antihomophobic inquiry and racial hermeneutics that directly inform the theories of identity, sexuality, gender, love, and (de)coloniality alive in each page.

In the case of *The Brief Wondrous Life of Oscar Wao*, Díaz paints a deliberate, critical understanding of a pair of US "black, Latino, migrant Dominican Jersey, smart boys"²⁶ through the lenses and projects of decolonial love. In "The Cheater's Guide to Love," Díaz changes gears by working through Yunior's philosophical praise of decolonial love and amplifying the critical, near-psychoanalytic self-analysis involved in expressing decolonial love in fiction. Like Toni Morrison and Sandra Cisneros, Díaz uses his central character Yunior de Las Casas—reminiscent of *Beloved*'s Paul D or *Caramelo*'s Celaya Reyes—to bear witness to what really happens to young US Latinx men of color who have been traumatized by economic migration, racial oppression, sexual abuse, and rape. Grappling with this culture of sexual violence and abuse is what Díaz sees as his characters' doomed search for love. As I explained in chapter 3, for instance, Díaz's "Ysrael" involves a nine-year-old Yunior being instructed by his older brother, Rafa, to sit at the back of the bus; Yunior obeys Rafa and sits next to an older Dominican man: "I lowered myself stiffly into my seat but the pastelito [I was eating] had already put a grease stain on my pants. . . . You have to watch out for stains like that, the man said to me. He had big teeth and wore a clean fedora. . . . These things are too greasy, I said. Let me help. He spit on his fingers and started to rub at the stain but then he was pinching at the tip of my pinga through the fabric of my shorts. You pato, I said." This scene of sexual molestation where a man with "big teeth" gropes the preadolescent Yunior ends with the young boy's testimony: "The man squeezed my biceps, quickly, hard, the way my friends smack me in church. I whimpered." Also, in "Drown," the titular story of the collection set in New Jersey, Yunior's college-bound best friend, Beto, gives him a hand job and more: "We had just come back from the pool and were watching a porn at his parents' apartment.... We were an hour into the new movie ... when he reached into my pants. What the fuck are you doing? I asked, but he didn't stop. His hand was dry. I came right away, smearing the plastic covers."²⁷ As these scenes powerfully suggest, part of Yunior de Las Casas's charm, vulnerability, and contradictions as a developing character in Díaz's fictional matrix is not that he is a dishonest chronicler of his erotic and sexual intimacies but rather that Díaz often paints Yunior as being too incredibly honest and fantastically observant about what he sees as his reality.

Still later, in Díaz's award-winning *Times of London* story "Miss Lora," Yunior's high school "profesora" frequently invites him to her flat for sex. Among other things, Díaz's "Miss Lora" investigates Yunior's teenage "ambivalences" about having sex with an older woman who has power over him. Although we often think of adolescent teenage boys of color as already hypersexualized, Díaz suggests that Yunior is not yet capable of seeing his couplings with a teacher at his high school as potentially criminal. Many years later, it is only after Yunior recounts his couplings and travails with Miss Lora to his Rutgers University girlfriend, Lola de León, that he begins to see how abusive this doomed coupling with the high school "profesora" had been.

As these episodes reveal, Yunior de Las Casas is a complex, contradictory protagonist that Díaz uses in his linked fictional work to create intricate narratological "character-spaces" and an evolving "character-system."²⁸ With these tools, Díaz weighs the sexual abuses and transgressions that Yunior experiences growing up in Santo Domingo and New Jersey, as well as how this abuse has centrally shaped who he is and how he feels as a subject. As Díaz noted in the *New Yorker*, "Yunior's been with [him] a long time," and he has "watched this frustrating fool grow up"; Díaz has, as a result, a "pretty good sense of his kinks and contradictions."²⁹ Moreover, Yunior's particular insights and blind spots allow us to see how his toxic masculinist ideas about women and his culture's sedimented heteronormativity often leave him feeling utterly "disconnected": alienated from lovers, family, and community. As Díaz said to Moya, "Yunior's desire for communion with self and with other" is often "tragic" because he's continually "undermined" by his own "unwillingness to see women in his life as fully human." If Yunior fails to recognize "the women parts of his identity as human," as Díaz describes, then how in the world can Yunior begin to "recognize himself as fully human"?[30]

Díaz's painting of Yunior's fraught, developing character is important to the overall argument in this final chapter because Yunior's preadolescent life in Santo Domingo and his teenage years in New Jersey constitute a rent, fragmented, nonlinear history in which he searches for decolonial hope, love, and compassion. But there is no real understanding of Yunior's full development as a character "without viewing him," as Díaz suggests to the playwright Gregg Barrios, "through the lens of these [sexual scenes of abuse and rape]"—lenses not only carefully thematized in the linked stories "Ysrael," "Drown," and "Miss Lora" but also fully examined in the extended, predatory rape culture of the dictator Trujillo's Dominican Republic in *The Brief Wondrous Life of Oscar Wao*.[31] In Díaz's fiction, Yunior learns how to "work through" his own wounded traumas of economic migration and criminal, sexual abuse; by working through his past experiences, he learns to become a writer.

More recently, philosopher Linda Martín Alcoff has argued that Díaz's fiction provides readers with "an account of the way that sexual violence is part of a colonial context, and the way in which sexual subjectivity is likely formed for men under these circumstances."[32] If there is an intergenerational transfer of trauma, from mothers who are rape victims to their daughters, as we see in *The Brief Wondrous Life of Oscar Wao*, is there also an intergenerational transfer of rape trauma between mothers and their sons? In Díaz's characters' search for decolonial love, then, do they have to ask themselves whether it is possible to love one's broken-by-the-coloniality self in the other's broken-by-the-coloniality-of-power person?

Yunior "will not need lots of talent," Díaz suggests, "to succeed." What Yunior needs "is more humanity. Yunior becomes very aware that part of what he lacks both in a relationship as a lover and perhaps even as an artist, what he lacks is not training, not will, but humanity, or what we would call sympathy or compassion."[33] Moreover, Yunior, Rafa, and Lola teach us that in their fighting against the cultures of US imperialism, and fighting for social justice, they also insist that they are fighting against rape.

On another level, do Oscar de León's excessive affectations (especially in reading the speculative genres) in *The Brief Wondrous Life of Oscar Wao* help Yunior begin "disidentifying,"[34] to use José Muñoz's term, with all of the racist, heteronormative structures that hail them? Before I return to the disidentifications in "The Cheater's Guide to Love," in the following section I briefly revisit Díaz's novel and examine how Yunior works through Oscar de León's epistemology of the closet.

Oscar Wao's Spectacular Barrio Closet

> [Oscar] wanted to blame the books, the sci-fi, but he couldn't—
> he loved them too much.
> DÍAZ, *The Brief Wondrous Life of Oscar Wao*, 50

What does Yunior de Las Casas in *The Brief Wondrous Life of Oscar Wao* tell us about Oscar de León's excessive love of reading? I approach this question not in the current, fashionable flourishing that intellectual historians of the book use to turn up a great deal of information about what Robert Darnton calls "the external history of reading"[35]—or what Franco Moretti and his digital humanities team of researchers at Stanford University call "quantitative formalism."[36] Instead, I answer this question in the most literal (and imaginative) way by reading a terrific footnote by Díaz—a footnote that shows Oscar reading the "speculative genres"[37]: science fiction and heroic fantasy. This slant approach begs a few questions: Does Oscar's reading—the J. R. R. Tolkien, Octavia Butler, and other heroic-fantasy books' storylands—arrest his development, like Cervantes's Don Quixote's reading of chivalrous literature and romances that fry the narrator-protagonist's brain? Does Oscar's reading in the barrio closet thematize for Díaz's Yunior an antihomophobic and dissident way of receiving, interpreting, and recoding science fiction's alien cultures otherwise? I will not argue below that Oscar de León's "closeted" identification suggests a transparent meaning of Oscar's erotic and sexual orientations; instead, I aim to demonstrate that Yunior's allegory of Oscar's reading in the closet helps him initiate a dissident way of understanding Oscar's gendered feelings and how they relate to their racist, heteronormative worlds in New Jersey and the Dominican Republic. Queer meaning, as David Halperin says, is a characteristic "recoding" of hegemonic heteronormative "meanings already encoded in that culture."[38] Thus, Yunior observes that unlike other teenage boys on the mean streets of Paterson who, say, "pitched quarters," "played wall balls," or "drove their older brothers'" fast cars, Oscar preferred to "gorge himself [in the closet] on a steady stream of Lovecraft, Wells, Burroughs, Howard, Alexander, Herbert, Asimov, Bova, and Heinlein, and even the old ones who were already beginning to fade—E. E. Doc Smith, Stapledon, and the guy who wrote all the Doc Savage books."[39]

In response to Oscar's reading this vast quantity of science fiction and heroic fantasy texts—Yunior estimates that by the time Oscar was in middle school, he had read Tolkien's modernist *The Lord of the Rings* hundreds of times, "one of his greatest loves and comforts of his life he'd first discovered"—his Dominican grandmother, La Inca, insists proudly that he "showed the genius" that "was part of the [de León-Cabral] family's patrimony." But not everyone in the de León family agrees with La Inca's sense of Oscar's "genius." Yunior, in one of the novel's thirty-three remarkable footnotes, suggests that Oscar's thick love for the "speculative genres" might have been a sociological consequence of Oscar's deep diasporic and oceanic feelings—that is, the hero's "being Antillean (who more sci-fi than us?)." Alternatively, Yunior speculates that Oscar's love of reading "jumped off" when, having lived "the first couple of years of his life" in the global South (the Dominican Republic), he "abruptly" and "wrenchingly" had to relocate to the global North (Central New Jersey): "a single green card," Yunior notes, "shifting not only worlds" geoculturally from the global South to the global North, but also spatiotemporally "centuries (from almost no TV or electricity to plenty of both)."[40]

In *The Brief Wondrous Life of Oscar Wao*, Yunior sets this extraordinary scene of decolonial reading within a "spacy"[41] epistemology of the closet as well as the hidden, secret spaces and encoded meanings in their Paterson barrio house. In the paratextual passage, Yunior attempts to explain to his readers why Oscar loves to read so much and, as a "smart bookish" Dominicano boy of color, what "the [sociocultural] consequences" of too much reading are for Oscar's decolonial "aesthetic education"[42] and his emergent queered, dissident gender formation. Yunior suggests that for those muchachos of color living on the mean streets of Paterson—where "the pure products of America go crazy,"[43] as the great Latinx poet laureate of New Jersey William Carlos Williams put it in his modernist poem "To Elsie"—Oscar's bookishness is as if he had enormous "bat wings or a pair of tentacles growing out of [his] chest." In other words, Yunior testifies to how Oscar's bookishness and dissident queerness led to his always being victimized by Paterson's ill-read barrio street toughs: they would kick, punch, and belittle him; worse, they would violently tear his "new Scholastic books" in half: "You like books, the urchins asked him?" They would then rip his books "in half before his very eyes. Now you got two."[44] In this passage, Díaz's Yunior demonstrates how Oscar's immersive reading in the closet illuminates Oscar's Dominican American queerness not as something that he is but as something that he does.[45]

Díaz's Yunior thus stages and investigates how Oscar's bookishness and his reading (and writing) are performative activities loaded with survivance and imaginative regeneration. On the one hand, Oscar carrying his books on the streets of Paterson makes "him stick out even more than he already did" as a nerdy, overly booksmart Dominican barrio boy. Oscar's mother, Belicia, also finds his bookish reading preoccupations "nutty," and she often belittles him. But Yunior frames some of the novel's central questions about why Oscar de León prefers the safe, secret spaces of his Paterson home's upstairs closet. There, secluded "in the upstairs closet,"[46] Oscar is afforded a special kind of well-being: a distance from the Paterson street cats and a proximity to his older sister, Lola, and his mother. And by honing in on the realities of Oscar's closet, Yunior calls our attention to one of the most powerful, catalyzing aspects of queer theory's emergent "antihomophobic inquiry" that we know through Eve Kosofsky Sedgwick's work on the epistemology of the closet.[47] Like Sedgwick's fight against heterosexism's dominance, Díaz's Yunior also uses the insights of antihomophobic queer inquiry to help him dissect the regime of Oscar de León's closetedness and what Belicia calls her muchacho Oscar's "nuttiness," especially through the closet's structuring of power, knowing, and not knowing (heteronormativity's willful ignorance), as well as the experiences and possibilities of queer dissidence. Moreover, Yunior asks what it is possible to know or say about Oscar's closeted "nuttiness." Are Oscar's racial and gendered identities inherent or socially hardwired? Why are his inner feelings and desires for others so unpredictable? And why so strong for Yunior?

I want to suggest that Yunior seizes this opportunity early in the paratextual lower frequencies of *The Brief Wondrous Life of Oscar Wao* to explore Oscar's inner life, allowing him, in effect, to map his own evolving, fraught male subjectivity. If we accept that Oscar's closet does not conceal his queered subjectivity, we might then argue that it stands in for Yunior as a way of highlighting Oscar's masculine sensibility, affect, pleasure, and identifications as a reader of speculative realist fantasy. This, again, begets a question: how do desire and the decolonial aesthetics of science fiction and dissident queerness entwine for Oscar de León and Yunior de Las Casas? At the beginning of the novel, Yunior is determined to crack open Oscar's love and shame for the solitary pleasures of reading; in the process, he wants us to understand how and why Oscar's feelings for culture and aesthetics are assiduously closeted in the barrio. Yunior proceeds to let the light in the closet by means of a distant social and literary analysis—an allegory of barrio reading—revealing Oscar's hopes of light and darkness in Paterson as a bookish young boy of color, demonstrating that it may in fact be possible to approach his friend's subjectivity without recourse to ego psychology. He is also able to begin painting the pathogenic consequences of Oscar's living in a racist, misogynist, and homophobic world.

Through metaphor, Yunior links this safe, secret space to the restorative "slat of light" where Oscar reads science-fiction books, tranquilly bathing him in a sublime, "razored" light that rushes in "from the cracked door" of the closet.[48] Yunior sees Oscar reading in solitude and wonders what joyous opportunities for imaginative contemplation exist in Oscar's acts of reading. Can the strengthening of the power-knowledge couplet brought on by reading aid in shaping the thick love Oscar has for the "speculative genres"—genres that have traditionally helped readers challenge their culture's hegemonic social, sexual, and ethnoracial codes of conduct? Yunior suggests that by closeting himself in his home and reading by the chiaroscuro crack of "razored light," Oscar's soaring imagination finds portals to other worlds and galaxies free from the real razors and brutal, "normalized" gendered identifications of the Paterson world outside. Rather than dismissing Yunior's nuanced, antihomophobic allegory of Oscar's closeted reading as outrageous, I aspire to understand what Yunior thinks Oscar's reading in the closet means for the Cabral-de León family, for his neighborhood childhood friends, and for him. What exactly is at stake for Yunior? What are the larger implications of Oscar's clandestine reading?

Yunior gets at these questions by first highlighting how Belicia's reaction to Oscar's reading in the upstairs closet sets off other metaphorical and figural chains of signifying connotations: "Pa' 'fuera! [Oscar's] mother roared. And out he would go, like a *condemned* [italics added] boy, to spend a few hours being tormented by the other boys—Please I want to stay; he would beg his mother but she shoved him out—You ain't a woman to be staying in the house."[49] In contrast to the interiorized, symbolic pleasure of Oscar's secret hiding space—the refuge where the immigrant-rising hero is free to feel, fantasize, and love, the figuration that fuses the closet and the imaginative mind—the weathered-yet-resolute Belicia "shoves" Oscar out of the closet and "roars" at him to go "Pa' 'fuera." Yunior, the novel's central "humble watcher,"[50] as he dubs himself, observes all of this and highlights Oscar's coming out as a performative staging of what philosopher María Lugones terms "the coloniality of gender."[51] Oscar obeys his mother and, as he says, goes out "like a condemned [and damned] boy." (Oscar as a Fanonian damné de la terre?) With his beautifully wrought, quasi-Proustian flourish, Yunior brilliantly plays the "inside," secret space of Oscar's closet's recuperative powers, where his reading of the "speculative genres" helps him attain his aesthetic education, against the harsh, male-centered, and violent urban spaces "outside" ("Pa' 'fuera") on the Paterson streets, where a multitude of hypermasculinized and homophobic boys "torment" the hero Oscar.[52] If we have not yet felt the full weight of Belicia's rigid, normalizing familial practices, or dispositifs—a conservative mindset of a popular barriocentric and heteronormative tíguere latinidad[53] formed both in the Dominican Republic and in New Jersey, where she equates Oscar's love of reading with a gendered domesticity—this scene dramatizes for Yunior the harsh, heteronormative ideology implicit in Belicia's comments: an ideology that implies that every human being must be assigned "a binarized identity," to use Sedgwick's terms, based on the gender of object choice. Yunior de Las Casas then goes on to quote Belicia's bilanguaging and stigmatizing interpellation of her closeted son: "Pórtate como un muchacho normal," for "you ain't a woman to be staying in the house."[54] Belicia prohibits Oscar's reading and spontaneous fantasizing in the closet; Yunior emphasizes this prohibition by using Michel Foucault's iconic discourse, suggesting that Oscar's family and public-school cultures want to "normalize" and discipline him as a "straight" subject within their gender regime.[55] Alas, only Oscar's sister Lola, a serious and capacious book reader herself and a loca in decolonial love to boot, consoles her brother by bringing him more "books from her own school, which had a better library."[56]

Although Yunior offers his readers no explanation for the emergence of Belicia's normalized gendered categorization and language—"un muchacho normal" to shame Oscar into straight normalization—he expertly traces its impact on Oscar's development both in New Jersey and the Dominican Republic, as well as on the aesthetic figural and tropological ways we come to know those cultures. Oscar's secrecy and disclosure in the closet, his imaginative wholeness and fragmentation inside his secret space, and his mental health and suicidal ideations come to mean what they mean in *The Brief Wondrous Life of Oscar Wao* through their figural relationship to the matrix of the "muchacho normal" and the dissident queered boy's reading in the closet. What Díaz's Yunior's complex meditation does here in *The Brief Wondrous Life of Oscar Wao* is thus allegorically *illuminated*, like the "razored" light rushing in through "the cracked [upstairs closet] door," the dizzying, contradictory significance of the secret signified by Oscar's barrio closet. Yunior enlarges his portrait of Oscar's identification as a bookish, alienated, "bloated," and "dyspeptic"[57] Dominicano "nerd" growing up on the mean streets of Paterson by problematizing the complex varieties of oppression—ethnic, sexual, racial, classed, and gendered—from which he seeks to free himself. Yunior's incomparable interpretation of Oscar's closeted reading in the footnoted passage is largely in agreement with a feminist focus on the intersectionality of oppression; as Sedgwick insisted, "all oppressions ... are differently structured and so must intersect in complex embodiments."[58]

If we now turn from the domestic, gendered economy of the barrio closet to the commercial, heteronormative economy that Belicia "condemns" him to, Oscar's being shoved out of his closet forces him to face the contours of his prescribed normalization on the brutal, gendered, urban streets of Paterson. Oscar thus metamorphosizes before Yunior's eyes: from a "nutty" and "smart bookish" young boy of color ("who ain't a woman") into a young, queered, dissident, and "oppressed" muchacho who appears to the straight boys on the Paterson's mean streets as if he had "bat wings ... growing out of his chest." Alas, "no one," Yunior concludes in his allegory of reading, was "more oppressive than the oppressed."[59] When Oscar's mother pushes him "Pa' 'fuera," he experiences how his iconic, gendered latinidad is defined, constrained, and designed by the patriarchal culture around him and, importantly, routed through the Paterson streets determining his social horizons. The chronotope of Oscar's spectacular closet and the domestic de León oikos that Yunior so rigorously routes, via metonymy, through the streets refers less to a poetics of insularity than to the mutually overdetermining spheres of private spaces and what historian Mike Davis calls the "magical urbanism"[60] of the global North's social barrioscape. Here the spatialized temporalities of Oscar's everyday barrio life—figured by Yunior as the closet and the house—stand out against the institutionalization of the subject into the heteronormativity of his culture and society. Thus envisaged, Yunior stages Oscar's reading science fiction texts in the secret, sheltered spaces of the closet—both a cradle and a retreat—that not only protects him against the invasion of the outside world but also borrows from this outside world some of its qualities: the fragile but razored light offered by the sun. Yunior valorizes Oscar's rich inner world—an alternative world where he is able to feel freely—as vastly preferable to the violent outside: the turbulent streets that cradle and corrode them both.

This primal paratextual scene, footnoted in the novel, gives us one of the text's first tropologically rigorous indications of how the inner-national and the outer-national—and, for that matter, outer-planetary—aesthetic alternative worlds operate for Oscar and Yunior in *The Brief Wondrous Life of Oscar Wao*. More importantly, this primal scene explores the limited range of "maleness" available in Oscar's culture and society, dramatizing the normative and normalizing structures of relation for Oscar within the larger sex-gender system. Yunior, in brief, investigates the normalizing tactics and strategies that Oscar's family, schooling, and society employ.

In Praise of Yunior's Cheater's Guide to (Sucio/a) Love

In this final section on Yunior's midlife search for decolonial love, I analyze the final story in Díaz's *This Is How You Lose Her*: "The Cheater's Guide to Love." What kind of "love event" is the creative-writing professor Yunior working through in this "guide"? Is he grappling with any new philosophical "truth procedures"? Why is the summative philosophical "event" for him an understanding of the radioactive "half-life of (decolonial) love"?[61]

Although "The Cheater's Guide to Love" reads as a nucleus of *This Is How You Lose Her*—an anchor for all of the other cuentos showcasing Yunior's ideolectical virtuosity and narratological energy—the other linked stories in the book are far from simple pretexts or wonderful fictional shards of "The Cheater's Guide to Love." In stories such as "Nilda," for example, Díaz's cuento not only tells two stories in one by painting the teenage Yunior yearning for sucio/a love but also embeds him in the cuento's "interstices," where the cuento's secret historia is encoded by having him (nine years later) work through a deep, soulful love and mourning for his older brother, Rafa. Rafa, we learn, dies not only from the destructive effects of leukemia but also from the radioactive treatments he receives to stop this destruction. Díaz's Yunior thus works the tension between the two historias without ever resolving it. He recounts the reactions of his mother, Virta, and his own reactions to Rafa—once a terrific "overmuscled" boxer and "papi chulo"—as he lays dying in their forlorn London Terrace apartment in Parlin, New Jersey.

At night, Rafa, "the hardest dude in the nabe" and the cruelest, most abusive, and most monstrous[62] older brother to Yunior, regularly sneaks the Dominicana Nilda and other barrio girls "orbiting around him" into the apartment's basement bedroom, which he shares with Yunior, and has sex with them. Fourteen-year-old Yunior endures all of this embarrassment because his mother does not allow her sons to sleep upstairs on the living-room couch. But "Nilda" begins years later, when twenty-three-year-old Yunior runs into Rafa's former girlfriend in a laundromat years after his brother's death and thinks that anything in his London Terrace metamundo—even escape from their downtrodden world—is still possible. However, this moment closes quickly.

Nilda once had long black hair and "world-class looks." Some nights she and Yunior would sit on the couch while Rafa was clocking hours at the carpet factory or working out at the gym. But as soon as Rafa showed up, Nilda jumped into his arms. Díaz's teenage Yunior has an "I. Q. that would have broken you in two," but he would have traded his smarts in for a halfway-decent face in a second. The story then loops back to earlier times when Nilda had been visiting Yunior and first met Rafa. Rafa noticed Nilda because she was wearing a tank top that "couldn't have blocked a sneeze." They went out that whole summer. Rafa was pale and tired all the time. Some mornings, Yunior remembers, Rafa's "leg bones hurt so much he couldn't get out of bed." The heartbroken Yunior can do nothing to "soothe Rafa's pain," not even "massag[ing] Rafa's shins." Rafa eventually quits high school, works manual labor jobs, and dreams of going to California. One night, at the end of summer, Yunior overhears Nilda telling Rafa about her plans for the future: she wants to get away from her mom and their downtrodden world and open up a group home for runaway kids. "Listening to her imagining herself," Yunior writes, "was about the saddest thing you ever heard." Rafa didn't even say "wow."[63] An hour later she gets up and leaves. A week later, Rafa is seeing some other London Terrace "nabe" girl.

But why was Nilda so doomed, Yunior asks? Why did the cruel man scoop her up when she had just gotten back from the group home? Why had Nilda been tossed out when the older barrio cat "bounced" and then handed around from man to man? Two years later, Rafa dies. Yunior, friendless, is out of school most of the time, smoking superweed at the toxic Global Landfill next to the London Terrace Apartments and chronicling in his mind everything about Rafa and Nilda's woes, incapable of effecting any change for them. Yunior's sad story records Nilda's downward spiral: how she fell in with more "stupid" street cats, got a "Brick city beat down," and lost some of her teeth. She continues to be in and out of school until she finally drops out completely. She loses her world-class looks; she "cuts her hair down to nothing."[64]

The story concludes when Yunior, now twenty-three, is washing his clothes up at the mini-mall and happens to run into Nilda. She tells him she misses his brother: "He treated me the best." What else can they really say about their London Terrace mundo, Yunior muses? They then walk back through the old New Jersey neighborhood, and Yunior, "his heart beating fast," has an epiphany: Could they do anything? Even marry and drive off together to the West Coast, as Rafa once desired, and start off in a better California world? But this moment in "Nilda" closes quickly. They are soon back in the downtrodden London Terrace world they have always known. "Remember the day we met?" Nilda asks. Nilda had been wearing a tank top, and Yunior, who wanted to play baseball, made her put on a shirt before he would let her be on his team. "I remember," Yunior the chronicler says. They never speak again. Many years later, Yunior goes away to a local community college and then transfers to Rutgers University, and he discovers "he didn't know where the fuck she went." Indeed, "Nilda" is one of saddest, best-wrought stories that Yunior de Las Casas narrates about the brutalizing inequality of wealth for those like Nilda living in Parlin's London Terrace Apartments; it is sadder still when we recall that in "Nilda," Yunior ingeniously chronicles the two historias of Nilda and the cuento of how Rafa was mourned for as if they were one historia. It "broke my heart,"[65] he writes.

Like Nilda and the multitude of other young, doomed women painted in *This Is How You Lose Her,* Yunior yearns for a better life: it "was the summer when everything we would become was hovering just over our heads. . . . In another universe," he philosophizes, he might have "come out OK, ended up with mad novias and jobs and a sea of love in which to swim, but in this world I had a brother dying of cancer and a long dark patch of life like a mile of black ice waiting for me up ahead." Yunior's captivating "dark patches of life," sucio/a love and loss—like the miles of black ice waiting ahead for him—are at the very heart of Díaz's prodigious book of short stories. Yet there is a deeper feeling still that Yunior stitches together in "Nilda": Yunior madly loves his dying brother, and Nilda's love for the "papi chulo" Rafa makes Yunior fall madly in love with her, too. As he agonizes over Rafa's death, he cannot suppress his memories about the doomed Dominicana Nilda. Every time he runs into her in their London Terrace "nabe," she acts as a painful reminder to him of everything he has lost in his world. At the funeral that he and his mother arrange for Rafa, a toothless, broken Nilda spectrally appears: "What a short skirt she'd worn," Yunior writes, "like maybe she could still convince" the dead Rafa "of something." Virta cannot easily place this forlorn Nilda, and all she can remember about her, she says to Yunior, is that "she was the one who smelled good.... It wasn't until Mami said it that I realized it was true." The story ends with an older but still unwise Yunior remembering his London Terrace world and attempting to make sense of his dark, icy patch of kinks and contradictions—and to chronicle Rafa's loss: "He's gone; he's gone, he's gone."[66] In stories such as "Nilda" from *This Is How You Lose Her*, Yunior cannot offer us an epic or grand anatomy of healthy reciprocity. But in stories like "Nilda" and "The Cheater's Guide to Love," Yunior sheds some refracted, even "razored," light on the matter, illuminating his search for decolonial love.

"The Cheater's Guide to Love" is the most philosophically and aesthetically nuanced of Díaz's short stories. His model of storytelling is nearly autoethnographic, in which the autopoetic reflexivity of postcontemporary narrative is inflected by an ethnographic understanding of writing cultural collectivity. It is also Díaz's most unstinting analysis of Yunior's culpability for a long-standing relationship he did not want to see collapse. Does Yunior's sucio love disrupt? Or does sucio/a love refashion the self in love with the other? In posing these questions, I am also reminded of why "The Cheater's Guide to Love" may be at this stage in his writing career Díaz's most legible story in doubtful praise of decolonial love, where Yunior's lost love is never usefully described or represented. Indeed, Yunior's fiancée is irrevocably lost to him; he has to learn from this "cheater's guide" how to paint the irrevocable loss. Ingeniously, he does this by literally making his fiancée invisible to readers in the cuento's two logics of causality throughout the story. And this is why it takes Yunior six years to grapple with the longitudinal complexity.

Now, the long and short of the cheater's guide: the story is divided by Yunior into the last six "years" of his life in praise of sucio/a love, where he works on his shattered heart on his own terms, wishing to chronicle those heartbreaks that never leave him. The overall scope of the "guide" allows Yunior to both measure this open wound—its own blank or página en blanco—and to simultaneously pose questions about decolonial (sucio/a) love that his imaginative cheater's guide cannot possibly answer through his self-centered, misogynistic, and hypermasculinist focalizations. In other words, if Yunior's serial cheating opened such a gaping hole in his forty-something immigrant heart, what ugly feelings and pain had his cheating carved into his fiancée?

Yunior's "The Cheater's Guide to Love" blasts off with "Year 0"—a ground zero where Yunior's knowledge about love has been hidden in the transparency and worldliness of a naught, a void, a "0." Six numbered years in Yunior's midlife crisis in love and loss follow. "Year 0" chronicles the collapse of Yunior's adult life as a professor of writing in Cambridge, where he feels himself "exiled" from New Jersey and Harlem's conviviality and racial diversity. His fiancée, a successful Latinx lawyer working in New York, has called off their engagement for his rampant "cheating" on her. Yunior, as writer-chronicler, has forgotten to delete the emails still stored on his computer's desktop trash can, and his fiancée finds an archive fever of trashed-but-not-erased emails documenting his love affairs with some fifty women. To begin the real gathering of his broken pieces, Yunior tells his fiancée he will change his cheating ways. He begins his rehabilitation by closing his Facebook account, giving his intended all of his email passwords, and taking her to salsa dance classes so that they can begin living a life from the lovers' perspective of twoness. If Yunior's intended is "immensely sad[dened]" by his reckless infidelities, he tries to apologize for his cheating by blaming it on the patriarchy, his having been groomed for misogyny and cheating by the serial offenses of his Dominican military-police father, and his struggling with the pressures of life as an assistant professor, struggling to move up the university's ranks and secure tenure. "It was the book," he confesses—the great American novel he is in the process of completing in Cambridge—that he blames as the root of all his amorous troubles. Wearied by Yunior's pitiful prevarications, the fiancée finally says what she must: "Ya," as in the Zapatists' "Ya Basta." For Yunior, this is likely a critical scene of ruptured difference. "Ya" suggests he must stop showing up at his fiancée's New York City apartment "at odd hours." "Ya" indicates he must "stop the phoning and emails." "Ya" marks the consequences awaiting the self-absorbed: as his (ex-)fiancée's sister informs him, any more contact, and his intended will put "a restraining order on you."[67]

Sections one through five in "The Cheater's Guide to Love" document Yunior's attempts to reconstruct how he has ended up a cheating, serial shagger. Yunior's cheating life implodes, and he tries to pull himself together by addressing his foolish immigrant infidelities, knavish kinks, and contradictions. Does Yunior's tortured search for decolonial love end up any better at the end of his story? Or is his life one huge, doomed mess in which he can't possess something one could call an authentic human self? Why has he always cheated on his girlfriends, and why does he continue his infidelities? Lola de León? Magda? Veronica? Cassandra? Alma? Paloma? His fiancée? The list is partial.

Whereas the first eight linked stories of *This Is How You Lose Her* are in part Yunior's attempt to fill gaps and contextualize shortcomings—as we might recall, Yunior dutifully and lyrically documents all of his failed commitments and his major infidelities—in his "cheater's guide" he commits to leaving all out in the open, stating that he "needs to finish" his guide to show the reader "what kind of fool I was." This final push for transparency confirms Yunior's slow—though perceivable—development into a self-critical, self-aware individual who sees himself and his life's relatively longue durée as "weak" and "full of mistakes." He even comes to imagine seeing himself as others, including the many ex-novias mentioned in the book, truly see him: as a "typical Dominican man," as Magda says in the book's opening story, "The Sun, the Moon, the Stars." Although he is not only a typical Dominicano male; he is also, importantly, a "sucio" and an "asshole," as his novia puts it. By the time that the forty-something Yunior chronicles the trauma of his younger, high school affair with Miss Lora, he has transformed into a radioactive, "totally batshit cuero"[68] without the discipline to commit himself to his fiancée. A hard truth come too late.

Despite the doom and heartbreak that precipitates it, Yunior's retrospection models how difficult (and necessary) personal excavations of memory and falsehood are to the enterprise of decolonial love. In the story "Miss Lora," for example, an analytic Yunior looks back on his life and asks "Are you your father's son and your brother's brother?" Are all of the de Las Casas men "genetically" "batshit" "sucios"? And, reflecting on his affair in high school, "You wonder if she feels like you do. Like it might be love."[69] Although the hypersexualized sixteen-year-old Yunior does not yet have any real understanding of human caritas or erotic lovemaking,[70] the forty-something writing professor Yunior recalls the ugly "panic" born of his couplings with Miss Lola: "Now it's official." Yunior writes about himself in the third person: "He's the worst of sucios"—just like his abusive and corrupt father, Ramón, who used to take him with him "on his pussy runs," and his monstrous brother, Rafa, who "banged girls in the bed next to his." In listening to all of Yunior's fulsome confessions and revelations about his sexual peccadilloes and pain, another girlfriend, Paloma, grows weary and tells him to stop; she has not the time or the energy to entertain his maldito loco "craziness."[71] Yunior's "The Cheater's Guide to Love," then, attempts to address "the dark patches of black ice" that constitute his downtrodden, immigrant life as well as salvage his swiftly shattered love.

As I have underscored in this chapter, one might understand Yunior de Las Casas's linked stories from *Drown* and *This Is How You Lose Her* as more than linked, rescripted stories that work well on their own terms; indeed, one might interpret them as collective historias working with and against one another, producing an arresting surplus of feeling that transcends the ordinary sum of its parts. This is the wonderful liminality that Díaz's Yunior, in his own Dominican-like island odyssey, spins out in his linked-story collections of a son abandoned on his island by his father and in his novel about a ghettonerd's brief wondrous life—texts in which he chronicles his and his interlocutors' journeys through heartbreak, historias that strive toward human, decolonial love.

To recap: in "Year 1," Yunior documents his journey through the initial stages of heartbreak following the breakup with his intended. In "Year 2," Yunior chronicles how after the worst of his heartbreak is over, he begins to date Naomi, a nurse. But he wrecks this budding relationship, too, when one day he "classlessly" and foolishly asks Naomi if "she is planning to give him some ass anytime soon." In "Year 3," Yunior recounts how he wishes to take better care of himself: he takes up running along the Charles River, and he tries to finish the Great American Novel he is writing. The year ends with yet another doomed love affair Yunior has with a married, upper-class woman from the Dominican Republic who is studying at the Harvard Graduate School of Business. In "Year 4," Yunior's off-and-on law-school girlfriend tells him she is pregnant and that he is the father, adding to what he describes as his life's "berserkería."[72] She moves in with Yunior and takes over his bedroom.

Should we perhaps pursue a Gabriel García Márquez–inspired adaptation and simply write out, like Melquíades at the end of *Cien años de soledad*, the entire section of events that make up "Year 5" of "The Cheater's Guide to Love"? Should we filter our reading of the totalizing, multiply reinforced ending of Yunior's cheater's guide, his fiancée, and himself through Aureliano Babilonia in *One Hundred Years of Solitude*—a character who reads about himself reading about the end of the guide where he is reading about his end as a cheater and cheating and so on? Should we use this to underscore the central philosophical point that Yunior's "guide" makes about the radioactive "half-life" of decolonial love?[73]

Near the story's end, Yunior reads what he calls the "Doomsday Book," a book he has hidden in a folder under his bed. Yunior's "Doomsday Book" consists of "copies of all the emails and fotos" from the cheating life we have been reading about—the dumped and trashed emails Yunior's fiancée found in his computer's trash, printed out, and then "compiled, [bound,] and mailed to [him] a month after she ended it." "Dear Yunior," the ex-intended explains, "for your next book."[74]

Yunior reads "the whole thing cover to cover." "You are surprised," he later writes in the second-person present, "at what a fucking chickenshit coward you are. It kills you to admit it but it's true. You are astounded by the depth of your mendacity." Many days later, after Yunior and Elvis are pulled over by the Boston police for driving while Brown, Elvis encourages Yunior to think seriously about writing "The Cheater's Guide to Love," that is, the doomsday book of emails and photographs his intended sent him. In the months that follow, Yunior obliges: "You bend to the work, because it feels like hope, like grace—and because you know in your lying cheater's heart that sometimes a start is all we ever get."[75]

But why does Díaz's "The Cheater's Guide to Love" underscore the philosophical conclusion in praise of the radioactive "half-life of love" with which Yunior ends his book? Why does Yunior believe that the "half-life of love is forever"?[76] Does this revelation mark the central turning point of Yunior's redemption or mutual reciprocity? Does it mark a passionate restoration expressed in the stories he composes in *This Is How You Lose Her*? When we finish reading Yunior's book of linked stories, do we comprehend that, in addition to creating a greater, cooler distance between himself and his readers, his many second-person stories are not simply focalized cuentos but rather stories he has been writing to his "sucio," cheating, prevaricating self? Díaz calls this his "writer's trick," one of the master techniques he uses through his character Yunior: "It's that the book we are reading is not directly from me. It's Yunior de Las Casas's book. He, at the end of the book, is seen writing the book that now we realize we have been reading."[77]

Before offering answers to some of these key questions, allow me to sketch some of the philosophical frameworks informing my argument—namely, that Yunior's "The Cheater's Guide to Love" lays bare his search for decolonial love. Much of this argument is enabled not only by the critical work of decolonial feminists such as Vargas and Moya that I discussed earlier, but also by the work of a philosopher who praises love as a kind of "communism": the French postexistentialist philosopher Alain Badiou. Badiou's work, which I turn to in the remaining pages, helps unlock Junot Díaz's definition of decolonial love as a kind of revolutionary hope: a praxis of Fanonian reciprocity and mutual recognition. Badiou's writings on the matter help generate fruitful questions about Yunior's life, works, and hang-ups: Does Yunior's hesitation about sucio/a love incite an interpersonal wisdom for himself and others? Can we frame Yunior's search for rehabilitated love as his transformation into a philosopher of quotidian intimacies? Here I turn to Badiou to reframe that fundamental question posed by Yunior, the strung-out sucio sage: why is the "half-life of love" "forever"?

In his *In Praise of Love,* Badiou uses the Western philosophical concepts that he developed in *Theory of the Subject* (1982) and *Being and Event* (1988) to construct a comprehensive theory of love, arguing that our late-capitalist epoch threatens to destroy love's passions, risks, and buoyant unpredictability. Like Yunior's guide to "the half-life of love," Badiou's book—a long 2009 interview with Peter Truong—praises love despite the emergent love market's "cozi[ness]," globalization, and "consumerist permissiveness."[78] Some of the themes that Badiou covers are the interplay of love and politics, love and aesthetics, love and online, commodified, ostensibly risk-free dating agencies.

For Badiou, one of the main features of heteronormative love is its incitation of risk; for Badiou, love is an "event," and events contain volatility and instability. More precisely, an event is a radical break with an existing state of affairs: "It's something that doesn't enter into the immediate order of things."[79] Events are thus totally new, Badiou suggests. The philosopher then looks at the structure of what he calls the "love event" and its transformation into a "truth procedure." With respect to the love event, the site is not to be found in our risk-free, online dating services but rather in our everyday relations with others at school, work, meetings, and political rallies. For Badiou, love is an encounter based entirely on chance—on, as with a Mallarmé poem, a totally random encounter. One cannot forecast love events, for they are often impossible to imagine.

The philosopher also defines love according to the difference between the lovers who, by chance, meet and fall in love. Their different standpoint locations and world epistemologies demand what we might call their pluritopical perspectives. "Love," Badiou writes, "is a decision to live a life . . . no longer from the perspective of One but from the perspective of Two," for "you have two. Love involves two." And it is precisely this critical difference between the two lovers that makes love so risky for Badiou; this riskiness gives love its potential to create "a different way of living in life" and a "desire for an unknown duration."[80]

Briefly, for Badiou, it is through chance encounter that lovers transform the love event into a "truth procedure": a declaration of their love and fidelity to the other. This performative declaration "seals the act of the encounter" and constitutes a lasting "commitment." By naming the void that structures the encounter, one makes oneself vulnerable to the other and risks losing everything. Love is thus "the proof of two." Thus, for Badiou, love has the same structure as "minimal communism," making clear that love and politics concern the emergence of a collectivity rather than the blooming of an individual. "People in love," he concludes, "put their trust in difference rather than being suspicious of it." "To love" is thus "to struggle, beyond solitude, with everything in the world that can animate existence."[81]

Are Yunior's love encounters in *This Is How You Lose Her*—and, in particular, "The Cheater's Guide to Love"—what constitute his truth procedures as a writer? Does it follow that the radioactive "half-life" of Yunior's search is a swiftly shattered love? Can Vargas's incisive feminist reading of sucio/a love serve as our guide to men's uncertainty about reciprocity and help us make some sense of Yunior's manifesto on decolonial love?

I want to suggest here that in "The Cheater's Guide to Love," Yunior dramatizes a questioning man's propensity to provoke—and struggle to end—what he calls the "half-life" of love. What good is it, for Yunior, to theorize sucio/a love? Does it help him understand his manhood? Can Yunior ever be sagacious about sucio/a love? Is part of the point of Yunior's "The Cheater's Guide to Love" to make a philosophical-decolonial claim? To articulate that love is unreliable under systems of the coloniality of power and gender?[82]

All things considered, it should come as no surprise that Yunior de Las Casas cannot tell us that love is judicious. That is just the way that Díaz's thinking about Yunior's "kinks and contradictions" works in his linked texts. But Díaz's decolonial readers can also glean that when Yunior explores his sucio love and masculinist self-formations through writerly, critical self-analysis, he might also be exploring the scene of decolonial love. Yunior's forty-something self-analysis, then, is itself an expression of decolonial love; Yunior's "guide" and linked, rescripted historias in *Drown*, *The Brief Wondrous Life of Oscar Wao*, and *This Is How You Lose Her* might well be, too. Whereas Yunior's critical self-analyses are not exactly models or schemas of love, they are relationships that resemble dreams, fantasies, wish fulfillments, drives, affects, and structures of feeling. When desire becomes speech in Yunior's linked texts, desire and meaning consort amicably while continually displacing each other through aesthetics and figuration.

This is why it is crucial to ground Díaz's search for decolonial love in his fiction in both aesthetic and corporeal terms that emerge, he emphasizes, out of the poetics of the Greater Antilles and the women-of-color feminism in the United States, which he carefully read as a student at Rutgers and Cornell. In his poignant interview with Moya, "The Search for Decolonial Love," Díaz recounts the genesis of his search for decolonial love by first quoting from the insights of the "prayer" with which Frantz Fanon famously ended his classic *Black Skin, White Masks*: "O my body, always make me a man who questions."[83] Like Fanon's prayer, Díaz's personal and intimate questioning of his embodied humanity leads to a decolonial philosophy of embodiment. For Fanon's prayer, as the philosopher Lewis Gordon suggests, "is not to an outside force, a god, but to the anxieties of the embodied self. His body is called upon to release itself from the enmeshed web of social pathologies to the expression that best suits a mature, free consciousness—the embodiment of questioning."[84] Díaz then updates Fanon's prayer of the embodied decolonial self by explaining how US women-of-color writers have supplemented Fanon's work on embodied love. Can Fanon's revolutionary, transcultural revolutionary psychiatry help us define decolonial love as a questioning human enterprise? Like Fanon and the Chicana feminists Gloria Anzaldúa and Cherríe Moraga that Díaz carefully read and cites often in his interviews, Díaz's imaginative writings touch his readers affectively, bodily, and sensually. Words and writing have a charge; they exhibit the color of "quivering flesh" and emblematize what Moraga and Anzaldúa called a "theory in the flesh."[85] Fanon, Moraga, Anzaldúa, and Díaz all critically diagnose societies whose pathological, heteronormative, and raciological cultures have created alienated peoples: Black, Brown, mixed-race, and White.

Whether or not everyone today shares either Fanon's phenomenological-existentialist dialectic of mutual reciprocity and liberation or Anzaldúa and Moraga's bodily theory in the flesh and feminist conocimientos, Díaz suggests that by acknowledging and supplementing Fanon's rich psychiatry of questioning from the body—and by turning to the ways that US women-of-color feminists have, in their theorizing in the flesh, "wield[ed] a genius that had been cultivated of their raced, gendered, sexualized subjectivities"—we can better understand his novel and collection of stories as a search for decolonial love. Like Anzaldúa and Moraga, Díaz attempts to forge in his characters' very "bodies" what he envisions as "a source code" for their own "future liberation." Thus envisaged, decolonial love, for Díaz, involves a radical questioning from the body, a radical decolonial love, with all of its "oppressions," "interpellations," and contrapuntal "liberatory counter-strategies." This is the "quantum leap" that US women-of-color feminists have made since Fanon's decolonial questioning from the body in 1952; this is the astonishing leap that Díaz himself wishes to join and elaborate on with his own fiction. It is the aesthetic, epistemological ground for his enunciations, the very "basis" of his art. As he affirms, "The kind of love that I [am] interested in, that my characters long for intuitively, is the only kind of love that [can] liberate them from that horrible legacy of colonial violence."[86]

Conclusion and Coda

"Monstro" and *Islandborn*

> It seems easier for us to imagine the thoroughgoing deterioration of the earth and of nature than the breakdown of late capitalism; perhaps that is due to some weakness in our imaginations.
>
> FREDRIC JAMESON, *The Seeds of Time*, xii

> William Gibson has famously declared, "The future is already here—it's just not very evenly distributed." Gibson's words have been much on my mind of late. How could they not be?
>
> JUNOT DÍAZ, introduction to *Global Dystopias*, 5

As I have argued throughout this book, Díaz's life and work invite us to grapple with many of the forces shaping postcontemporary experience: migration, trauma, the history of climate change, disaster, and diasporic invisibility. Born in 1968, he was raised by his family in bustling Santo Domingo; he came of age as an immigrant in Central New Jersey, silently dealing with the scars of sexual abuse; he turned to writing to give form to his worlds and visions, steadily crafting his writerly voice; and with the much-acclaimed *The Brief Wondrous Life of Oscar Wao* he helped articulate the new, revelatory, transmodern American literature we today call historical fantasy.[1]

Díaz's writings—and in particular his characters—similarly invite us to consider what it means to live with danger. For instance, *Drown* and *This Is How You Lose Her* make clear that very few of Díaz's characters are ever really safe; most are, instead, always at the risk of slipping off the edge of the world, always poised to vanish into some terrifying "abyss."[2] As I and others have argued, this is a defining precarity: not even neoliberalism, as Deborah R. Vargas has insisted, can wash away the human suciality of Díaz's characters.[3] Such characters, like Oscar de León, are emblematic of many of the major themes in Díaz's fiction. And perhaps most importantly: they are united not only in their suffering but also, as we see consistently, in their courage, their willingness to risk oblivion.

As I have noted in previous chapters, Díaz's career as a writer started relatively early. He completed his MFA at Cornell in his mid-twenties, and his talent and good fortune quickly vaulted him into the highest literary circles in the United States, winning praise from Nobel Prize–winning writer Toni Morrison and President Barack Obama. However, what seems truly lasting about his story thus far is not his Ivy League pedigree or literary fame; rather, it is that as a young writer his experience found expression in a new, highly original negative aesthetics and an emerging Black and Brown Dominican (Afro-Atlantic-Latinx) voice. And although it is impossible to predict how the subjects of his future literary works may change—or if he will continue to experiment with his methods—we can state with some certainty that the essential nature of Díaz's literary, philosophical, and ideological repertoire or signature has been firmly established.[4]

For instance, although the literary devices of symbolic deciphering, negative aesthetics, and decoding—gaps, páginas en blanco, and literal blanks, as I explained in chapter 4—might not be used again on the same scale as in *The Brief Wondrous Life of Oscar Wao*, the diasporic, cosmopolitan, and symbolic directions of his writing are continuing in other forms. Díaz's most recent fiction, as his short story "Monstro" and his picture book *Islandborn* suggest, remains dense with concrete and often monstrous images of the Dominican Republic, Haiti, and Nueva York: his diasporic and apocalyptic emplotments also impel readers to envision larger decolonial meanings. Díaz, ever the boundary pusher, continues to use his idiosyncratic decolonial imagination for great purposes.

And in the pages that follow, I will unpack Díaz's sci-fi cuento "Monstro" and his picture book *Islandborn* before concluding with a brief coda.

Since his early childhood emigration from Santo Domingo, Dominican Republic, to Parlin, New Jersey, Díaz has been fascinated by end-of-the-world stories and outbreak narratives. Since his early days of watching doomsday thrillers on television and reading them in comic books, he has been imagining how the eschatological mode interfaces with his lived experiences in Hispaniola.[5] Because so many near apocalypses had already taken place over the last five hundred years on Díaz's Caribbean home island—including the fukú americanus that incubated modernity and shaped our transmodern world—Díaz identified a critical dystopian project he was game to pursue: "Monstro," a science-fiction historia about the zombification of our planet.

What sparked Díaz's "Monstro" was his sense that privileged populations routinely and intentionally erase many people and places from view, frenetically (re)fashioning the planet without regard for serious "blind spots." What might happen, Díaz wondered, if some global plague or menace were to coalesce in the oscuro, marginalized spaces? Would our unseeing world blind us to the danger? Were these very spaces and geographies also the planet's most mistreated, neglected, and vulnerable areas? How might one envision an "opportunistic infection on the 'global body'"?[6] Like other contagion narratives he had read and seen on screen, Díaz immediately saw what his story's two outbreaks and infections wanted to say, how they would work, and how they would defend themselves from all humans. It was out of these concerns that Díaz's "Monstro" was born.

"Monstro's" break with linear teleological progression—its use of a consciously complicated fábula—reflects Díaz's sense of the fragmentary, elusive quality of individual experiences for those on the receiving end of late capitalism's flows, or what Díaz calls "vulture capitalism."[7] It is not entirely clear when the apocalyptic events in "Monstro" take place, but other signals in the text, such as global post-Fordism and the current planetary crises of Anthropogenic climate change—escalating social, gender, and racial inequalities: radical disruptions of natural and human history—indicate that Díaz's short story is set in the near future decades of the early twenty-first century.[8] Set on the cusp of a catastrophic ecological collapse—an apocalypse of the "third kind"—"Monstro" occurs "a year or so" before "things really go down the chute for humanity."[9] In its objective and prophetic form, this sense of our planet's doom—this take on things gone "down the chute"—guides much of the story's action.

As I have suggested earlier in this book, the apocalyptic geography and timescape of "Monstro," the doom of the pasts and futures to come, also looms in the plots and settings of *The Brief Wondrous Life of Oscar Wao* and the ecologically radiated New Jersey wastelands of *Drown* and *This Is How You Lose Her*. However, it remains to be seen what catastrophic threads will unite Díaz's future work. Will he continue to develop the disjunctions between his Afro-Atlantic Dominican American characters' individual double consciousnesses and the enormity of the planet's ailments? Will Díaz continue to write fictions directly and recognizably concerned with his alter ego Yunior de Las Casas—fiction that is largely based on his own experiences? "Negocios," *Drown*, *The Brief Wondrous Life of Oscar Wao*, and *This Is How You Lose Her*, I've argued, are distillations both of a particular Dominican American odyssey and of his immigrant life in the diaspora; the protagonists of his works to date are like either Yunior de Las Casas or Oscar and Lola de León—on the one hand, embodiments and imaginative transferences of their creator, and on the other, characters driven by some of his pressing aspirations and nightmares. I've argued, too, that many of Díaz's characters, situations, and themes are not projections of his *literal* biography but instead projections of his spiritual and imaginative decolonial biography. His fictional works to date, as I've explicated, draw most directly upon his experiences of impoverishment, suffering, sexual abuse, exile, and alienation in Santo Domingo's Villa Juana or Parlin's London Terrace. Given the intensity of these local and planetary forces, it remains to be seen, after having already developed his own autopoetic ways of dealing with youth, early adulthood, professional dealings, and public life, what new paths that Díaz will pursue in his future writings.

That said, if Díaz's short story "Monstro" (phonetic for "monstruo" in Spanish)[10] is representative of a new path—and if indeed he finds the courage to develop his *New Yorker* science-fiction story into a full-fledged utopian novel—one might go out on a limb and suggest that the general nature of Díaz's imaginative ideological outlook remains almost recognizably the same. To recapitulate: "Monstro" focuses on the ways that late capitalism (or globalization) has penetrated human lives at the deepest level, arguing that the only way one might destroy late capitalism's out-of-control pathology may be to radically treat its host body: our entire planet. Does Díaz's "Monstro" suggest that it is far easier, as Jameson famously put it, to imagine the end of the world than to imagine the end of late capitalism?[11] Is late capitalism and its historical (periodizing) cultural logic of postmodernity so stable and omnipotent that not one of our greatest writers and radical theorists can imagine its ending?

With "Monstro," Díaz extends his world-building techniques to create the sense of a world "way more messed up than ours but equally delusional." He offers a historia so caught up "in the vampire logic of late capitalism," he says, that it cannot stop eating itself alive. Its low-key futurity is at once charming and disarming, and to develop it, Díaz leans heavily on cyberpunk writer William Gibson's pronouncement that "the future is already here—it's just not evenly distributed."[12] Díaz, in line with Gibson, grounds his sci-fi short story with the worst scenarios of our present twenty-first-century ecological and economic disasters, distributing them in Hispaniola and across the planet.

Díaz's tragic awareness of the reciprocal but dialectical demands of what it means to write historical fantasy, sci-fi, and the utopian—to write in the face of the planet's deteriorating climate change; our contemporary culture and society's class, gender, and race inequalities; our economic system's cruel buoyancy; and our planet's increasing local and global femicides—makes his imaginative art so politically and aesthetically relevant today. And in my view, "Monstro" clarifies that historical fantasy and the utopian aspiration are not incompatible discourses but instead imaginative modes cut out of the same cloth. The story's dialectics and details, at once unsettling and hopeful, actually dramatize what Díaz calls "the utopian imagination."[13] This imagination, we might recall, was forged for him during the long 1970s and 1980s—the moment, it has been argued, that the idea of a postcontemporary late-capitalist aesthetics, with its waning of named emotions and history itself, was established.[14] Learning and writing in these formative years, moving between Santo Domingo and Parlin, Díaz effectively joined a generation of writers grappling with the zombification of the planet.

A quick dive: "Monstro" takes place in a future Port-au-Prince, Santo Domingo, and the 234-mile-long border between the Dominican Republic and Haiti, where double fencing and new border controls, including facial-recognition technology, motion detectors, and infrared cameras, are used to keep unauthorized Haitians out of the Dominican Republic.[15] An unnamed nineteen-year-old narrator, an Ivy League Afro-Atlantic Dominican, returns to Santo Domingo the summer after completing his year's coursework at Brown University, arriving in time to care for his ailing mother. While the teenage narrator is on Hispaniola, a "mysterious disease"—"La Negrura," the Blackness—breaks out. Initially, the disease is characterized as a "black mold-fungus blast" and infects only the Haitians who are subaltern, wasted, and immunocompromised. Hey, "Diablo," they'd ask, "que te pasó?" Not initially a lethal outbreak, La Negrura at first paralyzes a few infected Haitians and shocks them into near silence. Díaz's island-afflicted Haitians—stylized by the narrator as "viktims"[16]—do not suffer their infectious disease in solitude but rather are drawn to one another in solidarity. Like Fred Moten, Díaz suggests that "La Negrura," or Blackness itself, fluctuates, circulates, and levitates in a way that is not "articulated" to it. Thus envisaged, Blackness, or "La Negrura" throughout "Monstro," is what Moten says about Blackness as a "disruptive surprise moving in the rich nonfullness of every term it modifies."[17]

Doctors and medical anthropologists mistakenly determine that La Negrura isn't transferred by physical contact; when they dismiss it, local interest in Hispaniola fades. The narrator, a faithful "time witness," captures the motivating factors behind this quick dismissal: La Negrura, after all, was "just a horrible Haitian disease." However, island interest is sparked when the infection no longer remains a "slow leprous spread" and the muted "viktims" begin to exhibit what Díaz characterizes as bizarre symptoms that induce a horrific collective shrieking and wailing: "Shortly after the Silence, the phenomenon that became known as the Chorus began. The entire population simultaneously let out a bizarre shriek—two, three times a day. Starting together, ending together." Meanwhile, medical experts from around the world begin to study Hispaniola's possessed and form "a ninety-nation consortium," flooding "one another with papers and hypotheses,"[18] and all to no avail.

As the narrative unfolds, La Negrura begins to transform the body temperatures of the population it has infected: those with body temperatures lower than normal are described as "blue," and those with normal body temperatures are called "red." When "shit" goes awry, as Díaz's narrator testifies, bloody, homicidal violence and the deportation of Haitians in the Dominican Republic escalates. "Borders are sealed,"[19] and people are massacred in the relocation camps surrounding Port-au-Prince. Camps, as Paul Gilroy reminds us, "always operate under martial rules."[20] Haiti is quarantined as it moves toward the totalitarian condition of permanent emergency. Two hundred thousand Haitians attempt to flee from the outbreak. And, eventually, a US-controlled Air Force bomber squad, based in Puerto Rico, no less—drops a nuke on Port-au-Prince. The resulting pulse "fritz[es]" all "flatline communicators,"[21] freezing all electrical and mechanized activity on the entire island.

Díaz's *New Yorker* sci-fi "Monstro" ends with a second outbreak story in which a hot dead zone fully envelops Hispaniola and "a six hundred-mile chunk of the Caribbean." The second outbreak narrative in "Monstro" describes how the human species itself metamorphosizes: "forty-foot-tall cannibal motherfuckers running loose," wreaking a revolutionary havoc and what Díaz calls "an outbreak of homicidal violence."[22] And Díaz's Afro-Atlantic Dominican Ivy League narrator and his two best friends, Alex and Mysty, prepare to embark for the island's hot zone—an infected borderlands—to see for themselves, Polaroids and Leicas in hand, what the zombification of the planet really looks like.[23]

As with *The Brief Wondrous Life of Oscar Wao*, Díaz's outbreak fiction is embedded in the logic of historical sociologist Aníbal Quijano's concepts of the coloniality of power and Americanity. It fulfills the sci-fi story's impulse to imagine an end of the world by narrativizing a disruptive event and eliciting a revelation—the textbook definition, as Díaz reminds us, of an apocalypse. Very much like the work of ecological disasters, including the uptick in killer floods and hurricanes our planet is currently enduring, the outbreak event in Díaz's "Monstro" not only washes away the surfaces of our culture and society but also, in the secret logic embedded in the cuento's simultaneity, exposes what Díaz has described as "the underlying power structures, the injustices, the pattern of corruption and unacknowledged inequalities"[24] of our planet.

As I have argued in this book, Díaz's decolonial imagination developed largely from his childhood years growing up in Santo Domingo. There he learned that since its invasion by the killer tyrant Colón in 1492, Hispaniola had "ended multiple times." With Almirante Colón's invasion and conquest, "all of the Indigenous peoples were killed," Díaz says. "I mean think about that, the ground zero, the extermination of Indigenous people of the world, begins in Santo Domingo. One world, done." With the transatlantic slave trade that ensued, "millions of Africans were enslaved and imported to work to death. World two, ended."[25] Meanwhile, he suggests, the "Spanish empire abandoned Santo Domingo to focus on Cuba, Mexico, Peru and Colombia. World three, ended." Thus envisaged, Hispaniola is an island "that has apocalypse written in its very bones."[26] And it is this very sense of apocalypse (and its afterlife), emblematized by Hispaniola, that allows Díaz to respond to the Jamesonian provocation via "Monstro"—not only imagining the ending of the world but also envisioning the destruction of the "vulture capitalism" driving the coloniality of power in our present times. The apocalypse in "Monstro" is thus a historia that allows him and his readers "to see ourselves, to take responsibility for what we see, [and] to change" the world we have inherited.[27]

What I have said in this book's previous chapters about Díaz's poetics of indeterminacy and his signature use of negative aesthetics in his linked mature fictions also applies to his best-selling picture book *Islandborn* (2018). A children's cuento, *Islandborn* focuses on a young girl named Lola who was born in the Dominican Republic and lives in Nueva York's Washington Heights. When Ms. Obi, Lola's Asian American teacher, asks the students in her international elementary classroom to "draw a picture of the country you are originally from, your first country,"[28] Lola struggles to paint an image of the island, which she left as a baby. So she asks family members in the Heights about their memories of home. Some relatives share joyful stories of "bats as big as blankets" and more music than air and water; other relatives recall heartbreaking and disquieting moments from the island's dark totalitarian past. Very much like an ethnographer who collaborates with everyday informants to produce a rich cultural description, Lola fills up her notebook, draws pictures, and begins to assemble her own version of the island out of the conflicting fragments of her family's historias.

Like Díaz's short stories and novel, *Islandborn* thus begins with a call to historical consciousness. However, Lola's acute crisis of memory—she had moved from the island when she was just an infant—launches the picture book into an exploration of complex narrative tension, as well as political and ideological concerns that place Lola's cuento firmly alongside Díaz's previous fiction. For in *Islandborn*, as Lola strives to reestablish ties with a place she had "never known," the familiar threads of collective memory, exile, the impossibility of returning home, and the rewinding of history once again draw attention to the distance between a familiar-yet-inaccessible "word" and "an entire world."[29] Throughout the book, Lola spends her time collecting the fragmented historias, recording and painting the spectral and lyrical memories of a diasporic US Latinx community gazing toward the global South. And like Yunior's campus bildungsroman in *The Brief Wondrous Life of Oscar Wao*, Lola constructs her world around the negative aesthetics of the blank space, the página en blanco that appears throughout Díaz's fiction as historia's contested space of articulation.

From the cuento's first figurative melancholy of the island's mangoes—the "fruit that makes you cry"[30]—to the nightmarish threat of the "monster" who ruled the island for decades with an implacable, ruthless brutality, the ruptures in the island history that Lola paints for Ms. Obi are the scars and "heridas abiertas" (open wounds) left by a ruler who controlled nearly every aspect of the island's political, cultural, social, and economic life through a potent mixture of intergenerational sexual violence, intimidation, censorship, and terror. Lola responds to these ruptures through what Díaz has described as the young girl's acts of "imaginative courage," ultimately replacing the cuento's logic of common sense and its "gaps and the silences"[31] with a beautiful story of decolonial feminist solidarity and consciousness.

Díaz thus paints his children's picture book with figures of resistance and re-existence drawn from his own personal symbology and emergent authorial canon. For example, Díaz's young Dominican American Nelson, the class clown, announces to Ms. Obi and her class that in his assignment "there's gonna be a mongoose."[32] Alongside the Black and Brown Atlantic ships, Egyptian pyramids, and waterways of the other students' pictures, Nelson's mongoose not only represents the distinctive animal character systems of the transatlantic world but also recalls Oscar and Beli's supernatural encounters with the Black feminist Mongoose, or baká, in *The Brief Wondrous Life of Oscar Wao*, what Díaz recounted in his novel as "one of the greatest particles" of their metamundo and also "one of its greatest travelers."[33] For Díaz's Lola, who is pictured on the book's jacket, Nelson's mongoose also emerges as a potent symbol for the Dominican clan that helped him intuitively fight against the intense feelings of his sense of homelessness that is diaspora culture's hold on the schoolchildren. Whenever he searched for the possibility of sighting his island mongooses in his Central Jersey childhood, Díaz beautifully recalls in his essay "The Mongoose and the Émigré" that "the distances inside me lessened." More than a voodoo-like baká, however, Nelson's mongoose in *Islandborn* is surely an intertextual planetary traveler for Díaz, "an enemy of kingly chariots, chains, and hierarchies,"[34] and a principal animal character in Díaz's world making. It is not surprising that young Lola invokes the intergalactic super animal after hearing about the vanquishing of "the Monster" from Mr. Mir, the building superintendent: "'*Wao*,'" Lola whispered. "'What happened to the [island's] heroes?'"[35]

When Lola returns to her Washington Heights home, "look[ing] at the blank page in her hands," she begins to paint the island where she was born; her world-making picture book conjures up not only Díaz's own home island but also a diasporic children's practical past, a counterhistoria in which she cannot ever return or rewind the tapes of her exiled family's history.[36] Against the grand narratives of the US culture of imperialism and its anarchy of empire, Lola cobbles together the home island anew. Her simple cuento paints two stories simultaneously: first, the commonsense story of how her island's monster rose and fell, and second, the secret historia that is embedded in the children cuento's very interstices—a history of the Hispanophone Caribbean diaspora in which the island was finally liberated, as Mr. Mir tells Lola, through the collective struggle of "strong smart young women just like [you]."[37] The explosion of colorful paintings and memories that emerges from Lola's ethnographic-like interviews bursts through at the cuento's end (beautifully illustrated by Colombian American artist Leo Espinosa), passing from the cuento's logic of fabulation into the cuento's secret historia of the island's totalitarian dystopia.

BECAUSE OF THE still-developing reach of his Afro-Atlantic Latinx activist and literary vision, Díaz is not just another writer in the United States. He is instead one of the many prime exemplars of the postcontemporary surge of US Latinx literary creativity. This surge's representatives are demonstrably remarkable: the Chicana writers Sandra Cisneros from Chicago, Helena Viramontes from Los Angeles, and Gloria Anzaldúa from Hargill, Texas; the Cuban American writer Oscar Hijuelos from Havana and New York; the Dominican American writer Julia Alvarez from New York and Santo Domingo; the Nuyorican writers Julia de Burgos and Nicholasa Mohr; the spoken word and hip-hop poet, librettist, composer of musicals and mixtapes as well as Broadway actor extraordinaire Lin-Manuel Miranda; and the Dominican American writer from New York Angie Cruz all come readily to mind.[38]

Yet as I have also argued in this book, Díaz belongs to no coterie: he seems to have no interest in abandoning the narrative and generic constraints that he mobilizes. Far from flaunting his differences in taste, aesthetics, and ideology from writers who want to build "realist" worlds to address reality, he often attempts in his imaginative texts to evoke reality through what he calls "unreal worlds." "When I write," he suggests, "what I long for is not more realism or fiction but more courage. That's what I find myself short on and what I have to struggle to achieve in order that the work might live."[39]

By writing about our menacing present through alternative "unreal worlds," Díaz is able to express the problems of his own time with an energy and "courage" unique even among his contemporaries. These problems, experienced firsthand in Santo Domingo and Parlin, could perhaps be represented through the literary technologies of the unreal. The traumas of loss, alienation, coloniality, and the invidious cultures of US imperialism—the very experiences Díaz has explored as writer in diasporic exile—guide his calls for decolonial resistance, re-existence, intercultural solidarity, and courageous affirmation. Each call, each provocation, again articulates our co-implications in a shared tomorrow.

As I have aspired to argue here: perhaps it is this historically informed futurity that might be key to recuperating our communities and decolonizing, at long last, our bodies, our hearts, and our souls.

Coda: "Monstro" in the Age of COVID-19

I recently taught "Monstro" online via Zoom, a few weeks into the spring 2021 quarter and a year into the real-world viral apocalypse of COVID-19. Our group's discussion questions about Díaz's speculative short story, which he published nearly a decade before the current pandemic began, felt unfortunately timely: How does one respond to the end of the world? What happens when a sci-fi story's state of emergency and metaphors of virulence become the realism of the times? Have the terms *virus*, *La Negrura*, and *SARS-CoV 2* fully converged as symbols of realist dystopia? How are readers in the age of COVID-19 interpreting Díaz's literary vision of a terrifying pathogen that both warps *and* reveals Port-au-Prince and Santo Domingo?

My students felt at first that what Díaz's short story, and by extension sci-fi in general, builds seems almost specifically designed to predict the future. I disagreed gently, of course: that would be too high an expectation for any human author or text to meet. What Díaz's "Monstro" does seem to offer, I countered, is a kind of temporal-agential consciousness, a way of orienting oneself to past, present, and future possibility through critical modeling and creative experimentation. Texts like Díaz's, I offered, though not capable of *literally* predicting the future, might help us all contextualize world-historical events—including the current pandemic, which is now one of the most planetary disruptive plagues in recorded history—such that we might actually *build* a future out of calamity. Stories like Díaz's, which both critique and hope in the face of catastrophe, might help us understand, radically, that we're not just living through a terrifying sci-fi narrative but also that we are ourselves sci-fi speculators, writers with the powers of vision and perspective. We all have hopes, I said, and we plan to fulfill them by doing things in the present to shape the future. That's utopian thinking. All the while, we also have fears that keep us from sleeping, that keep us awake in the dead of the night, frightful that everything is disintegrating, falling apart. That's dystopian thinking. And that shapes our hopes and futures, too.[40]

Díaz's "Monstro," like his other fictions, reminds us of these powers and, in effect, of the role that literature can have in helping cultivate communal resilience amid the human-wrought deterioration of the Earth.[41] His writings, drawing from memory, dream, fantasy, and imagination, develop a racially/ecologically attuned hermeneutic that decenters the human and attends to the ethical dimensions of scale, the materiality of the humanimality body, the practical past. Such a past, as Hayden White once framed it, is of course grounded in *doing*, the necessary action of the ethical-political as opposed to the cool detachment of the abstract.[42] The future visions that such practical pasts open up animate what Díaz's writing keeps prompting us to ask: at the end of the world, what are we to do? So too do they remind us, just when all seems lost, of what we might still create together, gently, amid this half-life of love.

Notes

PREFACE

1. Michiko Kakutani, "How Reading Nourished Obama during the White House Years," *New York Times*, January 16, 2017, A15.
2. Masks and Michel Foucault's poetics of "(ab)normalcy" figure prominently across Díaz's short stories, essays, and novel, from the very first story he published as a graduate student, "Ysrael," through *The Brief Wondrous Life of Oscar Wao*, to his most recent autobiographical essays "The Silence" (2018) and "Old Masks, New Face," published in *Radcliff Magazine* in 2020. In *Drown*, for example, Díaz's characters use masks to hide pain, shame, personal identifications, and loss, whereas the actual mask in the story "Ysrael" screens his past and present traumas. In "The Silence," Díaz implies that figurative masks function as a deeply flawed coping mechanism for his own trauma: "The mask was strong. I kept that shit on for over twenty years." Díaz, "The Silence." Briefly, although the masks offer Díaz and his literary characters a short reprieve from their past pains, they come at the cost of forestalling the decolonial love that he and his characters long for. In his novel, Díaz's "the Man without a Face" who appears to Beli and her son Oscar is another representation of the writer's constellation of masked characters. "The Man without a Face" embodies the mask so thoroughly fixed that it leaves him without a face. In *Discipline and Punish*, Foucault outlines three kinds of control that "normalize" the human subject: hierarchy, observation (which normalizes judgment), and examination. All of these are functions of our modern disciplining systems used to correct deviant or abnormal behavior. The examinations of patients or of students combine hierarchical observation with normalizing judgment. They are prime examples of what Foucault calls "power/knowledge" because they combine into a unified whole: "the development of force and the establishment of truth." Foucault, *Discipline and Punish*, 184. Finally, in "Old Masks, New Face," Díaz analyzes his daily seven-month wearing of a medical mask in Cambridge and Boston to help him "slow the spread" and protect those around him in case he was unknowingly infected with the coronavirus. As in his previous literary work, the mask serves as a mirror of his and his fictional characters' dis-

alienation. Returning from a six-month sabbatical in Tokyo, Díaz grapples with his social-distancing alienation in the United States by going on long walks to combat his severe anxiety, often "blowing out" his shoes in the process of walking around his city streets. By also wearing a medical mask "a lot," at first "uncomfortable" until it became "routine," Díaz feels that his face "was cracking open" behind the mask. Just as he explained in "The Silence," Díaz here tells the reader that as a result of having grown up in a poor, immigrant Dominican family during "the Crack Kills '80s" and learning how to survive in his risky environment, he quickly learned how to turn his "face into a mask." In "Old Masks, New Face," he adds that he "learned quick" how to regulate this "facial affect"—weighing when to frown and smile, because everything "you did or didn't do with your face was open to misinterpretation and might put you in [mortal] danger." Díaz ends the essay by reflecting on what it means for him in our global pandemic to wear his medical mask "for large chunks" of his days and months. Although he imagines that "he had no face at all," he realizes that wearing the medical mask during our coronavirus pandemic helped him unveil his "real face," a "face that's free," his "decolonial face." For Díaz, the process of his mask veiling and unveiling is a progress in decolonial self-consciousness. It is a progress from his nonspecular or "irreal" identification to his "real," "free," and "decolonial "identification. In other words, the subject must free itself from the roles it mimics through the alienation imposed on it by the imagos of our culture and society. In "Old Masks, New Face," Díaz truly recognizes himself in his delusionary image and passes from ignorance to knowledge.

3 Through his agent, Nicole Aragi, Díaz said that he accepts responsibility for his behavior, although he denies ever forcibly kissing Zinzi Clemmons. See Alexandra Alter, Jonah Engel Bromwich, and Damien Cave, "The Writer Zinzi Clemmons Accuses Junot Díaz of Forcibly Kissing Her," *New York Times*, May 4, 2018, https://www.nytimes.com/2018/05/04/books/junot-diaz-accusations.html.

4 Alter, Engel Bromwich, and Cave, "The Writer Zinzi Clemmons Accuses Junot Díaz of Forcibly Kissing Her." For a rebuttal of the accusation of Díaz's subjecting an audience member at the University of Iowa to an enraged rant, see Mark Shanahan and Stephanie Ebbert, "Junot Díaz's Case May Be a #MeToo Turning Point," *Boston Globe*, June 30, 2018, accessed July 12, 2018, www.bostonglobe.com/metro/2018/06/30/junot-diaz-case-may-metoo-turning-point/3TMFseenE4G01eVsqbFSxM/story.html. Shanahan and Ebbert's investigative reporting suggested that this accusation against Díaz had "withered under scrutiny."

5 Subramanian, "In the Wake of His Damage."

6 See, for example, Figueroa-Vásquez, *Decolonizing Diasporas*, 79; and Moya, "Dismantling the Master's House," 233.

7 "Open Letter against Media Treatment of Junot Díaz."

8 "Open Letter against Media Treatment of Junot Díaz."

9 Two of the "letter to the editor" Latinx signatories, Linda Martín Alcoff, a professor of philosophy at CUNY and the Graduate Center, and Coco Fusco, a professor of creative writing at the University of Florida and renowned performance artist, then followed up their collective critiques of the media and expanded their support of

Díaz. Alcoff, in a *New York Times* op-ed piece, argued that "we must situate individual perpetrators within larger political systems" and further that "we need to go beyond easy binaries. . . . Sexist behavior, whether slight or severe, is never acceptable or excusable. Sexism in every form weakens liberatory movements, fractures solidarity and exacerbates the oppression of the oppressed." See Linda Martín Alcoff, "This Is Not Just about Junot Díaz," *New York Times*, May 2, 2018, accessed June 4, 2018, www.nytimes.com/2018/05/16/opinion/junot-diaz-metoo.html. Fusco, in several Facebook responses to critics of her signing of the *Chronicle of Higher Education* letter to the editor (the open letter), called out some of the cultural and literary conversations surrounding Díaz. In particular, she found the short-story writer Machado's accusations of Díaz's bullying of her and subjecting her to an "enraged" rant at the University of Iowa to be wholly inappropriate. Fusco, Facebook, May 17, 2018, and June 18, 2018.

Because Latinx and women-of-color feminist theorizing is far from essentialist or homogeneous, the various letters to the editors and Facebook and Twitter responses by Díaz's Latinx feminist supporters were interpreted by a group of other women-of-color feminists as an attempt to silence Díaz's accusers and them. A younger (and less senior) group of women-of-color academics and public intellectuals rebutted the senior Latinx scholars by writing a letter to the editor published in *Medium* magazine. While they did not reject the possibility of reparative justice for Díaz, they argued that "survivor support should take precedence. We must work to build a culture in which all survivors feel that they will be protected by us even if their stories make us uncomfortable." "In Scholarly Debates on #MeToo Survivor Support Should Take Preference" explains that MIT, where Díaz is a professor of writing, had launched an investigation in May 2018 (as required by Title IX) into Díaz's behavior toward women students and staff, and on July 18, 2018, reported that "to date, MIT has not found or received information that would lead us to restrict [Díaz] in his role as a MIT faculty." Shanahan, "Junot Díaz Is Cleared in MIT Investigation." MIT's judgment in favor of Díaz was also echoed by a similar finding by the editors Deborah Chasman and Joshua Cohen of the *Boston Review*, when they announced in early June 2018 that they would retain Díaz as fiction editor after a careful "review of complaints" and interviews with "women of color in the world of literary fiction." Chasman and Cohen, "A Letter from Deborah Chasman and Joshua Cohen." Finally, for a critical and nuanced plea for analyzing Díaz's "complex reality" as a "survivor" of rape and as a culprit of aggressive behavior, see de León, "Reconciling Rage and Compassion."

10 Alcoff, "This Is Not Just about Junot Díaz."
11 During the five-month inquiry, the Pulitzer Board noted that the outside law firm William & Connolly had interviewed dozens of witnesses and analyzed hundreds of pages of documents, as well as audio recordings. The inquiry by the law firm "did not find evidence warranting removal" of Díaz from the Pulitzer Prize board's ranks. See Julia Jacobs, "Junot Díaz Remains on Pulitzer Prize Board after Review of Misconduct Allegations," *New York Times*, November 16, 2018, accessed December 1, 2018, www.nytimes.com/2018/11/16/us/junot-diaz-pulitzer-board.html.
12 For a thorough recapitulation and investigation of the Junot Díaz case, see Deborah Chasman, "Why I Didn't Fire Junot Díaz," forthcoming. Chasman, the editor of the

Boston Review, not only explains in detail why she didn't fire Díaz from his position as the fiction editor of the *Boston Review* but also suggests that after her own investigation of the accusations made against Díaz by Zinzi Clemmons, Maria Carmen Machado, Monica Byrne, and others that if the case against Díaz "wasn't about the truth of the facts, then there was something about the emotional truth of women's experiences that seemed to matter more." Furthermore, Chasman writes that after own investigation at the *Boston Review*, she "found no evidence that [Díaz] had behaved improperly in his capacity as our fiction editor." Throughout her essay, Chasman asks readers why the mainstream media seemed "reluctant to investigate the allegations." Many magazines and almost every major newspaper in the United States published their own versions of the allegations against Díaz, all "with no new information or investigation"; Chasman criticizes the mainstream media for relying on "social media and the reporting by *Buzzfeed*." I am grateful to Chasman for sending me her forthcoming essay and for allowing me to quote from it.

13 Fluck, "Role of the Reader and the Changing Functions of Literature."
14 Díaz, email message to author, March 11, 2011.
15 Díaz, email message to author, March 11, 2011. Díaz's life matters, not only because President Obama somehow felt saved and enthralled by reading his pages during his presidency but also because of the work he has accomplished.
16 For Gumbrecht, the German word *Stimmung* can refer to the fine-tuning of musical instruments, but it also more commonly stands in for the word *mood*, indicating the atmosphere of a particular era or artistic work. Gumbrecht, *Atmosphere, Mood, Stimmung*, 10.
17 The theoretical concept of the decolonial turn has been formulated by the theorist Nelson Maldonado-Torres to refer to what he calls "the activity of decolonization, generally, and to decoloniality, more specifically." Decoloniality makes reference, Maldonado-Torres explains, "to the insurgent optionality of subjects and to the possibilities of decolonization in the *longue durée* of modern/colonial cultures and structures." Defined in this way, decoloniality is "intrinsically related to coloniality, which different from colonialism, refers to the specific matrix of power, being, and knowledge that became a central, if not constitutive, dimension of Western modernity, and its hegemonic civilization project." Maldonado-Torres, "Decolonial Turn," 111. See also Martínez-San Miguel, *Coloniality of Diasporas*.
18 The relationship between literary critic and imaginative writer is invariably a difficult one, and this is why, I believe, Díaz didn't comment on my interpretations of his work.
19 In fact, three years after the allegations against Díaz, his life remains, in Deborah Chasman's words, "partially cut off from the literary world. Where he used to receive forty to fifty invitations for lectures and readings, the number has dropped to one or two, where it remains. . . . Since 2002, *The New York Times Book Review* has invited him to write two pieces." See Chasman's aforementioned forthcoming piece, "Why I Didn't Fire Junot Díaz."
20 My use and understanding of the term *Afro-Atlantic* is indebted to Figueroa-Vásquez's coining of the term in *Decolonizing Diasporas*: "The term 'Afro-Atlantic' rather than 'Black Atlantic' as a way to call attention to how 'Afro' as a prefix has been used

throughout the Caribbean and Latin America to signal or claim afrodescendencia, or Afro-descendance.... I add the prefix 'Afro' to the term 'Hispanic Atlantic' in order to more directly address the ways that Atlantic modernities are contingent upon forms of racialization and domination that are most often expressed through modes of anti-Blackness." Figueroa-Vásquez, *Decolonizing Diasporas*, 3–4.

21 As Roberto Bolaño's character Amando Salvatierra says in *The Savage Detectives*, "I saw our struggles and dreams all tangled up in the same failure, and that failure was called joy." Bolaño, *Savage Detectives*, 336.

22 In chapters 4 and 5, I tarry with Díaz's Fanonian decolonial knowledge of the self and other that is rendered possible by what he calls "sucio" (dirty, unclean) and "sucia" love. As we know, Frantz Fanon, whom Díaz loves to cite in his interviews (when he discusses his notions of decolonial love in his fictions), devoted some five pages to Hegel in *Black Skins, White Masks*. Like Hegel's bildungsroman *Phenomenology of Spirit*, Fanon's work thematizes what the Fanon scholar Irene L. Gendzier called "the long journey of coming to consciousness." Gendzier, *Frantz Fanon*, 22. Through Fanon's reading of Hegel in France, the dialectical tussle for recognition, reciprocity, and struggle became crucial for his thinking about the nature of dependence and the relevance of the other. The Hegelian tussle—the risking of life—that existed between two individuals facing each other and dependent on each other was recognition. But for Fanon, reciprocity needed to take center stage. As I argue in chapter 5, this Hegelian-Fanonian tussle for recognition and reciprocity between Díaz's sucio and sucia lovers is central to his literary-philosophical conceptualization of decolonial love. See Fanon, *Black Skin, White Masks*; and Hegel, *Phenomenology of Spirit*. My thinking on (decolonial) love has also profited from Paul Kottman's *Love as Human Freedom*. For Kottman, the kind of knowledge of the self and the other that is made possible by the experience of love is the basis for what he calls human freedom. The philosophical underpinnings of Kottman's discourse on love are bolstered not only by Hegel but also Judith Butler. Last, but not least, I rely here on Andrew Cole's capacious reading of Hegel's dialectic of reciprocity. See Cole, *Birth of Theory*.

INTRODUCTION

1 See Quijano and Wallerstein, "Americanity as a Concept"; and Saldívar, *Trans-Americanity*.

2 See Roorda, Derby, and González, eds., *Dominican Republic Reader*; Ramírez, *Colonial Phantoms*; and Martínez-San Miguel, *Coloniality of Diasporas*. In her comparative work on Caribbean "archipelagic dislocations," Martínez-San Miguel suggests how buccaneering, pirating, and filibustering were central to Carlos de Sigüenza y Góngora's *Infortunios de Alonso Ramírez* and Pere Labat's *Memoirs of Pere Labat*.

3 Martínez-San Miguel, *Coloniality of Diasporas*. Martínez-San Miguel tracks the intracolonial migrations in the Caribbean. Like her comparative work, Díaz's fiction grapples with ethno-racial gender definitions and linguistic identity as symbolic elements in a collective Afro-Atlantic Dominican identification.

4 In his discussion of Wolfgang Iser's *Act of Reading*, Winfried Fluck refers to the potential

of literature to "expose the limitations" and "deficiencies of accepted systems of thought." For Fluck, a text's "negative aesthetics" allows readers to conceive how the imagination functions in relation to history to create a vision that goes beyond the formulations of realism, modernism, and magical realism to articulate precisely what is absent in each. Fluck, "Role of the Reader and the Changing Functions of Literature," 256.

5 Díaz, *Oscar Wao*.

6 In October 1937, Trujillo ordered the massacre of all Haitians and the descendants of Haitians in the Dominican Republic. The event lasted several days and is often called in the Dominican Republic "El Corte" in reference to the machetes used to kill and maim the victims. Robert Crassweller, Trujillo's biographer, suggests that "the number of those who perished in these October hours will never be known with accuracy.... Estimates range from a low of 5,000 to a high of 25,000." Crassweller, *Trujillo*, 156. According to Haitian American novelist Edwidge Danticat, "October 2015 marks the 78th anniversary of what Haitians call the 1937 'Parsley' Massacre, where thousands of Haitians and their Dominican-born descendants were murdered in what the US Ambassador in Santo Domingo, R. Henry Norweb, described as 'a systematic campaign of extermination.'" According to Megan Jeanette Myers, the term *Parsley Massacre* refers to the test that Dominican soldiers forced upon Haitians and Haitian Dominicans: they would hold up some parsley and ask what it was. Because the Spanish word for parsley, *perejil*, "is difficult for Haitians to pronounce as Kreyol pronounces the letter 'r' differently," this test was used by Dominican soldiers to determine the Haitians' fate. "Those who could not roll the 'r' were killed." Moreover, Myers notes, Díaz thematizes the 1937 massacre in one of his paratextual footnotes (225n27) to *The Brief Wondrous Life of Oscar Wao*. Myers, "Dos rayanos-americanos Rewrite Hispaniola," *Confluencia: Revista Hispánica de Cultura y Literatura* 32, no. 1 (2016): 168–81.

On October 3, 2015, Border of Lights—a group of artists, activists, students, teachers, and parents—commemorated as well as brought light to the current situation with a virtual Twitter and Facebook chat. This was an opportunity to ask questions from activists and leaders of the Dominican Haitian diaspora as well as those who are working on the ground.

7 A group of American literary critics named Díaz's *The Brief Wondrous Life of Oscar Wao*, an ingenious take on the life of an overweight Dominican-American nerd, as the best novel of the twenty-first century to date. BBC Culture, the arts section of the international BBC site, polled "several dozen" US critics to find the greatest novels written so far this century, with 156 novels in all named by experts from papers including the *New York Times*, *Time*, *Newsday*, *Kirkus Reviews*, and *Booklist*. Díaz's first novel was top of the list for the most critics, said BBC.com, "with the Latin author's Pulitzer-winning creation Oscar Wao, a 'hardcore sci-fi and fantasy man desperate to get laid,' compared to Philip Roth's Portnoy and John Updike's Rabbit by one respondent...." See Alison Flood, "*The Brief Wondrous Life of Oscar Wao* Declared 21st Century's Best Novel So Far," *Guardian*, January 20, 2015, accessed February 22, 2015, www.theguardian.com/books/2015/jan/20/brief-wondrous-life-of-oscar-wao-novel-21st-century-best-junot-diaz.

8. Stavans, ed., *Norton Anthology of Latino Literature*, liii.
9. Díaz, *Oscar Wao*, 1, 4.
10. Díaz, *Oscar Wao*, 1.
11. Danticat, "Junot Díaz by Edwidge Danticat."
12. Díaz, *Oscar Wao*, 184, 20, 43, 190.
13. Gloria E. Anzaldúa coined the term *autohistoriateoría* to describe women-of-color's interventions into and transformations of traditional Western autobiographical forms.
14. Díaz, *Oscar Wao*, 55, 60, 72, 127, 142, 159.
15. Díaz, *Oscar Wao*, 180.
16. Díaz, *Oscar Wao*, 2–3n1.
17. Díaz, *Oscar Wao*, 224–25n27.
18. Díaz, "Q&A."
19. The late Oscar Hijuelos was the first US Latinx writer to win the Pulitzer Prize, for his 1989 novel *The Mambo Kings Play Songs of Love*.
20. In his iconic 1963 essay on Richard Wright, "Black Boys and Native Sons," Irving Howe claimed that "the day *Native Son* appeared American culture was changed 'forever.'" In much the same way that Howe envisioned Wright's text reinvigorating African American, Anglo American, and modernist traditions, thereby integrally connecting the US Black experience to the experiences of other cultures, I argue that the day Junot Díaz's *The Brief Wondrous Life of Oscar Wao* appeared likewise changed forever American culture by broadening the interconnections of Afro-Atlantic Latinx, Anglo American, Greater Antillean, and Latin American experiences, along with transmodernist literary traditions, at the dawn of the twenty-first century. Howe, "Black Boys and Native Sons," 100.
21. For a similar argument about Latin American literature (after 1987) as an exemplary world literature, see Hoyos, *Beyond Bolaño*.
22. Díaz, email message to author, March 28, 2013.
23. Quoted in Ch'ien, *Weird English*, 212.
24. Sam Anderson, "Junot Díaz Hates Writing Short Stories," *New York Times Magazine*, September 27, 2012, accessed October 20, 2012, https://www.nytimes.com/2012/09/30/magazine/junot-diaz-hates-writing-short-stories.html.
25. Danticat, "Junot Díaz by Edwidge Danticat."
26. Anderson, "Junot Díaz Hates Writing Short Stories."
27. Díaz, email message to author, June 28, 2015.
28. Jeffrey Pierre, "Authors Junot Díaz, Edwidge Danticat Decry Dominican Efforts to Remove Haitians," *Miami Herald*, June 24, 2015, accessed July 12, 2015, www.miamiherald.com/news/nation-world/world/americas/haiti/article25460362.html.
29. Pierre, "Authors Junot Díaz, Edwidge Danticat Decry Dominican Efforts to Remove Haitians."
30. Pierre, "Authors Junot Díaz, Edwidge Danticat Decry Dominican Efforts to Remove Haitians."
31. Pierre, "Authors Junot Díaz, Edwidge Danticat Decry Dominican Efforts to Remove Haitians."

32 Sibylla Brodzinsky, "Dominicans of Haitian Descent Fear Mass Deportation as Deadline Looms," *Guardian*, June 16, 2015, accessed September 23, 2015, https://www.theguardian.com/world/2015/jun/16/dominican-republic-haiti-deportation-residency-permits.

33 Díaz, *Oscar Wao*, 273.

34 See Ramírez, "Great Men's Magic."

35 Field notes, September 3, 2015, Santo Domingo, Dominican Republic.

36 See Julia Alvarez's historical novel about the Mirabal sisters and their murders: *In the Time of the Butterflies*.

37 Ch'ien, *Weird English*, 222, 322n41.

38 DiTrapano, "A Brief History of Junot Díaz," 100–102, 130.

39 Ch'ien, *Weird English*, 223.

40 Ch'ien, *Weird English*, 222.

41 Junot Díaz, email message to the author, March 28, 2013. Díaz, it turned out, needed one class to complete an additional degree in history.

42 See Junot Díaz's opening remarks for his conversation with Toni Morrison at the New York Public Library on December 13, 2013. Díaz, "Conversation with Toni Morrison."

43 O'Neill, "Junot Díaz on the Game of Fiction and Intimacy."

44 The only story from Junot Díaz's 1995 MFA thesis that did not appear in *Drown* was "London Terrace." It appeared under the new title "Invierno" in *This Is How You Lose Her*, published in 2012.

45 See the interview with Díaz's literary agent Nicole Aragi. Lee, "Literary Culture Clash." Like the late literary superagent Carmen Balcells—who represented the Latin American Boom writers Gabriel García Márquez, Julio Cortázar, and Mario Vargas Llosa, among others—Aragi is one of the US's most influential literary agents of our times. Many of the US writers she represents and works with are radical experimenters—Edwidge Danticat, Colson Whitehead, and Alexander Heiman—but first they are young, brash, and smart, and they have all been awarded MacArthur Fellowships. Briefly, Aragi—via Libya, Lebanon, London, and New York—has become known for the range and diversity of the US literary voices she has helped introduce to world literature. As she notes, Junot Díaz was "a very early client" who helped her emerge as an agent: "I feel like [Díaz's] first story collection [*Drown*] was when editors began, for the first time, returning my calls with any speed." Aragi, quoted in Lee, "Literary Culture Clash."

46 Díaz, "Global Dystopias, Critical Dystopias."

47 National Institute of National Policy.

48 Quoted in Lavanya Ramanathan, "Artists in the Age of Trump," *Washington Post Magazine*, July 27, 2017, www.washingtonpost.com/lifestyle/magazine/the-cauldron-of-creation/2017/07/26/f83a3bfa-61ba-11e7-84a1-a26b75ad39fe_story.html.

49 Glass, "Literary Giants Junot Díaz and Toni Morrison on Their Refusal to Surrender."

50 For a trenchant analysis of Díaz's activism at Rutgers and Cornell (and beyond), see Dávila, "Against the 'Discursive Latino.'"

51 Grandin, "Junot Díaz Just Lost an Award for Speaking Out against the Dominican Republic's Anti-Haitian Pogrom."

52 Grandin, "Junot Díaz Just Lost an Award for Speaking Out against the Dominican Republic's Anti-Haitian Pogrom."

53 In a Univision interview on November 12, 2015, Díaz, alas, responded to Selman by saying, "I'm not going to be silenced because someone's taking away an award. I've been in this country how many years now, and when people want to silence you, they'll give you a fuetazo [lash]." Díaz, who described himself as "nothing big, just a small-time writer," was not worried about Selman's weak threat because he had been through worse. Simón, "Junot Díaz Won't Back Down from Criticizing DR's Immigration Crisis."

54 See Iser, *Act of Reading*; and Fluck, "Role of the Reader and the Changing Functions of Literature."

55 Moya, "Search for Decolonial Love, Parts I and II."

56 According to Díaz, "The footnotes are there for a number of reasons; primarily, to create a double narrative. The footnotes, which are in the lower frequencies, challenge the main text, which is the higher narrative. The footnotes are like the voice of the jester, contesting the proclamations of the king. In a book that's all about the dangers of dictatorship, the dangers of the single voice—this felt like a smart move to me." O'Rourke, "Questions for Junot Díaz."

57 Díaz, *Oscar Wao*, 20–21n6.

58 McGurl, *Program Era*.

1. "WRESTLING WITH J. R. R. TOLKIEN'S LORD OF THE RINGS"

1 To read the fruits of our Junot Díaz Symposium, see Hanna, Harford Vargas, and Saldívar, eds., *Junot Díaz and the Decolonial Imagination*. Our book considers how Díaz's writing illuminates the world of Latinx cultural expression and trans-American and diasporic literary history. Interested in conceptualizing Díaz's decolonial imagination and his radically reenvisioned world, the contributors show how his aesthetic and activist practices reflect a significant shift in American letters toward a hemispheric and planetary culture. We examine the intersections of race, Afro-Latinidad, gender, sexuality, disability, poverty, and power in Díaz's work. Collectively, we situated Díaz's writing in relation to American and Latin American literary practices and reveal the author's activist investments. The book concludes with Paula M. L. Moya's interview with Díaz. The entire interview is cited frequently in this book: Moya, "Search for Decolonial Love, Parts I and II." I want to give my mil gracias to my co-editors, Jennifer Harford Vargas and Monica Hanna, and to the contributors, Glenda R. Carpio, Arlene Dávila, Lyn Di Iorio, Junot Díaz, Ylce Irizarry, Claudia Milian, Julie Avril Minich, Paula M. L. Moya, Sarah Quesada, Ramón Saldívar, Silvio Torres-Saillant, and Deborah R. Vargas, for their splendid contributions to the book and for helping me hone in on the complexities and joys of Díaz's imaginative work. When Duke University Press sent Díaz copies of our book on January 15, 2016, he posted a photograph and generous comments on his Facebook page. One couldn't dream of a better critical reception.

2. Stanford's CCSRE Kieve Lecture aims to bring scholars, public intellectuals, and imaginative writers from around the world to Stanford to address (post)contemporary issues in race, ethnicity, and power.
3. Díaz, "Dark America." Subsequent quotations attributed to Díaz in this section all come from this address unless otherwise noted.
4. For the best essay on how the imaginative work of Thomas, Mohr, Laviera, and River helped Díaz hear the roar of Black Spanglish, see Carpio, "Now Check It."
5. Díaz, *Oscar Wao*, 3, 225.
6. In Kant's iconic *Observations on the Feeling of the Beautiful and the Sublime*, specifically section 4, the Enlightenment philosopher compromised himself by "associating the figure of the 'Negro' with stupidity and connecting differences in color to differences in mental capacities." Gilroy, *After Empire*, 9. Other scholars have also disputed Kant's racial "common sense": Eze, *On Reason*; Mignolo, *Darker Side of Western Modernity*; and Elden and Mendieta, eds., *Reading Kant's Geography*.
7. Li, *Signifying without Specifying*.
8. For a critique of the turn in US literary studies toward a "surface reading," see Moya, *Social Imperative*.
9. Díaz, "Dark America."
10. See McGurl, *Program Era*. Pointing to the proliferation of degree-granting "creative-writing programs" in US universities after World War II, McGurl requires us to take into account the institution of the university and the processes of the democratization of higher education in the United States to fully understand the nature of contemporary literature. Throughout his 2012 Stanford lecture, Díaz used Quijano's iconic concept of "coloniality" to ground his claims about the speculative genres in general and J. R. R. Tolkien's *Lord of the Rings* in particular. In his theory of coloniality and the coloniality of power, Quijano gives a new hemispheric (and planetary) meaning to the historical periodization known as "colonialism," particularly as it was explored during the Cold War together with the social movements of decolonization. For Quijano, coloniality emerged with European (Iberian, British, French) invasions of the Américas—of Abya Yala, Tawantinsuyu, Anáhuac, and, of course, Díaz's home island known in the Renaissance as Hispaniola (now Haiti and the Dominican Republic)—that is, with the formation of the Caribbean and the Américas. For Díaz, Quijano's concept of coloniality is a decolonial idea and project that can be traced back to the sixteenth century. For an overview of Quijano's project, see Quijano, "Colonialidad y modernidad/racionalidad" and "Coloniality of Power, Ethnocentrism, and Latin America."
11. Foucault, *History of Sexuality*, 93.
12. For Tolkien, the function of his heroic fantasy fiction is "consolation." If one reads his essay "On Fairy-Stories," one finds that, for him, central to heroic fantasy is "the Consolation of the Happy Ending." He pretends that such a happy ending is something that occurs miraculously, "never to be counted on to recur." It's no surprise that this kind of heroic fantasy is mostly conservative. Tolkien's essay is as close as it gets to the manifesto of most modern fantasy, and he has defined fantasy as literature that overindulges the reader rather than challenging them. Tolkien, "On Fairy-Stories," 12.

13   Suvin, *Metamorphoses of Science Fiction*; Jameson, *Archaeologies of the Future*. In *Positions and Presuppositions in Science Fiction*, Suvin's definition of science fiction's novum (as opposed to fantasy or the speculative genres) became a staple of its field imaginary: science fiction's necessary and sufficient conditions are "the presence and interaction of estrangement and cognition, and whose main device is an imaginative framework alternative to the author's empirical environment." Suvin, *Positions and Presuppositions in Science Fiction*, 37. By *cognitive novum*, Suvin means "a central and informing concern for conceiving and discussing radically new views and understandings of human relationships and potentialities." Suvin, *Positions and Presuppositions in Science Fiction*, 30. Suvin believes that science fiction is potentially the best literary form in which to explore cognition, partly because what he calls "paraliterature" subverts and reverses the dominant literary forms, which are under the hegemony of Western imperialism.
14   Suvin, *Metamorphoses of Science Fiction*, 408.
15   Tally Jr., "Places Where the Stars Are Strange."
16   Quoted in Peeters, *Derrida*, 1.
17   Okie, "Mil Máscaras."
18   Okie, "Mil Máscaras."
19   Díaz, *Oscar Wao*, 209.
20   Dávila, "Against the 'Discursive Latino,'" 41.
21   Mark Kurlansky, Junot Díaz, Edwidge Danticat, and Julia Alvarez, letter to the editor, *New York Times*, October 31, 2013, https://www.nytimes.com/2013/11/01/opinion/two-versions-of-a-dominican-tale.html.
22   Edwidge Danticat and Junot Díaz, "The Dominican Republic's War on Haitian Workers," *New York Times*, November 20, 1999, accessed January 31, 2000, http://www.nytimes.com/1999/11/20/opinion/the-dominican-republic-s-war-on-haitian-workers.html.
23   Quoted in Dávila, "Against the 'Discursive Latino,'" 42.
24   Dávila, "Against the 'Discursive Latino,'" 39.
25   For a definition of what Foucault means by "normalization" in the classical age, see his *Discipline and Punish*. Briefly, "the regime of disciplinary power," for Foucault, "imposes . . . the constraint of a conformity to be achieved. [It] traces the limit that will define difference in relation to all other differences, the external frontier of the abnormal. [It] compares, differentiates, hierarchizes, homogenizes, excludes. In a word, it normalizes." Foucault, *Discipline and Punish*, 182–83. For a provocative discussion of Foucault's notions of power and the ways of identifying and countering normalization in our postcontemporary context, see Gratton, "Foucault's Last Decade."
26   O'Rourke, "Questions for Junot Díaz."
27   Hao Ying, "Writing Wrongs," *Global Times*, April 14, 2010, accessed May 5, 2010, https://www.globaltimes.cn/content/522054.shtml.
28   Díaz, "Stanford Humanities Center Presidential Lecture." Subsequent quotations attributed to Díaz in this section come from this address unless otherwise noted.

2. DÍAZ'S PLANET MFA

1. Duany, *Blurred Borders*, 7.
2. Davis, *Magical Urbanism*. According to Davis, US Latinx immigrants from the global South are, in the most fundamental sense, struggling to reconfigure the cold frozen geographies of the old spatial orders in the global North to accommodate a "hotter," more exuberant, and magical urbanism.
3. Throughout this chapter and my book as a whole, I follow Hayden White's arguments that the historical past is a theoretically motivated construction, existing only in the books and articles published by professional historians. By contrast, the "practical past," for White, is basically the past as most people who are not professional historians perceive the past. In White's words, it refers to those "notions of the past which all of us carry around with us in daily life and which we draw upon, willy-nilly and as the best we can, for information, ideals, models and strategies for solving all the practical problems. . . . This is the past of memory, dream, and desire as much as it is of our present situation." White, *Practical Past*, 14.
4. See Levitt, *Transnational Villagers*; Portes and Bach, *Latin Journey*; and Roger Waldinger, *Between Here and There*.
5. See Vanessa Pérez-Rosario's *Becoming Julia de Burgos* for a superb way of understanding how the mass culture industry and media often flatten "all Latinos and Latinas into one group." Pérez-Rosario, *Becoming Julia de Burgos*, 27.
6. I have profited from Josh Kun's US-Mexico borderlands theory of the "más allá" in border sonics. Just as the spatial politics of mobility in the border sonics of the "Sonideros" thematize the possibility of the "más allá," so, too, I believe that Díaz's politics of the aquí and allá in his diasporic cuentos link up the transnational spaces of the here and there for Yunior de Las Casas's literary imaginary. Kun, "Allá in the Mix."
7. In an email, Junot Díaz recalled how in his MFA thesis, "Negocios," and his first book, *Drown*, the depictions of New Jersey were inspired by the artist and critic Robert Smithson and his iconic essay "Monuments of Passaic." Like Smithson's Passaic, which emblematized a late-industrial banality, Díaz said his stories were interested in the "elsewheres" of Santo Domingo and Parlin as opposed to the "somewheres" of New York City. Díaz, email message to author, March 2, 2020. See also Smithson, "Entropy and New Monuments."
8. According to a document discovered in Valladolid by Spanish historians, Columbus, "as governor and viceroy of the Indies, imposed iron discipline on the first Spanish colony in the Américas, in what is now the Caribbean country of Dominican Republic. Punishments included cutting off people's ears and noses, parading women naked through the streets and selling them into slavery." See Giles Tremlett, "Lost Document Reveals Columbus as Tyrant of the Caribbean," *Guardian*, August 7, 2007, accessed September 1, 2007, www.theguardian.com/world/2006/aug/07/books.spain.
9. See Ortiz, *Cuban Counterpoint*. The neologism *transculturation* is Ortiz's substitute for the sociological term *acculturation*. He used his term "to express the highly varied phenomena that have come about in Cuba as a result of the extremely complex transmutations of culture." Ortiz, *Cuban Counterpoint*, 97–98.
10. Roorda, Derby, and González, eds., *Dominican Republic Reader*, 6.

11 Harford Vargas, "Dictating a Zafa."
12 See Quijano for an overview of his theory of the coloniality of power: "Colonialidad y modernidad/racionalidad" and "Coloniality of Power, Ethnocentrism, and Latin America." For María Lugones, the coloniality of gender involves the process of how "the colonized became subjects" in the first modernity—that is, "the tensions created by the brutal imposition of the modern, colonial gender system." Lugones, "Toward a Decolonial Feminism," 743.
13 In a March 2, 2020, email, Díaz paid tribute to Robert Smithson's Passaic, New Jersey's "center with no center." Instead, Smithson's New Jersey, as Smithson remarked in "Monuments of Passaic," was an "abyss" that echoed "a cliched idea of infinity" and perhaps "the secrets of the universe." See Smithson, "Monuments of Passaic," 50.
14 In recent decades, advances in cosmology have suggested the existence of a metamundo, or multimundo. A theory called inflation suggests that in the instant after the Big Bang, space inflated quickly and then expanded, creating the bubble and space we now live in. Similar big bangs occurred many times, creating numerous other bubbles of space—the multimundo. Díaz's metamundo is full of metaphorical bubbles of space and black holes that leak radiation. This is why the half-life of love is forever for him.
15 For an account of postwar American literary minimalism, see McGurl, *Program Era*. According to McGurl, Raymond Carver and his Pacific Northwest Carver country—thematized in his short stories—rose to "prominence in the late 1970s and 1980s under the banner of the ordinary, the modest, the minimal, and the real." McGurl, *Program Era*, 279–80. The hegemonic politics of literary minimalism is, McGurl argues, that of "white culture," the silencing, by shame, of the voice of the lower-middle-class worker, trained to shut up and do his shit job." McGurl, *Program Era*, 315.
16 The US Census Bureau determines poverty thresholds. The poverty threshold for a family of four in the 1980s was $13,465. See US Bureau of the Census, "Poverty Thresholds."
17 For a history of the Dominican diaspora, see Nwosu and Batalova, "Immigrants from the Dominican Republic in the United States."
18 According to Ruth Wilson Gilmore, men and women of color in the racist US prison industrial state have a greater "vulnerability to a premature death" than do White people. Gilmore, *Golden Gulag*, 28.
19 Díaz, "Introduction," xii.
20 Andrews, *Roberto Bolaño's Fiction*, 71.
21 Piglia, "Theses on the Short Story," 63, 64.
22 Díaz, "Introduction," xiii, xiv.
23 Díaz, "Introduction," xv, xvi.
24 Díaz, "Negocios," 68, 72, 75.
25 Díaz, "Negocios," 83, 70.
26 Díaz, "Negocios," 71, 84.
27 Díaz, "Negocios," 84.
28 Díaz, "Negocios," 84, 76, 79.
29 Díaz, "Negocios," 82, 84.

30 Díaz, "The Silence."
31 "State of the Art: Junot Díaz, Author."
32 "State of the Art: Junot Díaz, Author."
33 See Cosgrove and Daniel, eds., *Iconography of Landscape*; Engler, *Designing America's Waste Landscapes*; Latour, *Politics of Nature*; and Miller, *Fat of the Land*.
34 "Global Landfill May 2010 Fact Sheet."
35 Throughout Díaz's linked books, Yunior de Las Casas learns how to manipulate the signs of his metamundo (of the environment in Parlin's London Terrace and Santo Domingo, of society, of decolonial art, culture, and aesthetics) that will allow him to translate his impressions into language and thus create his texts. More importantly, these signs (through imaginative transfer) are crucial for Díaz's readers, for the signs allow them to gain practical knowledge of their pluriversal world.
36 Díaz, "Negocios," 15, emphasis added. These six sentences were dropped from "Ysrael" in *Drown*. When I wrote to Díaz to inquire why he had edited them out, he answered: "As for the missing lines this is a sore spot with me to this day. My editor Julie Grau pushed me to cut it and dumbly I gave in—the version I had in the final [manuscript] had the brother in the hospital dying but the editor felt it would bring up too many questions since I never mentioned that he was sick etc. Dumb rookie error on my part. I want to put those lines back in one day." Díaz, email message to author, May 18, 2020.
37 Appadurai, *Modernity at Large*, 4.
38 Marina De Chiara, email message to author, November 18, 2019.
39 William Faulkner famously wrote that "the past is never dead. It's not even past." Faulkner, *Requiem for a Nun*, 73.
40 Díaz, "Negocios," 85.
41 Díaz, "Negocios," 91.
42 Díaz, "Negocios," 92. Penny dreadfuls—what Ramón de Las Casas loves to read in "Negocios"—were a type of British fiction in the nineteenth century that featured lurid serial stories appearing in parts over a number of weeks, each part costing a penny. Ramón read dime novels, the American equivalent: self-contained dime novels, ten cents apiece.
43 Díaz, "Negocios," 95, 88.
44 Vega, *Memoirs of Bernardo Vega*.
45 Sánchez Korrol, *History of Puerto Ricans in the U.S.*
46 Díaz, "Negocios," 90, 94.
47 Trouillot, *Silencing the Past*, 2.
48 Díaz, "Negocios," 105, 104.
49 Díaz, "Negocios," 107.
50 Díaz, *Drown*, 70.
51 Díaz, "Negocios," 105.
52 Lowe, *Immigrant Acts*, 13–14.
53 Díaz, "Negocios," 108.
54 Díaz, "Negocios," 111.
55 Díaz, "Negocios," 113, 114, 119.

56   Díaz, "Negocios," 121.
57   Díaz, "Negocios," 121.
58   White, *Practical Past*, 61.
59   Pratt, "Short Story."
60   Wallace, "Fictional Futures and Conspicuously Young."
61   Díaz's short story "London Terrace" originally appeared in his 1995 Cornell University MFA thesis, "Negocios," but it was published by the author under a new title, "Invierno," in *Glimmer Train* in 1996. "Invierno" was then included in Díaz, *This Is How You Lose Her*, 119–46.
62   Díaz, "Negocios," 50.
63   Díaz, "Negocios," 48.
64   Díaz, "Negocios," 52. My analysis here has profited from Ginetta Candelario's "Hair-Race-ing: Dominican Beauty Culture and Identity Production." As Candelario suggests, pelo malo, "tightly coarsed, soft, and kinky," as opposed to pelo bueno, "silky, straight, wavy," are racial connotations: "the notion of pelo malo implies outright denigration of African-origin hair textures, while pelo bueno exalts European, Asian and indigenous hair textures." Candelario, "Hair-Race-Ing," 128.
65   Díaz, "London Terrace," in "Negocios," 56, 67.
66   "Global Landfill May 2010 Fact Sheet," 1.
67   See Bowker, *Memory Practices in the Sciences*.
68   Díaz, "London Terrace," in "Negocios," 58.
69   Engler, *Designing America's Waste Landscapes*, 30.
70   Jameson, *Postmodernism*, 411–12.
71   Latour, *Politics of Nature*, 24.
72   Díaz, "London Terrace," in "Negocios," 61, 67.
73   See Tolkien, "On Fairy-Stories."

3. DÍAZ'S PLANET POC (PEOPLE OF COLOR)

1   Quoted in Barbara Stewart, "Outsider with a Voice," *New York Times*, December 8, 1996, https://www.nytimes.com/1996/12/08/nyregion/outsider-with-a-voice.html.
2   Díaz, "Junot Díaz Writes about Moving to Brooklyn."
3   Díaz, email message to the author, August 30, 2015. In response to my questions about his first book deal with Grau, Díaz said: "oh yes i received a two-book deal for both drown and the novel that would be oscar wao. 150k for both if i remember right. 15 percent for agent. 35 percent for taxes. and then of course the 11 years it took me to deliver the novel meant that it amounted to not a lot at the end."
4   Quoted in Stewart, "Outsider with a Voice."
5   Díaz, *Drown*, 14, 5, 6.
6   Díaz, *Drown*, 4, 15.
7   Díaz, *Drown*, 8, 6, 9, 12, 10.
8   Díaz, *Drown*, 14, 18, 14–15.
9   See John Riofrio's incisive essay "Situating Latin American Masculinity."
10 Levinas, *Alterity and Transcendence*, 23, 25.

11 Pérez, "Racial Spills and Disfigured Faces in Piri Thomas's *Down These Mean Streets* and Junot Díaz's 'Ysrael,'" 93.
12 Quoted in Stewart, "Outsider with a Voice."
13 Díaz, *Drown*, 32.
14 Díaz, *Drown*, 27, 23.
15 Díaz, *Drown*, 41, 43.
16 Díaz, *Drown*, 70.
17 Díaz, *Drown*, 84.
18 Díaz, *Drown*, 69, 71.
19 Díaz, *Drown*, 73. In *Oscar Wao*, Belicia de León, early in the novel, describes her son Oscar "as our little Porfirio Rubirosa." Díaz, *Oscar Wao*, 12. In the fourth footnote, Yunior explains why Rubiroso was so famous: "In the forties and fifties, Porfirio Rubirosa—or Rubi, as he was called—was the third-most-famous Dominican in the world (first came the Failed Cattle Thief, and then the Cobra Woman herself, María Montez). A tall, debonair pretty boy whose 'enormous phallus created havoc in Europe and North America,' Rubirosa was the quintessential jet-setting car-racing polo-obsessed playboy, the Trujillato's 'happy side' (for he was indeed one of Trujillo's best-known minions)." Díaz, *Oscar Wao*, 12n4.
20 Lowenthal, *Dominican Intervention*.
21 Lowenthal, *Dominican Intervention*, 78, 88.
22 Lowenthal, *Dominican Intervention*, 132, 139.
23 See Saldívar, "Conjectures on 'Americanity' and Junot Díaz's 'Fukú Americanus' in *The Brief Wondrous Life of Oscar Wao*."
24 Díaz, *Drown*, 87.
25 Díaz, *Drown*, 106.
26 Díaz, *Drown*, 92, 99.
27 Díaz, *Drown*, 93.
28 Díaz, *Drown*, 94. In an interview with Hilton Als, Díaz claims that his story "Drown" is an allegory of what it means to be a pato. Als, "Junot Díaz."
29 Díaz, *Drown*, 103, 104.
30 Díaz, *Drown*, 104, 105.
31 Díaz, *Drown*, 107.
32 Irizarry, "This Is How You Lose It," 150.
33 Díaz, *Oscar Wao*, 68.
34 See Orr, ed., *Joyce, Imperialism, and Postcolonialism*.
35 Joyce, *Ulysses*, 4, 46.
36 Jameson, *Antinomies of Realism*, 152–53.
37 Díaz, *Drown*, 112.
38 Díaz, *Drown*, 113.
39 Díaz, "MFA vs. POC."
40 Personal interview with Stephanie Vaughn (professor of English at Cornell University), April 2014.
41 Lamar Herrin, "Novels."
42 Gumbrecht, "Roads of the Novel," 614.

43 McGurl, *Program Era*, 131.
44 McGurl, *Program Era*, 131, 364.
45 Díaz, "MFA vs. POC."
46 Díaz, "MFA vs. POC." Whereas it is true that Díaz throughout his personal essay frames his critique of the Cornell MFA program in its strictest institutional formation, his essay might have grappled more with the presence of Black scholars in Cornell's Department of English such as Hortense Spillers, who was teaching African American literature at the time Díaz was there. I thank this manuscript's Anonymous Reader 1 for this insight. When I queried Paula M. L. Moya, who was a PhD student in Cornell's English Department when Díaz was an MFA graduate student, about the department's engagement with the teaching of race and writers of color, she informed me that the teaching of race and writers of color in Cornell's English Department at that time was "inadequate." Personal Interview with Paula M. L. Moya (professor of English at Stanford University), October 2020.
47 Díaz, "MFA vs. POC."
48 Díaz, "MFA vs. POC."
49 Cortázar, *Cronopios and Famas*, 25.
50 Díaz, *Drown*, 143.
51 Moya, "Dismantling the Master's House," 241. See also Marisel Moreno's "Debunking Myths, Destabilizing Identities."
52 Díaz, *Drown*, 14, 143, 144.
53 The "name 'racial imaginary' is meant to capture the enduring truth of race: it is an invented concept that nevertheless operates with extraordinary force in our daily lives, limiting our movements and imaginations." Díaz thus represents Yunior's teenage naïveté, misogyny, and failure to understand truly feminist intersectionality and shows us how we must understand, as Rankine emphasizes, that our "perceptions, resources, rights, and lives themselves flow along racial lines that confront some of us with restrictions and give others uninterrogated power. These lines are drawn and maintained by white dominance even as individuals and communities alike continually challenge them." Rankine et al., "About the TRII."
54 Alim, Ibrahim, and Pennycook, eds., *Global Linguistic Flows*, 2.
55 Díaz, *Drown*, 147.
56 Moya, "Dismantling the Master's House," 244.
57 Riverhead Books 1996 catalog.
58 David Gates, "English Lessons," *New York Times*, September 29, 1996, accessed January 20, 2010, www.nytimes.com/1996/09/29/books/english-lessons.html.
59 Quoted in Stewart, "Outsider with a Voice."

4. BECOMING "OSCAR WAO"

1 See writer Alan Moore, artist Dave Gibbon, and colorist John Higgins's limited comic-book series *Watchmen*. Díaz's Yunior de Las Casas draws inspiration from Oscar de León's love of reading *Watchmen* for its sense that "nothing ever ends" in the prose of the world's graphic novels. Moore, *Watchmen*.

2. Hall, "Cultural Identity and Diaspora."
3. Ciabattari, "21st Century's 12 Greatest Novels."
4. For the San Francisco adaptation of Díaz's novel, see Campo Santo Theatre Company, *Fukú Americanus*, performed at the Intersection for the Arts, Glide Memorial Church, San Francisco, 2011. For the New York one-person adaptation of Díaz's text, see Eloise Thoron, *Oscar Wao*, performed at the American Player Theatre in New York, 2012.
5. Moya, "Search for Decolonial Love, Parts I and II."
6. Díaz, "The Brief Wondrous Life of Oscar Wao."
7. Díaz, *Oscar Wao*, 177.
8. Carpio, "Now Check It"; Ch'ien, *Weird English*; Sommer, *Bilingual Aesthetics*.
9. Saldívar, "Chiste Apocalyptus."
10. See Hanna, "'Reassembling the Fragments'"; and Lanzendorfer, "Marvelous History of the Dominican Republic in Junot Díaz's *The Brief Wondrous Life of Oscar Wao*."
11. Julie Minich, "Cheater's Guide to Disability."
12. Harford Vargas, "Dictating a Zafa."
13. Valderrama, "Reading for the Anthropocene."
14. Although I generally agree with Gónzalez's strong reading of the ways in which Díaz's narrators Yunior, Lola, and Oscar insist on "alternatives to de-colonizing strategies of resistance to power with emancipatory ends" in the novel, my hesitation with her argument is that she relies too exclusively on Michel Foucault's Eurocentered theorizations of power and biopolitics to explain Díaz's representation of the dictator Trujillo. See González, "'Only Way out Is In,'" 280. As we know, many of the terms that come from Foucault's work—*biopolitics, governmentality, technologies of the subject*, and so on—are historically particular and geographically specific to France and its environs. Sometimes these keywords and concepts are then transplanted into analyses of other times and places in uncritical ways. This is why I think Díaz carefully supplements his playful allusions to Foucault in his critical metacommentaries on *The Brief Wondrous Life of Oscar Wao* with explicit references to Americanity theorists of the coloniality of power and the coloniality of gender such as Aníbal Quijano and María Lugones.
15. See Ramírez, "Great Men's Magic."
16. Di Iorio Sandín, "Laughing Through a Broken Mouth in *The Brief Wondrous Life of Oscar Wao*."
17. See Torres-Sallaint, *Intellectual History of the Caribbean*; García Peña, *Borders of Dominicanidad*, 84–85; Figueroa-Vásquez, *Decolonizing Diaspora*, 26–27; and Graulund, "Generous Exclusion."
18. For a few examples, see Grosfoguel, *Colonial Subjects*; Lao-Montes, *Contrapunteos diaspóricos*; Pérez-Rosario, *Becoming Julia de Burgos*; Martínez-San Miguel, *Coloniality of Diasporas*; and Figueroa-Vásquez, *Decolonizing Diaspora*.
19. Objects of literary and cultural study that once called for a postcolonial frame of analyses—studies that chiefly focused on nineteenth-century and twentieth-century colonization and decolonization practices in the global South—now demand a focus on colonization and decolonization in the Américas, which originated centuries

earlier in the transoceanic adventures of the Spanish colonialists from which Junot Díaz's concept of the fukú americanus (or "the Curse and Doom of the New World") and Aníbal Quijano's theory of coloniality were born. See Hanna, Harford Vargas, and Saldívar, introduction to *Junot Díaz and the Decolonial Imagination*.

20 Díaz's fiction largely works through the four interlinked domains of the human experience that Aníbal Quijano theorized as the coloniality-of-power matrix in the New World Américas: (1) the appropriation of land, the exploitation of labor, and the control of finance by the Iberians; (2) the control of authority; (3) the control of gender, ethnicity, and race through the Iberians' classification and reclassification of the planet's population; and (4) the control of subjectivity and knowledge through an epistemological perspective from which the Iberians articulated the meaning and profile of the matrix of power that placed them at the top of the hierarchy and Indigenous and African subjectivities and epistemologies at the very bottom. See Quijano, "Colonialidad y modernidad/racionalidad" and "Coloniality of Power and Eurocentrism in Latin America."

21 Moya, "Search for Decolonial Love Parts I and II."
22 Moya, "Search for Decolonial Love Parts I and II."
23 Díaz, email message to author, July 31, 2016. Although Díaz met often with professors Silvio Torres-Saillant and Arlene Dávila, his colleagues at the time at Syracuse, he told me that he "never burdened them with what I was working on because they were both so prolific and so busy and because I'm always afraid of being a bother."
24 "New Faces of 1996."
25 Díaz was chosen as one of the *New Yorker*'s "20 Under 40" in 1999.
26 Brues, "Chasing the Whale."
27 Quoted in Brues, "Chasing the Whale."
28 Brues, "Chasing the Whale."
29 Quoted in Brues, "Chasing the Whale."
30 Junot Díaz, "Had I Been 70, I Would Have Been Dead," *Guardian*, November 8, 1996, A27.
31 O'Rourke, "Questions for Junot Díaz."
32 Danticat, "Junot Díaz by Edwidge Danticat."
33 In 1895 the Marquis of Queensberry filed legal charges against Oscar Wilde, accusing him of having "posed as a sodomite" and of having solicited the Marquis's son, Lord Alfred Douglass, to commit sodomy and "other acts of gross indecency." In the Wilde's sex scandal's aftermath, as literary scholar Ed Cohen suggests, Britain's bourgeoisie attempted to "legitimate limits for the sexual deployment of the male body" and to define "a form of male sexuality . . . [and] ensure standards for the health" of their nation. Cohen, "Writing Gone Wilde," 801. For comprehensive surveys of the Oscar Wilde trial and the critical appraisals of Wilde as a "dandy" and "decadent," see Cohen, "Typing Wilde"; and Gagnier, *Idylls of the Marketplace*.
34 For the underpinnings of this argument, see Foucault, *History of Sexuality*. As we know, Foucault analyzed the positive strategies that enveloped the body within particular historical discursive dispositifs.
35 Díaz, *Oscar Wao*, 176, 181, 170, 264.

36   For Díaz's proselytizing comments on his love of the "beauty" and "extraordinary mutability and generativity" of the short-story form—"there's never a week when [he] doesn't have a story [he's] just reading kicking around inside [his] head," see the introduction he wrote for *The Best American Short Stories 2016*, xii.
37   Díaz, "The Brief Wondrous Life of Oscar Wao," 100, 101, 104, 103, 106.
38   Díaz, "The Brief Wondrous Life of Oscar Wao," 106.
39   Sandín Di Iorio, "Laughing Through a Broken Mouth in *The Brief Wondrous Life of Oscar Wao*."
40   Díaz, "The Brief Wondrous Life of Oscar Wao," 107, 108.
41   Díaz, "The Brief Wondrous Life of Oscar Wao," 113, 115.
42   The twenty-seven days in Santo Domingo that Oscar pursues and woos Ybón is a reference to Toni Morrison's *Beloved*, when Sethe experiences twenty-seven days of freedom in the novel.
43   Díaz, "The Brief Wondrous Life of Oscar Wao," 117.
44   According to Evelyn Ch'ien, Oscar's exclamation of the beauty at the end of *The Brief Wondrous Life of Oscar Wao* (in contrast to Conrad's obscurity, "The horror, the horror," at the end of *Heart of Darkness*) is what she calls "infinitely clear about what it is describing: Oscar's one experience of sexual intercourse." Ch'ien, *Weird English*, 228. Melissa M. González adds that Oscar's final words at the end of *The Brief Wondrous Life of Oscar Wao*, "The beauty! The beauty!," "have two referents: the inverted allusion to Conrad and Oscar's delight at the "little intimacies" that he finally experienced in a sexual relationship before his death. Taken together, the references signal the ultimate and interdependent importance of both the text and the body, reminding us that Oscar's experience of pleasure is shaped by his reading life, be it Conrad or The Fantastic Four." Díaz, *Oscar Wao*, 335; González, "'Only Way out Is In,'" 291.
45   Díaz, introduction to *Beacon Best of 2001*, xii.
46   Piglia, "Theses on the Short Story."
47   Andrews, *Roberto Bolaño's Fiction*, 40.
48   O'Rourke, "Questions for Junot Díaz."
49   O'Rourke, "*Brief Wondrous Life of Oscar Wao*."
50   To approach the making or becoming of Junot Díaz's *The Brief Wondrous Life of Oscar Wao* as a well-wrought *New Yorker* story or script and then to see how Díaz radically rescripted the story into one of this century's best epic novels is to begin by establishing how the genres he turned to—the extended short story or novella and the novel—have to be specified relationally in terms of each other. Was his *New Yorker* scripting of "The Brief Wondrous Life of Oscar Wao" noteworthy for its economical unity of effect? Was it a loosely extended script structured like a dream?
51   O'Rourke, "Questions for Junot Díaz."
52   O'Rourke, "Questions for Junot Díaz."
53   Díaz, "The Brief Wondrous Life of Oscar Wao," 99, 100.
54   For a history of the *New Yorker* magazine as a sociocultural institution of literary taste, from its founding in 1925 to 1987, see Yagoda, *About Town*. However, Díaz's Yunior de Las Casa's unapologetic use of the N-word or racial slurs in the *New Yorker* stories raises other concerns about his "style." Although US modernists like Heming-

way, Stein, Dos Passos, and Faulkner all used the N-word in their canonical texts as a slur and as a disparaging word for Blacks, it is not enough for Díaz—I believe—to say, as he has often remarked in defense of the criticisms of Yunior's use of the N-word, that "there's a difference between representing a thing and endorsing it." Nor is it enough for him to explain that Yunior uses the N-word in *The Brief Wondrous Life of Oscar Wao* because "that's how Central New Jersey kids (like Yunior) talked back then." The term is a slur—understood by all—and Díaz the writer and philologist has to be more attuned to the disparagement. The question remains why Yunior de Las Casas feels more at home in using his N-bombs, whereas Oscar de León would never use the slur. For Díaz's response to the criticism of Yunior's use of the N-word, see his discussion with Danticat, "Junot Díaz by Edwidge Danticat," and his Colorlines presentation, Díaz, "Keynote Speech."

55 Yagoda, *About Town*, 12.
56 Danticat, "Junot Díaz by Edwidge Danticat."
57 Díaz, "The Brief Wondrous Life of Oscar Wao," 108, 100, 106.
58 Ch'ien, *Weird English*, 228.
59 Danticat, "Junot Díaz by Edwidge Danticat."
60 Danticat, "Junot Díaz by Edwidge Danticat."
61 Danticat, "Junot Díaz by Edwidge Danticat."
62 Brues, "Chasing the Whale."
63 Brues, "Chasing the Whale."
64 Brues, "Chasing the Whale."
65 Brues, "Chasing the Whale."
66 Brues, "Chasing the Whale."
67 The best studies of this type of allegorical rewriting of Díaz's novel are Barradas, "El realismo cómico de Junot Díaz"; Bautista, "Comic Book Realism and Genre in Junot Díaz's *The Brief Wondrous Life of Oscar Wao*"; and Mahler, "Writer as Superhero."
68 Fluck, *Romance with America*? According to Fluck, negative aesthetics exemplifies literature's potential to expose the ideological and hegemonic deficiencies of our accepted systems of thought.
69 Díaz, *Oscar Wao*, 225.
70 De Maeseneer, *Seis ensayos sobre narrativa dominicana contemporánea*, 117.
71 O'Rourke, "Questions for Junot Díaz." Díaz continues: "The footnotes are like the voice of the jester, contesting the proclamations of the king. In a [novel] that's all about the dangers of dictatorships, the dangers of a single voice—this felt like a smart move to me."
72 Genette, *Paratexts*, Kindle edition.
73 Carpio, "Now Check It," 275, 280.
74 Alvarez, *A Wedding in Haiti*, 177.
75 For a rich comparative reading of Julia Alvarez's *In the Time of the Butterflies* and Díaz's *The Brief Wondrous Life of Oscar Wao*, see Preziuso, "Rewriting the Caribbean Nation."
76 Saldívar, "Historical Fantasy, Speculative Realism, and Postrace Aesthetics in Contemporary American Fiction," 586.
77 Tolkien, *Fellowship of the Ring*, 276, 176, 373.

78   See, for example, "Beowulf: The Monsters and the Critics," a 1936 lecture by J. R. R. Tolkien that was published in *The Monsters and the Critics and Other Essays*.
79   Lanzendorfer, "Marvelous History of the Dominican Republic in Junot Díaz's *The Brief Wondrous Life of Oscar Wao*," 128.
80   Díaz, *Oscar Wao*, 2n1, 224.
81   Lanzendorfer, "Marvelous History of the Dominican Republic in Junot Díaz's *The Brief Wondrous Life of Oscar Wao*," 138.
82   Díaz, *Oscar Wao*, epigraph.
83   Saldívar, "Historical Fantasy, Speculative Realism, and Postrace Aesthetics in Contemporary American Fiction," 586.
84   For a discussion of the classics and the reception of Caribbean writers among themselves, see Greenwood, *Afro-Greeks*.
85   See Ramírez, "Great Men's Magic."
86   Danticat, "Junot Díaz by Edwidge Danticat."
87   Díaz, "Dark America."
88   The Enlightenment, in other words, displaced our impulses for wonder and magic. In the West, the Enlightenment—Díaz argued—"knocked the shit out of wonder," and then these very impulses "began to express" themselves in and "find a home" in "the sub-sub-zeitgeist in comic books, movies, and the speculative genres." Díaz, "Dark America."
89   Díaz, "Dark America."
90   Throughout his 2012 Stanford Kieve Lecture, Díaz employed Quijano's concept of coloniality in discussing the speculative genres in general and Tolkien's *Lord of the Rings* in particular. Quijano endowed the historical periodization known as colonialism, particularly as it was explored during the Cold War together with the social movements of decolonization, with new meaning. For Quijano, coloniality emerged with European invasions of the Américas—Abya Yala, Tawantinsuyu, Anáhuac, and, of course, Díaz's home island, known as Hispaniola during the Renaissance (now Haiti and the Dominican Republic). Coloniality, for Díaz, is a decolonial idea and project stemming from the sixteenth century.
91   Díaz, "Dark America."
92   See Fimi, *Tolkien, Race and Cultural History*.
93   Díaz, "Dark America."
94   According to Dixa Ramírez, Díaz's mongoose is reminiscent of a baká identity in the novel, for it is a large animal, usually black, of the dog family and with eyes glowing. The baká is an imaginary hybrid animal that is created by a sorcerer that enables people to become dogs, cats, pigs, and goats to amass wealth. Ramírez, "Great Men's Magic," 6. For an autoethnographic-like essay on Díaz's memories of the juron or mongoose in the Dominican Republic, see "The Mongoose and the Émigré," where he compares the mongoose "brought over to the Caribbean in chains" to "his own people." The Mongooses "managed to slip empire's bonds and become free, and flourish." In other words, throughout Díaz's text, if the mongoose is a "baká," Yunior casts it as feminine, Black, and all-powerful. Díaz, "The Mongoose and the Émigré." In fact, in an interview with Lu Sun, Díaz suggests that the baká, a shape-shifting being, is "the

guiding metaphor of the novel, which means, I wanted it to take on different forms with each reading." Sun, "Every Novel Is a New Country," 250.
95 Díaz, *Oscar Wao*, 301.
96 Díaz, *Oscar Wao*, 327.
97 Díaz, *Oscar Wao*, 107.
98 The implied reader, for Wolfgang Iser, does not refer to an individual, to the empirical, or to the ideal reader of the literary text, but to its strategies and structures of communication, or its "guiding devices" that exert a certain control over the reader's response. Iser, *Act of Reading*.
99 Díaz, *Oscar Wao*, 132n17. In footnote 17, Yunior confesses that his facts in previous drafts of the novel we are reading are occasionally fast and loose: "In my first draft Samaná was actually Jarabacoa. But then my girl Leonie, resident expert in all things Domo, pointed out that there are no beaches in Jarabacoa. Beautiful rivers, but no beaches."
100 This is why literature truly matters, and this is how I teach it.
101 Iser, *Act of Reading*, 10.
102 Iser, *Act of Reading*, 34, 14, 85, 87.
103 Iser, *Act of Reading*, 33, 97.
104 Iser, *Act of Reading*, 158.
105 Fluck, "Why We Need Fiction," 367.
106 Fluck, "Imaginary and the Second Narrative," 241.
107 Iser, quoted in Fluck, "Imaginary and the Second Narrative," 241.
108 Fluck, "Imaginary and the Second Narrative," 242.
109 Fluck, "Imaginary and the Second Narrative," 242.
110 Comité Clandestino Revolucionario Indígena-Comandancia General del Ejército Zapatista de Liberación Nacional, "Cuarta Declaración de la Selva Lancandona."
111 Fluck, "Imaginary and the Second Narrative," 256.
112 Díaz, *Oscar Wao*, 5.
113 The neologism *global South* goes back to the 1970s. It is entangled with other terms that post–World War II modernization discourse and revolutionary social movements generated to describe the economic and political goals of capitalist and socialist modernity. I am using the term throughout this chapter to replace older neologisms like the 1950s terms *first world*, *second world*, and *third world*. My sense of the roots and routes of the term *global South* has profited from Arif Dirlik's incisive essay "The Global South."
114 Moretti, "Conjectures on World Literature."
115 Cohen, "Narratology in the Archive of Literature," 59.
116 Quijano and Wallerstein, "Americanity as a Concept."
117 Moretti, "Conjectures on World Literature."
118 Díaz, *Oscar Wao*, 15, 1.
119 Saldívar, *Trans-Americanity*.
120 Quijano and Wallerstein, "Americanity as a Concept," 550.
121 Quijano and Wallerstein, "Americanity as a Concept," 550. Briefly, throughout their essay "Americanity as a Concept," Quijano and Wallerstein closely identify colonial-

ity, ethnicity, and racism with capitalism and with capital's consolidation in Europe and the Américas from the fifteenth century to the eighteenth century. Moreover, coloniality constitutes itself, they propose, through the Iberian and British classification and reclassification of the planet's population—hence, the concepts of culture and ethnicity become foundational in this task of classifying and reclassifying. As they put it, "all the major categories" of ethnicity and race "into which we ethnically divide today in the Américas and the world (Native Americans or 'Indians,' Blacks or 'Negroes,' Whites or 'Creoles'/Europeans, *Mestizos* or other names given to a so-called 'mixed' category)—all these categories did not exist prior to the modern world-system," and, by extension, prior to the invention of Americanity. Additionally, the so-called ideological state apparatuses such as the church and the universities served to manage and control such classifications. Thus envisaged, the Iberian and British coloniality the colonists brought with them from Europe's empires figured an epistemological and standpoint positionality from which they signified the ethnic and racialist absolutist meaning of this new matrix of power. From my perspective, one could therefore conceptualize Quijano and Wallerstein's concept of the coloniality of power as sharing axes of both domination and of subjectification, articulated with labor, exploitation, and capital. Ethnicity and coloniality from the perspective of Americanity delineated what the authors call "the social boundaries corresponding to the division of labor. And it justified the multiple forms of labor control, invented as part of Americanity: slavery for the Black Africans, various forms of coerced cash-crop (*repartimiento*, *mita*, peonage) for the Native Americans, indentured labor (engagés) for the European working class." Americanity established a series of institutions and worldviews that sustained the system, and it invented all of this out of the *American crucible.*

122 My understanding of our planet's "historico-structural heterogeneity" is indebted to the historical sociologist Aníbal Quijano. In his reading of Miguel de Cervantes's *Don Quixote*, he argues that one of the greatest "epistemological and theoretical lessons" thematized for us in the novel is when Don Quixote attacks the hegemonic power of the windmills. It is here, he suggests, where one can see the following: "The historico-structural heterogeneity, co-presence of historical times and structural fragments of forms of social existence, of varying historical and geo-cultural origins, are the primary modes of existence and movement of all society and all history. Not as in the Eurocentric vision, with its radical dualism paradoxically associated with homogeneity, continuity, unilinearity and one directional evolution; in a word: "progress." Because it is power—and thereby power struggles and their shifting balances—that articulates the heterogeneous forms of social existence produced at different historical moments and in distant spaces, brings them together and structures them within one and the same world, in a concrete society, into historically specific patterns of power. This is also precisely the issue regarding the specific space/time that today we refer to as Latin America. Due to its historical and structural constitution as dependent on the current pattern of power, it has been constrained all this time as the privileged space where the coloniality of power plays itself out. And since in this pattern of power the hegemonic mode of production and control of knowledge is Eurocentrism, it is

a history replete with combinations, contradictions and (non)encounters that are analogous to those that Cide Hamete Benengeli could identify in his own space/time. By its very nature, the Eurocentric perspective distorts (when it does not block altogether) perception of our social and historical experience, all the while taking its own time to admit that the latter is real. It operates in today's world, and particularly in Latin America, in the same way that the chivalrous life did in Don Quixote's view of things. As a consequence, our problems cannot be perceived in any other way but through this distorted form" (Quijano, "Of *Don Quixote* and Windmills in Latin America," 14–15).

123 Díaz, *Oscar Wao*, 285.
124 Pérez, *Decolonial Imaginary*.
125 Díaz, *Oscar Wao*, 330.
126 Grafton, *Footnote*, 233, 235.
127 Díaz, *Oscar Wao*, 3.
128 Díaz, *Oscar Wao*, 21.
129 Díaz, *Oscar Wao*, 6.
130 Díaz, *Oscar Wao*, 1.
131 Díaz, *Oscar Wao*, 3, 2.
132 Díaz, *Oscar Wao*, 285.
133 Fanon, *Les damnés de la terre*.
134 Díaz, *Oscar Wao*, 6.
135 Trouillot, *Silencing the Past*, 115.
136 Díaz, *Oscar Wao*, 209.
137 Díaz, *Oscar Wao*, 2–3.
138 In Fernando Ortiz's classic *Cuban Counterpoint: Tobacco and Sugar*, the Cuban social scientist writes that "I have chosen the word transculturation [instead of acculturation] to express the varied phenomena that came about in Cuba as a result of the extremely complex transmutation of culture that has taken place here." Ortiz, *Cuban Counterpoint*, 98.
139 Díaz, *Oscar Wao*, 6.
140 Enrique Dussel uses the neologism *transmodernity* as an alternative to the Eurocentric formulation of *postmodernity*. As he sweepingly puts it, "The overcoming of cynical managerial reason (planetary administration), of capitalism (as economic system), of liberalism (as political system), of Eurocentrism (as ideology), of machismo (in erotics), of the reign of the white race (in racism), of the destruction in nature (in ecology), and so on presupposes the liberation of diverse types of the oppressed and/or excluded. It is in this sense that the ethics of liberation defines itself as transmodern (because the postmoderns are still Eurocentric)." Dussel, "Beyond Eurocentrism," 19.
141 Díaz, *Oscar Wao*, 57.
142 Díaz, *Oscar Wao*, 78, 257, 261, 121.
143 Davis, *Magical Urbanism*, 54.
144 Díaz, *Oscar Wao*, 167.
145 Díaz, *Oscar Wao*, 276.
146 Díaz, *Oscar Wao*, 243, 215, 217, 219.

147 Díaz, *Oscar Wao*, 239.
148 Gómez-Barris, *Where Memory Dwells*, 77.
149 Díaz, *Oscar Wao*, 240, 243.
150 See Abrams, *Natural-Supernaturalism*.
151 Díaz, *Oscar Wao*, 275n24, 245.
152 Saldívar, "Chiste Apocalyptus," 380.
153 Díaz, *Oscar Wao*, 245, 243.
154 Jameson, *Archaeologies of the Future*, 66.
155 Díaz, *Oscar Wao*, 275, 277.
156 Césaire, "Notebook of a Return to the Native Land," 67.
157 Díaz, *Oscar Wao*, 49.
158 Depestre, *Bonjour et adieu à la négritude*, 144–45.
159 Mignolo, *Local Histories/Global Designs*. According to Mignolo, border thinking in the Américas is "the consequence of the power differential that constitutes the colonial difference." Mignolo, *Idea of Latin America*, 10.
160 Agamben, *State of Exception*.
161 Gómez-Barris, *Where Memory Dwells*, 6.
162 See Robben and Suárez-Orozco, eds., *Cultures under Siege*; Vargas Llosa, *Feast of the Goat*; Manz, *Paradise in Ashes*; Gómez-Barris, *Where Memory Dwells*; Nelson, *Reckoning*; and Derby, *Dictator's Seduction*.
163 Díaz, *Oscar Wao*, 323, 324.
164 Díaz, *Oscar Wao*, 325.
165 Díaz, "Becoming a Writer."
166 Díaz, "Becoming a Writer."
167 Díaz, "Conversation with Toni Morrison."
168 Díaz, *Oscar Wao*, 181.
169 In an earlier version of this chapter's conclusion, I hadn't sufficiently addressed Yunior de Las Casas's callous, saturnine, and pitiless representations of Oscar de León's fulsome life of struggle, but in reflection I found Yunior's near absencing of Oscar in writing their bildungsroman to be part of his general coldheartedness. For an analysis of the limitations of Yunior's literary imagination and the state of fantasy in Díaz's text, see Saldívar, "Historical Fantasy, Speculative Realism, and Postrace Aesthetics in Contemporary American Fiction."

5. JUNOT DÍAZ'S SEARCH FOR DECOLONIAL LOVE

1 See Alberto Fuguet and Sergio Gómez's anti-magical realism and postmodern manifesto, where they suggest that "Latin America is, irremediably, MTV América Latina, that luminous consensus, that wave that colonizes our consciousness by way of cable, and which is being converted, in the grandest version of Bolivar's dream imaginable into a unity, more concretely and effectively than a hundred treaties or international forums ever could." Fuguet and Gómez, eds., *McOndo*, 15–16.
2 Als, "Junot Díaz."
3 In other words, Díaz's *The Brief Wondrous Life of Oscar Wao* and his two rescripted

books of short stories, *Drown* and *This Is How You Lose Her*, are not exactly the same as the texts and the most recent cheater's guide to love that the near-forty-something-year-old Yunior de Las Casas writes because Díaz's imaginative literary works are (to a considerable degree) works of imaginative fantasy and not moralistic parables. The result is that readers cannot entirely determine Díaz's literary project by only contemplating Yunior's promises and gifts as a writer, where he enjoys writing a terrific Bartolomé de Las Casas–inspired meta-crónica-in-progress, historias with gaping central absences (or lacunae) chiseled into them. As I have argued, in *Drown*, Yunior's father, Ramón, and his brother, Rafa, are absences at the very heart of the book; and in *The Brief Life of Oscar Wao*, Díaz's novel is largely constructed out of a series of absences, gaps, erasures, and páginas en blanco.

4   Moya, "Search for Decolonial Love, Parts I and II."
5   I am saying that in Junot Díaz's fiction to date there are aspects that simply exceed or leave the knavish, "kooky," unwise, and befuddled Yunior and his historias in the dust.
6   Besides responding to critics of his imaginative literature (as I outlined in chapter 4), Díaz, like the Dominican American writer Julia Alvarez, has had to deal with criticisms made by nationalist Dominican politicians who have branded both of them as "traitor[s]" to the Dominican Republic for criticizing the nation's immigration policies as racist. As I explained in the book's introduction, Díaz (along with intellectuals like Alvarez and Edwidge Danticat) publicly criticized Dominican politicians for enacting a 2012 law that stripped the citizenship of Haitian Dominicans registered in the country legally. The "sentencia," as it is called in the Dominican Republic, revoked the citizenship of all Dominicans born to undocumented parents after 1929.
7   Quoted in Moya, "Search for Decolonial Love, Parts I and II."
8   For more on Díaz's sense of the challenge of conjuring his work around Yunior de Las Casas's adolescence in *Drown*, his early adulthood's sentimental education in *The Brief Wondrous Life of Oscar Wao*, and his writing about Yunior's heartbreaks on the deep side of middle age, see Cressida Leyshon's *New Yorker* interview with Díaz. Leyshon, "This Week in Fiction."
9   Quoted in Kachka, "Junot Díaz's Counterlife."
10 "Near-Riot in NYC Book Store for Junot Diaz."
11 Kachka, "Junot Díaz's Counterlife."
12 Kachka, "Junot Díaz's Counterlife."
13 Quoted in Kachka, "Junot Díaz's Counterlife."
14 See, for example, Carol Campanile, "Best-Selling Author Junot Díaz in Lover's Quarrel over Townhouse," *New York Post*, September 4, 2016, accessed October 2, 2016, http://nypost.com/2016/09/04/best-selling-author-junot-diaz-in-lovers-quarrel-over-townhouse. As Campanile explains, "Díaz was locked in a long-running lovers' quarrel with his ex, Manhattan state Senate candidate Marisol Alcantara—and the saga was full of enough heartache to fill any romance paperback. At the heart of the dispute was a townhouse that the couple bought in Washington Heights in 2002, three years after meeting through a youth group at City College, court records show. Alcantara said she and Díaz planned to 'own the property together in contemplation of marriage and starting a family,' according to court papers. Díaz said it was simply

a purchase of convenience—and he put more money into it, anyway. They broke up shortly after they bought the four-story, three-apartment building at 529 W. 141 St."

15 Leyshon, "This Week in Fiction."
16 Díaz, *This Is How You Lose Her*, 45, 82, 213.
17 Piglia, "Theses on the Short Story."
18 A literary signature to be sure, yes, but is it like a killer radioactive isotope that lasts forever? Perhaps it is precisely Díaz's desire to reach a global audience and have his audience love him and his characters—by writing about love and its half-life—that has allowed him to win over a planetary readership and to thematize different kinds of decolonial loving practices—dispositifs—in his texts: sucia and sucio love, familia love, love and heartbreak, and sexual love. Decolonial love—eros, caritas, amor, or philos—embodies practices of reciprocity and recognition for Díaz.
19 This builds off the term *sucio/a* as used by Deborah Vargas (and Díaz himself) but rendered playfully as *suciality* to mark its difference from the term *suciedad* in Spanish.
20 Vargas, "Sucia Love," 352, 353.
21 Moya, "Search for Decolonial Love, Parts I and II."
22 As I noted in chapter 4, Díaz has explained that "the footnotes are there for a number of reasons; primarily, to create a double narrative. The footnotes, which are in the lower frequencies, challenge the main text, which is the higher narrative. The footnotes are like the voice of the jester, contesting the proclamations of the king. In a book that's all about the dangers of dictatorship, the dangers of the single voice—this felt like a smart move to me." Díaz, quoted in O'Rourke, "Questions for Junot Díaz."
23 Díaz, *Oscar Wao*, 92.
24 As we know, the closet emblematizes and spatializes the sense that "power is everywhere." Why does Oscar read in the closet? Why does he need to protect himself in the closet from all kinds of familial, social, and cultural disqualifications?
25 See McGurl, *Program Era*. As I have noted, McGurl asks us to take into account the institution of MFA creative-writing programs and the processes of the democratization of higher education in the United States to fully understand the nature of American postcontemporary literature from the postwar period to our present moment.
26 Díaz, email message to author, March 11, 2011.
27 Díaz, *Drown*, 11–12, 103–4.
28 See Woloch, *One vs. the Many*. Here Woloch develops a powerful new theory of the novel and imaginative fiction by demonstrating that the representation of any character takes place within a shifting field of narrative attention and obscurity. Each character—whether the central character or a subordinated one—emerges as a character only through his or her contingent space within the narrative as a whole. If character spaces mark the dramatic interaction between a character and his or her delimited position within a narrative, the totality of the organization and clashes between many character spaces constitutes the text's character system.
29 Díaz, "The Brief Wondrous Life of Oscar Wao."
30 Quoted in Moya, "Search for Decolonial Love, Parts I and II."
31 Gregg Barrios, "'He Is a Writer of Fiction. He Puts on Masks for a Living.' An Interview with Junot Díaz," *Los Angeles Review of Books*, October 7, 2012, accessed October

12, 2012, https://lareviewofbooks.org/article/he-is-a-writer-of-fiction-he-puts-on-masks-for-a-living-an-interview-with-junot-diaz/. For an exploration of the rape culture of the Trujillato thematized in Diáz's work, see Saldívar, "Conjectures on 'Americanity' and Junot Díaz's 'Fukú Americanus.'"

32 I have profited immensely from Linda Martín Alcoff's analysis of the colonialities of power and gender in Díaz's fiction. See Alcoff, *Rape and Resistance*.
33 Díaz, "Baseline Is, You Suck."
34 José Esteban Muñoz uses the concept of "disidentification" to get at the multiple ways in which queer subjects produce and flip the hegemonic identity scripts in order to work on, with, and against them. Muñoz, *Disidentifications*, 23.
35 Darnton, "First Steps toward a History of Reading," 157.
36 Allison et al., "Quantitative Formalism: An Experiment." Allison and colleagues define quantitative formalism as "formalism, because all of us, in one way or another, were interested in the formal conventions of genre; and quantitative, because we were looking for more precise—ideally, measurable—ways to establish generic differences." Allison et al., "Quantitative Formalism," 6.
37 Díaz, *Oscar Wao*, 20–21n6.
38 Halperin, *How to Be Gay*, 12.
39 Díaz, *Oscar Wao*, 20–21n6.
40 Díaz, *Oscar Wao*, 307, 20–21n6.
41 For one of the best studies of space, spacey-ness, and the spatial imagination and how it flourishes in postcontemporary literature, see Brady, *Extinct Lands, Temporal Geographies*.
42 In addition to the decolonial work on aesthetics by Fanon, Mignolo, and Pérez that I have discussed above, let me mention just a few more texts that take up the issues of aesthetics and aesthetic education in substantial ways: Kant, *Critique of the Power of Judgment*; Ngai, *Our Aesthetic Categories*; Schiller, *On the Aesthetic Education of Man*; and Spivak, *Aesthetic Education in the Era of Globalization*. An aesthetic education—from Kant and Schiller to Spivak and Ngai—seems to be most easily defined by what it is not. It is not the teaching of logical form or matters of fact, and it is not satisfied to remain at the level of surface text. Kant and Schiller saw the central task of aesthetic education as the improvement of taste, claiming that this required the development of two dispositions: the capacity to obtain aesthetic gratification from increasingly subtle and complex objects that are characterized by various forms of unity, and an increasing dependence on beautiful objects as sources of aesthetic satisfaction.
43 Williams, "To Elsie," 221.
44 Díaz, *Oscar Wao*, 21–22n6.
45 Díaz may also be addressing another, more complex educational issue of why boys in our US schools are in academic trouble. Unlike Oscar and Yunior, boys are lagging behind girls from early primary to secondary school. Why are boys doing poorly in reading in early grades, and why do they fail to complete their higher education programs at a higher rate than their female counterparts? Are boys' brains somehow hardwired differently from girls'? Are there no role models for the boys? In all of Díaz's work his central characters—Yunior, Oscar, Lola—champion reading and writing skills, for

our world has become increasingly verbal. For an overview of why boys are failing, see Whitmore, *Why Boys Fail*.

46 Díaz, *Oscar Wao*, 22, 21n6.
47 See Sedgwick, *Epistemology of the Closet*.
48 Díaz, *Oscar Wao*, 22n6.
49 Díaz, *Oscar Wao*, 22n6, emphasis added.
50 Díaz, *Oscar Wao*, 92. In other words, Yunior de Las Casas is not only coldhearted and distant, but as a self-proclaimed "Watcher" he prides himself in holding to something like the *Star Trek* doctrine called the prime directive. That is to say, in the fictional universe of *Star Trek*, the prime directive is the guiding principle of the United Federation of Planets. It prohibits Starfleet personnel from interfering with the internal development of alien civilizations.
51 For María Lugones, the coloniality of gender involves the process of how "the colonized became subjects" in the first modernity, that is, "the tensions created by the brutal imposition of the modern, colonial gender system." Lugones, "Toward a Decolonial Feminism," 743.
52 Later, Díaz's Yunior rewrites the Madeleine-allegorical experience in Proust's *À la recherche du temps perdu*, contrasting young Marcel's dipping a piece of the French cake in tea and tasting it and undergoing a vision of inner gardens and alleys that marvelously grow out of the cup of tea like Japanese paper flowers by depicting Oscar's experiences of resurrecting his Caribbean past through a different geocultural dynamic. Once Belicia and Oscar arrive in Santo Domingo to visit their island family, Oscar breathes in the island's "fecund tropical smell that he had never forgotten, that to him was more evocative than any madeleine . . . like a whole new country was materializing atop the ruins of old ones." Díaz, *Oscar Wao*, 273. In this Antillean island setting, the planet's exteriority does not lose its privileged position but helps release the impulse through smell and sight for Oscar's imaginative production of a completely internal world which is that of his own past that is reborn and transfigured. Can whole historical periods and other worlds, Yunior suggests, be hidden in the "dilapidated" tropicalized streets of the Dominican Republic and the global South? Is Santo Domingo the ontological site of unfolded remembered time for Oscar? As Yunior brilliantly suggests, Oscar's dynamic of the involuntary memory is tropologically metonymical: the whole of the Dominican Republic emerges from the Caribbean heat and smell of Santo Domingo's "pollution and the thousands of motos and cars" on the city's roads. Díaz, *Oscar Wao*, 273. Oscar thus compares his inner world that is largely shaped by his reading of the speculative genres with his Caribbean island's spatialized urban smells and sounds. Thus envisaged, in footnote 6, Yunior models Oscar's interiority as a hiding place of secrecy and ideality, of dense aesthetic atmosphere.
53 In her study of the popular Dominican masculine imagination in the age and afterlife of the Trujillato, anthropologist Lauren Derby incisively defines the *tíguere* as "the figure of the popular hero from the barrio—the quintessential Dominican underdog who gains power, prestige, and social status through a combination of extrainstitutional wits, force of will, sartorial style and cojones. The *tíguere* seduces. . . .

A man of the street, the *tíguere* operates through cunning, frequently via illicit means." Derby, *Dictator's Seduction*, 114.

54 Díaz, *Oscar Wao*, 22n6.
55 Yunior de Las Casas (like Díaz himself) is well versed in queer theory and decolonial feminism's theorization of power and gender. Here he is conjuncturally uniting Michel Foucault's iconic work on power and gender—which, far from enslaving their objects, constructs them as subjective agents—with his rewriting of Marcel Proust. Foucault's idea of power does not only indirectly terrorize its subjects; it also directly "normalizes," "responsibilizes," and disciplines. Foucault, *History of Sexuality*.
56 Díaz, *Oscar Wao*, 22.
57 Díaz, *Oscar Wao*, 22, 28.
58 Sedgwick, *Epistemology of the Closet*, 33.
59 Díaz, *Oscar Wao*, 22n6.
60 Davis, *Magical Urbanism*.
61 Díaz, *This Is How You Lose Her*, 213.
62 Díaz, *This Is How You Lose Her*, 34.
63 Díaz, *This Is How You Lose Her*, 30, 31, 33, 37, 38.
64 Díaz, *This Is How You Lose Her*, 32, 40.
65 Díaz, *This Is How You Lose Her*, 42, 43, 40.
66 Díaz, *This Is How You Lose Her*, 38, 40, 41.
67 Díaz, *This Is How You Lose Her*, 175, 177.
68 Díaz, *This Is How You Lose Her*, 25, 3, 175.
69 Díaz, *This Is How You Lose Her*, 163.
70 I am saying that forty-something Yunior de Las Casas is searching for a sense of the challenges of (decolonial) love as a praxis of (Hegelian-Fanonian) reciprocity and mutual recognition. For a rich philosophical-historical cultural anthropology of love (from Plato's *Symposium* to Annie Proulx's "Brokeback Mountain"), see Kottman, *Love as Human Freedom*. I have also relied on Andrew Cole's capacious reading of Hegel's dialectic of reciprocity. See Cole, *Birth of Theory*.
71 Díaz, *This Is How You Lose Her*, 165.
72 Díaz, *This Is How You Lose Her*, 185, 193.
73 García Márquez, *One Hundred Years of Solitude*, 420–22.
74 Díaz, *This Is How You Lose Her*, 212.
75 Díaz, *This Is How You Lose Her*, 212, 213.
76 Díaz, *This Is How You Lose Her*, 213.
77 Díaz, "Growing the Hell Up."
78 Badiou and Truong, *In Praise of Love*, 7.
79 Badiou and Truong, *In Praise of Love*, 28.
80 Badiou and Truong, *In Praise of Love*, 29, 32, 33.
81 Badiou and Truong, *In Praise of Love*, 36, 14, 49, 90, 98, 104.
82 My readings of Díaz and the coloniality of gender, theory in the flesh, and sucia/o love draw on the decolonial intersectional works by Paula M. L. Moya, María Lugones, Gloria Anzaldúa, Cherríe Moraga, and Deborah R. Vargas.
83 Fanon, *Black Skin, White Masks*, 206.

84 Gordon, *What Fanon Said*, 70.
85 Moraga and Anzaldúa, eds., *This Bridge Called My Back*, 22.
86 Moya, "Search for Decolonial Love, Parts I and II."

CONCLUSION AND CODA

1 Saldívar, "Historical Fantasy, Speculative Realism, and Postrace Aesthetics in Contemporary American Fiction."
2 In the speech he gave in Caracas, Venezuela, upon receiving the Premio Rómulo Gallegos for his novel *Los detectives salvajes* (1999), Roberto Bolaño said that a "writer's homeland is his language." It is also "the people he loves, plus whatever he is writing at the moment and the courage to face the abyss and accept what he finds." Later in his discurso, Bolaño ended by asking, "So, what is great literature? It is the same thing it has always been: the ability to peer into the darkness, to leap into the void, to know that literature is basically a dangerous undertaking. The ability to skate along the edge of the precipice: to one side the bottomless abyss and to the other the faces you love.... Literature is danger." Bolaño, "Discurso de Caracas (Venezuela)."
3 Vargas, "Sucia Love," 352.
4 A signature is an indicator and measure of the presence of the writer or author. The signature denotes the writer as the source of the text, or the speaker of an utterance, and they hold the form of regulation for the sign or words that are spoken or written.
5 Leyshon, "This Week in Fiction: Junot Díaz."
6 Leyshon, "This Week in Fiction: Junot Díaz."
7 Leyshon, "This Week in Fiction: Junot Díaz."
8 For my understanding of how humans have become a force of nature, a geophysical force comparable to, say, a massive asteroid, with a capacity to move things, I have profited from Chakrabarty, *Climate of History in a Planetary Age*.
9 Leyshon, "This Week in Fiction: Junot Díaz."
10 For a transatlantic reading of the "decolonial monstro" in Díaz's text, see Quesada, "A Planetary Warning." For a "Calibanic" reading of the colonial trope of the monstrous cannibal in Díaz's dystopian short story, see Figueroa-Vásquez, *Decolonizing Diasporas*, 169–73.
11 Jameson, *Seeds of Time*, xii.
12 Leyshon, "This Week in Fiction: Junot Díaz."
13 Leyshon, "This Week in Fiction: Junot Díaz." It isn't hard to tell—as I've argued in this book—how Díaz's voracious reading of decolonial theorists such as María Lugones, Walter Mignolo, Paula M. L. Moya, and Aníbal Quijano inhabits many nuanced turns of his fiction. Furthermore, the sci-fi (or utopian) discourse of "Monstro" suggests that he has carefully read nearly all of Fredric Jameson's iconic work on science fiction and the utopian imagination I've cited throughout this book, and he fully understands how science-fiction discourse (or utopia) allows writers to imagine a radical alternative to our present by allowing them to think its limits.
14 Jameson, *Postmodernism*.
15 In 2021 the Dominican Republic president Luis Abinadar fortified the 234-mile-long

border with Haiti to "bring to an end" what he considers "the serious problems of illegal immigration, narco-trafficking and the movement of stolen vehicles"— problems he claims Dominicans "have been suffering for years." See "Dominican Republic: Border to Be Fortified," *San Francisco Chronicle*, March 1, 2021, A4.

16   Díaz, "Monstro."
17   Moten, *In the Break*, 255.
18   Díaz, "Monstro."
19   Díaz, "Monstro."
20   Gilroy, *Between Camps*, 84.
21   Díaz, "Monstro."
22   Díaz, "Monstro."
23   In the sci-fi novel in progress that Díaz has been writing (off and on) based on his story "Monstro," his world-building canvas expanded. He added new chapters focusing on a Mujerista movement; the Witch War; a new character, a sixteen-year-old girl named Isis, who finds herself standing "alone between the world and its destruction"; and more terrible intimations that are coming out of the island's hot zone. His central protagonists, Alex, Mysty, and the unnamed time witness and narrator, Díaz once insisted, are not going to like "what they meet at the border" and will "wish they had paid attention to the world" from the get-go. More recently, however, in a radio interview that aired on June 9, 2015, Díaz confessed that he had killed off his sci-fi novel in progress just as, many years earlier, he had slain "Akira," his sci-fi thriller in progress. See Leyshon, "This Week in Fiction: Junot Díaz"; and Chacón and Hernandez, "Words on a Wire: Junot Díaz." For Díaz's comments on Afro-Dominican dystopias, see his essay introducing *Global Dystopias*.
24   Díaz, "Apocalypse."
25   Díaz, "Apocalypse."
26   Sheppard, "Identity, Dictators, and Apocalypse."
27   Díaz, "Apocalypse."
28   Díaz, *Islandborn*, 3. Díaz told Alexandra Alter of the *New York Times* that his picture book, *Islandborn*, was aimed at four- to eight-year-olds and that it grapples with themes Díaz has explored in his previous texts: immigration and diasporic identity as well as feelings of displacement and belonging. See Alexandra Alter, "Next from the Novelist Junot Díaz? A Picture Book," *New York Times*, July 18, 2017, accessed September 19, 2018, https://www.nytimes.com/2017/07/18/books/junot-diaz-islandborn.
29   Díaz, *Islandborn*, 6.
30   Díaz, *Islandborn*, 6.
31   Vera Castaneda, "Q&A: Talking to Junot Díaz about 'Islandborn,' His First Book for Kids," *Los Angeles Times*, April 9, 2018, accessed May 1, 2018, https://www.latimes.com/books/la-ca-jc-fob-junot-diaz-20180409-htmlstory.html.
32   Díaz, *Islandborn*, 10.
33   Díaz, *Oscar Wao*, 151n18.
34   Junot Díaz, "The Mongoose and the Émigré," *New York Times Magazine*, May 17, 2017, accessed May 30, 2017, www.nytimes.com/2017/05/17/magazine/the-mongoose-and-the-emigre.html.

35 Díaz, *Islandborn*, 20.
36 In a 1994 interview the British theorist Paul Gilroy explained the strategy of how he was using the concept of diaspora in *The Black Atlantic: Double Consciousness and Modernity*: "First we have to fight over the concept of diaspora and to move it away from the obsession with purity and invariant sameness. Very often the concept of diaspora has been used to say, 'Hooray! we can rewind the tape of history, we can get back to the original moment of our dispersal!' I'm saying something quite different. That's why I didn't call the book diaspora anything. I called it the Black Atlantic because I wanted to say, 'If this is a diaspora, then it's a very particular kind of diaspora. It's a diaspora that can't be reversed.'" This version of an Afro-Dominican diaspora "that can't be reversed" is what I take to be Lola's invocation of her practical past in *Islandborn*. See Lott, "Black Cultural Politics."
37 Díaz, *Islandborn*, 22.
38 Likewise, a terrific literary criticism on these US Latinx writers has come of age. See, for example, González, *Reading Junot Díaz*; Gabriella Gutiérrez Muhs, ed., *Rebozos de palabras*; Hanna, Harford Vargas, and Saldívar, eds., *Junot Díaz and the Decolonial Imagination*; Irizarry, *Chicana/o and Latina/o Fiction*; Méndez, *Narratives of Migration and Displacement in Dominican Literature*; Miranda and McCarter, *Hamilton the Revolution*; Moya, *Social Imperative*; Olguín, *Violentologies*; Ostman, *Fiction of Junot Díaz*; Pérez Firmat, *Life on the Hyphen*; Pérez-Rosario, *Becoming Julia de Burgos*; and Sommer, *Bilingual Games*.
39 Leyshon, "This Week in Fiction: Junot Díaz."
40 My pedagogy builds upon the theorizing of science fiction by Kim Stanley Robinson: "If you think of science fiction as just a kind of modeling exercise, everybody is a science fiction writer in their own lives. You make plans based on modeling in your mind. When you're feeling hopeful, you have a kind of utopian plan: if you do these things, you'll get to a good place. And then when you're afraid, you have these worries that if you do these things, you'll get to a bad place." See Robinson, "We Asked Kim Stanley Robinson."
41 My understanding of the Anthropocene was sharpened by Patricia Valderrama's PhD dissertation, "Reading for the Anthropocene."
42 White, *The Practical Past*.

Bibliography

Abrams, M. H. *Natural-Supernaturalism: Tradition and Revolution in Romantic Literature*. New York: W. W. Norton, 1973.

Agamben, Giorgio. *State of Exception*. Translated by Kevin Attell. Chicago: University of Chicago Press, 2005.

Alcoff, Linda Martín. *Rape and Resistance: Understanding the Complexities of Sexual Violation*. Medford, MA: Polity, 2018.

Alim, Samy H., Awad Ibrahim, and Alastair Pennycook, eds. *Global Linguistic Flows: Hip Hop Cultures, Youth Identities, and the Politics of Language*. New York: Routledge, 2009.

Allison, Sarah, Ryan Heuser, Matthew Jockers, Franco Moretti, and Michael Witmore. "Quantitative Formalism: An Experiment." *Literary Lab Pamphlet 1*, Stanford University. January 15, 2011. https://litlab.stanford.edu/LiteraryLabPamphlet1.pdf.

Als, Hilton. "Junot Díaz" (Interview by Hilton Als). In *Upstairs at the Strand: Writers in Conversation*, edited by Jessica Strand and Andrea Aguilar. New York: W. W. Norton, 2016. E-book.

Alvarez, Julia. *In the Time of the Butterflies*. Chapel Hill, NC: Algonquin, 1994.

Alvarez, Julia. *A Wedding in Haiti*. Chapel Hill, NC: Algonquin, 2012.

Andrews, Chris. *Roberto Bolaño's Fiction: An Expanding Universe*. New York: Columbia University Press, 2014.

Appadurai, Arjun. *Modernity at Large: Cultural Dimensions of Globalization*. Minneapolis: University of Minnesota Press, 1996.

Badiou, Alain, and Nicolas Truong. *In Praise of Love*. Translated by Peter Bush. London: Serpent's Tail, 2012.

Barradas, Efraín. "El realismo cómico de Junot Díaz: Notas sobre *The Brief Wondrous Life of Oscar Wao*." *SECOLAS* 53, no. 1 (2009): 99–111.

Bautista, Daniel. "Comic Book Realism and Genre in Junot Díaz's *The Brief Wondrous Life of Oscar Wao*." *Journal of the Fantastic in the Arts* 21, no. 1 (2010): 41–53.

Bolaño, Roberto. "Discurso de Caracas (Venezuela)." Speech presented upon receiving the Premio Rómulo Gallegos, Caracas, Venezuela, October 31, 1999. www.letraslibres.com/mexico/discurso-caracas-venezuela.

Bolaño, Roberto. *The Savage Detectives*. Translated by Natasha Wimmer. New York: Farrar, Straus and Giroux, 2007.

Bowker, Geoffrey. *Memory Practices in the Sciences*. Cambridge, MA: MIT Press, 2005.

Brady, Mary Pat. *Extinct Lands, Temporal Geographies: Chicana Literature and the Urgency of Space*. Durham, NC: Duke University Press, 2002.

Brues, Frank. "Chasing the Whale: A Profile of Junot Díaz." *Poets and Writers*, September 1, 2007. Accessed September 2, 2010. www.pw.org/content/chasing_whale_profile_junot_díaz.

Candelario, Ginetta E. B. "Hair-Race-ing: Dominican Beauty Culture and Identity Production." *Meridians* 1, no. 1 (2000): 128–56.

Carpio, Glenda R. "Now Check It: Junot Díaz's Wondrous Spanglish." In *Junot Díaz and the Decolonial Imagination*, edited by Jennifer Harford Vargas, Monica Hanna, and José David Saldívar, 257–90. Durham, NC: Duke University Press, 2016.

Césaire, Aimé. "Notebook of a Return to the Native Land." In *The Collected Poetry*. Translated by Clayton Eshleman and Annette Smith. Berkeley: University of California Press, 1983.

Chacón, Daniel, and Tim Z. Hernandez. "Words on a Wire: Junot Díaz." *Words on a Wire* (podcast interview), June 9, 2015. Accessed June 30, 2015. http://ktep.org/post/words-wire-junot-d-az.

Chakrabarty, Dipesh. *The Climate of History in a Planetary Age*. Chicago: University of Chicago Press, 2021.

Charney, Noah. "Junot Díaz: How I Write." *Daily Beast*, July 11, 2017. Accessed July 21, 2017. https://www.thedailybeast.com/junot-diaz-how-i-write.

Chasman, Deborah. "Why I Didn't Fire Junot Díaz." Forthcoming.

Chasman, Deborah, and Joshua Cohen. "A Letter from Deborah Chasman and Joshua Cohen." *Boston Review*, June 5, 2018. Accessed July 16, 2018. http://bostonreview.net/editors-note/boston-review-letter-deborah-chasman-and-joshua-cohen.

Ch'ien, Evelyn Nien-Ming. *Weird English*. Cambridge, MA: Harvard University Press, 2004.

Cibattari, Jane. "The 21st Century's 12 Greatest Novels." *BBC Culture*, January 19, 2015. Accessed January 23, 2015. www.bbc.com/culture/story/20150119-the-21st-centurys-12-best-novels.

Cohen, Ed. "Typing Wilde: Constructing the 'Desire to Appear to Be a Person Inclined to the Commission of the Gravest of All Offenses.'" *Yale Journal of Law & the Humanities* 5, no. 1 (1993): 1–101.

Cohen, Ed. "Writing Gone Wilde: Homoerotic Desire in the Closet of Representation." *PMLA* 102, no. 5 (1987): 801–13.

Cohen, Margaret. "Narratology in the Archive of Literature." *Representations* 108 (2009): 51–75.

Cole, Andrew. *The Birth of Theory*. Chicago: University of Chicago Press, 2014.

Comité Clandestino Revolucionario Indígena-Comandancia General del Ejército Zapatista de Liberación Nacional. "Cuarta Declaración de la Selva Lancandona." January 1, 1996. Accessed December 10, 2009. http://palabra.ezln.org.mx/comunicados/1996/1996_01_01_a.htm.

Cortázar, Julio. *Cronopios and Famas*. Translated by Paul Blackburn. New York: New Directions, 1999.

Cosgrove, Denis, and Stephen Daniel, eds. *The Iconography of Landscape*. Cambridge: Cambridge University Press, 1988.

Crassweller, Robert D. *Trujillo: The Life and Times of a Caribbean Dictator*. New York: Macmillan, 1966.

Danticat, Edwidge. "Junot Díaz by Edwidge Danticat." *BOMB*, October 1, 2007. Accessed November 2, 2007. https://bombmagazine.org/articles/junot-d% C3% ADaz.

Darnton, Robert. "First Steps toward a History of Reading." In *The Kiss of Lamourette: Reflections in Cultural History*, 154–87. New York: W. W. Norton, 1990.

Dávila, Arlene. "Against the 'Discursive Latino': On the Politics and Praxis of Junot Díaz's Latinidad." In *Junot Díaz and the Decolonial Imagination*, edited by Jennifer Harford Vargas, Monica Hanna, and José David Saldívar, 33–48. Durham, NC: Duke University Press, 2016.

Davis, Mike. *Magical Urbanism: Latinos Reinvent the US Big City*. New York: Verso, 2000.

de León, Aya. "Reconciling Rage and Compassion: The Unfolding #MeToo Moment for Junot Díaz." *Aya de León* (blog). May 5, 2018. Accessed December 1, 2020. https://ayadeleon.wordpress.com/2018/05/05/reconciling-rage-and-compassion-the-unfolding-metoo-moment-for-junot-diaz.

De Maeseneer, Rita. *Seis ensayos sobre narrativa dominicana contemporánea*. Santo Domingo: Banco Central, 2012.

Depestre, René. *Bonjour et adieu à la négritude*. Paris: Robert Lafont, 1980.

Derby, Lauren. *The Dictator's Seduction: Politics and the Popular Imagination in the Era of Trujillo*. Durham, NC: Duke University Press, 2009.

Di Iorio Sandín, Lyn. "Laughing Through a Broken Mouth in *The Brief Wondrous Life of Oscar Wao*." In *Junot Díaz and the Decolonial Imagination*, edited by Jennifer Harford Vargas, Monica Hanna, and José David Saldívar, 69–88. Durham, NC: Duke University Press, 2016.

Díaz, Junot. "Apocalypse: What Disasters Reveal." *Boston Review*, May 1, 2011. Accessed May 5, 2011. www.bostonreview.net/junot-diaz-apocalypse-haiti-earthquake.

Díaz, Junot. "Becoming a Writer." *O, the Oprah Magazine*, November 2009. Accessed December 1, 2009. http://www.oprah.com/spirit/Junot-Diaz-Talks-About-What-Made-Him-Become-a-Writer/2.

Díaz, Junot. "The Brief Wondrous Life of Oscar Wao." *New Yorker*, January 1, 2000.

Díaz, Junot. *The Brief Wondrous Life of Oscar Wao*. New York: Riverhead, 2007.

Díaz, Junot. "Conversation with Toni Morrison." New York Public Library, December 13, 2013. Accessed April 22, 2015. www.nypl.org/events/programs/2013/12/12/toni-morrison-junot-d%C3%ADaz.

Díaz, Junot. "Dark America." The Anne and Loren Kieve Distinguished Lecture. Stanford University, May 18, 2012. M4A file.

Díaz, Junot. *Drown*. New York: Riverhead, 1996.

Díaz, Junot. "Global Dystopias, Critical Dystopias: A Podcast with Junot Díaz." Interview by Avni Majithia-Sejpal, *Boston Review*, October 31, 2016. Accessed November 1, 2016. http://bostonreview.net/podcast/global-dystopias-critical-dystopias-podcast-junot-d%C3%ADaz.

Díaz, Junot. Interview by Joe Fassler. "The Baseline Is, You Suck: Junot Díaz on Men Who Write about Women." *Atlantic*, September 12, 2012. Accessed March 10, 2013. https://www

.theatlantic.com/entertainment/archive/2012/09/the-baseline-is-you-suck-junot-diaz-on-men-who-write-about-women/262163/.df.

Díaz, Junot. Interview by Richard Wolinsky. "Growing the Hell Up: From Middle Earth to NJ." *Guernica*, November 1, 2012. Accessed November 30, 2012. www.guernicamag.com/interviews/growing-the-hell-up-from-middle-earth-to-nj.

Díaz, Junot. Introduction to *The Beacon Best of 2001: Great Writing by Women and Men of All Colors and Cultures*, vii–xi. Boston: Beacon, 2001.

Díaz, Junot. Introduction to *Dismantle: An Anthology of Writing from the VONA/Voices Writing Workshop*, 1–8. Edited by Marissa Johnson-Valenzuela. Philadelphia: Thread Makes Blanket, 2014.

Díaz, Junot. Introduction to *Global Dystopias*, 5–6. Edited by Junot Díaz. Cambridge, MA: MIT University Press, 2017.

Díaz, Junot. *Islandborn*. New York: Dial, 2018.

Díaz, Junot. "Junot Díaz Writes about Moving to Brooklyn." *Time Out: New York*, September 26, 2017. Accessed April 2, 2018. www.timeout.com/newyork/blog/junot-diaz-writes-about-moving-to-brooklyn-in-1995-092617.

Díaz, Junot. "Keynote Speech." Colorlines, Facing Race: A National Conference, November 15–17, 2012, Baltimore. Accessed April 13, 2013. www.colorlines.com/articles/facing-race-2012-bonus-junot-d%C3%ADazs-press-conversation-video.

Díaz, Junot. "Loving Ray Bradbury." *New Yorker*, June 6, 2012. Accessed June 30, 2012. www.newyorker.com/online/blogs/books/2012/06/loving-ray-bradbury.html.

Díaz, Junot. "MFA v. POC." *New Yorker*, April 30, 2014. Accessed May 5, 2012. www.newyorker.com/online/blogs/books/2014/04/mfa-vs-poc.html.

Díaz, Junot. "Monstro." *New Yorker*, May 28, 2012. Accessed July 12, 2012. http://www.newyorker.com/fiction/features/2012/06/04/120604fi_fiction_diaz.

Díaz, Junot. "Negocios." MFA thesis, Cornell University, 1995.

Díaz, Junot. *Negocios*. Translated by Eduardo Lago. New York: Vintage, 1997.

Díaz, Junot. "Old Masks, New Face." *Radcliffe*, December 1, 2010. https://www.radcliffemagazine.org/contents/old-masks-newface.

Díaz, Junot. "The Silence: The Legacy of Childhood Trauma." *New Yorker*, April 18, 2018. Accessed June 5, 2018. www.newyorker.com/magazine/2018/04/16/the-silence-the-legacy-of-childhood-trauma.

Díaz, Junot. "Stanford Humanities Center Presidential Lecture." Stanford University, May 24, 2017.

Díaz, Junot. *This Is How You Lose Her*. New York: Riverhead, 2012.

Díaz, Junot. "Under President Trump, Radical Hope Is Our Best Weapon." *New Yorker*, November 14, 2016. Accessed December 20, 2016. https://www.newyorker.com/magazine/2016/11/21/under-president-trump-radical-hope-is-our-best-weapon.

Dirlik, Arif. "The Global South: Predicament and Promise." *Global South* 1, no. 1 (2007): 12–23.

DiTrapano, Giancarlo. "A Brief History of Junot Díaz." *Playboy*, September 2013, 100–102, 130.

"Dominican Republic: Border to Be Fortified." *San Francisco Chronicle*, March 1, 2021.

Duany, Jorge. *Blurred Borders: Transnational Migration between the Hispanic Caribbean and the United States*. Chapel Hill: University of North Carolina Press, 2011.

Dussel, Enrique. "Beyond Eurocentrism: The World-System and the Limits of Modernity." In *The Cultures of Globalization*, edited by Fredric Jameson and Misao Miyoshi, 3–31. Durham, NC: Duke University Press, 1998.

Elden, Stuart, and Eduardo Mendieta, eds. *Reading Kant's Geography*. Albany: State University of New York Press, 2011.

Engler, Mira. *Designing America's Waste Landscapes*. Baltimore: Johns Hopkins University Press, 2004.

Eze, Emmanuel Chukwudi. *On Reason: Rationality in a World of Cultural Conflict and Racism*. Durham, NC: Duke University Press, 2008.

Fanon, Frantz. *Black Skin, White Masks*. Translated by Richard Philcox. New York: Grove, 2008.

Fanon, Frantz. *Les damnés de la terre*. Paris: Éditions La Découverte, 2002.

Faulkner, William. *Requiem for a Nun*. New York: Vintage, 2012.

Figueroa-Vásquez, Yomaira C. *Decolonizing Diasporas: Radical Mappings of Afro-Atlantic Literature*. Evanston, IL: Northwestern University Press, 2020.

Fimi, Dimtra. *Tolkien, Race and Cultural History: From Fairies to Hobbits*. New York: Palgrave Macmillan, 2010.

Fluck, Winfried. "The Imaginary and the Second Narrative: Reading as Transfer." In *The Imaginary and Its Worlds: American Studies after the Transnational Turn*, edited by Laura Bieger, Ramón Saldívar, and Johannes Volez, 237–64. Hanover, NH: Dartmouth College Press, 2013.

Fluck, Winfried. "The Role of the Reader and the Changing Functions of Literature: Reception Aesthetics, Literary Anthropology, Funktionsgeschichte." *European Journal of English Studies* 6, no. 3 (2002): 253–71.

Fluck, Winfried. *Romance with America? Essays on Culture, Literature, and American Studies*. Edited by Laura Beiger and Johannes Voelz. Berlin: Universitätsverlag Winter, 2006.

Foucault, Michel. *Discipline and Punish: The Birth of the Prison*. Translated by Alan Sheridan. New York: Pantheon, 1978.

Foucault, Michel. *The History of Sexuality*. Vol. 1, *An Introduction*. Translated by Robert Hurley. New York: Vintage, 1980.

Fuguet, Alberto, and Sergio Gómez, eds. *McOndo*. Barcelona: Mondadori, 1996.

Gagnier, Regina. *The Idylls of the Marketplace: Oscar Wilde and the Victorian Public*. Stanford, CA: Stanford University Press, 1986.

García Márquez, Gabriel. *One Hundred Years of Solitude*. Buenos Aires: Editorial Sudamericana, 1967.

García Peña, Lorgia. *The Borders of Dominicanidad: Race, Nation, and Archives of Contradictions*. Durham, NC: Duke University Press, 2016.

Gendzier, Irene L. *Frantz Fanon: A Critical Study*. New York: Pantheon, 1973.

Genette, Gérard. *Paratexts: Thresholds of Interpretation*. Translated by Jane E. Lewis. Cambridge: Cambridge University Press, 1997. Kindle edition.

Gilmore, Ruth Wilson. *Golden Gulag: Prisons, Surplus, Crisis and Opposition in Globalizing California*. Berkeley: University of California Press, 2007.

Gilroy, Paul. *After Empire: Melancholia or Convivial Culture*. London: Routledge, 2004.

Gilroy, Paul. *Between Camps: Nations, Cultures, and the Allure of Race*. London: Routledge, 2004.

Glass, Joshua. "Literary Giants Junot Díaz and Toni Morrison on Their Refusal to Surrender." *Document*, April 20, 2017. Accessed February 28, 2010, www.documentjournal.com/2017/04/literary-giants-junot-diaz-and-toni-morrison-on-their-unwillingness-to-surrender.

"Global Landfill May 2010 Fact Sheet." https://nj.gov/dep/srp/community/sites/pi/g000003352.pdf.

Gómez-Barris, Macarena. *Where Memory Dwells: Culture and State Violence in Chile*. Berkeley: University of California Press, 2009.

González, Christopher. *Reading Junot Díaz*. Pittsburgh: University of Pittsburgh Press, 2015.

González, Melissa M. "'The Only Way out Is In': Power, Race, and Sexuality under Capitalism in *The Brief Wondrous Life of Oscar Wao*." *Critique: Studies in Contemporary Fiction* 57, no. 3 (2016): 279–93.

Gordon, Lewis. *What Fanon Said: A Philosophical Introduction to His Life and Thought*. New York: Fordham University Press, 2015.

Grafton, Anthony. *The Footnote: A Curious History*. Cambridge, MA: Harvard University Press, 1999.

Grandin, Greg. "Junot Díaz Just Lost an Award for Speaking Out against the Dominican Republic's Anti-Haitian Program." *Nation*, October 26, 2015. Accessed November 1, 2015. www.thenation.com/article/archive/junot-diaz-just-lost-an-award-for-speaking-out-against-the-dominican-republics-anti-haitian-pogrom.

Gratton, Peter. "Foucault's Last Decade: An Interview with Stuart Elden, Eduardo Mendietta, and Diana Taylor." *Symposium* 20, no. 2 (2016): 181–211.

Graulund, Rune. "Generous Exclusion: Register and Readership in Junot Díaz's *The Brief Wondrous Life of Oscar Wao*." *MELUS* 39, no. 3 (2014): 31–47.

Greenwood, Emily. *Afro-Greeks: Dialogues between Anglophone Caribbean Literature and Classics in the Twentieth Century*. Oxford: Oxford University Press, 2010.

Grosfoguel, Ramón. *Colonial Subjects: Puerto Ricans in a Global Perspective*. Berkeley: University of California Press, 2003.

Gumbrecht, Hans Urlich. *Atmosphere, Mood, Stimmung: On a Hidden Potential of Literature*. Stanford, CA: Stanford University Press, 2012.

Gumbrecht, Hans Urlich. "The Roads of the Novel." In *The Novel*. Vol. 2, *Forms and Themes*, edited by Franco Moretti, 611–46. Princeton, NJ: Princeton University Press, 2006.

Hall, Stuart. "Cultural Identity and Diaspora." In *Stuart Hall: Selected Writings on Race and Difference*, edited by Paul Gilroy and Ruth Wilson Gilmore, 257–71. Durham, NC: Duke University Press, 2021.

Halperin, David. *How to Be Gay*. Cambridge, MA: Harvard University Press, 2012.

Hanna, Monica. "'Reassembling the Fragments': Battling Historiographies, Caribbean Discourse, and Nerd Genres in Junot Díaz's *The Brief Wondrous Life of Oscar Wao*." *Callaloo* 33, no. 2 (2010): 498–520.

Hanna, Monica, Jennifer Harford Vargas, and José David Saldívar. "Introduction." In *Junot Díaz and the Decolonial Imagination*, edited by Monica Hanna, Jennifer Harford Vargas, and José David Saldívar, 1–32. Durham, NC: Duke University Press, 2016.

Harford Vargas, Jennifer. "Dictating a Zafa: The Power of Narrative Form in Junot Díaz's *The Brief Wondrous Life of Oscar Wao*." *MELUS* 39, no. 3 (2014): 8–30.

Hegel, G. W. F. *Phenomenology of Spirit*. Translated by A. V. Miller. Oxford: Oxford University Press, 1977.

Hemingway, Ernest. *The Short Happy Life of Francis Macomber and Other Stories*. London: Penguin, 1970.

Hijuelos, Oscar. *The Mambo Kings Play Songs of Love*. New York: Farrar, Straus and Giroux, 1989.

Howe, Irving. "Black Boys and Native Sons." In *A World More Attractive: A View of Modern Literature and Politics*, 98–122. New York: Horizon, 1963.

Hoyos, Héctor. *Beyond Bolaño: The Global Latin American Novel*. New York: Columbia University Press, 2015.

"In Scholarly Debates on #MeToo Survivor Support Should Take Precedence." *Medium*, May 23, 2018. Accessed May 28, 2018. https://medium.com/@nsscollectiveeditorial/collective-editorial-survivor-support-should-take-precedence-71a2f6230157.

Irizarry, Ylce. *Chicana/o and Latina/o Fiction: The New Memory of Latinidad*. Urbana: University of Illinois Press, 2016.

Irizarry, Ylce. "This Is How You Lose It: Navigating Dominicadidad in Junot Díaz's *Drown*." In *Junot Díaz and the Decolonial Imagination*, edited by Monica Hanna, Jennifer Harford Vargas, and José David Saldívar, 147–72. Durham, NC: Duke University Press, 2016.

Iser, Wolfgang. *The Act of Reading: A Theory of Aesthetic Response*. Baltimore: Johns Hopkins University Press, 1979.

Jameson, Fredric. *The Antinomies of Realism*. London: Verso, 2013.

Jameson, Fredric. *Archaeologies of the Future: The Desire Called Utopia and Other Science Fictions*. New York: Verso, 2005.

Jameson, Fredric. *Postmodernism, or, the Cultural Logic of Late Capitalism*. Durham, NC: Duke University Press, 1991.

Jameson, Fredric. *The Seeds of Time*. New York: Columbia University Press, 1994.

Joyce, James. *A Portrait of the Artist as a Young Man*. New York: Penguin, 2003.

Joyce, James. *Ulysses*. New York: Vintage, 1961.

Kachka, Boris. "Junot Díaz's Counterlife." *New York*, August 12, 2012. Accessed September 1, 2012. http://nymag.com/guides/fallpreview/2012/junot-diaz-2012-8#print.

Kant, Immanuel. *Critique of the Power of Judgment*. Translated by Paul Guyer and Eric Matthews. Cambridge: Cambridge University Press, 2000.

Kant, Immanuel. *Observations on the Feeling of the Beautiful and the Sublime*. Translated by John T. Goldthwait. Berkeley: University of California Press, 1960.

Kottman, Paul A. *Love as Human Freedom*. Stanford, CA: Stanford University Press, 2017.

Kun, Josh. "Allá in the Mix: Mexican Sonideros and the Musical Politics of Migrancy." *Public Culture* 27, no. 3 (2015): 533–55.

Lamar Herrin Blog. "Novels." Accessed September 1, 2018. http://www.lamarherrin.com/novels.html.

Lanzendorfer, Tim. "The Marvelous History of the Dominican Republic in Junot Díaz's *The Brief Wondrous Life of Oscar Wao*." *MELUS* 38, no. 2 (2013): 127–42.

Laó-Montes, Agustín. *Contrapunteos diaspóricos: Cartografías políticas de Nuestra Afroamérica*. Bogota: Universidad Externado, 2020. Kindle edition.

Latour, Bruno. *The Politics of Nature: How to Bring the Sciences into Democracy*. Translated by Catherine Porter. Cambridge, MA: Harvard University Press, 2004.

Lee, Jonathan. "Literary Culture Clash." *Guernica*, July 1, 2013. Accessed July 12, 2013. www.guernicamag.com/literary-culture-clash.

Lee, Stan, and Jack Kirby. *Fantastic Four* 1, no. 13. Marvel, 1963.

Levinas, Emmanuel. *Alterity and Transcendence*. Translated by Michael B. Smith. New York: Columbia University Press, 1999.

Levitt, Peggy. *The Transnational Villagers*. Berkeley: University of California Press, 2001.

Leyshon, Cressida. "This Week in Fiction: Junot Díaz." *New Yorker*, June 1, 2012. https://www.newyorker.com/books/page-turner/this-week-in-fiction-junot-daz-2.

Li, Stephanie. *Signifying without Specifying: Racial Discourse in the Age of Obama*. New Brunswick, NJ: Rutgers University Press, 2011.

Lott, Tommy. "Black Cultural Politics: An Interview with Paul Gilroy." *Found Object* 4 (Fall 1994): 56–57.

Lowe, Lisa. *Immigrant Acts: On Asian American Cultural Politics*. Durham, NC: Duke University Press, 1996.

Lowenthal, Abraham F. *The Dominican Intervention*. Baltimore: Johns Hopkins University Press, 1972.

Lugones, María. "Toward a Decolonial Feminism." *Hypatia* 25, no. 4 (2010): 742–59.

Mahler, Anne Garland. "The Writer as Superhero: Fighting the Colonial Curse in Junot Díaz's *The Brief Wondrous Life of Oscar Wao*." *Journal of Latin American Cultural Studies: Travesia* 19, no. 2 (2010): 119–40.

Maldonado-Torres, Nelson. "The Decolonial Turn." In *New Approaches to Latin American Studies: Culture and Power*, ed. Juan Poblete, 111–27. New York: Routledge, 2018.

Manz, Beatriz. *Paradise in Ashes: A Guatemalan Journey of Courage, Terror, and Hope*. Berkeley: University of California Press, 2004.

Martínez-San Miguel, Yolanda. *Coloniality of Diasporas: Rethinking Intra-colonial Migrations in a Pan-Caribbean Context*. New York: Palgrave Macmillan, 2014.

McGurl, Mark. *The Program Era: Postwar Fiction and the Rise of Creative Writing*. Cambridge, MA: Harvard University Press, 2009.

Méndez, Danny. *Narratives of Migration and Displacement in Dominican Literature*. New York: Routledge, 2012.

Mignolo, Walter. *The Darker Side of Western Modernity: Global Futures, Decolonial Options*. Durham, NC: Duke University Press, 2011.

Mignolo, Walter. *The Idea of Latin America*. London: Blackwell, 2005.

Mignolo, Walter. *Local Histories/Global Designs: Coloniality, Subaltern Knowledges, and Border Thinking*. Princeton, NJ: Princeton University Press, 2000.

Miller, Benjamin. *Fat of the Land: Garbage of New York—The Last Two Hundred Years*. New York: Four Walls Eight Windows, 2000.

Minich, Julie. "The Cheater's Guide to Disability." In *Junot Díaz and the Decolonial Imagination*, edited by Monica Hanna, Jennifer Harford Vargas, and José David Saldívar, 49–68. Durham, NC: Duke University Press, 2016.

Miranda, Lin-Manuel, and Jeremy McCarter. *Hamilton the Revolution: Libretto of Broadway Musical, with a True Account of Its Creation, and Concise Remarks on Hip-Hop, the Power of Stories, and the New America*. New York: Grand Central, 2016.

Moore, Alan. *Watchmen*. Illustrated by Dave Gibbons. New York: DC Comics, 2005.

Moraga, Cherríe, and Gloria Anzaldúa, eds. *This Bridge Called My Back: Writings by Radical Women of Color*. New York: Kitchen Table Women of Color, 1983.

Moreno, Marisel. "Debunking Myths, Destabilizing Identities: A Reading of Junot Díaz's 'How to Date a Browngirl, Blackgirl, Whitegirl, or Halfie.'" *Afro-Hispanic Review* 26, no. 2 (2007): 9–23.

Moretti, Franco. "Conjectures on World Literature." *New Left Review* 1 (2000).

Moten, Fred. *In the Break: The Aesthetics of the Black Radical Tradition*. Minneapolis: University of Minnesota Press, 2003.

Moya, Paula M. L. "Dismantling the Master's House: The Decolonial Literary Imaginations of Audre Lorde and Junot Díaz." In *Junot Díaz and the Decolonial Imagination*, edited by Monica Hanna, Jennifer Harford Vargas, and José David Saldívar, 231–56. Durham, NC: Duke University Press, 2016.

Moya, Paula M. L. "The Search for Decolonial Love, Parts I and II: An Interview with Junot Díaz." *Boston Review*, June 26–27, 2012. Accessed October 6, 2012. http://bostonreview.net/books-ideas/paula-ml-moya-decolonial-love-interview-junot-d%C3% ADaz.

Moya, Paula M. L. *The Social Imperative: Race, Close Reading, and Contemporary Literary Criticism*. Stanford, CA: Stanford University Press, 2015.

Muhs, Gabriella Gutiérrez, ed. *Rebozos de palabras: An Helena Maria Viramontes Reader*. Tucson: University of Arizona Press, 2013.

Muñoz, José Esteban. *Disidentifications: Queers of Color and the Performance of Politics*. Minneapolis: University of Minnesota Press, 1999.

Myers, Megan Jeanette. "Dos rayanos-americanos Rewrite Hispaniola: Julia Alvarez and Junot Díaz." *Confluencia: Revista Hispánica de Cultura y Literatura* 32, no. 1 (2016): 168–81.

"Near-Riot in NYC Book Store for Junot Díaz." *Writers Institute Blog*, September 13, 2012. Accessed November 1, 2012. http://nyswiblog.blogspot.com/2012/09/near-riot-in-nyc-book-store-for-junot.html.

Nelson, Diane M. *Reckoning: The Ends of War in Guatemala*. Durham, NC: Duke University Press, 2009.

Nelson, Victoria. *The Secret Life of Puppets*. Cambridge, MA: Harvard University Press, 2003.

"New Faces of 1996." *Newsweek*, January 14, 1996. Accessed December 3, 2010. www.newsweek.com/new-faces-1996-177174.

Ngai, Sianne. *Our Aesthetic Categories: Zany, Cute, Interesting*. Cambridge, MA: Harvard University Press, 2012.

Nwosu, Chiamaka, and Jeanne Batalova. "Immigrants from the Dominican Republic in the United States." Migration Policy Institute, July 18, 2014. www.migrationpolicy.org/article/immigrants-dominican-republic-united-states-2012.

Okie, Matt. "Mil Máscaras: An Interview with Pulitzer-Winner Junot Díaz (*The Brief Wondrous Life of Oscar Wao*)." *Identity Theory*, 2008. Accessed January 20, 2010. http://www.identitytheory.com/interviews/okie_Díaz.php.

Olguin, Ben. *Violentologies: Violence, Identity and Ideology in Latina/o Literature*. New York: Oxford University Press, 2021.

O'Neill, Tracy. "Junot Díaz on the Game of Fiction and Intimacy." New York Public Library, January 19, 2016. Accessed February 1, 2016. http://www.nypl.org/blog/2016/01/19/podcast-junot-diaz?utm_campaign=SocialFlow&utm.

"Open Letter against Media Treatment of Junot Díaz." *Chronicle of Higher Education*, May 14, 2018. Accessed May 18, 2018. www.chronicle.com/blogs/letters/open-letter-against-media-treatment-of-junot-diaz?cid2=gen_login_refresh&cid=gen_sign_in.

O'Rourke, Meghan. "Questions for Junot Díaz: An Interview with the Pulitzer Prize-Winning Author." *Slate*, April 8, 2008. Accessed May 1, 2008. http://www.slate.com/id/2188494/.

Orr, Leonard, ed. *Joyce, Imperialism, and Postcolonialism*. Syracuse, NY: Syracuse University Press, 2008.

Ortiz, Fernando. *Cuban Counterpoint: Tobacco and Sugar*. Translated by Harriet de Onís. Durham, NC: Duke University Press, 1995.

Ostman, Heather. *The Fiction of Junot Díaz: Reframing the Lens*. London: Rowman and Littlefield, 2017.

Peeters, Benoit. *Derrida: A Biography*. Translated by Andrew Brown. Cambridge, UK: Polity, 2013.

Pérez, Emma. *The Decolonial Imaginary: Writing Chicanas into History*. Bloomington: Indiana University Press, 1999.

Pérez, Richard. "Racial Spills and Disfigured Faces in Piri Thomas's *Down These Mean Streets* and Junot Díaz's 'Ysrael.'" In *Contemporary U.S. Latino/a Literary Criticism*, edited by Lyn Di Iorio Sandín and Richard Perez, 93–112. New York: Palgrave Macmillan, 2007.

Pérez Firmat, Gustavo. *Bilingual Blues*. Tempe, AZ: Bilingual Press/Editorial Bilingüe, 1995.

Pérez Firmat, Gustavo. *Life on the Hyphen: The Cuban American Way*. Austin: University of Texas Press, 2012.

Pérez-Rosario, Vanessa. *Becoming Julia de Burgos: The Making of a Puerto Rican Icon*. Urbana: University of Illinois Press, 2014.

Piglia, Ricardo. "Theses on the Short Story." *New Left Review* 70 (2011).

Portes, Alejandro, and Robert L. Bach. *Latin Journey: Cuban and Mexican Immigrants in the United States*. Berkeley: University of California Press, 1985.

Pratt, Mary Louise. "The Short Story: The Long and Short of It." *Poetics* 10 (1981): 175–94.

Preziuso, Marika. "Rewriting the Caribbean Nation: Literary Authorship and the Diasporic Imagination." In *The Routledge Companion to Anglophone Caribbean Literature*, edited by Michael A. Bucknor and Allison Donnell, 526–33. London: Routledge, 2011.

Proust, Marcel. *À la recherche du temps perdu*. Paris: Gallimard, 2002.

Quesada, Sarah. "A Planetary Warning? The Multilayered Caribbean Zombie in 'Monstro.'" In *Junot Díaz and the Decolonial Imagination*, edited by Monica Hanna, Jennifer Harford Vargas, and José David Saldívar, 291–320. Durham, NC: Duke University Press, 2016.

Quijano, Aníbal. "Colonialidad y modernidad/racionalidad." In *Los conquistadores: 1492 y la población indígena de América*, edited by Heraclio Bonilla. Bogotá: Tercer Mundo/FLASCO, 1992.

Quijano, Aníbal. "Coloniality of Power, Eurocentrism, and Latin America." *Nepantla: Views from the South* 1, no. 3 (2000): 533–80.

Quijano, Aníbal. "The Coloniality of Power and Eurocentrism in Latin America." *International Sociology* 15, no. 2 (2000): 215–32.

Quijano, Aníbal. "Of *Don Quixote* and Windmills in Latin America." Translated by Meryl Adelman. *Estudos avançados* 21, no. 55 (2007): 9–31.

Quijano, Aníbal, and Immanuel Wallerstein. "Americanity as a Concept, or the Americas in the Modern World-System." *International Social Science Journal* 29 (1992): 549–97.

Ramírez, Dixa. *Colonial Phantoms: Belonging and Refusal in the Dominican Americas, from the 19th Century to the Present*. New York: New York University Press, 2018.

Ramírez, Dixa. "Great Men's Magic: Charting Hyper-masculinity and Supernatural Discourses of Power in Junot Díaz's *The Brief Wondrous Life of Oscar Wao*." *Atlantic Studies Journal* 10, no. 3 (2013): 384–405.

Rankine, Claudia, LeRonn P. Brooks, Monica Youn, Stephen Wilson, Emily Skillings, John Lucas, Sara'o Bery, Nuar Alsadir, and Simon Wu. "About the TRII: An Interdisciplinary Cultural Laboratory." Accessed June 4, 2018. https://theracialimaginary.org/about/.

Riofrio, John. "Situating Latin American Masculinity: Immigration, Empathy and Emasculation in Junot Díaz's *Drown*." *Atenea* 28, no. 1 (2008): 23–36.

Riverhead Books. *1996 Catalog*.

Robben, Antonius C. G. M., and Marcelo M. Suárez-Orozco, eds. *Cultures under Siege: Collective Violence and Trauma*. Cambridge: Cambridge University Press, 2000.

Robinson, Tasha. "We Asked Kim Stanley Robinson: Can Science Fiction Save Us?" *Polygon*, October 20, 2020. Accessed on July 8, 2021. https://www.polygon.com/2020/10/20/21525509/kim-stanley-robinson-interview-science-fiction-utopias.

Roorda, Eric Paul, Lauren Derby, and Raymundo González, eds. *The Dominican Republic Reader: History, Culture, Politics*. Durham, NC: Duke University Press, 2014.

Saldívar, José David. "Conjectures on 'Americanity' and Junot Díaz's 'Fukú Americanus' in *The Brief Wondrous Life of Oscar Wao*." *Global South* 5, no. 1 (2011): 120–36.

Saldívar, José David. *Trans-Americanity: Subaltern Modernities, Global Coloniality, and the Cultures of Greater Mexico*. Durham, NC: Duke University Press, 2012.

Saldívar, José David, Monica Hanna, and Jennifer Harford Vargas, eds. *Junot Díaz and the Decolonial Imagination*. Durham, NC: Duke University Press, 2016.

Saldívar, Ramón. "Chiste Apocalyptus." In *Junot Díaz and the Decolonial Imagination*, edited by Monica Hanna, Jennifer Harford Vargas, and José David Saldívar, 377–90. Durham, NC: Duke University Press, 2016.

Saldívar, Ramón. "Historical Fantasy, Speculative Realism, and Postrace Aesthetics in Contemporary American Fiction." *American Literary History* 23, no. 3 (2011): 574–99.

Sánchez Korrol, Virginia. *History of Puerto Ricans in the U.S.: Part Four*. Center for Puerto Rican Studies, Hunter College, City University of New York. Accessed November 4, 2019. https://centropr.hunter.cuny.edu/education/story-us-puerto-ricans-part-four.

Schiller, Friedrich. *On the Aesthetic Education of Man*. Translated by Reginald Snell. New York: Dover, 2004.

Sedgwick, Eve Kosofsky. *The Epistemology of the Closet*. Berkeley: University of California Press, 1990.

Sheppard, Tiye. "Identity, Dictators, and Apocalypse: An Interview with Junot Díaz." *Divisadero*, 2012. Accessed December 1, 2012. www.usfca.edu/artsci/las/divisadero/fall2102/interview-with-junot-diaz.

Simón, Yara. "Junot Díaz Won't Back Down from Criticizing DR's Immigration Crisis." *Remezcla*, November 12, 2015. Accessed December 1, 2015. https://remezcla.com/culture/junot-diaz-wont-back-down-from-criticizing-drs-immigration-crisis/.

Smithson, Robert. "Entropy and New Monuments." In *Robert Smithson: The Collected Writings*, edited by Jack Flam, 10–24. Berkeley: University of California Press, 1996.

Smithson, Robert. "The Monuments of Passaic." *Artforum* 7, no. 4 (1967): 48–51.

Sommer, Doris. *Bilingual Games: Some Literary Investigations*. New York: Palgrave, 2003.

Spivak, Gayatri Chakravorty. *An Aesthetic Education in the Era of Globalization*. Cambridge, MA: Harvard University Press, 2012.

"State of the Art: Junot Díaz, Author." PBS. www.pbs.org/video/21832223790.

Stavans, Ilan, ed. *The Norton Anthology of Latino Literature*. New York: W. W. Norton, 2011.

Subramanian, Shreerekha. "In the Wake of His Damage." *Rumpus*, May 12, 2018. Accessed June 5, 2018. https://therumpus.net/2018/05/in-the-wake-of-his-damage.

Sun, Lu. "Every Novel Is a New Country: A Conversation with Junot Díaz." *Critique: Studies in Contemporary Fiction* 61, no. 3 (2020): 249–61.

Suvin, Darko. *Metamorphoses of Science Fiction: On the Poetics and History of a Literary Genre*, edited by Gerry Canavan. Oxford: Peter Lang, 2016.

Suvin, Darko. *Positions and Presuppositions in Science Fiction*. Kent, OH: Kent State University Press, 1988.

Tally Jr., Robert. "Places Where the Stars Are Strange: Fantasy and Utopia in Tolkien's Middle-earth." In *Tolkien in the New Century: Essays in Honor of Tom Shippe*, edited by John Wm. Houghton, Janet Brennan Croft, Nancy Martsch, John D. Rateliff, and Robin Anne Reid, 5–65. Jefferson, NC: McFarland, 2014.

Tolkien, J. R. R. "Beowulf: The Monsters and the Critics." In *The Monsters and the Critics and Other Essays*, edited by Christopher Tolkien, 5–48. London: HarperCollins, 1997.

Tolkien, J. R. R. *The Fellowship of the Ring: Being the First Part of The Lord of the Rings*. New York: Houghton Mifflin, 1954.

Tolkien, J. R. R. "On Fairy-Stories." In *The Tolkien Reader*, 3–84. New York: Ballantine, 1973.

Tolkien, J. R. R. *The Return of the King: Being the Third Part of Lord of the Rings*. New York: Houghton Mifflin, 1954.

Tolkien, J. R. R. *The Two Towers: Being the Second Part of Lord of the Rings*. New York: Houghton Mifflin, 1954.

Torres-Saillant, Silvio. *An Intellectual History of the Caribbean*. New York: Palgrave Macmillan, 2006.

Trouillot, Michel-Rolph. *Silencing the Past: Power and the Production of History*. Boston: Beacon, 1995.

US Bureau of the Census. "Poverty Thresholds." October 8, 2021. www.census.gov/data/tables/time-series/demo/income-poverty/historical-poverty-thresholds.html.

Valderrama, Patricia. "Reading for the Anthropocene: Humanimality as Resilience." PhD diss., Stanford University, 2018.

Vargas, Deborah R. "Sucia Love: Losing, Lying, and Leaving in *This Is How You Lose Her*." In *Junot Díaz and the Decolonial Imagination*, edited by Jennifer Harford Vargas, Monica Hanna, and José David Saldívar, 351–76. Durham, NC: Duke University Press, 2016.

Vargas Llosa, Mario. *The Feast of the Goat*. Translated by Edith Grossman. New York: Farrar, Straus and Giroux, 2001.

Vega, Bernardo. *Memoirs of Bernardo Vega: A Contribution to the History of the Puerto Rican Community.* Edited by Cesar Iglesias. Translated by Juan Flores. New York: Monthly Review Press, 1984.

Waldinger, Roger. *Between Here and There: How Attached Are Latino Immigrants to Their Home Countries?* Washington, DC: Pew Hispanic Center, 2007.

Wallace, David Foster. "Fictional Futures and Conspicuously Young." In *Both Flesh and Not: Essays*, 37–72. New York: Little, Brown, 2012.

White, Hayden. *The Practical Past.* Evanston, IL: Northwestern University Press, 2014.

Whitmore, Richard. *Why Boys Fail: Saving Our Sons from an Educational System That's Leaving Them Behind.* New York: AMACON, 2010.

Williams, William Carlos. "To Elsie." In *Collected Poems, Volume 1: 1909–1939*, edited by Walton Litz and Christopher MacGowan, 217–19. New York: New Directions, 1991.

Woloch, Alex. *The One vs. the Many: Minor Characters and the Space of the Protagonist in the Novel.* Princeton, NJ: Princeton University Press, 2003.

Yagoda, Ben. *About Town:* The New Yorker *and the World It Made.* New York: Scribner, 2000.

Index

Abinadar, Luis, 222n15
Abrams, M. H., 141
The Act of Reading (Iser), 127–29, 213n98
Adichie, Chimamanda Ngozi, 100
Aesthetic Education in the Era of Globalization (Spivak), 219n42
African Americans: violence against, 12
Afro-Atlantic Dominican identity: in *The Brief Wondrous Life of Oscar Wao*, 114–15, 143–46; in Díaz's work, xvi, 17, 20, 25, 48, 66–68, 78, 87, 94–96, 180–85, 187–88, 193n20; in "Monstro," 183–85; premature death and, 52, 203n18
Agamben, Giorgio, 143
"Aguantando" (Díaz), 13–14, 49, 79–82
"Akira" (unfinished Díaz novel), 32, 104–5, 115–16
Alcantara, Marisol, 217n14
Alcoff, Linda Martín, xiii, 162, 192n9
Allison, Sarah, 219n36
"Alma" (Díaz), 157
Als, Hilton, 73, 151
Alterity and Transcendence (Levinas), 77–78
Alvarez, Julia, 39, 120, 187, 217n6
Americanity: in *The Brief Wondrous Life of Oscar Wao*, 131–46; in Díaz's work, 1–2, 50; in "Monstro," 185; scholarship on, xv–xvi, 131–33, 213n121
Andrews, Chris, 52, 112
Anzaldúa, Gloria, 178, 187
apocalypse: in Díaz's work, 182–85
Appadurai, Arjun, 60
Appleton, Victor, 17
Aragi, Nicole, 20, 76, 154, 198n45
"Aurora" (Díaz), 50, 53–56, 61, 66

Badiou, Alain, 175–77
Balaguer, Joaquin, 8, 13, 15
Balcells, Carmen, 198n45
Barrett, Frances, 141
Being and Event (Badiou), 176
Beloved (Morrison), 160, 210n42
Bennett, W. Tapley, Jr., 81
Beowulf, 29
Big Bang theory, 203n14
"Big Two-Hearted River" (Hemingway), 112
The Black Atlantic: Double Consciousness and Modernity (Gilroy), 224n36
Blackness: Díaz's alignment with, 120, 138, 183–85
Black Skin, White Masks (Fanon), 177–78, 195n22
body-corpus borders: in "Aurora," 55–56; Díaz's discussion of, 37–38
Bolaño, Roberto, xvi, 21–22, 52, 100, 112, 222n2
Bosch, Juan, 49, 81–82
Boston Review, 193n12
"Boyfriend" (Díaz), 87–88
Bradbury, Ray, 17
The Brief Wondrous Life of Oscar Wao (novel) (Díaz), xiv–xvi; Americanity in, 131–46; apocalyptic imagery in, 182; autobiographical elements in, 86–87, 182; blanks and erasures in, 124–29, 180–81, 216n3; characterization in, 58–59, 112–15, 121; closet imagery in, 41–42, 110, 163–68, 218n24; coloniality in, 2–5, 24–25, 123–26, 131–46; critical analysis of, 117; dark consciousness in, 33–38; decolonialism in, 103–5, 177; density of text in, 5; diasporic world in, 71–72, 103–5;

The Brief Wondrous Life of Oscar Wao (continued)
Dominican Republic in, 12–13, 101–5, 113–15, 132, 136–38, 143–46; footnotes in, 49, 119, 134, 163, 218n22; fukú americanus in, xvi, 4, 6–7, 100–105, 119–20, 131–46; grimoire in, 141–42; Haitian genocide in Dominican Republic and, 118–19; half-life of love in, 158–78; as historia, 112; impact on Latinx literature of, 1, 3, 7–8; language in, 19; narrative structure in, 32; negative aesthetics and imaginary transference in, 126–31; New Jersey in, 107–16, 121–26, 131–32, 137–38; paratexts in, 117–23, 163–68; past and present in, 60; plotlines in, 5–6; publication of, 20–21; Santo Domingo in, 12–13, 57–59, 67, 113–15, 121–23, 138; science fiction elements in, 31–38; sucio/sucia love in, 159–62; Tolkien's influence in, 31–32; torture depicted in, 15–16; Trujillo as figure in, 29, 103–5, 112–15, 118, 120–23, 132, 137, 139–42; women in, 120, 138–39, 158; writing of, 7, 23–24, 99–105, 116–19, 146–47, 210n50

"The Brief Wondrous Life of Oscar Wao" (Díaz) (short story), 23–24, 100–113, 115–16, 118–20, 123, 210n50
Brues, Frank, 104
Buford, Bill, 75
Burgos, Julia de, 188
Butler, Octavia, 142
Byrne, Monica, 193n12

Campanile, Carole, 217n14
Candelario, Ginetta, 205n64
capitalism: in Díaz's work, 1
Caramelo (Cisneros), 100, 160
Caribbean history and aesthetic: in *The Brief Wondrous Life of Oscar Wao*, 2, 4, 13, 35–38, 101, 113–15, 118, 121–23, 131, 139–46; in Díaz's writing, 17–18, 48, 75–77; Dominican Republic and, 9, 49; fantasy and, 129; fukú americanus and, 135–38; US imperialism and, 61, 67, 81–82; in Walcott's writing, 122–23
Carpio, Glenda R., 119–20
Carver, Raymond, 51, 67, 204n26
Catedral Primada de América, 13
Cather, Willa, 89
Cervantes, Miguel de, 100, 109, 214n122
Césaire, Aimé, 5, 129, 140, 142–43
Chamoiseau, Patrick, 60

Chasman, Deborah, 192n9, 193n12, 193n19
"The Cheater's Guide to Love" (Díaz), xvii, 25, 88–89, 153, 157–60, 168, 171–78
Ch'ien, Evelyn, 17, 19, 210n44
chisme (gossip), 63–64
Chronicle of Higher Education, xiii
Cien años de soledad (*One Hundred Years of Solitude*) (García Márquez), 4, 8, 174
Cisneros, Sandra, 5, 19–20, 100, 120, 160, 187
Clemmons, Zinzi, xii, 193n12
Clinton, William Jefferson, 103, 131
closet imagery: in Díaz's work, 41–42, 110, 163–68, 218n24
cognitive novum: Suvin's concept of, 201n13
Cohen, Joshua, 192n9
Cohen, Margaret, 131
coloniality: in *The Brief Wondrous Life of Oscar Wao*, 2–5, 24–25, 102–5, 123–26, 131–46; Díaz's analysis of, 25, 200n10; in Díaz's work, 1–2, 4, 49–50, 208n19; of gender, 166, 203n12, 220n51; in Tolkien's *Lord of the Rings*, 29–38; transnationalism and, 47–48
Columbus, Christopher (Almirante Colón), 3–4, 13, 24, 101–2, 118, 132–36, 185, 202n8
Columbus, Diego, 13
Conrad, Joseph, 111
Cornell University: Díaz in MFA program at, 47–48, 50–58, 67, 71–72, 89–93, 103, 112, 207n46; Latinx student activism at, 38–44
The Corrections (Franzen), 100
Cortázar, Julio, 93
cosmology: inflation theory in, 203n14
COVID-19 pandemic: "Monstro" (Díaz) in age of, 188–89
creative writing programs, 20, 25, 41, 88–93, 109, 153, 168, 202n10, 218n25
Critique of the Power of Judgment (Kant), 219n42
Cruz, Angie, 188
Cuba: Castro in, 81–82; Guantanamo in, 145; migration to US from, 48, 61; plantation system in, 2; Spanish-American War and, 16, 187; transculturation in, 202n9, 215n138
cuento form: Díaz's use of, 52–58, 65–66

danger: in Díaz's writings, 180–85
Danticat, Edwidge, xiv, 2–3, 10–11, 22, 39, 60
Darnton, Robert, 163
Das Rheingold (Wagner), 32–34, 123–24

Dávila, Arlene, 38–39
Davis, Mike, 139, 168, 202n2
De Chiara, Marina, 60
decolonial feminism: Díaz and influence of, xiii, 178, 221n55
decolonial turn: aesthetics and, 219n42; in *The Brief Wondrous Life of Oscar Wao*, 123–26; in Díaz's work, xv, 2, 7–8, 24–25, 85, 102–5, 193n17, 195n22, 199n1; love in Díaz's fiction and, 151–53, 174–78; self and other in, 195n22; sucio/sucia love in Díaz's writing and, 159–62; in Tolkien's *Lord of the Rings*, 30–38
De Maeseneer, Rita, 118
de Peña, Luisa, 10, 15–16
Depestre, René, 143
Derby, Lauren, 2, 220n53
Derrida, Jacques, 37–38
diaspora: in Díaz's work, 2, 5, 20, 59–60, 102–5, 223n28; from Dominican Republic, 51–52; Gilroy's discussion of, 224n36; Latin American writers on, xvi
Díaz, Junot: at Berkeley, xiv, 2–3; critical analysis of, 21–22, 96, 217n6; *Drown* published by, 20–21; early Cornell fiction by, 49–50; early life in Dominican Republic, 8–14; emigration to United States, 17–19; interviews with, 155–59; Joyce's influence on work of, 85–86; literary influences on, 19–20; MFA creative writing programs critiqued by, 91–93; "Negocios" thesis and, 20; Obama's praise of, xi; political activism of, 21–23, 28–36, 38–44; racist slurs in writing of, 210n54; readings by, 156–59; sexual assault experience, xi–xii; short stories published by, 20–21; Stanford Presidential Lecture by, 27–28, 39–44, 200n2; student identification with, 40–44; suicide attempts by, xii; women's relationships with, 156–59; on writing of *The Brief Wondrous Life of Oscar Wao* (novel) (Díaz), 99–105
Díaz, Marisabela, 8
Díaz, Maritza, 8
Díaz, Paul, 8
Díaz, Rafael (brother), xii, 8, 17, 157
Díaz, Rafael (father), 8–9, 17
Díaz, Virtrudes, 8
Discipline and Punish (Foucault), 191n2, 201n25
Document magazine, 21–22
Dominican Americans: in Díaz's fiction, xi, xvi, 3–4, 21–22, 49–50, 152–54, 186–87; Díaz's political activism in, 38–44
The Dominican Intervention (Lowenthal), 81
Dominican Republic: criticism of Díaz in, 10–11, 217n6; Díaz's early life in, 8–14; in Díaz's work, 1–3, 6–7, 48–49, 59, 81–82, 101–5, 113–15; DREAM project in, 39; fukú americanus and, 135–36, 140–46; Haitian border fortifications by, 222n15; Haitian citizenship revoked in, 217n6; Haitian deportation and genocide in, 2–3, 10–12, 22–23, 39, 118–19, 141; large-scale migration to US from, 51; Ruling 168 in, 39; in "The Brief Wondrous Life of Oscar Wao" (Díaz) (short story), 107–16, 118, 132, 138–39, 143–46; trans-American scholarship on, 2; US invasion of, 13–16, 49, 81–82; women in, 120
"The Dominican Republic's War on Haitian Workers" (Díaz and Danticat op-ed), 39
Dominican Youth Union, 39
Don Quixote (Cervantes), 100, 109, 214n122
Doyle, Arthur Conan, 17
DREAM project (Dominican Republic), 39
Drown (Díaz): apocalyptic imagery in, 182, 185; autobiographical elements in, 85–87, 182; blanks and erasures in, 216n3; characterization in, 48, 58–59, 93; critical praise for, 104; danger in, 180; decolonial love in, 177; diasporic world in, 71–72, 103; Díaz's discussion of, 153–54; Dominican Republic in, xiv, xvi, 2–3, 12, 23, 191n2; drowning man imagery in, 86–87; as historia, 112; literary influences in, 19–20; London Terrace in, 57–58; mask imagery in, 191n2; narrative tension in, 53; New Jersey images in, 202n7; past and present in, 60; publication of, 76, 96; short-story form in, 67, 174
"Drown" (short story) (Díaz), 20, 76, 82–85, 161–62
Duany, Jorge, 47–48
Dussel, Enrique, 215n140

"Edison, New Jersey" (Díaz), 74, 88
Eggers, David, xi, 155
Engler, Mira, 70
Enlightenment: Díaz's discussion of, 33, 212n88
Epoch (Cornell creative writing journal), 89
Eurocentric hegemony: fukú americanus in context of, 144–46

Fanon, Frantz, 136, 177–78, 195n22
The Fantastic Four (Kirby and Lee), 5, 120–23, 129
fantasy: in Díaz's *Brief Wondrous Life of Oscar Wao*, 121–23, 163; Díaz's discussion of, 31–38; Tolkien on function of, 200n12
Faulkner, William, 60, 89
feminist writing: defense of Díaz in, 192n9; influence on Díaz of, 120
"Fiesta, 1980" (Díaz), 76, 78–79
Figueroa-Vásquez, Yomaira C., xiii, 102
"The Figure in the Carpet" (James), 128
"Flaca" (Díaz), 85, 157
Flaubert, Gustav, 5, 100, 129
Florida Immigrant Coalition, 11
Fluck, Winfried, xiv, 24, 127, 129–30
The Footnote (Grafton), 134
footnotes: in *The Brief Wondrous Life of Oscar Wao* (Díaz), 49, 119, 134, 163, 218n22
Foucault, Michel, 35, 107, 167, 191n2, 201n25, 208n14, 209n34
Franzen, Jonathan, 100
Free University (Berlin), 127
Fuguet, Alberto, 216n1
fukú americanus: in *The Brief Wondrous Life of Oscar Wao*, xvi, 4, 6–7, 100–105, 119–20, 131–46; Díaz's concept of, xvi, 4, 24, 153–54, 208n19
Fukú Americanus (adaptation of *The Brief Wondrous Life of Oscar Wao*), 208n4
Fusco, Coco, 192n9

García Márquez, Gabriel, 4, 8, 89, 174
García-Peña, Lorgia, 102
Gates, David, 96
gender: coloniality of, 166, 203n12, 220n51
Genette, Gérard, 117–19
Gibson, William, 183
Gilroy, Paul, 184, 224n36
Glimmer Train (Díaz), 157
Glissant, Édouard, 5, 60, 113, 129
Global Landfill, in Díaz's fiction, 48–49, 57–59, 64, 68–72
Global South journal, xiv
Goldman, Francisco, 7, 104
Gómez, Sergio, 216n1
Gómez-Barris, Macarena, 140, 143
González, Raymundo, 2, 208n14
Gordon, Lewis, 177
Grafton, Anthony, 134

Grau, Julie, 76, 96
grimoire: in *The Brief Wondrous Life of Oscar Wao*, 141–42
Grosfoguel, Ramón, 102
Guardian newspaper, 10–11
Guggenheim Fellowship: Díaz as recipient of, 7, 31–32, 104–5
Gumbrecht, Hans Ulrich, 90–91

Haitians: Dominican Republic deportation and genocide of, 2–3, 10–12, 22–23, 39, 118–19, 141; in "Monstro," 182–85
Half of a Yellow Sun (Adiche), 100
Hall, Stuart, 99–100
Halperin, David, 163
Hanna, Monica, xv, 27, 199n1
Harford Vargas, Jennifer, xv, 27, 199n1
Harry Potter series, 32, 35, 123
Heart of Darkness (Conrad), 111
Hegel, G. F. W., 195n22
Heidegger, Martin, 37–38
Hemingway, Ernest, 105–6, 111–12
Hernandez, Jaime, 105–6
Herrin, Lamar, 71, 89–91
heteropatriarchy: in Díaz's fiction, xiii
higher education, democratization of, 200n10
Hijuelos, Oscar, 187
historias: of Díaz and Danticat, 2–3; Díaz's stories as, 60–66. *See also* cuentos
The History of Sexuality (Foucault), 35
Homer, 5, 85, 129
homosexuality: in Díaz's work, 83–85, 163–68
"How to Date a Brown Girl (Black Girl, White Girl, or Halfie)" (Díaz), 20, 58, 76, 87–88, 93–96

imaginary transference: in *The Brief Wondrous Life of Oscar Wao* (Díaz), 126–31; in Díaz's work, xv, 2
immigrant experience: in Díaz's fiction, 3–4, 21–22, 61; Latin American writers on, xvi
Indigenous groups: Díaz's alignment with, 120, 185
In Praise of Love (Badiou), 176
"Instructions on How to Wind a Watch" (Cortázar), 93
International Coalition of Historic Sites of Museums of Conscience, 15
Intersection for the Arts, 155
In the Time of the Butterflies (Alvarez), 120

"Invierno" (Díaz), 67, 157, 205n61
Irizarry, Ylce, 85
Iser, Wolfgang, 24, 127–29, 213n98
Islandborn (Díaz), xvi, 2, 25, 112, 180, 185–87, 223n28
Islas, Arturo, 89

James, Henry, 128
Jameson, Fredric, 36, 87, 179, 222n13
Johnson, Lyndon Baines, 17, 82
Joyce, James, 60, 85–87
"Junot Díaz" (Als), 73, 151
"Junot Díaz: A Symposium" (Stanford University), 27–28
Junot Díaz and the Decolonial Imagination (Hanna, Harford Vargas, and Saldívar), 27, 199n1
"Junot Díaz Writes about Moving to Brooklyn," 73

Kakutani, Michiko, xi
Kant, Immanuel, 30, 200n6, 219n42
Kennedy, John F., 131, 134
King, Stephen, xii, 17
Kingsolver, Barbara, xi
Kirby, Jack, 5, 120, 129
Konstance School of Reception Aesthetics (Germany), 127
Kottman, Paul, 195n22
Krik? Krak! (Danticat), xiv
Kun, Josh, 202n6

Lahiri, Jhumpa, xi
Lanzendorfer, Tim, 121–22
Lao-Montes, Agustín, 102
Late Night with Seth Meyers (television talk show), 155
Latinx identity: in Díaz's writing, xv–xvi, 21–22, 129–31, 187–88; student activism and, 38–44
Latinx literature: Díaz's impact on, 3–4, 7–8, 152–54
Latour, Bruno, 70
Laviera, Tato, 29
Lee, Stan, 5, 120, 129
Levinas, Emmanuel, 77–78
literary minimalism, 51, 67, 114, 203n15
"London Terrace" (Díaz), 23, 50, 67–72, 157, 205n61. *See also* "Invierno" (Díaz)
London Terrace apartments: in Díaz's fiction, 48–50, 54–59, 64, 67–72, 78–79, 83–87, 94–96, 169–70, 204n35
Lorde, Audre, 120
The Lord of the Rings (Tolkien), 100, 121–23, 129, 163–64; Díaz's discussion of, 5, 28–38, 124–26
love: Díaz on half-life of, 154–78; Díaz's experiences with, 156–59; sucio and sucia love, 159–62
Love as Human Freedom (Kottman), 195n22
Lovecraft, H. P., 29, 32, 123–24
Lowe, Lisa, 63
Lowenthal, Abraham, 81–82
Lugones, María, 166, 203n12, 220n51

MacArthur Fellowship: Díaz as recipient of, xv, 20–21
Machado, Carmen María, xii, 192n9, 193n12
magical urbanism: in Díaz's work, 39, 168, 202n2
Magical Urbanism (Davis), 139, 168, 202n2
The Magus (Barrett), 141
Maldonado-Torres, Nelson, 193n17
Martí, José, 120
Martínez-San Miguel, Yolanda, 2
"más allá" US-Mexico borderlands theory, 48, 202n6
masculinity: in Díaz's works, xiv–xv, 37–38, 106–15, 154–55, 219n45; in Dominican culture, 220n53
masks: in Díaz's writing, 38, 191n2; in "Ysrael," 75–78
Massachusetts Institute of Technology (MIT): Díaz at, 35–37, 53, 116–17, 192n9
McGurl, Mark, 25, 91–92, 200n10, 218n25
Medium magazine, 192n9
memory: in *Islandborn* (Díaz), 185–87
Metamorphoses of Science Fiction (Suvin), 36, 201n13
metamundo: Díaz's London Terrace neighborhood and, 50, 69, 204n35; in Díaz's work, 86, 112, 122, 130, 138, 153, 169, 187, 203n14
Mexican War of 1848, 16
"MFA vs. POC" (Díaz), 51, 88, 92, 207n46
Miami Herald, 11
Mignolo, Walter, 143, 216n159
Miranda, Lin-Manuel, 188
misogyny: accusations against Díaz of, xii–xiii, 153, 192n9, 193n12
"Miss Lora" (Díaz), 153, 161–62, 173
Mohr, Nicholasa, 29, 188
"The Mongoose and the Émigré" (Díaz essay), 187

"Monstro" (Díaz), 2, 25, 180–85, 188–89, 222n13, 223n23
"Monuments of Passaic" (Smithson), 202n7, 203n13
Moraga, Cherrie, 178
Moretti, Franco, 131–32, 163
Morrison, Toni, 5, 19–22, 60, 85, 120, 145–46, 160, 180, 210n42
Moten, Fred, 183–85
Moya, Paula M. L., xiii, 24, 94–96, 102, 158–59, 177, 199n1, 207n46
Moyers and Company (television talk show), 155
Muñoz, José Esteban, 219n34
Museo Alcazár, 13
Museo de la Resistancia, 14–16
My Ántonia (Cather), 89

narrative tension: in Díaz's short stories, 52–58; in "Ysrael," 77–78
National Book Award: Díaz shortlisted for, 20–21
National Institute of Latino Policy, 21
negative aesthetics: in *The Brief Wondrous Life of Oscar Wao* (Díaz), 126–31; in *Islandborn*, 185–87; trans-Americanity and, xv–xvi, 24–25
"Negocios" (Díaz short story), 60–66
"Negocios" (Díaz's MFA thesis), xv–xvi; Afro-Atlantic Dominican identity in, 17, 20, 78, 103; autobiographical elements in, 182; characterization in, 48–50, 58–59, 89–93; coloniality in, 2; Dominican Republic in, 12, 23, 49, 59, 90; drowning imagery in, 87; narrative tension in, 53, 56–59; New Jersey places in, 57–59, 90, 202n7; past and present in, 60–61; short-story form in, 65–68
négritude, 140, 142–43
Nelson, Victoria, 33, 124
New Jersey: Díaz's early life in, 17–19, 57; images in Díaz's writing of, 50, 57–59, 64–72, 202n7; in "The Brief Wondrous Life of Oscar Wao" (Díaz) (short story), 107–16, 121–26, 131–32, 137–38
Newsweek magazine, 104
New York City: Cuban and Puerto Rican migration to, 61
New Yorker magazine, 20; Díaz's short stories in, xi–xii, 51, 58, 74, 93, 210n54; "The Brief Wondrous Life of Oscar Wao" published in, 23–24, 100–113, 115–16, 118–20, 123, 210n50
Ngai, Sianne, 219n42
"Nilda" (Díaz), 157, 169–71

non-identity, Fluck's concept of, 129–30
Norton Anthology of Latino Literature, 3
"Notebook of a Return to My Native Land" (Césaire), 142–43

Obama, Barack, xi, xvi–xvii, 30–31, 180, 193n15
Observations on the Feeling of the Beautiful and the Sublime (Kant), 200n6
Odyssey (Homer), 5, 86–87, 129
"Old Masks, New Face" (Díaz), 191n2
Omeros (Walcott), 5, 129
"One Last Poem for Richard" (Cisneros), 19
On the Aesthetic Education of Man (Schiller), 219n42
Order of Merit (Dominican Republic): Díaz as recipient of, 22–23
Ortiz, Fernando, 137, 139, 202n9, 215n138
Otomo, Katsuhiro, 104
"Otravida, Otravez" (Díaz), 59, 157
Our Aesthetic Categories (Ngai), 219n42

paratext, in *The Brief Wondrous Life of Oscar Wao* (novel) (Díaz), 117–23, 163–68
Paris Review, 76
Partido de los Trabajadores Dominicanos, 39
past and present: in Díaz's fiction, 60
Peña, José Francisco, 49
Pérez, Richard, 77–78
Pérez-Rosario, Vanessa, 102
Phenomenology of Spirit (Hegel), 195n22
Piglia, Ricardo, 52–53
Pinochet, Augusto, 140
place, in Díaz's writing, 47–48, 57–58, 70–72
Poetics (Aristotle), 52
political activism: Díaz's engagement in, 21–23, 38–44
The Politics of Nature (Latour), 70
Portrait of the Artist as a Young Man (Joyce), 86
Program Era (McGurl), 25, 91, 200n10, 203n15, 218n25
program era in creative writing, 25, 91–93, 96, 160, 203n15, 218n25
ProLibertad social movement, 38–39
Proust, Marcel, 220n52
Puerto Rican migration to US, 61
Pulitzer Board: Díaz's membership on, xiii, 193n11
Pulitzer Prize: Díaz as recipient of, xv, 7
"The Pura Principle" (Díaz), 157
Pynchon, Thomas, 68

quantitative formalism, 163, 219n36
queer theory: Díaz's work and, 41–42
Quijano, Aníbal, 24, 33–34, 102, 124, 131–36, 184–85, 200n10, 209n20, 212n90, 213n121, 214n122

race: in Tolkien's *Lord of the Rings*, 29–38
racial double consciousness: in Díaz's work, 67
racial imaginary: in Díaz's work, 95, 207n53
Ramírez, Dixa, 2, 13, 212n94
Ranke, Leopold von, 134
Rankine, Claudia, 95
rape culture: coloniality and, 102–5; in Trujillo's Dominican Republic, 138–42, 162
reading: in *The Brief Wondrous Life of Oscar Wao*, 127–29, 163–68, 213n98
Reagan, Ronald, 5–6, 24, 103, 105, 131
Reid Cabral, Donald, 81
Riverhead Books, 76, 96
river metaphor: in "Negocios" (Díaz's MFA thesis), 90–91
Robinson, Kim Stanley, 234n40
Rodriguez, Maria, 11
Roman, Edilberto, 11
Romance with America (Fluck), 127–28
Roordia, Eric Paul, 2
Rosenthal, Lois, 76–78
Rowling, J. K., 29, 31, 32, 123
Rubirosa, Porfirio, 206n19
Rutgers University: Díaz's attendance at, 6, 19, 31, 87–88; in "The Brief Wondrous Life of Oscar Wao" (Díaz) (short story), 107–9

Saldívar, Ramón, 121–22, 141–42, 199n1
Sandín, Lyn Di Iorio, 110
Santo Domingo: in Díaz's writing, 12–13, 57–59, 67, 113–15, 121–23, 138
The Savage Detectives (Díaz), xvi, 21–22
Schiller, Friedrich, 219n42
"The Schooner Flight" (Walcott), 122–23
science fiction: in Díaz's work, 1, 41–42, 142–46, 163–68, 181–85, 222n2; Suvin's discussion of, 201n13; theories of, 234n40
"The Search for Decolonial Love" (Díaz), 177
The Secret Life of Puppets (Nelson), 33, 124
Sedgwick, Eve Kosofsky, 41, 165–66
Selman, Eduardo, 22, 199n53
Sentimental Education (Flaubert), 5, 100, 108–9, 129

sexual violence: Díaz's experience with, xi–xii; in "Ysrael," 76–78, 160–62
"The Short Happy Life of Francis Macomber" (Hemingway), 105–6
"The Silence: The Legacy of Childhood Trauma" (Díaz), xi–xii, 57, 102, 191n2
Silencing the Past (Trouillot), 62, 137
slavery: Díaz on, 185; in Dominican Republic, 2; in Tolkien's *Lord of the Rings*, 33–34
Smith, Zadie, xi, 8, 100
Smithson, Robert, 202n7, 203n13
social media: criticism of Díaz on, xiii, 153, 192n9; Díaz's political activism on, 39
Song of Solomon (Morrison), 19
Spanglish: Díaz's use of, 28, 66, 110, 113–14, 155, 159
Spanish American War (1898), 16
speculative genres: Díaz on, 163–64
Spillers, Hortense, 207n46
Spivak, Gayatri, 219n42
Stanford Center for Comparative Studies in Race and Ethnicity (CCSRE), 27–28, 200n2
State of Exception (Agamben), 143
Stavans, Ilan, 3
Stegner, Wallace, 89
Stewart, Barbara, 96
Story magazine, 76, 78
student activists: identification with Díaz among, 39–44
Subramanian, Shreerekha, xii–xiii
sucio and sucia love: Díaz's decolonization of, 159–62, 168–78
"The Sun, the Moon, the Stars" (Díaz), 157
Suvin, Darko, 36, 201n13
Syracuse University: Díaz at, 103–5, 116, 209n23

Tally, Robert, Jr., 36
Theory of the Subject (Badiou), 176
"Theses on the Short Story" (Piglia), 52–53
This Is How You Lose Her (Díaz), xvi, 25, 49; apocalyptic imagery in, 182; autobiographical elements in, 83, 86–87, 157, 182; blanks and erasures in, 216n3; capitalism depicted in, 71; coloniality in, 25; danger in, 180; decolonial love in, 177; Díaz's readings of, 156; Dominican Republic in, 2, 59; half-life of love in, 154, 176–78; as historia, 112; "Invierno" in, 67; London Terrace in, 57; narrative tension in, 53; past and present in, 60; publication of, 76, 157–58;

This Is How You Lose Her (Díaz), *(continued)* sucio and sucia love in, 159–62, 173–78; vernacular in, 19–21

Thomas, Piri, 29

Time Out, 87–88

"To Elsie" (Williams), 164

Tolkien, J. R. R., 5, 17, 23, 100; Díaz's discussion of, xv, 28–38, 124–26; on function of fantasy, 200n12; influence in Díaz's *The Brief Wondrous Life of Oscar Wao*, 121–23

Torres-Saillan, Silvio, 102

torture in: in *The Brief Wondrous Life of Oscar Wao* (Díaz), 140–41

transculturation, 202n9, 215n38; coloniality and, 47–48

transculturation and transnationalism: in Díaz's work, 49–50, 67–68

transmodernity: fukú americanus and, 145–46, 215n40

Trouillot, Michel-Rolph, 62, 137

Trujillo Molina, Rafael Leónidas, 3, 49; assassination of, 14, 51, 81; in *The Brief Wondrous Life of Oscar Wao* (Díaz), 5–6, 29, 103–5, 112–15, 118, 120–23, 132, 137–42; in Díaz's writing, 5–6, 9–10, 24, 29, 49, 103–5, 112–15, 118, 120–23, 131; monumentalization of, 13

Trump, Donald: anti-immigration policies of, 21; Díaz's discussion of, 39, 42–44

Truong, Peter, 176

2666 (Bolaño), xvi, 100

Ulysses (Joyce), 85–87

United States: Díaz's criticism of, 29–36; in Díaz's work, 1, 143–46; Dominican large-scale migration to, 51; English academia and literary production in, 31; invasion of Dominican Republic by, 13–16, 49, 81–82

University of Iowa Workshop, xii

US Immigration and Customs Enforcement, 40

Vargas, Deborah R., 158–59, 177, 180

Vaughn, Stephanie, 71, 89–91

Vega, Edward, 29

vernacular: Díaz's use of, 51; in Díaz's writing, 19–21

Villa Juana neighborhood (Santo Domingo): in Díaz's stories, 59

Viramontes, Helena María, 38, 187

Wagner, Richard, 32–33, 123–24

Walcott, Derek, 5, 60, 85, 122–23, 129

Wallerstein, Immanuel, 24, 131–36, 213n121

Watchmen comic book series, 207n1

Weber, Max, 132

Weird English (Ch'ien), 19

Where Memory Dwells (Gómez-Barris), 140

White, Hayden, 202n3

Whitehead, Colson, xi

Whiteness: in creative writing programs, 91–93, 96; Díaz's relationship to aesthetics of, 1, 92–93

White supremacy: Díaz's activism against, 22–23, 28–36, 42–44

White Teeth (Smith), 8, 100

Wilde, Oscar, 6–7, 106–7, 209n33

Williams, William Carlos, 164

Woloch, Alex, 218n28

Yarrul, Miguel, 10, 14

"Ysrael" (Díaz), 20, 59, 74–78, 204n36

"zafa" counternarrative, xvii

www.ingramcontent.com/pod-product-compliance
Lightning Source LLC
Chambersburg PA
CBHW070839160426
43192CB00012B/2239